Studia Fennica
Historica 8

The Finnish Literature Society was founded in 1831 and has from the very beginning engaged in publishing. It nowadays publishes literature in the fields of ethnology and folkloristics, linguistics, literary research and cultural history.
The first volume of Studia Fennica series appeared in 1933.
Since 1992 the series has been divided into three thematic subseries: Ethnologica, Folkloristica and Linguistica. Two additional subseries were formed in 2002, Historica and Litteraria.
In additional to its publishing activities the Finnish Literature Society maintains a folklore archive, a literature archive and a library.

Editorial board
Anna-Leena Siikala
Rauno Endén
Teppo Korhonen
Pentti Leino
Auli Viikari
Johanna Ilmakunnas

Editorial office
Hallituskatu 1
FIN-00170 Helsinki

Northern Revolts

Medieval and Early Modern
Peasant Unrest in the Nordic Countries

Edited by Kimmo Katajala

Finnish Literature Society • Helsinki

Medieval and early modern history –
Nordic countries – political culture –
forms of protest – treason legislation

ISBN 951-746-643-9
ISSN 1458-526X

www.finlit.fi

Hakapaino Oy
Helsinki 2004

Foreword

This book is a result of a joint research project "Peasant Revolts in the Nordic Countries 1300–1800." The project was funded by the Joint Committee of the Nordic Research Councils for the Humanities (NOS-H) in 1998–2000. Partial financing for writing the chapters concerning Finland came from the Academy of Finland. The partners in this project were the Universities of Joensuu and Helsinki, Finland, the Universities of Lund and Uppsala, Sweden, the University of Trondheim, Norway and the University of Copenhagen, Denmark.

Originally, all five Nordic countries were to be represented in the project. Unfortunately, the Danish specialist in the field of peasant revolts, Hans Henrik Appel, had to regrettably withdraw from the project. As a result there is no separate chapter about the Danish revolts, as there is about those in the other Nordic countries. Thus, the Danish case is handled on a more general level.

It has taken a long time to edit the manuscript and get it ready for publication, and the time has now come to thank all those who contributed to bringing it to birth. First, I want to thank all the authors. In the most heated moments of the project, I think we were a good team. Brian Fleming has unstintingly checked the language of the book, and has also offered many valuable comments on the manuscript. The Karelian Institute in Joensuu has been the headquarters of the project and provided the use of its facilities. And, finally, I wish to thank the Finnish Literature Society, which is publishing the book in a long-established and respected series.

22 April 2004,
Karelian Institute, Pielisjoki Castle, Joensuu, Finland

Kimmo Katajala
Project Leader

Contents

FOREWORD 5

KIMMO KATAJALA
CHAPTER I: INTRODUCTION 11

HARALD GUSTAFSSON
CHAPTER II: THE NORDIC COUNTRIES, SO
SIMILAR AND YET SO DIFFERENT 16
    Three kingdoms, two states 16
    Politics: the emergence of the State 19
    Economy: the agrarian crisis and its legacy 21
    Culture: tensions and mutuality 25
    A region of overlapping divisions 29

KIMMO KATAJALA
CHAPTER III: AGAINST TITHES AND TAXES,
FOR KING AND PROVINCE
Peasant unrest and medieval Scandinavian
    political culture 32
    Protest in autonomous peasant society 32
    The Kalmar Union in crisis 37
    The contentious Swedes 39
    Interpretations of the Engelbrekt uprising 41
    The tumultuous Union 44
    Against taxes, for shelter: the Danish and
        Norwegian uprisings 47
    Towards the early modern era. 49

KENNETH JOHANSSON
CHAPTER IV: "THE LORDS FROM THE PEASANTS OR
THE PEASANTS FROM THE LORDS"
The Dacke War and the concept of communalism 53
    Sweden enters the early modern era 53
    Early summer 1542: the rise of Dacke and the
        truce in Bergkvara 56
    August: collapse of the fragile truce 60
    September and October: the attack by the royal army . . . 63
    November: the Linköping agreement that was never
        intended to stand 64
    The new truce: suspicions and preparations on both
        sides 67

The war and the end 70
Understanding the Dacke War 72
    Geographical extent of the uprising.............. 74
    Social range of the uprising 76
    Economy of the uprising 77
Preludes and post-mortems............................ 80
The contents of communalism: organisational principles,
egalitarian and horizontal ideals 81

Magne Njåstad

CHAPTER V: RESISTANCE IN THE NAME OF THE LAW
Peasant politics in medieval and early modern Norway...... 90
Violent Norwegians? 91
Conflicts in the legal arenas 94
Medieval local political cultures in conflict with the
central authorities 97
The triumph of the Crown in the post-Reformation
period.. 103
    Trøndelag: controlling the local authorities 103
    Jemtland: controlling the peripheries 105
    Bratsberg: controlling the finances 106
    *Rogaland: draft-dodging, a case of everyday
    resistance*....................................... 108
The eighteenth century – subordination or consensus? . 112
Law, custom and resistance 114

Árni Daníel Júlíusson

CHAPTER VI: PEASANT UNREST IN ICELAND........ 118
Rebellion, unrest and conflict....................... 119
The Sturlungar era 120
    Conflict in the Sturlunga....................... 122
    *Conflicts between the peasantry and chieftains
    in the Sturlunga*................................ 123
'Patriotic' unrest and rebellion in the late
Middle Ages, 1300–1550............................ 125
    Unrest 1301–1320 125
    *The battle of Grund in 1361 and other conflicts
    of the late seventeenth century* 126
    *The drowning of a bishop and other events of
    the fifteenth century*........................... 128
    Bishops against the king, the Reformation war ... 130
Conflicts between peasants and elites 1300–1550 132
    Conflicts over cow rent in the late Middle Ages... 132
    Conflicts over duties........................... 133

Consequences of the plague in the fifteenth century	133
The 'patriotic' struggle for rights 1550–1800	134
The struggle against the trading monopoly	134
Taxes	138
Conflict between the peasants and the elite 1550–1800	139
Rents 1550–1800	139
Cattle rents, duties and taxes	141
Conflicts in the period 1680–1710	143
The late eighteenth century	144
Peasant unrest and rebellions: a useful idea in the history of Iceland?	145

KIMMO KATAJALA

CHAPTER VII: THE CHANGING FACE OF PEASANT UNREST IN EARLY MODERN FINLAND ... 149

The state enters local society: the unrest in Karelia 1551–1553	149
Bitter fruits of the 25-year war: the Club War of 1595–1596	153
The peasantry and the emergence of the Swedish state	159
Fixing a hole in the Crown's purse: the struggle for reduction	162
Varieties of local unrest	167
Elimäki: struggle over meadows and fields turns into defence of holdings and peasant freedom	167
Jokioinen: struggle against fixed tax turns into fight for the holdings	172
Ostrobothnia: disputes over the tax tar and local autonomy	175
Karelia: protests against tax farming lead to armed food riots	178
Entering the Age of Liberty	181

KARIN SENNEFELT

CHAPTER VIII: MARCHING TO STOCKHOLM
Repertoires of peasant protest in eighteenth-century Sweden. 188

The Dalecarlia uprising	189
The Hofman uprising	190
Repertoires of protest and how they change	191
The political conditions of the Age of Liberty	193
The state-building process thus far	194
Peasant political identity in the Age of Liberty	196
The march as a form of protest	198
The goal of the march	202

Kimmo Katajala

CHAPTER IX: FOR THE KING, FARMS AND JUSTICE
Swedish peasant politics and tenant movements in
    the eighteenth century 206
        Peasants at the Diet and in the law courts 206
            Jokioinen. 208
            Joensuu. 210
        The restoration of absolutism in 1772 211
        Tenant movements of the 1770s 212
            Elimäki 212
            Nastola 214
            Pälkjärvi. 216
            Scania and Halland 218
        The peasant unrest tamed 219

Mia Korpiola

CHAPTER X: SWEDISH MEDIEVAL AND EARLY MODERN TREASON LEGISLATION
A consequence of peasant uprisings? 222
        Revolt and the law 222
        The crime of treason. 224
        The emergence of treason legislation in Sweden:
            when, what and why? 226
        How to deal with non-violent protest? 232
        Treason legislation and the state-building process in
            early modern Sweden 238
        Nipping discontent in the bud. 244
        Continuity and interpretation 248

Kimmo Katajala

CHAPTER XI: CONCLUSIONS
Peasant unrest and political culture 258
        Economics 258
        Religion 260
        Instigation. 262
        The pacification of society 263
        Peasant communalism 264
        Political culture. 266

SOURCES AND REFERENCES. 270

AUTHORS 288

INDEX OF PERSONS 289

INDEX OF PLACES AND NAMES 293

SUBJECT INDEX 298

CHAPTER I

Introduction

Kimmo Katajala

About 5000 'peasants' march along the main street of the capital. Some of the men have severed goat heads impaled on the tips of long sticks. Here you can see an axe handle sticking out of a knapsack, and there, some of the 'peasants' carrying long wooden clubs in their hands. One man is carrying the carcase of a slaughtered pig. Some of the protesters slip from the row into a tavern called the Happy Pig. Men from the countryside are crowding the tavern, drinking beer and discussing politics. In particular, they curse the government. But the march carries on towards the parliament building. Slogans fill the air. Black smoke is rising from hay bales that have been set on fire. Some protesters, fortified with spirits, rush against the fences erected to close the road. They scuffle with the police and some are arrested.

Where does this description come from? Is it from London during the English Rising in 1381 or from revolutionary Paris in 1789? Or does it describe the unrest in Stockholm in 1743? No, the description of this protest march is from the events in Helsinki, the capital of Finland, at the beginning of December 1999.[1] Finland at that time held the Presidency of the European Union and the leaders of the Union were meeting in the city. The usually very calm Finnish farmers expressed their anger to these leaders in an exceptionally strong way. This, by Finnish standards, extreme action had a simultaneous counterpart in France, where the streets were covered not only with smoke but with open flames.

How did this come about? Should we understand these rather strong acts as pale northern reflections of the heated European political situation? Or was it just a spontaneous movement of angry Finnish farmers worrying about their income? It is clear that, although both explanations contain an element of truth, they capture only a very small part of the processes behind these kinds of movement. The protest was organised by the Central Union of Agricultural Producers and Forest Owners (MTK). As well as exerting a strong influence in Finnish politics, the MTK also plays a role in the politics of the European Union. However, it would be too simple to claim that the Finnish farmers were merely incited and used for political purposes. They clearly had their own reasons to protest. Discontent is a precondition for successful agitation.

The farmers marching on the streets of Helsinki were not cottagers or small farmers from the east and north, the poorest and least fertile parts of the country. No, they were farmers from the fertile plains of southern Finland, holders by Finnish standards of rather large farms. This was not a protest of the poor. But why did they *march*? I mean, why did they march rather than expressing their protest in other ways? Was it an echo of Finland's quasi-military movements of the 1920s and 1930s, or should we see the decision to march as a borrowing from the labour movement? Or is it perhaps relevant to ask if the protest march carried traits from the pre-modern peasant protests? Did the peasantry also march in the past?

The aim of this book is not to resolve these questions in relation to this or any other present-day protest. However, the example does clearly highlight the main issues essential to understanding any protest, whether present-day or in the past. And the focus of the book is on the past, in pre-modern northern Europe. The period under study extends from medieval Scandinavia at the end of the Viking age through to the birth of the modern era at the end of the eighteenth century. The area treated consists nowadays of the five Nordic nation states: (in alphabetical order) Denmark, Finland, Iceland, Norway and Sweden. This was not the case in history, as we shall see. Sometimes all these areas were united under the same king, but for most of the period the area contained two kingdoms: Denmark-Norway, which also held sway over Iceland, and the Swedish kingdom, including the land of the Finns as the 'eastern half of the realm'.

The main aims of this book can be crystallised in three concepts: 1) political culture, 2) forms of protest and 3) organising principles.

The concept of political culture is defined here as the political 'patterns of the game' of an era. Although the concept of 'political culture' shares a lot with the concept of 'mentalities', not all of these patterns are necessarily shared with every group in society, as is often said in reference to mentalities.[2] These political patterns can be seen to some extent to have a general European ideological basis, but they also contain a great deal which is specifically Nordic. The framework of political praxis varied from one country to another. At the same time as the Swedish Diet held the main power in the realm, in Denmark the king was an absolute ruler. So there is always also a 'national' character in the rules of the political game.

There were inequalities between the various strata in society. The opportunities the peasants of the past had to act in society differed from those of the nobility. So they also acted in different way to the nobles. The totality of the political culture of the medieval or early modern era contains characteristics from at least three levels: 'general', 'national' and 'estate'. A precondition for understanding any protest is to identify how the political culture of that specific society operates, the ideological presumptions behind the network of the political game. Only then can we discover why the protesting peasants acted as they did. We must ask what opportunities they had to influence their conditions and what means they had to take part in the decision-making processes in different eras and different parts of the area under study.

We must also ask how their protest was expressed in different political cultures. The changing repertoire of forms of protest is one of the threads followed in the chapters of this study. The nature of different protests can be analysed using the following dichotomies.

violent protests	—	non-violent protests
active protests	—	passive protests
offensive actions	—	defensive actions
illegal protests	—	legal protests
high degree of organisation	—	unorganised protests

We can isolate from the historical literature several concepts describing different peasant protests. The borderlines between these concepts are not always clear. We can find the concepts of peasant war (G. *Bauernkrieg*, S. *bondekrig*, F. *talonpoikaissota*), peasant uprising (G. *Bauernaufstand*, S. *bonderesning*, F. *talonpoikaisnousu*), peasant revolt or rebellion (G. *Bauernrevolt*, S. *bonderevolt* or *bondeuppror*, F. *talonpoikaiskapina*), peasant riot (G. *Tumult* or *Krawall*, S. *tumult* or *upplopp*, F. *mellakka*), popular disturbance or peasant unrest (G. *Bauernunruhe*, S. *bondeorolighet*, F. *talonpoikaislevottomuus*) and peasant resistance (G. *Bauerlichen wiederstand*, S. *bondemotstånd*, F. *talonpoikainen vastarinta*). The contents of these concepts and their relations to each other can to some degree be clarified by reference to the above dichotomies.

The difference between peasant war/uprising, peasant revolt/rebellion, and peasant riots can be assessed through their degree of violence. Peasant wars and uprisings are understood as large-scale violent events that move great masses of armed peasants over an extensive area, while revolts and rebellions are, while also always a violent phenomenon, more localised in focus. Peasant wars and uprisings can last a long time: a month, several months, or even several years. Revolts and rebellions are always over in a matter of weeks or months. Peasant riots are always very localised, short term disturbances lasting a day or a week and usually expressing violence of at least a symbolic nature. They are always violent, active and offensive actions, and as such are in modern societies also illegal acts. The distinctions between legality and illegality and between the concepts of peasant war, peasant revolt and peasant uprising in medieval society will be discussed in detail later on.

The degree of organisation is of course highest in peasant wars and uprisings and lowest in riots. The former can organise complicated and well-planned governmental structures, as witnessed, for example, in the French *Croquant* and *Nu-Pied* uprisings in the sixteenth and seventeenth centuries and the Great German Peasant War at the beginning of the sixteenth century. A local riot usually has leaders and instigators, but this organisation often vanishes as quickly as it emerged.

How, then, should we understand the concepts of peasant or popular disturbances, peasant unrest and peasant resistance? Perhaps the concepts of peasant disturbances and unrest can be seen as at least partly synonymous. They can be reserved as general concepts describing most peasant protests, extending perhaps from revolts to tax strikes or strikes in rent service. These acts may include violence, but they can also be non-violent. Disturbances and unrest are usually open acts, but passive forms of protest are also normally included under these concepts. Disturbances and unrest can be offensive acts, but they are usually interpreted as having been defensive and preventive protests against some external threats or activities. However, the concepts of disturbance and unrest view events from the perspective of the authorities and therefore presume at least some degree of illegality.

Finally we have the much used term of peasant resistance.[3] This concept (and its counterparts in German, Swedish and Finnish) has been coined to cover all peasant acts opposing the authorities. It covers peasant wars as well as the passive protest of a single serf in his landlord's field. Much has been written about everyday resistance. This fits well under the concept of peasant resistance, although it cannot be labelled as a disturbance or unrest. However, there are some fundamental problems with this concept. The word 'resistance' itself points to the presumption that peasant action was always a reaction to an act of the authorities, be it the Crown or a landlord. It implicitly denies the peasant an active role in the political culture. The peasant is subordinated to the status of reacting puppet. His own active part in the political culture of an era vanishes from the repertoire of analysis. We must be alert to this and bear it in mind when dealing with this widely used concept. When used in this book, the concept of resistance always includes the possibility of an autonomous peasant politics.

A protest cannot be organised if there is no room, conditions or organisational structure available for organising it. One of the main tasks in this book is to present the organising principles on which the protests of the Nordic peasantry were based. These principles are due to the fundamental patterns in the political culture of each era. This view originates from Peter Blickle's idea of the communalist organising-principles that developed in Europe after the period of medieval 'feudalism'. Blickle's idea, presented here in short, is that the feudal legal, protective and productive organisations were replaced with communalist ones during the fourteenth and fifteenth centuries. The town or village now took care of defence, criminal justice and organising those aspects of production dependent on communal cooperation. Under 'feudalism' all this had been organised by the landlord and the manor. This communal organisation was developed to operate during times of peace and for defence against outside enemies, but, according to Blickle, it was also possible to use it for purposes of attack.[4]

It is clear that nothing comparable to this developed in the Nordic countries, where medieval society differed a great deal from European 'feudalism'. In medieval Nordic society there were no manors, feudal lords or serfdom as in the countries of continental Europe. There was accordingly not such a need to develop new structures and organisations for defence, judicial process or production as on the Continent. And there were no such networks of towns and villages in the North to compare with those of Central Europe. However, there were other kinds of peasant organisation and organising principles in the North, and it is on these we must focus.

However, protest and resistance always come up against a counter-reaction in every society. The establishment, be it pope, bishop, king, government, landlord or whatever, is always constructing repressive and integrating systems to hinder or subdue the protests and disorder in society. These are usually the military or police forces and the law. In this book we shall concentrate on the latter. We shall approach the question from two angles. The final chapter will deal with how social disturbances were handled by the law and consider whether peasant disturbances had any influence on the law-making process. But before we can turn to the riots and revolts, we must take a look at the Nordic countries themselves, at the outlines of their history and nature, and the conditions under which the peasantry lived in these countries.

NOTES

1   See the newspaper Helsingin Sanomat (HS) 11.–17.12.1999.
2   For Swedish discussion on the concept of political culture see Österberg 1989, 76; Aronsson 1992, 337 passim.; Gustafsson 1994, 21–22; Linde 2000, 25–27; Sennefelt 2001, esp. 17–21.
3   The concept of peasant resistance has recently become well-known and entered general usage especially as a result of the fascinating works of James C. Scott. See Scott 1985; Scott 1990.
4   See Blickle 1986.

CHAPTER II

The Nordic countries, so similar and yet so different

Harald Gustafsson

The area known today as the Nordic countries – *Norden, Pohjoismaat* or *Norðurlönd* in the Nordic languages – covers a large part of northern Europe. Within it you find seemingly endless dark forests, but also vast fertile plains, wild mountains and pleasant archipelagos, grey lava fields and bright white glaciers. In terms of human geography the differences are nowadays great and were even greater in pre-industrial society. In some areas the people lived in towns and large country villages tilling the soil in much the same way as in the plains of continental Europe. In other places the farms were rather isolated and several miles from the closest neighbour. A living was eaked mostly from the meagre fields, but also from the sea, the forest and the mountains.

The purpose of this chapter is twofold: to give some background information on the Nordic countries in the period under consideration from the late Middle Ages to the end of the early modern era, and to discuss the question of the unity or disunity of this part of Europe, paying special attention to aspects important for understanding and explaining peasant unrest. How similar and how different were the Nordic countries?

A presentation of the Nordic countries in the period, and a discussion of differences and similarities, can be based on a rough division of spheres of human interaction into politics, economy and culture. But the first question is which were these 'Nordic countries' that were so different or so similar?[1]

Three kingdoms, two states

The term 'the Nordic countries' today usually refers to the present five member states of the Nordic Council: Denmark, Finland, Iceland, Norway, and Sweden (with the semi-independent Danish Greenland and Faroe Islands and the Finnish Åland Islands). These have, however, only existed as five independent states since 1918. There is a 'bad habit' in modern historiography of treating the Nordic region as consisting of these five equal entities in previous periods as well. It may sometimes be necessary to do so due to the different historiographic traditions in the modern Nordic countries, the present division of archival material and the presentation of printed sources, and also for simple reasons of funding. Be that as it may, although this division into the modern national states of the present prevails in this book too, we should never allow ourselves to forget that this is an anachronistic division when discussing medieval and early modern history.

In political terms the Nordic region during the Middle Ages consisted of three separate kingdoms, three kingdoms that continued later to form the base of Nordic state formation: Denmark, Norway and Sweden. This sounds simple enough. However, if we look closer the picture becomes more complicated.

The Duchy of Schleswig was gradually separated from Denmark and joined to Holstein, a duchy of the Holy Roman Empire. But these two duchies in turn became closely knitted to Denmark, closer in some periods and in some parts than in others. The North Atlantic islands settled by the Vikings – the Faroes, Iceland, and Greenland – accepted Norwegian rule but were regarded as 'tax lands' of the kingdom. They were outlying provinces with their own separate laws and political arrangements, not parts of Norway proper. The province of Jemtland was in much the same position before it was handed over to Sweden in the seventeenth century.

Medieval and early modern Sweden looked different on the map from the Sweden of today. The southern and western provinces in present-day Sweden were Danish and Norwegian until the seventeenth century. But it is most important to note that the present-day Finland was then an integral part of Sweden. It is important also to remember that 'Finland' was not a 'country' in the meaning of a separate unit, as Iceland was within the Norwegian kingdom. Instead, it was a name for eastern Sweden, an area that gradually became a part of the kingdom in the high Middle Ages like much of the rest of Sweden. When I speak below of 'Sweden', the territory of Finland is included unless otherwise stated.

There was, however, a notion of Finland, or 'Eastland' (the medieval term), as a somewhat special area of Sweden at quite an early stage. Not least was the language gap, greater, for example, than that between Swedish and Norwegian: most people in most areas of Finland spoke Finnish, a language diverging totally from the Scandinavian languages. In Finland, Swedish dominated only certain narrow ribbon-like strips along the coast, where everybody spoke Swedish. In the rest of the country language presented a social division. The language of the authorities, the nobility and the burghers was Swedish, while the common people spoke mostly Finnish.

During our period these political entities formed states in different ways. For the most of the fourteenth century, however, Norway, Sweden and eastern Denmark (the provinces of Scania) had the same king. Between 1389 and 1523 this was true for all three kingdoms. This Kalmar Union (named after the coronation of King Eric in Kalmar in 1397) was a very loose federation covering the whole Nordic region. Each kingdom kept its own laws, political institutions and political culture. In

Map 1. The Nordic countries in the early modern era

fact, after 1448, the Union monarchs were as a rule recognised fully only in Denmark and Norway. In Sweden, conflicts between different groups of the political elite prevailed, conflicts which at times gave the Union kings an opportunity to enter the country. For most of the time, however, Sweden was governed by the Council of the Realm and the regents of the Sture family.

After the Swedish and Danish rebellions against Christian II in the early 1520s, there followed a period of great uncertainty, mixed with the dramatic events of the Lutheran Reformation. When the decisive fight for power within the ruins of the old Union came to an end in 1537, two new states emerged: Denmark-Norway and Sweden. The cohabitation of Denmark and Norway thus continued, but Norway was now clearly reduced to the junior partner in this relationship, since the Norwegian Council of the Realm was abolished and the Lutheran Church transferred the leadership of the Church from the Archbishop of Trondheim to the King in Denmark. Denmark now spoke for Norway on the international scene, but the internal organisation of Norwegian society was left untouched.

These two princely and Lutheran states were to dominate northern Europe for the rest of the early modern era. The most important change was the Swedish conquest in the middle of the seventeenth century of most of eastern Denmark and parts of eastern Norway.

It is important to remember that early modern Denmark-Norway and Sweden were conglomerate states like most if not all other contemporary European states. They consisted of territories standing in different relations to the ruler, territories with different local elites, different laws, sometimes even different constitutions. The most important separate parts of the Danish conglomerate were Denmark proper, Norway, Schleswig-Holstein and Iceland. Sweden itself was more integrated, and the provinces conquered from Denmark-Norway were all soon integrated into Sweden proper, like Finland had always been. However, the acquisitions of the sixteenth and seventeenth century in the Baltic area and Germany – territories such as Estonia, Livonia and Pomerania – were all separate parts of the conglomerate state. The easternmost part of the present-day Finland, the province of Käkisalmi s. *Keksholm* (today the region of Northern Karelia) was only partially integrated into the Swedish realm during the seventeenth century.[2]

From the viewpoint of the peasantry this meant that they had to interact with different regimes, react to different laws and live in different political cultures in different parts of the Nordic countries. It is important to bear in mind that this was true also within a single state.

Politics: the emergence of the State

The political system was for most of the period very much alike in all three kingdoms and two states. In the late Middle Ages a strong counterweight to royal power emerged in the Council of the Realm consisting of the bishops and the most important members of the nobility. Formed in the late 13th and early fourteenth centuries, these councils were of great importance in the kingdoms integrated into the various Scandinavian Unions established during the following two centuries. The participation of the Council in political decisions became more or less obligatory for the legitimacy of decision-making. The Council spoke, in principal, for all the inhabitants of the realm. In the late Middle Ages when politics became more complicated, and when the military advantage of the knights over the infantry was declining, it became increasingly necessary to get a broader base for decisions. The greater part of the nobility, burghers, clergy and occasionally also peasants were summoned to the larger meetings.

The 1520s and 1530s were decisive. The monarchies of Gustavus Vasa in Sweden and Christian III in Denmark-Norway saw the centralisation of power. The Council was still important, but after the Reformation no clergymen took part in its meetings. The vast landholdings of the Church now became Crown property. The ever-rising tax burden contributed to the strengthened financial position of the Crown. Money was needed for hiring mercenaries and building up-to-date fortresses to replace the medieval castles. Both the military and the administrative capacity of the State to dominate its territory and to defend it against domestic and foreign competitors was greatly expanded, while the new Lutheran doctrine strengthened the religious legitimacy of the princely regimes.

New taxes could in principle be introduced only with the consent of the taxed. Other major decisions also needed the legitimacy of a meeting of the Estates. The Swedish Diet of four estates (*Riksdag*) took shape during the Vasa period and kept this form for the next 300 years. The four estates – the nobility, the clergy, the burghers and the peasant-freeholders (but not the tenants) – met separately. The Diet was less important in some periods than in others, as, for example, in the later reign of Gustavus Vasa or during the absolutist rule of Charles XII in the early eighteenth century. From time to time it achieved a central position in political life, as in the late sixteenth century, during the regency of the 1660s, and above all in the 'Age of Liberty' (1718–1772). In the latter period, Sweden was not in fact ruled by the King, but by the Diet. The Diet controlled the Council much in the same way as a modern parliament controls the government.[3]

In Denmark-Norway, political meetings with broader sections of the population never played the same role. However, they were occasionally summoned separately for Denmark and Norway all the way through until 1660. High politics were basically a game between the main powers in the state: the aristocratic Council of the Realm and the King. This dualism was put to an end in 1660 when Frederic III carried through a coup d'état with the help of the military and the burghers of Copenhagen and declared himself absolute ruler. From then on, Denmark-Norway was constitutionally perhaps the most absolutist state in Europe. When, after 1730, the kings' personal ability to rule declined, this increasingly became an absolutism of the high bureaucracy.[4]

It is important to note that state-building took a leap forward in both states in the seventeenth century. An advanced bureaucracy was created in Sweden in the times of the dynamic chancellor Axel Oxenstierna in the 1610s to 1630s, while a similar development in Denmark-Norway followed the introduction of absolutism in 1660. Sweden saw a new period of administrative growth during the absolutist rule of the last two decades of the century. All this enabled the regimes to extract more resources from their subjects, resources that mainly went to the respective armies and navies. The form of state created has been labelled 'power state' or 'military state'.[5] In the eighteenth century both states took on a more civilian complexion, but nevertheless retained their bureaucracies, which by contemporary European standards were unusually effective, centralised and reliable.

Although there were constitutional differences, the differences in praxis were not too great. Studies on the eighteenth century have shown a high degree of communication between the rulers and the ruled, even in absolutist Denmark-Norway.[6] It cannot be denied that the Swedish Diet gave broad groups in society ample opportunity to influence politics. However, the administrative and judicial systems were also used for political communication even in Denmark-Norway, although there were certainly regional differences. Norwegian society was more complex. Decision-making was a considerably more delicate business in Norway than in Denmark or Iceland. There were regional variations within the kingdoms too, and many regulations applied to parts of the country only. Norwegian peasants reacting, for instance, against State regulations in the timber trade did not have the same regulations to react against in different parts of Norway.

In political terms there were probably greater differences between the two early modern states than there had been between the three medieval kingdoms. Denmark-Norway came closer to continental absolutism, while Sweden showed more tendencies to constitutional development, although the latter also had its own short periods of absolutism too. But the differences in praxis were not overwhelming and regional differences within the states were considerable. However, we can safely assume that the usually more open Swedish political system gave the peasantry more scope to voice their demands and react to or even sometimes initiate central legislation.

Economy: the agrarian crisis and its legacy

The general crisis of the late Middle Ages did not spare the Nordic countries. Desertion of farms, in all probability explained by a demographic crisis, can be discerned in sources from many parts of the region during the fourteenth and fifteenth centuries. Norway appears to have been hardest hit, followed by Iceland. There are signs of a crisis also in Denmark and south and central Sweden, while north and east Sweden, Norrland and Finland, seem to have escaped with less damage. Here settlement seems to have spread further to the north, further up the river valleys and further into the forests during most of the late Middle Ages and also in the sixteenth century.

Declining population and abandoned farms meant falling rental incomes for the nobility. Their attempts to compensate this loss met resistance from the peasants. The late Middle Ages are a period of continuous social unrest. This is true on the continent as well as in the Nordic countries. It is a well-established fact that the consequences of the agrarian crisis were quite different in western and eastern Europe, with the river Elbe as a symbolic borderline. In Europe west of the Elbe the independence of the peasant family farm was strengthened. The peasant rebellions were harshly suppressed, but the policy of the landlords became more careful after the upheavals. Rents in kind and in day-labour gave way in many places to money rents. The formal ties between the peasantry and their lords were loosened. Servitude more or less disappeared from this part of Europe.

East of the Elbe the peasants were tied more firmly to their lords and their manors. Different varieties of formal servitude were introduced in one country after another. The landowners used the heavy labour dues of their peasants to cultivate their large manorial demesnes producing grain for export to western Europe. Of course, there were in reality many nuances that are lost in this picture of a total bifurcation of social development along two distinct paths. However, if we keep in mind that the division is a simplification, we can use it as an instrument to characterise developments in the Nordic countries.

The division between East and West continued north through the Nordic countries. Basically, Denmark and Iceland followed the Eastern path, and Norway, Sweden and present-day Finland the Western. This had far-reaching consequences for the following centuries.

In Denmark the losers of the late Middle Ages were the peasantry and the lesser nobility. The winners were the families of the higher nobility with the resources to buy manors and farms. They built up large, complex landholdings and took advantage of the economic turn of the tide in the late fifteenth century. Production and export of grain and especially oxen became a very lucrative activity over the next few centuries. The peasants became burdened with labour service and the duty to fodder the oxen of their lords. If there ever had been any large proportion of landowning peasants in Denmark, which is debatable, they more or less disappeared during this process.

In the late fifteenth and early sixteenth centuries a mild variety of servitude (*vornedskab*) came into force in the eastern Danish islands. This made it possible for the manorial lords to forbid their peasant families from leaving the manor. Gradually, from the late fifteenth century onwards, royal rights were transferred to the landowners. The manorial lords in many ways replaced the royal bailiffs in police and justice matters. They received the right to royal fines, the right to act as a tax-collector over their peasants, and often the right to hold their own courts. The ties between the peasant population and the Crown were loosened. Politics became to a greater extent an affair exclusively for the elite. After the introduction of absolutism in 1660, even more administrative duties were handed over to the landowners. *Vornedskab* was abandoned in 1702, but followed in 1733 by the *stavnsbånd*, which forbade males of an age suitable for military service from moving without the consent of their lords. This gave lords of the manor all over Denmark the power to control their peasants and labourers.[7]

The Icelandic peasants were tied to their lords more firmly than in the other Nordic countries, although not so firmly as in Denmark. As in Denmark, only a very small percentage of the peasants owned the farms they lived on. However, there were no manors of the Danish type in Iceland. Isolated farms were the rule. Only in the fishing districts did labour service play any significant role. The Icelandic landowners never took over any formal judicial or administrative functions in regard to their tenants, although royal officials were usually recruited from the landowning families.

In the rest of the Nordic countries there was no real counterpart to the expansion of nobility and manors in late medieval Denmark. With few exceptions, Swedish and Norwegian peasants kept their direct contact with Crown officials even if they were tenants. In Sweden, the seventeenth century was the period of expansion for the nobility. The expanding State often lacked money, and the new service nobility received payment in Crown land and the right to tax the peasants. Many new manors were established, especially in the central and southern parts of present-day Sweden, not least around Stockholm, but also in Finnish Ostrobothnia, southern Finland and Karelia. This undoubtedly led to various tensions in society, but it never placed the peasantry in the position of their Danish counterparts.

This picture of a Denmark 'east of the Elbe' and a Norway and Sweden 'west of the Elbe' should not be exaggerated. It is important to underline that all people in all the Nordic countries were legally free. In a judicial sense it is misleading to speak of servitude in Denmark. The Danish peasant, even when tried in the lord's court, was a free subject with rights and duties according to the laws of the realm. He could not be bought and sold and he could not be punished without a legal trial. But unlike many of his counterparts further north he lived directly under the eyes of his lord. Only seldom did he meet any royal officials, with the exception of the parish priest (who was often chosen by the lord).

There were also important regional differences. The acquisition of Scania and Halland, in particular, from Denmark in the seventeenth century meant that Sweden now had a share in 'Danish' social relations in its southern country areas. Important parts of the central plains of Sweden were also dominated by noble estates and a tenant peasantry. This was also true of smaller districts in Norway, as, for example, around the Oslo Fjord and in Trøndelag. In other parts of the country the State owned large areas and estates that were either directly run, as in southwest Iceland, or leased out, as in eastern Finland. In this latter case the tenants of the Crown under the leaseholders were in much the same position as the tenants of the nobility. In general, Nordic historiography has taken too little account of such regional differences. Especially in Sweden, the independent freeholder household (*skattebonde*) has dominated the picture, although it only accounted for a third of peasant households in the seventeenth century.

The same split between two parts of the Nordic region can also be discerned in commercial and industrial development. After the general expansion of the 'long sixteenth century' which benefited the whole Nordic region, the economic restructuring of the seventeenth century caused new lines of division. The traditional Danish agrarian exports met great difficulties on the German market. The export trade in oxen reached a climax in the late sixteenth century only to fall away sharply around 1620. Like much of central Europe, Denmark and the Duchies went into a long economic depression.[8] The Icelandic economy also entered a gloomy period. It was protected from the fluctuations of the international market by the Danish trade monopoly (1602–1787) that operated with fixed price lists unchanged for decades, but the same arrangement also deprived it of the stimulus of rising international fish prices.[9]

In contrast to Denmark, both Norway and Sweden (including Finland) had exports that were attractive on the European market: commodities such as tar, timber, iron and copper. Mining and forest product exports linked Norway and Sweden to the commercial centres of Europe: Holland and, later, England. This provided a great stimulus for the towns, the burghers and market relations in general.

The expansion of mining and forestry also meant a great deal for the peasant households in Norway and Sweden. The peasants made charcoal for the ironworks and metal industries, cut timber for their own trade or transported timber for other forest owners. In many cases, especially in Norway, they were themselves directly involved in foreign trade. This was a process that caused a lot of conflict between, for example, the peasants and the new metalworks on the use of the forests, or between the metalworks and the old towns over trading rights. But it also gave rise to many new opportunities. For instance, peasants in Finnish Ostrobothnia seem to have engaged in intensive tar production for export as a source of money to hire other people to serve in the army instead of serving themselves or sending their sons.[10]

These patterns prevailed until the economic growth in Europe after about 1720–1730. The general rise in population and the growing need for food in Europe also affected the Nordic region. Merchants thrived. The great wars between France and Britain provided excellent opportunities for shipping in the neutral countries. This was the golden age of Danish commerce. Agricultural production was stimulated by the rising international demand, but the old social organisation of farm labour was seen as an obstacle to expansion. The response was political reform.

With what Danish historians refer to as the great agrarian reforms (*de store landboreformer*), starting in 1788 with the abolition of the *stavnsbånd*, the Danish State embarked on a policy of reducing the great landholdings and encouraging the peasants to become modern-style freeholders. At about the same time the *skifte* movements (the Great Division) began in Sweden. This was a kind of Crown-led enclosure movement that allowed the peasants to gather their hitherto dispersed parts of the village fields into one consolidated farm. Both reforms paved the way for modern commercial farming. The Danish reforms steered Denmark decisively away from the 'eastern' path and back into the Nordic model. Up until then there had been a fundamental difference between the agrarian communities of Denmark and most of the rest of the Nordic countries.

Thus, we could perhaps argue that in economic and social terms the differences within the Nordic region grew significantly as a result of the late medieval agrarian crisis. This division continued to be significant during the early modern period. Denmark, and to some extent Iceland, followed an 'eastern' path, while Sweden (with Finland) and Norway experienced development more akin to western European. The peasants were more dependent on their lords in Iceland and, especially, Denmark than in large parts of Sweden and Norway. They had less opportunity to respond to the changes in their own economies, while many Norwegian and Swedish peasant households got involved in major economic issues in their everyday life, whether for good or ill.

Culture: tensions and mutuality

A fundamental aspect of people's thinking remained unchanged during the whole period: they were convinced that the ultimate meaning of life, and of society as a whole, was determined by supernatural powers. Although the precise form of Christianity changed, all shared a magic-religious world view. The right way of organising society, the right and honourable way of living, the right farming methods or legitimate sexual practices were all determined not by the will of men and women but by God. This is of course a fundamental fact for all pre-secular societies, not a special feature of the Nordic countries, but it is well worth bearing in mind.

This did not mean there was no discussion or conflict. It meant that conflicting standpoints were expressed in terms that were either openly religious or at least had their ultimate legitimacy anchored in religious constructions. There existed a 'common language' in which it was possible to voice conflicts, and this language was to a great extent religious.

In the late Middle Ages the Nordic region had for several centuries been an integrated part of Roman Christendom. With the Reformation in the 1520s and 1530s, the Nordic countries all converted to Lutheranism. In both Denmark-Norway and Sweden the Lutheran established churches operated under strong princely domination. It is, however, an open question as to when this new interpretation of Christianity became accepted at the level of the individual. Popular support for ecclesiastical reform existed only in Denmark. Here, the peasants and especially the townspeople had been fighting for a more radical change than the princely, authoritarian variety of Protestant church organisation that actually emerged. In the other Nordic countries the Reformation came almost exclusively from above. It met with violent popular resistance in Sweden. Several of the rebellions against the regime of Gustavus Vasa were explicitly directed against the new church regimen. The most notable were the rebellion of the lords of Western Gothia (described thus even though it also involved the common people) and the Dacke War in Småland. In Norway and Iceland it was rather the old Church as such that resisted the Reformation, but its resistance was violently suppressed in 1537 and 1550, respectively.[11]

The close connection of Church and State meant that the parish priests held a key position in the interaction between central authority and local society. Obedience to the new State was declared a Christian duty, and the clergy took over many tasks within secular administration, especially in Sweden. Here they also led the parish meetings, which developed into an important platform for local self-government. It is difficult to view the Church exclusively as either an instrument of the State and the elite for controlling the lower orders or a body serving the needs of parishioners. It was both at once. Indeed, much of the strengthened social control was carried out through the Church: for example in the field of sexual relations. This must have been in the interests of or even demanded by the local peasant elite. Other matters such as military conscription, carried out with the help of the parish registers kept by the vicar, were in all certainty viewed with more hostile eyes by most members of the local community.[12]

There is also good reason to regard the political culture from this double perspective. There existed both conflict and consensus at the same time. Throughout the Nordic region, the Middle Ages saw the emergence of a political culture of ordered interaction and communication between different groups in society. The kings of the fourteenth and fifteenth centuries had to negotiate with their councils and sometimes with larger meetings of various types. The national and regional law codes held a strong position in the minds of the people. This strong legalism is indeed one of the main features of Nordic political culture. Those in power had to argue repeatedly on behalf of their actions either in the Diet or in letters read out at local courts or in church. Even when open rebellion burst out, the unrest followed certain unwritten rules that made it 'readable' to other groups. Although the elite lived in constant fear of peasant rebellion, and rebellions did indeed sometimes break out, there was nevertheless a fundamental level of communication which held society together.

The traditionalist, legalist and legitimist political culture was marked by negotiations in accepted arenas.[13] The local courts and the Swedish parish meetings were probably the most important arenas for the peasants. Only slowly did the Diet of the four estates take over this role in Sweden. For instance, new taxes were as a rule still granted at local meetings at the beginning of the sixteenth century. In the course of the 'judicial revolution' of the seventeenth century the courts became more like courts in our sense of the word: run by professional State-appointed judges, and less like political assemblies. However, they still handled important matters of everyday life and probably retained some of this role for the local peasant elite well into the nineteenth century.

It is, however, important to remember that the new State administration built up from the sixteenth century onwards could also function as a legitimate channel of political communication. Many of the letters exchanged between local officials and central bodies in fact dealt with local reactions to centrally issued orders or even local initiatives. As mentioned above, this was true even for the Danish-Norwegian absolutist regime, which had little chance of implementing any central decisions that went contrary to the will of any large number of people in local society. In both states, every subject also had the right to petition the central authorities, or even the king directly.[14] However, simultaneously with the process of building representative structures for political discourse in Sweden, there was from the sixteenth century onwards a tendency to limit this right of direct petition.

All this communication between authorities and subordinates usually concerned locally limited issues and seldom any 'political' issues in the narrow sense. It was not new ideas of political or economic reform that made local peasants contact the authorities, but practical problems like conflicts over a forest common between a peasant district and a local ironworks. But the fact that the State was involved in solving such local problems contributed to reinforcing a political culture of interaction, communication and negotiation.

It is not my intention here to paint an idyllic picture of mutual respect and understanding between all groups in pre-industrial Nordic society. There did exist times when communication broke down and weapons were allowed to speak instead. And from the point of view of the peasantry it is fair to describe developments after the introduction of the new State structures in the early sixteenth century as a long and sometimes fruitless defensive struggle. Although they invoked all the fine concepts of fraternity, mutuality, law and ancient custom in the Christian, legalist and consensual political culture of the time, peasant households had to pay more in tax, their male members had to go off to war (which in most cases meant death of disease long before they reached the battlefield), they had to watch young noblemen coming from university to take over their old courts, and they had to change their faith according to the latest ideas of theologians and kings.

In Denmark the peasants probably had less reason to care about kings and politics while the local manor played a major role in their cultural universe.[15] This was certainly also true in some central parts of Sweden and smaller communities in Norway. In Iceland, it might be argued that the local lords and the merchants of the Danish trading monopoly played a much more important role in everyday life and culture than the distant king and his advisers.[16]

But nowhere were the peasants defenceless victims of the advances of State and lords. The existing culture gave them a role that was not totally passive. A good and loyal Christian subject had the right of defence by his lord or prince, the right to live safely under the recognised laws and the old customs and traditions, and to a certain although varying extent the right to pursue his own interests.

One might ask, then, if the Nordic countries were characterised by a widening gulf between elite culture and popular culture, as has been argued for Europe in general.[17] There indeed existed such a cultural gap. During the period as a whole there was a small stratum of the population which lived life on the level of the European elite. They were the 'lords' (*herrar*), and they and their womenfolk distinguished themselves from the commoners by their clothes, their buildings, their large households, their way of speaking and their larger geographical outlook.

Aristocrats and bishops in the fourteenth century knew at least something about how their counterparts lived in Germany, France or Italy and tried to partake of these continental conditions and, at least in part, their cultural ideals. In the eighteenth century, noblemen, wealthy burghers, officials and manufacturers were in even more direct contact with a wider world, dressed like gentlemen in Amsterdam or London, spoke French and read the philosophes. There are indeed many signs that this elite attempted to 'educate', 'civilise' or even 'enlighten' the common people – from medieval attempts to solicit support for pretenders to the throne, through the Reformation and the religious and moral campaigns of Lutheran orthodoxy and (in Denmark-Norway) pietism, to the Enlightenment of the late eighteenth century.

But it would be wrong to suggest there was an insurmountable gap between the 'lords' and the rest of society, and it would be just as wrong to assume that the rest of society could be characterised as one homogeneous 'popular culture'. There were many subdivisions, overlapping groups and floating changes in the course of time.

In continental perspective the Nordic elite was always rather small and furnished with modest means. With an exception of perhaps a handful of families in Denmark and even fewer in Sweden they could not match the living standards of the European nobility. There were no magnates on an eastern European scale with thousands of subject peasants and their own courts of princely standard. The social elite must have lived closer to the common people in the Nordic countries than in most of pre-industrial Europe. This would have made it more difficult to uphold and deepen a cultural gap, although the distinction was clearly presented. In the northern parts of the realms the only 'lord' you could find in a local society would probably be the vicar. If you had met him out in the field on a weekday you would probably not have been able to notice the difference between him and other peasants. But on Sundays he would put on his black coat and take his position in the community as the channel of communication between the parishioners and the higher authorities, with God and the King at the pinnacle.

Within peasant society there were probably major differences between the outlook of the wealthy peasant families and the families of crofters and labourers. We know as yet too little about such differences or differences depending on separate styles of life among the peasants. But in all the Nordic societies there would seem to have been a rather limited group of peasants who held positions such as church wardens, lay assessors in the courts, parish constables under the bailiffs, and so on. Regardless of whether they were freeholders or tenants, the wealthy peasants were often able to pass on their farms and their positions in local society to their sons and to marry their daughters within the same circles, or perhaps even to a clergyman.[18] It is above all among this social group that we find the participatory political culture described above. It is likely that crofters and labourers took less part in this political culture, although the differences might have been too small to constitute a real gap. Perhaps the crofters also felt involved and were proud when a wealthy farmer spoke for the whole village or parish at the local court meeting.

Pre-industrial Nordic society was closely knit, with overlapping loyalties and tensions and many conflicts, but also much essential cooperation.

All in the village or on the manor had to cooperate in certain phases of the work in the fields, and all parishioners had to live a Christian life to avoid the wrath of God (who was likely to punish the whole parish if one of the households behaved badly). All were to follow both God's law and the secular laws and customs. This also held true for the nobleman, the bailiff, the vicar, the merchant in the town, and ultimately for the king and his councillors in the distant city. Although there were certainly differences in cultural preferences and opportunities when it came to clothes, furniture, music or architecture, many basic conditions of material culture were still very similar for most people in an overwhelmingly agrarian rural society. When a peasant, a clergyman, a nobleman and a town burgher met at the Diet in Stockholm, they could all engage in lively conversation about the weather during the last harvest.

The peasantry was the lowest estate in the hierarchic self-image of pre-industrial society. But it was also the men and women of the peasant households who represented the foundation and backbone of society, and who provided the basic conditions of life under which all the rest also lived. "The peasant is the father of us all" as the old saying went.[19]

A region of overlapping divisions

There were many basic similarities in the Nordic region in the period covered here. Many of these were also part of a general European or at least western European pattern. This was true of such features as the development of the princely and relatively centralised conglomerate state, the basic social and economic characteristics of an agrarian society with family farms and a group of wealthy estate owners, and the magic-religious world view of Christian culture.

Other features common to the Nordic countries single them out from much of Europe. One such feature was the existence of large areas dominated by a 'lord-less' peasant society in direct contact with the State. This 'lord-less' society was less tied to traditional agriculture and more dependent on auxiliary occupations than in many other parts of Europe. This is also true of the special variety of the early modern State that developed after the breakdown of the Kalmar Union and the Reformation which set up the Lutheran State churches, the relatively slim but well-organised and efficient bureaucracies and the participatory political culture of interaction, communication and debate.

There were, however, also important differences within the Nordic region. In social and economic terms they can be divided into three zones.

In the southernmost zone, basically consisting of most of Denmark and Schleswig-Holstein, the landscape looked pretty much the same as south of the border in Germany. The plains here were scattered with many small towns, numerous manors and castles and many relatively large villages inhabited almost totally by peasant families more or less dependent on a manorial lord.

The counterpoint to this landscape was the vast stretches of forest or mountainous land in central and northern Sweden, Finland and Norway.

Here, people mostly lived in scattered farms. There were few or no towns. Manors or landlords were rare or in many cases did not exist at all. Even if the Crown was sometimes an important landowner, as in northern Norway, and even if noblemen in some areas owned individual farms, the tenants usually did not have a close relationship to their lords. They probably lived under much the same conditions as their neighbouring freeholders.

Between those two extremes there were smaller areas on the plains where conditions could be closer to one or the other of the two types, but usually in more mixed form. This was the case in the Mälaren valley in central Sweden, the Western Gothia and Eastern Gothia plains and several smaller areas in southern Sweden, and in southwest Finland. Indeed, around Mälaren and in Eastern Gothia the noble estates dominated some districts as much as in Denmark. In Norway, the largest estates were to be found in the southeast, and especially around the Oslo Fjord and north to the lake of Mjøsa, in certain districts on the west coast and in Trøndelag.

It is an interesting question as to where Iceland should be located in this typology. Its lack of towns, villages and manors in the continental sense should perhaps place it in the second category, but the dependence of almost all peasants on the local gentry would rather indicate the first.

As we have seen above, from the late Middle Ages onwards, Denmark came in many ways to develop in a different direction from the rest of the Nordic region. The landlords got a stronger grip over their subordinate peasants both economically and legally. We can perhaps speak of a 'German' period in Danish history between the early sixteenth and late eighteenth centuries.[20] This is true not only of the socio-economic structures, but also of the place of Denmark in the international economy, as it was hit hard by the central European recession of the seventeenth century. Denmark's political system developed in the direction of absolutism at about the same time as, for instance, Brandenburg-Prussia. During this period Denmark does not totally fit the picture of the special Nordic region outlined above.

We can clearly see that political borders do not follow social and economic borders. The late Middle Ages saw several attempts at putting together dynastic states across such dividing lines. Early modern Denmark-Norway contained both the 'eastern' Denmark and the dynamic and diversified Norway.

All these overlapping divisions must surely have influenced the desires and opportunities of the peasantry for making their voice heard in society. If it is true there was a more participatory political culture in Sweden (including Finland) and Norway, this must mean that the opportunities and ways in which the peasantry could voice their demands would have been different in Norway and Denmark within the same state. But they must have been different in Norway and Sweden too, due to the different political frameworks. Just as it was possible to operate with different socio-economic zones within the Swedish kingdom, so peasant politics would also seem to have taken a different form in different provinces.

From the point of view of peasant unrest, the most important conclusion of this discussion of the similarities and differences within the Nordic region is that there were many factors which created different settings in different parts of the countries and states. It is important to pay attention to the different socio-economic, institutional and cultural frameworks within which the peasants operated. The peasants had very different reasons for being dissatisfied in neighbouring provinces within the same realm. They perhaps also had different repertoires of resistance to choose from whenever they decided to act. They certainly had different adversaries. While it might have been perfectly rational for a group of Swedish or Finnish peasants to appeal to the authorities in the capital with their grievances and petitions, the same would perhaps in certain situations have been meaningless for a group of peasants on a Danish noble estate. Even when open violence erupted, it could have been interpreted differently in different contexts and by different groups. Violence could be seen as a legitimate last resort by some, as illegal rebellion by others.

This underlining of differences is not to say there did not exist a common substructure in the Nordic medieval and early modern societies. Kings, lords and peasants in the Nordic countries shared at least enough of a common 'language' (in the broadest sense of the term) and the same fundamental conceptions of society to make the interaction between rulers and ruled meaningful. The study of peasant unrest and peasant politics must look for common ground as well as conflict, just as we have done here on the similarities and differences in the Nordic region.

NOTES

1. There is no overview in English covering the entire Nordic region during the whole of this period that takes account of modern research in social and cultural history. In 'Scandinavian', see Gustafsson 1997. For the Middle Ages (until about 1500), Sawyer & Sawyer 1993 provides a good account in English. Danielsen et al. 1995 is an excellent book on Norwegian history in English, but there is no counterpart for the other countries.
2. Gustafsson 1998a.
3. Metcalf (ed.) 1987.
4. Jespersen 1987.
5. Ladewig Petersen (ed.) 1984.
6. Gustafsson 1994.
7. Skrubbeltrang 1978; Løgstrup 1987.
8. Feldbæk 1993, 28–106.
9. Gunnarsson 1983.
10. Villstrand 1992.
11. Grell (ed.) 1995.
12. See e.g. Villstrand 1992, passim.
13. Gustafsson 1994; Österberg 1995, 171–197.
14. Bregnsbo 1997.
15. Appel 1999, chapters 8 and 9.
16. Gustafsson 1985.
17. See Spierenburg 1991.
18. This local peasant elite is also found in a typical Danish manorial community: Appel 1999, 129–131, 403–406.
19. Bjørn 1981.
20. Gustafsson 1998b.

CHAPTER III

Against tithes and taxes, for King and province
Peasant unrest and medieval Scandinavian political culture

Kimmo Katajala

Protest in autonomous peasant society

The famous Snorri Sturlasson describes the oldest mentioned rising in the Nordic countries in his Heimskringla Saga. This uprising of slaves is dated approximately to AD 500. The saga tells us that an escaped slave of King Egil called Tunne gathered around him a group of robbers and begun to rob the villages. Egil was forced to fetch military help from Denmark. With the help of the Danes, Egil was able to defeat Tunne and his gang and return to the throne. Although the saga is an ancient folk tale and partly a construction of the poet Snorri, the nucleus of the story may contain some element of truth.[1]

The scanty sources on the eleventh and twelfth centuries bring us the first pictures of the conflicts between peasants and establishment in the Nordic countries. It would seem that the main contradictions were between the peasantry and the clergy. The Church was the main establishment force at local level. As an elected monarch, the king was in a weak position within the kingdom. The principles of Crown taxation were only just being developed, castle building was in its infancy and royal warfare was comparable to that of any of the major lords. The provinces had their own laws and still occupied a rather autonomous position under princely rule. The Church, bishops and local clergy in the new parishes had the most contact with the local peasant societies.

This being the case, it is obvious that most peasant protest would have been aimed at the demands of the clergy. Indeed, we have some implicit evidence on the violence and peasant protests against the clergy in this period. In 1171 or 1172, pope Alexander III ordered the archbishop of Uppsala to take steps to ensure the people paid their tithes to the Church. In this very same letter, the pope wrote that anyone who raised his hand against a clergyman would be put under the ban.[2]

Yet, on what occasions did these controversies lead to protests and even open violence? Some light can be thrown on this question from 'Eastland' (S. *Österland*) as the Swedes called the eastern part of their Swedish realm, Finland. The ballad of the death of Bishop Henry, written in the first half of the thirteenth century, tells of the crusade of Bishop Henry and King Eric from Sweden to Finland approximately during the years 1155–1157. Nowadays, we know that this 'crusade' was possibly just one of the many *ledung* journeys the Swedish medieval kings conducted overseas to the east to strengthen their power there.

This old ballad tells us how Bishop Henry was left in Finland to build churches and christen the people. He grew hungry and went to a peasant house. Only the mistress of the house was present, and, although it was her duty, she did not want to feed the bishop and his horse. However, it was also the case that the clergy and servants of the Crown had to pay for the food they took from the peasants during their travels. According to the ballad, Bishop Henry took bread, beer and hay for his horse and left some money in payment. When Lalli, the peasant proprietor, came home, his wife, lying, yelled out:

"a Swedish guest, German glutton
took a loaf from the oven top,
took some beer from the cellar,
ashes threw in their place;
hay he took from the hay shed,
oats he took from the oat bin,
ashes threw in their place".[3]

Lalli took his weapons, skied at a terrible speed, caught Henry on the ice of Lake Köyliö and furiously killed him. In the last scene of the ballad, Henry is a saint in heaven, while Lalli must ski forever in the flames of hell.

Whether there is much truth in this small tale or not has been a topic of keen debate between Finnish historians and folklorists for decades. Still, the story tells us something essential about the relationship between the clerical authorities and the peasantry in medieval Scandinavian society. Food, and tithes too, were not something a bishop or a clerk could simply take or demand. He had to have the peasant's permission to take the goods, and he had to pay for them. They also had to have an agreement on such payments and tithes with the peasants, parishes and provinces. Disagreement about these payments would seem to have been fairly frequent. Finland was still the 'wild east'. In 1209, pope Innocent III wrote in a letter that there had been a bishop in Finland but it had been hard to find a man to replace him after his death. The bishop was not honoured in Finland. Instead, according to Innocent, he was in great danger of dying a martyr's death.[4]

These conflicts seem to have continued down to the first half of the fourteenth century. Statements were repeatedly issued banning those who did violence to the clergy.[5] Conflict between bishops, local clergy and peasants was certainly not a rare event. King Magnus Ericsson sent a letter to the Finnish provinces of Karelia, Savonia and Tavastia urging them to pay their tithes to the clergy. The archbishop of Uppsala had to renew these demands several times.[6]

There was an extremely lengthy and heated dispute in the 1320s and 1330s between Bishop Bengt and the Tavastians over the four marten

Map 2. The provinces of Sweden in the sixteenth century

skins every peasant was obliged to give. The peasants were ready to pay the value of three skins in money, but Bishop Bengt demanded four skins in kind. One parish was even excommunicated when the peasants totally refused to pay the furs to the bishop. The resolution to this conflict by the archbishop of Uppsala in 1335 was a compromise, but also in practice a victory for the peasants. They were obliged to pay four skins, as Bengt wanted, but in money. However, because the value of one skin was estimated at a quarter lower than before, the actual payment was equal to the demands of the peasants.[7] The fur tax payable to the bishops was a constant source of dispute for a long time. In 1370, the bishop threatened the populace of Savonia with punishment because they did not pay the fur tax in the manner of Tavastia and Satakunta.[8]

Most of the conflicts occurred between local priests and the peasants in their parishes. Knowledge of these cases and written sources have survived only if a bishop, archbishop or pope was involved in the process. Even so, we know of several cases from every corner of the Finnish territory of those times.[9] In 1360, Archbishop Petrus of Uppsala rebuked the populace of Satakunta and Tavastia in a letter as follows: "Instead of fulfilling your duties and paying your tithes you have with a hard neck (L. *erectis ceruicibus*) promised to the guardians of your souls only losses and blows in reward for their fatherly care of you. All this you done have with loud noise."[10]

No true peasant uprising is known from the medieval Swedish realm. But during the thirteenth and fourteenth centuries recalcitrance in the payment of tithes was also quite common in the Swedish part of the kingdom.[11] The Uppland uprising in 1247 has been interpreted as a mixture of competition over the Crown of Sweden and a peasant protest against the developing system of taxation. The movement was led by the pretenders to the throne, local lords known as *folkungas*. The peasantry of Uppland rose up in arms and joined the mutineers. Royal troops smashed this joint noble-peasant army in a bloody battle.[12] However, this event looks like a prelude to the numerous uprisings of the turbulent Swedish fifteenth century. Late-medieval pretenders to the throne were often in alliance with and at the head of peasant armies, the latter having their own goals. This was characteristic of many late-medieval disturbances labelled as peasant uprisings.

The first half of the fourteenth century seems to have been a period of special unrest. The Norwegian historian Steinar Imsen has found about twenty occasions from that century where the common people came into conflict with the representatives of Crown or Church. This resistance seems to be concentrated in eastern Norway in the environs of the present-day Oslo. In the first half of the century the source of discord seems to have been payment for the clergy. The latter half of the century sees the common people dissatisfied with the representatives of the Crown. It would seem that the main cause of dispute was taxation, and the typical form of peasant protest was the tax strike.[13] In this sense, fourteenth-century Norway had much in common with Finland.

The picture of medieval peasant protest in Denmark looks quite different from the other Nordic countries. The last Viking king of Denmark, Saint Knut died at the hands of rebelling commoners in 1086. Knut's ill-starred voyage to England in 1085 and the taxes collected for a new looting expedition caused open violent resistance when he travelled around Denmark. Many local lords joined the opposition. The rebels encircled Knut in the Church of Saint Alban on the island of Fyn. Pushing their way into the church, they killed the king. Behind this rebellion there has been a tendency to see general contention against Knut's policies. Some Danish historians even claim the resistance was stimulated by the first traces of the process leading to the centralised state.[14]

The provinces of Scania and Halland, nowadays covering the southern parts of Sweden, belonged to the Danish realm down to the sixteenth century. These provinces were especially tumultuous parts of medieval Denmark. Two remarkable revolts took place in 1180 and 1182 against the bailiffs of Absalon, bishop of Lund. According to the chronicle, this unrest was caused by the collection of taxes and the communication to the peasants of a new obligation to work for the bishop. The local lords are said to have played an important role in the first phase of the uprising. Their discontent was due to Absalon overlooking them in favour of his relatives in appointments to the offices of bailiff. Soon the movement also began to oppose the local lords of Scania. The Danish historian Poul Holm interprets these revolts as serious signs of protest against the development of the Danish system of government in these areas. The peasants were totally defeated in the battles that ended these two revolts.[15]

The Danish peasantry protested during the thirteenth and fourteenth centuries against the extra taxes the kings were demanding. In 1249, Eric IV (r. 1241–1250) failed in his attempt to force the Danes to pay an extra tax of 'plough money' (D. *plovpenning*). In Scania a group of men drove the king and his soldiers out of the province. Resistance was still continuing in different parts of Denmark in the 1250s.[16]

In 1313 the 'plough tax' (D. *plovskat*) once again became an issue between the Danish peasantry and the king. King Eric Mendved needed money for war and wanted to collect an extraordinary tax. Crop failure made it difficult for the peasantry to pay even the ordinary taxes. Extraordinary taxes had already been a subject of dispute since 1311. In 1312, some recalcitrant peasants were hanged. Now the resistance became concentrated on the island of Jylland and the central parts of Denmark. Once again the movement was not led by peasants, but by local gentry opposed to the king. King Eric attempted to raise the tax by military force. The result was that his opponents also armed themselves. In the ensuing battle at Kolding, the well-organised peasant army in alliance with the local lords defeated the royal force. The king had to furnish a larger military force that was able to defeat the rebels. The leaders of the rebellion were hanged, the peasants were heavily fined and a new tax called 'gold corn' (D. *guldkorn*) was placed on the peasantry as a permanent monument to the rebellion. The king strengthened his power in these rebellious provinces by building new castles and repairing the old. Royal control over the area was tightened.[17]

There are traces in the sources of almost simultaneous tumult against King Albert of Mecklenburg (r. 1364–1389) in Finland. Unrest among the Finnish peasantry would seem to have been greatest in the provinces of Satakunta and Karelia during the years 1367–1369. Construction began on three new castles, while Turku Castle was enlarged. The costs were placed on the peasantry, and peasants were obviously also used in the building work itself. At the same time a new war tax was introduced. The result was protest. In Satakunta the protest was directed against the new castles. In 1367, men from Satakunta were sent to King Albert to complain about the new castle. It should be noted that King Albert saw the protest of the peasants as so strong that he decided not to irritate them any further. He ordered the demolition of the newly built small castle at Kokemäki and its removal to a more suitable site on Crown land.[18]

Taxation would seem to have been a general reason for unrest at this time. It is known that Albert of Mecklenburg wrote to his bailiffs in

Finland and urged them to negotiate with the peasants of Uusimaa and Karelia to get them to speedily pay their taxes for Viipuri Castle. In the same letter he confirmed the agreements the bailiffs had entered into with the peasants of the other Finnish provinces. From this we see clearly that the king could not impose the taxes on the peasants, but had (at least formally) to negotiate with the local peasant community. It is also believed these letters show there was general unrest at this time over taxes in the western parts of Finland, but that the disagreement there was resolved through negotiation.[19]

However, there is also one slight mention of violent turbulence from these very same years. A tax roll from the sixteenth century mentions that the parish of Jääski in Karelia in the environs of Viipuri Castle was to pay a permanent tax (the 'Ryes of Soini') because of the killing of the castle bailiff. It is thought this Soini must have been the bailiff Sune Hakonsson (the Swedish name *Sune* is rendered in Finnish as *Soini*), who was in charge of Viipuri Castle. We know he died violently during these turbulent years of 1368–1369. From these fragmentary sources, the historian Väinö Voionmaa proposed as far back as 1915 that this was a real event and the first known violent Finnish peasant tax revolt in Karelia during the reign of Albert of Mecklenburg.[20]

All this is guesswork. Nothing is known for certain about the tax revolt in Karelia in 1368–1369. However, it is clear that the taxes were a constant source of dissension, especially in the 1360s. The change is clear. During the twelfth and thirteenth centuries peasant protest was directed against the demands of the Church and clergy. This was especially so in Norway and Finland. Protests against king and Crown arrive on the scene during the thirteenth and fourteenth centuries, somewhat earlier in the politically more central areas in Sweden and Denmark. There, we can also find real rebellions with armed peasants led by the local gentry. In the more peripheral Norway and Finland the unrest was not linked to politics, being rather local, small-scale actions in direct response to the new taxes and castle building.

In medieval Sweden the taxes and tithes were clearly not simply dictated from above, but negotiated with the subjects. Where disagreements arose, the peasants would complain to the king, organise a tax strike or, where they felt a strong sense of injustice, finally rise up in arms. How should we understand all this? The above ideas on the medieval disturbances provide an important background to our attempts to figure out the political culture of the numerous violent movements involving the peasants of the fifteenth century.

The Kalmar Union in crisis

Margaret, Queen of Denmark and Norway, united the three northern kingdoms to form a loose federation in 1397. That year in the town of Kalmar, the young Eric of Pomerania was nominated as the common king of the new Union. However, Queen Margaret held the real reigns of government until her death in 1412. Denmark took the lead in the Union. The period of Union and especially the reign of Eric of Pomerania (r. 1397/1412–1441) was a time of great turbulence in all three kingdoms. Explanations vary as to the cause of these protests. Swedes especially stress Eric's system of government and the results of his policies. Approaching from this viewpoint, we must outline the character of the Union policies that may have been behind the protests that arose in Sweden.

Queen Margaret had already stepped on the toes of the Swedish clergy. She nominated what she considered to be reliable (often Danish) men to Swedish bishoprics. The intervention of the earthly ruler in church politics infringed the privileges of the clergy. The Church was (or sought to be) an autonomous power within the realm but outside the Crown. The bitterness of the deposed Swedish bishops was real. Queen Margaret had intensified taxation, and the Swedish clergy were already complaining in 1396 that the peasants were as poor as the Israelites enslaved in Egypt. This dissatisfaction broke out into open conflict in 1432 when the chapter of Uppsala chose a new archbishop from their own circles. Without a recommendation from the king, the new archbishop nevertheless travelled to Rome to solicit papal approval for his nomination.[21] This was tantamount to an open declaration of war.

Another dissatisfied group in Sweden was the nobility and the aristocratic Council of the Realm. Eric held his court in Denmark. He also used a lot of Danes and Germans as bailiffs and lords of his castles in Sweden and Norway. Ruling the castles was in essence the same as ruling the kingdom. The power of the Council of the Realm was diminished and, what is even more important, the Swedish gentry were set aside from the profitable offices of the bailiffs. When King Eric reclaimed some of the lands and rents of the nobility for the Crown to meet his need for money, there was no shortage of reasons for irritation among the Swedish nobility in the 1430s.[22]

Eric's tax reform and monetary policies caused special problems for the burghers and peasants. Besides the 'national' currencies, there were several local currencies minted in different parts of the Union. In Finland, for example, a mark was coined in Turku. Eric decided to devalue these local currencies by one third of their value against the 'official' currencies. The taxes were, however, counted in "good old money". Because the peasants paid their taxes in local coin, the effect was to raise their tax burden by half.[23]

Eric particularly needed money for his warfare on the Continent. The taxes were now demanded in money, which was in reality impossible. The many wars meant there was a continuous lack of money in circulation. The peasantry had no money, so they had to pay their taxes to the bailiff mainly in kind. A monetary tax value was put on the products. The bailiff sold these products in the market at a market price higher than the tax value. He could then deliver the taxes to the Crown in money and pocket the difference.[24]

This system of changing tax products into money led to a lot disputes and conflict between the peasantry and the bailiffs. We know, for example, of several peasants' complaints from Finland in the 1410s to King Eric about taxes and the system of taxation.[25] Eric's policies on the Continent led to conflict with the commercial power of northern Europe, the Hansa. The Union kingdoms were under commercial blockade by the Hansa during the years 1427–1432. This was detrimental to the economies of the towns, the burghers and those who produced goods for export. Eric's policies had thus upset all the key groups in late-medieval Swedish society. So it is no wonder there was protest. Even so, it is astonishing how strong the turbulence against Eric of Pomerania and his government was in all three Union kingdoms. The best-known of these is the Engelbrekt uprising in Sweden.

The contentious Swedes

Open violence broke out in the province of Dalecarlia at the beginning of the 1430s. The peasantry of Bergslagen district were in conflict with King Eric's Danish bailiff Jens Erikssøn. In the 1420s, the man had already caused peasant protests and complaints in Jemtland in Norway. Swedish folktales adopted this 'Jösse Eriksson' as an extreme example of the harsh foreign bailiffs. A Dalecarlian petty nobleman called Engelbrekt Engelbrektsson complained in spring 1432 to King Eric about Jens Erikssøn. The king passed the case on to the Swedish Council of the Realm. The Council organized an investigation into the abuses by the bailiff and found the accusations of the peasants well-grounded. However, nothing happened. The peasants of Dalecarlia then took the initiative, armed themselves and advanced on the town of Västerås. Negotiations with the Council of the Realm led this time to the withdrawal of the peasants. In spring 1433, Jens Erikssøn was still sitting in Västerås Castle. The hatred could not be blocked any longer. Armed peasant troops attacked and took Borganäs Castle and began to march towards Västerås Castle. Now the Council of the Realm finally took action and deposed Jens Erikssøn. The unrest seems to have settled down for a while.[26]

We know the situation in Dalecarlia was raised in Copenhagen at the common assembly of the nobles of the Union in summer 1433. Jens Erikssøn himself was also present. Jens did not return to Dalecarlia. However, a rumour spread to the province that King Eric was to send a new, even harder man to replace Jens Erikssøn. According to a chronicle, this rumour was enough to trigger the Engelbrekt uprising in June 1434. The peasant army recruited one man from each household. Midsummer saw the castles of Borganäs and Köpinghus in flames. The town and castle of Västerås fell to the rebels. The peasants and gentry of the province of Västmanland were summoned there to an assembly (*ting*). The province, including the gentry, joined the rebel army. Erik Puke, a son of a member of the Council of the Realm, was sent to the provinces of Hälsingland, Norrland, Osthrobothnia and Åland to make sure these areas would join the opposition against King Eric.[27]

The peasant army with Engelbrekt Engelbrektsson in the lead rolled into the province of Uppland. Simultaneously the peasants of the province of Södermanland rose against their German bailiff. The province of Uppland joined the rebel army. Numerous complaints about the bailiffs and taxes were brought to the assembly in the town of Uppsala. Engelbrekt promised the complainants that the taxes would be lowered. Now the peasant force comprised about 40 000 men. The walls of the town of Stockholm brought the army to a halt in July. The governor of the town, Hans Kröpelin was loyal to King Eric and negotiated an armistice with Engelbrekt. In August a meeting of the Council of the Realm was held in the town of Vadstena. Engelbrekt was also present. The chronicle tells us that Engelbrekt violently pressed the aristocrats to join the rebels. Be that as it may, three bishops and sixteen men of high nobility gave notice of resigning their allegiance to King Eric.[28] The Swedish political elite began to join the open opposition.

After the meeting in Vadstena the rebels roamed in three sections around the country. This army was no longer a mere gang of peasants with poor weapons. Armoured nobles were riding alongside armed peasants on foot. The rebels also had at least formal support from the Council of the Realm. The castles quickly surrendered and were often burned. If we exclude the town of Stockholm and several of the greatest fortifications, Englbrekt Engelbrektsson was the real ruler of Sweden in those days. King Eric arrived in Stockholm with several warships, but the only result was a two-year truce with Engelbrekt.[29]

A meeting of the Estates was convened in the town of Arboga at the beginning of 1435. About twenty Swedish nobles joined the rebels. Three men were named to lead the rebel troops into the heart of Sweden. One of these was Engelbrekt, the others being two high nobles. Engelbrekt took care of the troops from Uppland. In June he was elected military commander (S. *rikshövitsman*) of the kingdom. Now he really had power in his hands.[30] However, the Council of the Realm began to negotiate with King Eric without Engelbrekt. The consultations were long and difficult. Numerous complaints of the peasantry about the taxes and abuses by the foreign bailiffs were presented to the king. Eric promised to rule the country in accordance with its laws, to lower the taxes and to hear the Council of the Realm in his decisions. So, in May 1435 an agreement was made between the king and the Council of the Realm and Eric returned to the throne of Sweden.[31]

The result of the agreement was not what had been expected. Eric returned Danes and Germans to their offices. The Council of the Realm was investigated and many of those involved in the rebellion, for example Engelbrekt Engelbrektsson and Eric Puke, were dismissed from their posts. The promised tax reform was postponed. A young 27-year-old noble called Carl Knutsson was nominated to be military commander of the kingdom. Although Engelbrekt was not a member of the Council and no longer the official military commander of the kingdom, he was nevertheless still at the head of the rebel army. So it is no wonder that the discontent of the peasants of many provinces burst out again in November. The Council of the Realm was accused of this betrayal. An assembly of the Estates was convened in the town of Arboga again in January 1436. The oath of allegiance to King Eric was cancelled once again. The rebel army and the members of the Council, including many bishops, progressed from Arboga towards the capital. Carl Knutsson now rode beside Engelbrekt Engelbrektsson.[32]

The burghers and the commons in Stockholm took the side of the rebels. The gates were opened and the town was soon taken. Carl Knutsson and Engelbrekt Engelbrektsson were elected military commanders of the rebel army. Engelbrekt was sent to southern Sweden to conquer the castles still faithful to King Eric. On this journey he was murdered on March 4. This was clearly not a political assassination, but a murder for personal reasons. Soon the Council of the Realm began to negotiate about the restoration of the Union. In autumn 1436, Eric of Pomerania accepted the demands of the Swedes. The revolt was over. It was planned that Eric would return to the Swedish throne in September. However, this was not what finally happened.[33] Yet, we must first outline how the Swedes have attempted to explain the Engelbrekt uprising and then look at how the late-medieval uprisings in general have been explained in recent writings.

Interpretations of the Engelbrekt uprising

The late-medieval chronicles put great stress on the abuses and cruelty of Eric's foreign bailiffs as the reason for the peasant uprising.[34] Patriotic Swedish historical writing keenly accepted the view that the uprising was directed against the Kalmar Union, seeing the patriotic Swedes as having risen under national banners against foreign rule.[35] The German and Danish bailiffs undoubtedly handled the Swedish peasantry more roughly than they were used to. However, the uprising was clearly not directed against the Union. If this had been the case, it would be hard to explain why the rebels negotiated with King Eric and twice accepted his return to the throne. The rebels were not seeking to break the Union, but to change the government of King Eric and his bailiffs.[36]

Swedish historians were quite early in rejecting this national interpretation of the Engelbrekt uprising. In 1934, Erik Lönnroth suggested that the background to the revolt lay in the economic troubles into which Eric's policies on trade, finance and warfare had plunged all the key groups in late-medieval Swedish society: the nobility, the clergy and the peasantry. The trade blockade by the Hansa in 1427–1432 caused an increase in the price of grain and salt. This was especially irritating in Bergslagen, a district largely dependent on iron production. The price of iron fell and the blockade prevented iron exports just when the rising taxes and foreign bailiffs were upsetting the local peasantry. According to Lönnroth, this was the stimulus that caused the conflict to break out in Bergslagen.[37]

Although Lönnroth's view was generally accepted, there have been a number of critiques presented. According to Lars-Olof Larsson, the blockade can hardly have contributed to the uprising, because it was already in force several years before the revolt began. Instead, he stresses the long-term social and economic impact of the constant wars. Taxes rose and the war hampered the export trade. Most of all, Larsson focuses on the way the production of iron was organized in this area. The miners of Bergslagen were mostly free peasants. Many of them were partners in the mine in which they worked, and the organisation of the work was almost corporative in nature. According to Larsson, the revolt arose specifically in the mining areas of Dalecarlia because of the nature of the local productive organisation. Although the war affected the whole country, the Dalecarlians, whom Eric's politics had perhaps hit hardest of all, had both a suitable organisation ready to hand and the resources to raise a rebellion.[38]

Modern historical research has developed new approaches to late-medieval rebellions. Here, we shall outline three approaches that historians have presented to throw new light on the subject: revolts as 'alliances', revolts as 'uprisings' and the 'communalistic order' as the organising principle of revolt. The common feature of all these approaches is the notion of 'political culture'. They all look at the revolts as part of the era's way of 'doing politics'.

The young scholar Dick Harrison has divided the late-medieval Swedish revolts into two categories. On the one hand were the 'traditional' peasant revolts, and on the other the alliances between nobles, often pretenders to the throne, and armed peasants. In late-medieval Swedish society, the kings had little power. In contrast, the peasants in the provinces held a rather strong position. As already mentioned, the Crown had to negotiate over taxes, or at least the peasant assemblies (S. *ting*) in the provinces had to formally accept them. The late-medieval peasants were still armed and peasant armies were quickly assembled whenever needed, as we saw during the Engelbrekt uprising. So, in many cases during the fifteenth century when we see a noble at the head of a peasant rebellion, there was in fact an alliance. Nobles and peasants each had their own aims. However, they were seldom the same.[39]

Harrison's approach can be applied to several cases of unrest in late-medieval Sweden, and there were certainly plenty to choose from. A noble at the head of a peasant army has also been a problem for Continental researchers on peasant revolts. The traditional explanation has been that in such cases the peasantry had been 'lured' into rising. The nobles were supposedly using the simple peasants for their own ends. In Harrison's approach, the peasantry was allied with the nobles. Pretenders to the throne needed the armed force of the peasantry, and the peasants needed trained military commanders to lead their troops. In letters to the provinces by some pretenders to the throne, we can find examples of promises to lower the taxes. If the peasants thought the promise was worthy of support, an alliance was likely. This approach gives the peasantry the role of an active party in the late-medieval political culture.

Another Swedish historian of the younger generation, Peter Reinholdsson, has underlined the fact that late-medieval society was still based to a large extent on agreements. This strongly influenced the way in which conflicts were resolved. Protest was seen as acceptable if the other party did not follow the terms of the agreement and fulfil his duties. The result was a feud between the parties to the agreement. This feud (*fejd* in fifteenth-century Swedish) could be a dispute between persons, families or houses. The first stage would be a formal renouncing of friendship. There were then two possibilities: negotiations and a new agreement, or open violent conflict. The result of violent conflict would provide the setting for negotiations on a new agreement. In a European context, this medieval 'right of feud' was also possible in vertical feudal hierarchies, between the lord and his vassals.

This kind of 'agreement' was also understood to exist between monarch and subjects. The most important duty of the monarch was to protect his subjects, and this was the main argument for why the subjects had to pay taxes. If the king did not protect the peasants against the abuses of the bailiffs, this was, in Reinholdsson's approach, a proper reason for renouncing loyalty and rising in arms. This is why Reinholdsson states that the late-medieval turbulence should not be described as rebellions (S. *uppror*) but, using the terminology of the era, as uprisings (S. *resning*). Use of *resning* in the sense of 'rebellion', or a revolt against the legal government, dates back only to the beginning of the early modern era in the 1520s. The term 'uprising' embraces the idea that violent conflicts, feuds, were an integral part of late-medieval political culture.[40]

The well-known Swiss historian Peter Blickle presented his concept of 'communalism' in 1986. This refers to the new local organizations that emerged in the Holy Roman Empire during the fourteenth and fifteenth centuries. According to Blickle, the receding feudal systems of production, security and law were replaced with new local organizations in the towns and villages. Manorial production with serfs was replaced by productive family units of freeholders. Where necessary, production or parts thereof were organised in corporative forms. The Law of the Land (G. *Landsrecht*) came to replace manorial justice. An essential part of this process was that responsibility for security was transferred from the feudal lords to local organisations. Urban bylaws obliged the burghers and townsmen to provide armour and take part in the defence of the town. The peasantry held arms for the same reason. These new organisations were meant primarily for times of peace. But they could be quickly mobilized for military defence, and why not for attack, too.[41]

The Nordic countries differed in many ways from Continental Europe. The Swedish kingdom never had feudal structures like those in medieval Europe. The towns and villages did not develop into such autonomous units as further south. Blickle's model, if perhaps suitable for German areas, cannot be transferred whole to the late-medieval Swedish kingdom. However, this does not mean that Blickle's ideas are of no interest to our topic. When analysing the late-medieval German revolts, Blickle pays a lot of attention to the organisational structures the peasants and townsmen used in their protests. This should also be done for the northern revolts. The old organisations of the Swedish provinces and their system of gathering in popular assemblies (S. *ting*) were still strong alongside the new local government and judicial organisations of the establishment. As we saw from the Engelbrekt uprising, the corporative organisation of iron production probably served as the nucleus of the revolt. The popular assemblies of the Swedish provinces were used effectively in mobilising the enormous, rebellious peasant army. From this perspective, we can look from the Engelbrekt uprising forwards to the numerous later political crises of the Kalmar Union.

The tumultuous Union

An autumn storm prevented Eric of Pomerania from arriving in Sweden for his coronation. Despite his absence, he was still raised to the Swedish throne, but real power had already slipped from his hands. The real leaders of Sweden were now the young marshal (S. *marsk*), Carl Knutsson and the old governor of the realm (S. *drots*), Krister Nielsson. With the Council of the Realm they purged the Swedish castles of the foreign bailiffs and governors, replacing them with Swedes of the highest aristocracy. The only one of Eric's Danish governors to remain in office was Hans Kröpelin. However, he was moved from Stockholm to Finland to take charge of Turku Castle. Carl Knutsson ruled Stockholm and Krister Nielsson took over Viipuri Castle in the most easterly corner of Finland.[42]

Erik Puke, a member of a high aristocratic family but also a close partner of the late Engelbrekt Engelbrektsson, was also pushed out of high office. Although Puke now had no formal position, he remained in the good graces of the commons. The Puke uprising (1436–1437) has been seen as an epilogue to the Engelbrekt uprising. The peasantry were discontented because the taxes had not been reduced as promised. Erik Puke successfully agitated among the peasants, winning them over to his side in the provinces of Södermanland and Västmanland and around Lake Mälaren. In December 1436, Puke stirred up the commoners in Dalecarlia. Most of the aristocracy, bishops and burghers supported Carl Knutsson, who was therefore able to gather a large army. He marched to Västerås and suppressed the resistance of the local peasantry. Many of those involved in the rebellion were tried and sentenced to death. Yet only four leaders were executed, being burned at the stake.[43]

Erik Puke attracted new supporters from northern Dalecarlia and the provinces of Gästrikland and Hälsingland. The peasant army was now successful, and Carl Knutsson's military power was not enough to suppress the rebels. He therefore proposed negotiations and guaranteed the safety of the negotiators. But this was a betrayal. The bailiff Hans Mårtensson, who had joined Erik Puke, was executed immediately. Erik Puke himself was arrested, taken to Stockholm and executed at the end of January 1437.[44]

1436 and 1437 was also a time of unrest in other parts of the realm. The Danish bailiff Jens Erikssøn, familiar to us from the start of the Engelbrekt uprising, had now upset the peasants of Eastern Gothia. The peasants arrested him and carried him to the local assizes in the town of Motala. After a quick trial he was executed in December 1436. The only punishment Carl Knutsson could impose on the peasants were large payments to compensate for the life of the bailiff.[45] In Dalecarlia, a high noble owner of a manor and Carl Knutsson's bailiff were killed in summer 1437. In negotiations between Krister Nielsson and the Dalecarlians in January 1438, the peasants undertook once again to make large payments in compensation for the lives of the king's men and to carry the weight of the taxes. But the peace did not last, as Carl Knutsson had to send soldiers to the area as soon as November 1438. Autumn 1437 also saw unrest in the province of Värmland near Dalecarlia. The peasantry there rose in arms and killed the bailiff. The rebellion was spreading fast. This time Carl Knutsson answered with violence, and the royal troops defeated the peasant army in a bloody battle. The arrested leaders of the revolt, Torsten Ingelsson and Jösse Hansson, were burned at the stake in February 1438.[46]

There was also unrest rose during those years in the eastern half of the realm, in Finland. The sources on these two events, known as the Karelian tax revolt and David's uprising, are scanty. Much of the interpretation is sheer guesswork. Two men were sent to Carl Knutsson and the Council of the Realm from Karelia in autumn 1438 to complain about the taxes collected at Viipuri Castle. As mentioned, the lord of Viipuri Castle was the other strong man of the realm, Krister Nielsson. He had fallen out with Carl Knutsson, who aspired to the throne. Krister Nielsson saw these complaints as an attack on himself. He wrote to the council of Reval in Estonia and asked them to arrest these "criminal complainers" who had stirred up unrest in Karelia. He guessed right. The homeward-bound Karelian 'complainers', Philippus and Hyncze, were arrested in Reval and put in prison. Now they became pawns in the power politics of the kingdom. Carl Knutsson demanded the council of Reval to free these men, which they duly did. There was evidently widespread discontent over taxation in Karelia during those years and in all probability there was a tax strike. However, we have no evidence of open violent confrontation in Karelia.[47]

David's uprising took place at the same time as the Karelian unrest, but compared to the events in Karelia it was a violent revolt on the opposite side of Finnish territory, in the provinces of Satakunta and Tavastia. Few facts are known about this revolt. We know that on 9 January 1439 the peasants of six parishes in upper Satakunta met the governor of Turku Castle, Hans Kröpelin, probably the bishop of Turku, Magnus Tavast, and several members of the local aristocracy. In a document that has survived from this meeting they pledged never again to raise their hand against the local authorities as they had under the leadership of "crazy David and his crowd". The parishes then thanked the government for pardoning them of their crime. This document was confirmed later with the seal of the province of Satakunta.[48]

Several documents written almost two hundred years later give us some hint of what had really happened. In a court session at the beginning of the sixteenth century it was recounted that a peasant called David had roamed with his 'crowd' like a robber to the manor of bailiff Jöns Sturesson. In the attack, four soldiers of the bailiff were killed and the manor was robbed. The peasants had later compensated for these lives by giving some meadows to the manor. This was evidently not the only damage David and his men had caused to the manors. We know that he had also made his way with his men to the province of Tavastia. There, the peasants had attacked the manor of Porkkala and caused serious losses. It would be astonishing if they had completed this long journey without touching any other manors on the way.[49]

Historians have explained these events in several ways. Traditionally, David's uprising has been seen as a tax rebellion. However, although we have knowledge from Karelia of discontent over taxation, there is no evidence at all that this was the case in Satakunta. It has also been thought the Karelian complainants Philippus and Hyncze and David from Satakunta may have been agents provocateur sent by Carl Knutsson to stir up trouble for his opponents Krister Nielsson and Hans Kröpelin, the latter still faithful to the Union king, Eric of Pomerania. The case of Philippus and Hyncze is not indisputable, although it does seem quite improbable. The case of David is, however, clear. The Finnish historian Kaarlo Blomstedt has proved that David was the peasant proprietor of the wealthiest farm in the parish.[50] It seems that he was not at all 'crazy', but rather a wealthy peasant with special reasons for his behaviour. Yet, if these reasons were not taxes, as Blomstedt, among others, proposes, we must ask what they were.

Seppo Suvanto has interpreted David's uprising with a parallel explanation to that Erik Lönnroth applied to Engelbrekt uprising. In the 1430s, the province of Satakunta was a peripheral area. Although farming and slash-and-burn cultivation were the main source of livelihood, furs and the fur trade were also essential to peasant incomes. The peasants were frustrated because the taxes had not been lowered as promised by the Council of the Realm in 1436, but Suvanto suggests the situation was also exacerbated by the trade blockade that hindered the fur trade. On the other hand Suvanto ponders the effects on the peasant economy of the newly built manors of the bailiffs and judges. It seems there was keen competition between the manors and local peasant society over natural resources such as fisheries, meadows, forests for slash-and-burn cultivation and mill sites.[51]

The young Finnish scholar Tapio Salminen has like Seppo Suvanto stressed the conflict between the new local gentry and the peasants. Instead of the peasant economy, he sees the motive for the unrest as the changes in the economic conditions of the newly formed local gentry. The price of land, the basic economic pillar of the gentry, fell at the beginning of the fifteenth century. Because of this, sources of income for the gentry, such as rents, also decreased. This forced the gentry to look for new sources of income. This was the reason for their invasion of the wilderness areas previously utilised only by the peasantry. Alongside this explanation, Salminen also raises the traditional explanation of discontent over taxation.[52]

The thrust of interpretation is thus drawn from tax protests in the direction of conflict between the peasantry and the local gentry. The cause of discord was seen as competition over natural resources. Heikki Ylikangas, the well-known Finnish researcher into peasant revolt, has emphasized the conflict between the manors and peasants, especially on a general level.[53] However, Sweden and the Finnish territory were not the only areas inside the Kalmar Union to experience revolts during the 1430s. To get a full picture we must turn next to Norway and Denmark, who also had their share of these political tumults.

Against taxes, for shelter: the Danish and Norwegian uprisings

Steinar Imsen has found around twenty events from fifteenth-century Norway that can be described in terms of peasant unrest.[54] Until the 1420s these were usually quarrels between the parish commons and their priests, and they were often settled in the local assizes by the bishops or representatives of the king. Most of these local tumults occurred in the most densely populated areas of eastern or western Norway. The integrationist policies of the realm under Eric of Pomerania, new taxes and Eric's Danish and German bailiffs have been among the key factors quoted by Norwegian historians in interpreting the popular disorder of the 1420s and 1430s. In the 1420s, the peasantry complained a lot about the abuses of the foreign bailiffs. During this phase the leaders of the movement were the wealthy peasants.[55]

Inspired by the Swedish uprising, the peasants around the Oslo Fjord rose in arms in 1436–1437 under the leadership of a member of the gentry, Amund Sigurdsson Bolt. Nevertheless, the classic Norwegian researcher of peasant revolts, Halvdan Koht stresses it was the peasants who instigated the revolt. Amund Sigurdsson was simply chosen to lead the movement. The demands of the peasants were political reform and eviction of the foreign bailiffs, priests and bishops. The armed peasants progressed to the town of Akershus, where they had a battle with the men of the local bailiff, known as 'Black Jens'. Negotiations between the Norwegian members of the Council of the Realm and the Danes led to an armistice. The Norwegians used the tense situation and the threat of the peasants against the foreign bailiffs of King Eric. A 26-member Norwegian delegation under the leadership of Amund Sigurdsson extracted from the Danish Council a promise of a speedy inquest on the claimed abuses. A couple of the most hated bailiffs were evicted from the country. However, the archbishop rejected the demand to evict the foreign bishops and priests. The peasants promised for their part never again to rise against the Council of the Realm and the king.[56]

The promises of both parties were just empty words. The next year, 1438, saw the peasants west of the Oslo Fjord rising under the leadership of Halvard Gråtopp. The focus of protest was once again the foreign bailiffs, the local systems of governance and the bishop of Oslo. The peasants robbed manors and churches. Those who tried to oppose them were treated badly. The Crown and the establishment were no longer interested in negotiating. The former and present bailiffs of Akershus, Black Jens and Olav Bukk, united their forces and defeated the armed peasants. Knowledge of these events is scanty. Those involved in Halvard

Gråtopp's revolt were subjected to heavy fines. Some lost their farms and property.[57] According to Steinar Imsen, this was the turning point in the Crown's attitude to the peasant uprisings in Norway. From here on, violent suppression of the peasant opposition replaced negotiations as the means of solving open conflicts between peasant society and the Crown.[58] The unrest of the latter half of the fifteenth century in Norway consisted of local disputes between the peasants and the bailiffs or judges (N. *lagman*). On a couple of occasions the dispute led to the murder of an official. Although there were no serious large-scale disturbances, a relationship of conflict existed and was also carried through to the sixteenth century.[59]

In 1434, the leader of the Swedish uprising, Engelbrekt Engelbrektsson encouraged the peasants in other Union countries to attack the King's castles and bailiffs. The peasantry of the provinces in eastern Denmark willingly followed this advice. The uprisings in Sweden and Norway have traditionally been viewed through the national paradigm. This absolutely cannot be the case in Denmark. The king, the masters of the castles, the bailiffs and the rebels were all Danes. The most noteworthy unrest arose in Sjaelland, where the peasants opposed the severe taxes of the local lord of the castle. King Eric of Pomerania, hiding in Gotland, and the Danish Council of the Realm accused each other of fomenting the revolt. Yet, historians have shown that the discontent had grown over the years until, under suitable circumstances, it broke out in violence. The unrest spread from Sjaelland over the whole realm, especially to the central parts of Jylland.[60]

The Council of the Realm renounced its oath of allegiance to King Eric and began to negotiate over the throne with Count Christopher of Lübeck. The situation became even more critical in spring 1439. The peasantry burned at least one of the Crown castles. Soon after this a government military detachment plundered the province. It seemed to the peasants that neither king nor government were able to protect them against the soldiers and the bailiffs. Many of the peasants allied with Duke Adolf of Holstein who promised them shelter in return. The government was forced to negotiate, as the duke now had the peasantry behind him. He profited greatly as a result. The government and the fief-holders promised not to collect new or unlawful taxes from the peasants before the new king was elected. On these conditions, the responsibility for protecting the peasants was to be transferred from the duke to the new king. This demonstrates that the aims of this revolt/movement were not political as such, but pursuit of protection against the fief-holders and the Crown bailiffs. The politics of the realm were the framework within which these events took place, not the reason for the revolt.[61]

Count Christopher of Bavaria ascended the throne of Denmark. However, the unrest was not settled. At the end of April 1440, just after his coronation, he had to send a special military detachment to pacify the unrest in Sjaelland. Denmark was now in conflict with the Netherlands, and the king needed funds for warfare. The extra tax for this purpose stimulated a response from the peasants on Fyn island. They armed themselves against the tax collectors and the bailiffs who were to distrain their property for unpaid taxes. This disorder was settled in autumn 1440.[62]

However, the unrest continued. In spring 1441, peasant troops burned down several manors of the Crown and gentry in the northern parts of Jylland. At the head of the peasants was the lord of a local manor, Henrik Tagesen. It would seem his aim was to compete with another local manor-owning family. For the peasants, the riot was caused by a mixture of local tensions with the manors and discontent over the extra tax the king had once again placed on the peasantry. The peasants were successful in the initial battles against the landlords' troops. Following the model of the Hussites, the peasants had built a movable fortification. After hearing of the defeat, King Christopher himself travelled to Jylland, collected a vast army and rushed against the rebels. According to a folk song, the peasants were lured out from their fortification, after which they were easily defeated. Henrik Tagesen was executed on 12 June 1441.[63]

The last episode of large-scale unrest in Denmark was the revolt of Skipper Clemens in 1534. Traditionally, this has been linked with the War of the Counts between the king and the nobility. As a result, it is not always described as a peasant revolt. Christian II was exiled in 1523. His successor, Frederic I died in 1533, and his son Christian III succeeded him in 1534. However, there was a party supporting the restoration of Christian II. The leader of this party, Christopher of Oldenburg attacked the province of Holstein in summer 1534. Skipper Clemens, a well-known political adventurer and professional troublemaker, was sent to northern Jylland to make trouble for the other party. His earlier career had included time as a privateer harassing the ships of Frederic I.[64]

It was well known that the discontent among the peasantry and burghers against the rule of Frederic I and his son was widespread. In September 1534, Clemens took the town of Aalborg. The revolt soon spread to the surrounding areas. The peasant leaders were the wealthiest peasants, those whom the constantly rising taxes had hit hardest. This was not an uprising of the poor. The nobility gathered troops against the peasants and Clemens' men. However, they were pushed back in the battle. Everywhere the revolt took hold, the manors were robbed and burned. Christian III had to organize a large army to defeat Clemens' peasant troops. In Aalborg, a force of about 700–800 burghers and Clemens' men were defeated. The town was ransacked. The lesser leaders were executed immediately. The parishes that had joined the revolt had to pay high collective fines to save the lives of the rebels, and the freeholders lost their farms to the Crown. An oath of allegiance to Christian III was demanded. Clemens himself was tried and executed in 1536.[65]

Towards the early modern era

The rest of the fifteenth century seems to have been quite a calm period in Finland and Norway after the stormy 1430s. As we have seen, this was not the case in Denmark. However, Sweden was the hotbed of the Kalmar Union in the second half of the century. Revolts and riots followed each other in rapid succession. Almost every one of these events involved the armed peasantry. The competition for power and the throne was fierce. These movements were usually headed by pretenders to the throne, although sometimes the peasant troops were led by the bishops. Sometimes the peasant armies of different provinces fought on opposite sides, as for example in the civil war of the mid-1460s.

The peasants were still a power to be reckoned with in the late-medieval Nordic countries. They were numerous, they were armed and the ancient organizational principles of the local assizes (S. *ting*) gave them tools to take part in the politics of the realm. They were a party that had to be taken into account in the calculations of contenders for the throne or political power in the realm. The one who could win an oath of allegiance from the peasants of most provinces was strongly placed in the struggle for power. The peasantry pursued a variety of goals including lower taxes and getting rid of unpopular bailiffs, but they also fought for their political favourites, as evidenced by the rebellion launched by the peasants of Uppland on behalf their imprisoned bishop, Jöns Bengtsson (Oxenstierna).[66]

The keywords of late-medieval political culture were 'feud' and 'alliance'. A feud would lead to either an open fight or negotiations. After the violence died down, a new agreement would be made, oaths of allegiance given and received, and the stability of society (if such there was) re-established. The law and the courts played a very minor role in solving this turbulence.

However, the times were changing. The crisis of the 1430s can be seen as a turning point. The establishment began to rule the peasantry in new ways. In Sweden, the statutes of Strängnäs in 1437 forbade the peasantry from bearing arms in public places. Although these statutes were still a 'dead letter' at the end of the century, they can nevertheless be seen as the beginning of the process of disarming the Swedish peasantry. In Denmark, the tumults of the 1430s resulted in the prohibition of the peasant assemblies, thus denying the organisational principles of peasant society. As mentioned above, Steinar Imsen sees Halvard Gråtopp's uprising of 1438 as a turning point in establishment attitudes towards the peasant risings. From now on the answer was not negotiation but force.

Scandinavian union broke down in the bloody tragedies of the early 1520s. The Union king, Christian II was deposed from the Swedish throne and the Kalmar Union split into two realms, the Danish-Norwegian kingdom and the Swedish realm. The man who effectively ended the Union was Gustavus Ericsson, a member of the Swedish high nobility. The concept of coup d'état was an old one. Gustavus Ericsson, known later as Gustavus Vasa or King Gustavus I, managed to rally the peasantry of Dalecarlia and several other provinces behind him, defeated the Danish army with his peasant troops, and was elected regent of Sweden in 1521. He was the last Swedish king to rise to the throne with the help of a peasant army.

Gustavus Vasa was an energetic state-builder. He reinforced the local systems of governance. Local society was placed under tighter control. Taxation and tax-collecting were made more efficient. The room for manoeuvre and autonomy of peasant society became correspondingly more restricted. The disarmament of the peasantry proceeded. Gustavus initially used foreign mercenaries in his army, but it was soon to be based on the Swedish nobility.

Among other novelties, Gustavus Vasa introduced three essential innovations to Swedish society: hereditary monarchy, double-entry bookkeeping and the Reformation. Kingship was no longer elective; it was hereditary. This ended the constant bloody struggles for the throne that had marked the past and altered the political climate. The bailiffs and lords of the castles were no longer vassals taking care of their fiefs. They now became royal officials, and the bookkeepers of the castles and districts had to send their records to the king's Council for auditing.

Especially in Sweden and Norway, the Lutheran Reformation was introduced almost totally from above, as a Crown venture. There was no religious-social movement for reformation among the common people, as for example in Germany. The liturgy was simply changed and many of the Church's properties confiscated by the Crown. So it is no wonder that the new regime also encountered several opposition movements: the rebellion of the Western Gothian lords, the revolt of the young lord of Dalecarlia, the 'bell revolt' and so on. However, one Swedish revolt of the sixteenth century stands out above all the rest. The revolt of Nils Dacke in 1543 was the last significant peasant uprising on the territory of Sweden proper.

NOTES

1. Silvén-Garnert and Söderlind 1980, 24–26.
2. FMU I, no. 26.
3. Translation of the ballad according to *Piispa Henrikin surmavirsi* 1999.
4. Suvanto 1987, 37.
5. See FMU I, no. 121; FMU I, no. 498.
6. FMU I, nos 371, 373, 374, 383, 425.
7. FMU I, nos 372, 415, 424; Voionmaa 1916, 373; Suvanto 1987, 121.
8. FMU I, no. 781; REA, no. 211.
9. FMU I, no. 415; cf. Pirinen 1962, 119–120, 130–131; Voionmaa 1916, 374; Suvanto 1987, 120–121.
10. REA, no. 172.
11. See Silvén-Garnert and Söderlind 1980, 34–50.
12. Suvanto 1987, 50; Lindqvist 1988, 62; also Silvén-Garnert and Söderlind 1980, 33.
13. Imsen 1990a, specially 88–89; Imsen 1990b, 131–138.
14. Würtz-Sørensen 1983, 15–16; Wåhlin 1988, 46–71.
15. Würtz-Sørensen 1983, 15–16; Holm 1988, 72–89.
16. Würtz-Sørensen 1983, 16.
17. Würtz-Sørensen 1983, 18–20; Rasmussen 1988, 110–137.
18. FMU I, no. 761; REA, no. 202; Pirinen 1940, 36–47; Jaakkola 1944, 320–326; Suvanto 1987, 107.
19. FMU I, no. 740; REA, no. 196.
20. Voionmaa 1916, 374–375; Suvanto 1987, 106, 111.
21. Lönnroth 1934, 64–65, 92–102; Suvanto 1987, 140–141; Palola 1997, 47.
22. Lönnroth 1934, 63, 89–92; Suvanto 1987, 134–135.
23. Lönnroth 1934, 82; Larsson 1984, 116; Suvanto 1987, 138.
24. Lönnroth 1934, 73; Suvanto 1987, 136–138.
25. Renvall 1962, 48.

26 Rosén 1962, 273; Larsson 1984, 129; Harrison 1997a, 51; Koht 1926, 26.
27 Rosén 1962, 273; Larsson 1984, 129–130, 139–140; Harrison 1997a, 51.
28 Lönnroth 1934, 105–111; Rosén 1962, 273–274; Larsson 1984, 142–153.
29 Rosén 1962, 274–275; Larsson 1984, 154–162; Harrison 1997a, 52.
30 Kumlien 1933, 32; Rosén 1962, 276; Harrison 1997a, 52; Larsson 1984, 162–170.
31 Kumlien 1933, 37–40; Rosén 1962, 277; Larsson 1984, 178.
32 Kumlien 1933, 41–54; Rosén 1962, 279; Larsson 1984, 180–181, 185–189, 192.
33 Kumlien 1933, 55–75; Rosén 1962, 280; Larsson 1984, 195–218.
34 Lönnroth 1934, 72.
35 Lönnroth 1934, 121–122.
36 Lönnroth 1934, 69; Larsson 1984, 173.
37 Lönnroth 1934, 75–81, 85–88;
38 Larsson 1984, 67–68, 116–117, 131–132.
39 Harrison 1997a.
40 Reinholdsson 1998.
41 Blickle 1986a, 530–535.
42 Kumlien 1933, 80–83; Rosén 1962, 281–282; Larsson 1984, 216–218.
43 Kumlien 1933, 85–86; Larsson 1984, 222–224; Harrison 1997a, 53–55.
44 Kumlien 1933, 85–89; Rosén 1962, 282; Larsson 1984, 225–226; Harrison 1997a, 54–55.
45 Harrison 1997a, 55–56.
46 Kumlien 1933, 101–107; Larsson 1984, 231–234; Harrison 1997a, 56–57.
47 FMU IV, nos 2291, 2295, 2307, 2308, 2338; Kumlien 1933, 110–111, 126–127, 164; Rosén 1962, 283; Voionmaa 1916, 377–378; Blomstedt 1937, 5–7.
48 REA, no. 476; this famous letter has been published in translation in several publications: Suomen historian dokumentteja 1 1968, no. 24, 43–45; HArk IV 1874, 145–147; Voionmaa 1916, 376–377; Blomstedt 1937, 3–4; Blomstedt 1952, 14–15.
49 FMU IV, no. 3001; Blomstedt 1937, 24; Jaakkola 1950, 525–526; Blomstedt 1952, 16; Suvanto 1973, 361–361; Suvanto 1987, 145–146; Salminen 1995, 35; Palola 1997, 109–110.
50 Blomstedt 1937, 23–33.
51 Suvanto 1973, 360–361; Suvanto 1987, 146; cf. Kaukiainen 1978, 279.
52 Salminen 1995, 34–35.
53 Ylikangas 1990, 16.
54 Würtz-Sørensen 1983, 31–34; Imsen 1990a, 79–80, 89–90.
55 Koht 1926, 26–29; Imsen 1990b, 190.
56 Koht 1926, 29–32; Imsen 1990b, 173.
57 Koht 1926, 33–34.
58 Imsen 1990a, 86.
59 Imsen 1990a, 79.
60 Würtz-Sørensen 1983, 38–42.
61 Würtz-Sørensen 1983, 42–48.
62 Würtz-Sørensen 1983, 56–66.
63 Olesen 1980, 183–185; Würtz-Sørensen 1983, 72–94.
64 Tvede-Jensen 1983, 232–235.
65 Tvede-Jensen 1983, 234–243.
66 Olesen 1988, 172–173; Harrison 1997a, 67–68.

CHAPTER IV

"The lords from the peasants or the peasants from the lords"
The Dacke War and the concept of communalism

Kenneth Johansson

"...the lords from the peasants or the peasants from the lords."[1] This was how the chronicler Rasmus Ludvigsson summed up the speech given by the peasant leader Nils Dacke to his followers following the truce of Bergkvara in August 1542. The peasants of the province of Småland in southern Sweden had risen up against the new order imposed by their masters. Both before and during the uprising the Swedish nobility had laid claim to peasant land and property; during the Dacke War – the last major peasant rebellion in Sweden proper – the peasants took back what they could. In fact, they took the opportunity to gain rather more than they had lost; under the terms agreed at Bergkvara, property seized by each side before the truce was not to be returned. In this way the contract between the peasants and the king that guaranteed peace within the body politic was to be restored. Nils Dacke argued that it was the king who had broken the contract.[2] In the previous decade the king had made it shamefully easy for the lords to grab an ever increasing proportion of the peasants' land. This was the reason for the uprising and peasant war that began in the early summer of 1542.

Sweden enters the early modern era

With the accession of Gustavus Vasa, Sweden embarked on a very different path – be it political, economic, legal, or cultural – from the medieval period. After the War of the Counts (S. *grevefejden*, a war between Sweden – allied with Denmark and Prussia – and Lübeck concerning trade and navigation) Sweden entered what has been termed the 'German period', named both for the number of Germans who held office in Gustavus Vasa's government and for the numerous ideas that they, amongst others, introduced. At this juncture the king could contemplate many new choices. The future held many opportunities that his predecessors had not had, among them the choice between:

- general conscription or the use of mercenaries;
- a traditional policy towards the aristocracy, or a new approach that profited certain groups of aristocrats;

- the old weak central authority or a new strong one;
- the existing medieval state administration or the construction of a new, modern, centralised administration;
- elective or hereditary monarchy;
- further development of the medieval legal system or the creation of a new one;
- a medieval 'feudal' ideology or a modern, absolutist ideology;
- a strong, independent Church or one under state control.

Even without claiming this to be a comprehensive list, it clearly demonstrates that the choices Gustavus Vasa faced were many and complicated.[3] Across Europe, princes had approximately the same options. Princely power was expanding. State administration, the law, the economy, and ideology – in every context the prince's role was increasingly emphasised, but at the cost of administration, law, economy and so on that had previously stemmed from local needs. As we shall see, the term 'prince' itself expanded in meaning. It was not only kings who were princes, for there were now people in local society who increasingly behaved in a princely manner. The lords were ever more concerned to mark out their position and interests. None of this happened without protest. The peasants believed that since time immemorial they had been the political force that guaranteed both continuity and the security of the realm.

Swedish kings came and went, but the peasants were always there, ready to enter into a renewed contract with each new king as he came along. Every king had to make a traditional progress around Sweden (S. *eriksgata*) to gain the legitimacy he needed. Local self-government, representation in the Assembly of the Estates of the Realm, the right to bear arms, and an all-embracing local government were important pillars on which the entire authority of state power had long been based. The defenders of this tradition were only too aware of the growing threat posed by an increasingly despotic central government that implemented the will of the prince without a thought for peasant traditions.

The centre of the Dacke uprising was the ancient region of Värend that lay on the border between the Swedish and Danish kingdoms. It had long been known for its tendency to go its own way; particularism was a well-developed tradition here. As early as the middle of the eleventh century it is thought that the people of Värend had managed to assert their independence in the face of the Svea kings' determined efforts to expand their rule over ever larger areas. During the second half of the twelfth century there is evidence "within the heterogeneous Småland area"[4] of a separate legal enclave made up of Värend, Njudung, and Finnveden that became known as the *Decem provinciae* or *Tiohärad* (literally, the 'ten hundreds'). It was only in the thirteenth century that Värend and the other old regions were finally conclusively absorbed into the kingdom of Sweden.[5]

Much research on the Dacke War has concentrated on trying to identify its underlying causes and the factors that triggered its outbreak. Of the many reasons suggested, some researchers have argued that the rebellion broke out because Gustavus Vasa's policies imposed restrictions on the oxen trade or introduced similar obstacles,[6] or because of his policy

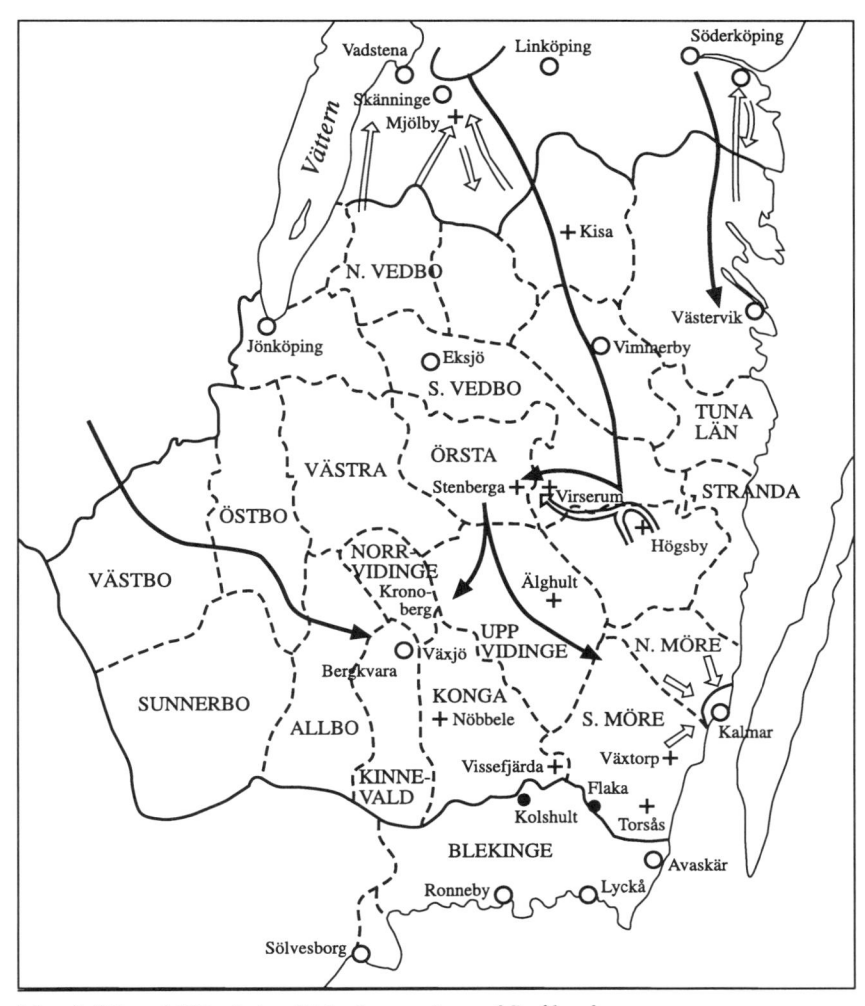

Map 3. Värend ('Dackeland') in the province of Småland

towards the Church,[7] or the increasingly severe taxation.[8] Given the complexity of the early sixteenth century, it is not surprisingly an extremely difficult task to identify one single factor, whether it be an underlying or an immediate cause.[9] Such an approach tends to be based on the idea that it was others who acted while the peasants, at least in this case, merely reacted.

An alternative would be to take the issues raised above as merely a point of departure and, instead of returning yet again to the discussion of the rebellion's causes, try to demonstrate the context in which the peasants addressed the king. Was the king afraid of the rebel forces? If so, what was it about the peasant's choice of words that made him afraid? What were the rebels' demands? What was the world view that informed those demands? What did they aim to achieve? These are some of the crucial questions that remain largely unanswered. Above all, Swedish research has neglected to set the rebels' demands and actions in the context of a broader world view, as an alternative political order at a time when a new order was being formulated.[10]

There are three main source types that deal with the Dacke uprising. There is a very limited body of primary material, principally the list of demands that the rebel forces sent to the King. There is also a small amount of correspondence dealing with the rebellion, and a number of relatively detailed narrative sources. Of the latter, comprising four different accounts, the chronicle of Rasmus Ludvigsson has been judged the most reliable.[11]

Early summer 1542: the rise of Dacke and the truce in Bergkvara

From the early summer of 1542, a small group of peasants and others, in all about thirty men, began to make violent attacks on selected bailiffs and noblemen. The king was informed fairly quickly, and he wrote a letter to the peasants of the province of Kalmar and the *Tiohärad* from which it is clear that he found the unrest extremely worrying, if not downright alarming. He began, however, by minimising its significance, announcing to his subjects that it was only a "gang of forest bandits and traitors" who had "ganged up" to attack bailiffs and royal officers. However, it soon became apparent that it was not only the forest bandits who excited his ire; instead, it was all Småland men who harkened to the call of Nils Dacke, the leader of the rebellion.

The king wrote that he could not understand why "those who are so ready and willing to wage war and fight amongst themselves" would not also take the lead in the war against Sweden's arch enemy, Denmark. Instead, the Småland men were dragging their feet, but, the king continued, "...to murder and strike Our servants, there are some of you who are quite willing and prepared to do so, which God knows is right troublesome and trying...". He went on that he even believed that the Småland men had shown themselves to be "like dumb creatures, that have neither souls nor sense" because they had not shown him the least humility. Yet, he warned them: "Where you turn to quarrel or unrest, then you should doubt that you will be the first and last to do so." However, he understood the seriousness of the situation, and concluded his open letter by promising to listen to the Småland men's grievances if they came to him instead of going to Dacke. Indeed, he announced that he had ordered three "loyal men and councillors" to consult with the peasants of all Småland, to "hear if you have any demands and complaints".

It is thus clear that Gustavus Vasa attempted at the start of the uprising to drive a wedge between the "forest bandits" and the majority of the Småland peasantry. The bandits were to be isolated at all costs, and with a combination of threats and inducements the king attempted to persuade the peasants not to listen to the rebels.[12] He was seriously concerned that the Småland peasants already sympathised with the rebels, and that it was too late to prevent them from joining the uprising. He therefore warned them of the consequences of their actions.

At the same time as he alternately threatened and reassured the peasants, the king embarked on a series of purely military preparations; he now faced the prospect of war against the peasants in large parts of Småland: thus, in actual fact, a peasant war. This is confirmed by a letter sent out from the royal chancery to the leading men of the realm a few days after the king's letter to the Småland men. A comparison shows how the king initially attempted to isolate the growing rebel force while at the same time attempting to increase the pressure on the rebels and crush the uprising by military means as quickly as possible. It also shows how seriously the king viewed the situation as it then stood. It was now scarcely a matter for the *ting*, the traditional local judicial assemblies and their peasant jurors to resolve in the courts, and it was far more than a few bandits on the rampage; it had become a matter of national security and a threat to the survival of the kingdom.

Germund Svensson Somme, governor of Kalmar, was responsible for the military measures taken against Dacke's forces. He had about seventy soldiers (S. *knektar*) at his disposal, and from 12 July, following a recommendation from the Council of the Realm,[13] reinforcements in the form of two small, fully manned ships, a number of boats and some arms. Councillor Gustavus Olsson Stenbock was instructed to send about a hundred soldiers to Småland. These were to proceed to the castle of Bergkvara to assist Ture Trolle, who had been given the task of consulting with the peasants of the *Tiohärad* and the province of Kalmar with the help of Jon Olsson Lilliesparre and Isak Birgersson Hjort. Meanwhile Måns Johansson, together with Jöran Eriksson and Sten Bengtsson, had been ordered to assist Ture Trolle. Yet once these measures were put in place, silence fell. The king heard nothing from Germund Svensson in Kalmar or Ture Trolle at Bergkvara. They were in the thick of the uprising and presumably had other things to concern them than keeping the king informed on what was happening. Perhaps there were no successes to report.

This greatly concerned the king. On 12 July he therefore wrote to the governor of Kalmar that "We have no intelligence from you ... which amazes Us greatly". Meanwhile, further letters were dispatched from the royal chancery. Birger Nilsson in Western Gothia was instructed to call out as many of the nobles in the province as he could muster, and shortly thereafter letters were sent to the bailiffs in Finland with orders to recruit as many soldiers as they could. The uprising had become a matter of state that affected the whole realm. The king, who at the outset had believed it was sufficient to direct the governor of Kalmar and Ture Trolle to take care of it, found scarcely a fortnight later that he would need all the resources of the realm to suppress the uprising.

While the king was taking these measures, he also began to consider what might lie behind the uprising. He wrote to several bailiffs and other royal officers in a manner that demonstrates his views on the matter. Addressing himself in particular to Hans Skrivare and Jören Nilsson, the king warned against extracting too much from the peasants, since then "it follows that, when they are impoverished, they have no other recourse, but are forced to quit house, home, wife, and children for the

Table 1. Measures taken by Gustavus Vasa during the early stages of the uprising until the truce of Bergkvara in 1542. Sources: GVR 1542, L.-O. Larsson 1964.

Date	Name	Measure
3 July	Ture Trolle	Consult with the peasants of the Tiohärad
-"-	Jon Olsson Lilliesparre	-"-
-"-	Isak Birgersson Hjort	-"-
-"-	Måns Johansson Natt och Dag	Consult with the peasants of the province of Kalmar
-"-	Jöran Eriksson	-"-
-"-	Sten Bengtsson	-"-
6 July	Birger Nilsson	Call out the nobles in the province of Western Gothia
-"-	Germund Svensson Somme	Take charge of the military response
10 July	Gustavus Olsson	Call out the nobles in the province of Western Gothia
11 July	Severin Kiil	Consult with the peasants of Småland
-"-	Peder Andersson	-"-
13 July	Måns Johansson Natt och Dag	Consult with the peasants of Vimmerby
-"-	Jöran Jönsson Svan	-"-
16 July	The bailiffs in Finland	Recruit as many soldiers as possible

forest bandits, who are now in Småland, at no small annoyance, damage, and disadvantage to Ourself and the Realm".[14] Four days later he wrote to Councillor Gustavus Olsson about something that had enraged the peasants in other parts of the country:[15] the levying of tithes in the provinces of Western and Eastern Gothia.

From Rasmus Ludvigsson's chronicle it is apparent that tithes were a problem in Småland too. The king wrote that there were a number of bailiffs who had "acted somewhat too harshly and unwisely" when they "demanded the accounts of the priests". The bailiffs had demanded information based on the actual amount of grain sown or harvested.[16] Previously, tithes had been based on the *mantal* (a fixed unit of land used to assess taxes), and the way in which they were recorded had not been particularly specific; it had sufficed to note that M or N had delivered this or that amount to the church. Now every person – as Rasmus Ludvigsson's chronicle put it – "was made to swear how much he had sown in his fields in the year, and how much grain had come of it." This novelty had created great unease amongst the peasants in both Western and Eastern Gothia.

The king thought that in future the approach should be much more cautious: He wrote: "Where you believe that it[17] could cause unrest amongst the common men, then We would rather see that it returns to the terms that were held earlier, while waiting for the outcome of this uprising." He probably did not consider this to be the single most important cause of the uprising, but he would seem to have believed that it was sufficiently serious to move carefully on this issue to prevent the uprising spreading even further. Taxation based on the actual amounts sown or harvested – and the demand that the peasants swore that they had delivered the correct tithe – made it impossible for peasant communities to decide themselves how the tithe burden should be divided amongst them. The *mantal* was a far more anonymous basis for division, leaving as it did a great deal of room for negotiation amongst the peasants, and making it possible for them to determine the individual farmer's share of each *mantal's* tithe.

The issue was thus one of the nature of the tithe: should it be a form of collective tax, or an individual tax that each was responsible for paying correctly? For peasant communities this was naturally an extremely important issue that reflected two different ways of organising society: the old pattern, where a local community administered its own financial transactions and paid for different kinds of protection and safeguards, be they spiritual or temporal; or the new pattern, where everyone was subject to the king and the new state in all kinds of issues.

Nils Dacke and his small band of peasants initially kept to the forests around his home parish. Here they had already managed to make contact with peasants in neighbouring parishes.[18] The band grew into a large body of peasants.[19] This force – then about a thousand strong[20] – seems to have descended on the town of Växjö to gauge their support with the peasants there, after which they advanced on nearby Kronoberg Castle. They occupied the castle and plundered Ture Trolle and other nobles, but when they heard that Gustavus Olsson and the royal troops had reached Småland and had begun to consult with the peasants in the hundreds of Västbo and Östbo, they abandoned Kronoberg, taking with them everything they could carry, and even persuading the priests in Växjö to give them a sum of money. They then moved south to the hundred of Konga to rally the peasants there.[21]

However, Nils Dacke had already taken a very important precaution prior to these events. He had summoned six or eight men from each parish in several hundreds, and peasants from Södra Möre, Konga, and Blekinge at least massed at a meeting in Kolshult in northern Blekinge on St. Knut's Day.[22] According to L.-O. Larsson, the sources that survive from this meeting reveal the context in which we should view both it and, indeed, the whole uprising.[23] At the meeting, a letter was drafted to the inhabitants of Ronneby, situated in Blekinge in what was then Denmark. "Good Danes all, may you know that we have had talk today in this manner, that we have sworn together that if there are those who will carry fire into Blekinge or Värend, then we will assist each other and punish them."[24] The letter expresses what was then the usual approach to border politics in the early sixteenth century, entered into by peasants on both sides of the national border.[25] However, it also shows that the hard core of Dacke's followers, who in the initial stages of the uprising had been made up of more or less marginalised forest peasants, often with a criminal record, had by this point joined up with the ordinary peasants of the border area.

When Gustavus Olsson arrived in Växjö, he set out to gauge his support amongst the local peasants. With a military force of about four hundred men, he tried to take over control of the area. He met with the response that the local peasants were only interested in 'dealing with him' if he could promise to restore to them all their old customs. Naturally he was not able to do this, as he lacked the authority to do so. If that were not enough, he soon heard that one of the Blekinge men, Krämare Pelle, as he was named in the oath sworn at Kolshult, had gathered about two thousand Blekinge peasants and planned to join Dacke to advance again on Växjö. On its way through Värend this force grew to about ten thousand men, at which point Olsson judged it wise to withdraw from the town.[26] With his four hundred men he made for Ture Trolle's fortified house at Bergkvara, followed by about two thousand of the rebels who "gave themselves in battle with those who were there ... and there was carnage at Herr Ture Trolle's mill, that lies outside Bergkvara", as Rasmus Ludvigsson put it, continuing "but God gave King Gustavus's men happiness and victory, so that Dacke's party left there with many men dead and wounded".[27]

It would seem that Dacke's forces were unable to take the stronghold at this point. The rebels dispatched several men together with Trolle's parish priest to try to reach a compromise with Councillor Gustavus Olsson and Ture Trolle. The lords answered that they could only come to a compromise if the rebels surrendered Nils Dacke. To this, the rebels retorted that Dacke was "a good man", who always wanted the "peasants' best", and so the first attempts at a truce foundered. However, once the king's men had found out that Krämare Pelle was en route to Bergkvara with at least five hundred men, gunpowder, and new hackbuts, they decided to talk to the peasants' representatives. "Therefore it seemed wise to them [the king's men] to meet with them [Dacke's men] on the terms that they demanded."[28] A truce was agreed on 24 July 1542. Shortly afterwards, Dacke gathered his men together and gave them an account of the substance of the truce. He went on to warn "the common men" that before the truce lapsed they should arm themselves adequately.[29]

It is also interesting to note in the source material and in Rasmus Ludvigsson's chronicle an episode that had occurred somewhat earlier. At the time of the retreat from Kronoberg,[30] Nils Dacke had written to a nobleman named Svante Sture at Stegeborg, asking if he wished to take command of the Småland men. Dacke clearly envisaged a future without Gustavus Vasa on the throne. The leadership of the Småland men should thus be taken by a descendant of the Sture family, thought Dacke.[31] If Svante Sture agreed, the Småland men "would yield him all the Crown's treasure and taxes, that they should yield to their lord and king, if he would hold them as by old law and right, as his father young Herr Sten had done".[32]

August: collapse of the fragile truce

Since the middle of July, the king had received many reports from the war in Småland, all of which reported that the situation was rapidly deteriorating. His response was to rush to mobilise the nobles in all corners of the realm. From Eastern Gothia, Södermanland and Uppland, the nobles were to gather in the town of Linköping and then join up with the nobles from Western Gothia to march together on Dacke's forces. As noted above, however, Gustavus Olsson had gone ahead on his own instead of waiting for the other troops. This did not please the king, who understood only too well a fact that eluded Gustavus Olsson: that Dacke's forces were far superior in numbers to his noble levies. The king wrote direct to Gustavus Olsson on 26 July:

> "And it is not a little strange to Us ... that you so dangerously and hastily ... have given yourself to such a course, not remembering that such peasants cannot be trusted."

The next day, 27 July, the king wrote to Abraham Eriksson Leijonhufvud and Axel Eriksson Bielke more fully on the same matter:

> "It does not appear wise to Us, that he or the others should put themselves up against the enemy before they have been further reinforced, therefore We have now written to Herr Gustavus, that he shall hold himself, with the small band that are with him, in some convenient and safe place, where he can be safe and secure till he can be further reinforced. ... And because you may well think, which God forbid, the same traitor's party is not to be at the first defeated, you can be certain of wider unrest, that will not then lightly be extinguished or dammed up."

At the end of July, a few days after the truce of Bergkvara – of which he was as yet unaware – it was clear to the king that the war against Dacke would have to be won by force, and as quickly as possible. Gustavus Olsson's efforts, however, had rendered this uncertain. If his expedition failed, and everything spoke for its failure, it would only serve to strengthen Dacke and his uprising, and prolong the conflict.

Gustavus Vasa received the news of the Bergkvara truce at the beginning of August.[33] The war had ground to a halt. The king now had the chance, if he had not had before, to solve the conflict by peaceful means. There are signs in the sources that may indicate he was in fact so inclined. He wrote to his commanders that the truce should be observed. But, he also added that the sensitive state of foreign affairs made negotiations with Denmark essential. These negotiations were to take place in Markaryd, on the border with Denmark. Meanwhile he wrote again to the peasants of Småland, ordering them to choose four men from each hundred and send them to negotiations with the king in Linköping. This all indicates that he did not intend to keep the Bergkvara truce a moment longer than necessary; the war against the Småland men was to be won by force.

The meeting with the Danish king, Christian III, that King Gustavus used as a pretext for continued mobilisation in the south had been under consideration for some time without the slightest effort made to see it to completion. Now it suited the king to use it as a justification for gathering his troops in Jönköping prior to an incursion into the area controlled by Dacke. In a later letter, he wrote to Christian III that it was impossible to hold a meeting until the war against the Småland men had been won. It was the same with the promised negotiations with the peasants: they were intended to lull them into a false sense of security, to give the impression that despite everything the king might want a peaceful solution.

The orders to attack Dacke were in fact issued about two days before the planned meeting was to have taken place, and when the peasants' representatives arrived in Linköping the king was not there. Instead, he had exhorted his men in the town to try to keep the peasants there as long as possible under the pretence that he was soon to return. In fact he was not to appear in Linköping until the middle of September. All this demonstrates Gustavus Vasa's cunning and rhetorical skill. Here was a prince acting fully in the spirit of Machiavelli.[34]

Nils Dacke and his followers seem to have observed the truce, even if some of his men continued to attack bailiffs and others who had distinguished themselves by their brutality. After the truce "he withdrew immediately towards Kalmar",[35] where many of his troops were based. Not until Gustavus Vasa dispatched his troops around St. Bartholomew's Day did Dacke resume his attacks on any significant scale. In fact, there is reason to think that Dacke at this point anticipated a peaceful outcome, and saw himself sitting down to negotiate with Gustavus Vasa. Rasmus Ludvigsson records one event that seems to indicate this:

> "At St. Lawrence's tide a peasant named Nils Bagge, born in Bergunda parish, committed a theft against a nobleman named Arffvet Trolle till Boo and was later called to justice and fined a sum of money before king Gustavus's bailiff. The same Nils Bagge went straightaway with six other forest bandits on Wednesday next before St. Lawrence's Day in the evening to the forenamed Arffvet Trolle's farm and shot him dead in his own manor as he sat and dined, and then took with them everything that he had, and, since they were not of Dacke's party, the forenamed Arffvet Trolle's brother, Herr Ture Trolle till Bergkvara, knight, sent two men to Dacke at the *ting* in Konga hundred to hear if it was his will and command that the forenamed Nils Bagge should commit such a murder on his brother and defy the truce and peace that he and his followers had made with King Gustavus's soldiers."[36]

Ture Trolle relayed this to the *ting* and asked that he, with Dacke's men, should punish the "gang of thieves" who had done the deed.[37] Dacke was prepared to acquiesce in this; together with one of the nobles whom he had previously plundered, he is seen here attempting to maintain order in the region. The episode says much about the local nobility's views on who had the real power. It was Nils Dacke.

Calm did not prevail, however. In the middle of the month, some of Dacke's men took prisoner the bailiff of the hundred of Östra, Anders Karlsson, and the local constables. They warned them and the peasants of the hundred not to attend the *ting* that Måns Johansson and Jöran Eriksson had called in Vimmerby to read out the king's various letters to the Småland peasants. Later it was reported that the bailiff Anders Karlsson together with another one of the king's bailiffs, Olof Larenson, were "slain by Dacke's party outside a village called Screffvaremåle in Hesleby parish".[38]

By the middle of the month the king's troops were on the move. The Master Purveyor, with the help of some knights, was ordered to gather the provisions that the king's army needed and that were then to be delivered to the troops that were to beat back Dacke's forces. When they reached Kisa in Eastern Gothia they were attacked by some of Dacke's men in the area, and in the battle twelve of the king's men were killed. The provisions intended for the king's soldiers went instead to Dacke's men. At the same time the peasants of the hundred of Tjust declined to send their oxen to the king, instead writing a letter – reproduced in Rasmus Ludvigsson's chronicle – to say that if the king wanted their oxen he could come and collect them himself.

At this juncture Dacke sent out an order – together with a threat of what would happen if it was not obeyed – summoning all the people of Småland to a meeting; they should make their way to Värend "and join him by St. Bartholomew's Day". Rasmus Ludvigsson concluded: "The whole of Värend joined him, and he then had all the lord's manors in Värend robbed and plundered."[39]

By St. Bartholomew's Day, 24 August 1542, Nils Dacke had raised his own army. He controlled all the approaches to Värend. In the parishes of Slätthög and Moheda in the hundred of Allbo, along the road between Jönköping and Växjö, there were two hundred men; between Ed and Rydaholm sixty men controlled the road; there were about eighty in the parish of Ryssby guarding the road that ran east into Värend. At this point Dacke was in contact with the peasants in several hundreds: Södra Möre, Konga, Uppvidinge, Norrvidinge, Allbo, and Kinnevald.[40]

The parishes in each of these hundreds had been divided into *fjärdingar* (literally, quarters). One man had been appointed to be responsible for each *fjärding*. "And he had them all written down, each with his name", wrote Rasmus Ludvigsson. This meant that Dacke had built up a new civil and military organisation in the region. Naturally it was based on the old pattern, but he had appointed his own men who were to answer for everything of importance in their particular area. He had also appointed two men from each parish to attend on him daily, "with the intent that as soon as he saw that King Gustavus's forces were on the road, then the two men were immediately to hasten night and day to their parishes and tell the *fjärding* men that each in his *fjärding* should leave that very moment and hurry to Dacke without delay".[41] Those who failed to do so would forfeit both life and goods, noted the chronicler.

September and October: the attack by the royal army

On 24 August the royal army decamped from Linköping and Jönköping and marched on the Småland interior. The army itself was a motley crew who were setting out on a mission that in fact they knew relatively little about. It appears that Gustavus Vasa tried to convince his captains that they were off to the old war against Christian 'the Tyrant' that had flared up again. His army included not only soldiers (S. *knektar*) from all of Sweden including Finland, but also German mercenaries (S. *landsknektar*) and possibly even Danish troops.[42] The latter may appear strange, but the new Danish King – unlike his predecessor – had good relations with Gustavus Vasa at this point, to the extent that there was peace between the two countries. There had been rumblings from the German mercenaries over their pay – it was too meagre – and after some bargaining it was raised slightly.

It was at this point that the march on the centre of the uprising and Dacke's home turf began. The exact course of events is very unclear. Rasmus Ludvigsson's chronicle mentions that the royal troops won a battle against the rebels outside Växjö, but nevertheless withdrew. A retreat despite a victory? L.-O. Larsson instead argues that the retreat was the result of a severe defeat suffered by the royal troops in Eastern Gothia.[43] The peasants of the hundred of Kinda in southern Eastern Gothia had made common cause with Nils Dacke. A small part of the royal army had remained behind in Eastern Gothia to prevent revolt in the province, while the larger force had marched on the Småland border and along the road to Kalmar. It was at this point that the peasants attacked those soldiers who had been left behind.

It would seem that this was the signal for the spread of the uprising into Eastern Gothia. The war was no longer confined to Småland. More and more peasants now joined the rebel troops, with the peasants of the hundreds of Hanekind and Göstring leading the way. There were consultations with peasants across the whole of Eastern Gothia, but the attempt to rally all the peasants in the province ultimately failed. Leadership of the rising in this area fell to Måns Hane and Tord 'the Knight'.[44]

The rising meanwhile spread to parts of Småland that had previously not been affected. The ancient district of Finnveden had earlier sworn to be faithful to the king, but a large number of peasants now abandoned this promise and joined the fray. Even in the hundreds around Jönköping the peasants came to an agreement with the local bailiffs and joined Dacke. Among the places that came under attack were the royal manor of Ettak in Western Gothia, and several nobles' and bailiffs' manors in western Småland were plundered and torched. However, many of the peasants in Finnveden and in the hundreds of Tveta and Vista chose to remain aloof from the uprising. For this they were later to receive warm thanks from the king, and the promise that in future he would listen more closely to their complaints.[45]

November: the Linköping agreement that was never intended to stand

By the beginning of November 1542 the uprising was widespread. The inhabitants of several hundreds had joined to a man. Running from south to north, these were the hundreds of Södra Möre, Konga, Kinnevald, and Allbo; Norrvidinge, Uppvidinge, and Norra Möre; the hundred of Stranda and the province of Tuna, together with the hundreds of Östra and Västra, and Norra and Södra Vedbo; all these districts had been drawn into the fighting on Nils Dacke's side. More lukewarm in their support were the hundreds of Sunnerbo, Västbo, and Östbo in Finnveden, the area around Jönköping, the southern parts of Eastern Gothia, and possibly also southern Western Gothia. Parts of the coastal region down towards Västervik had become involved, while Dacke had the support of both the peasants and the burghers of the coastal towns of Blekinge, the province that bordered on Denmark. Even the burghers of Västervik supported the uprising and provided Dacke's men with certain essential supplies. As far as may be judged, the burghers of Växjö had gone over to Nils Dacke at an early stage.

The sources do not mention any significant troop movements at the end of October and the first few days of November. Dacke's army is thought instead to have spent the time consolidating its hold over the areas already under its control. Efforts were made to prepare the peasant army, and contact was made with the burghers of the area. For example, the burghers of Västervik supplied the troops with gunpowder from Germany. Rasmus Ludvigsson records at least two such occasions when Dacke managed to get the gunpowder that he requested, and both indicate that there were large shipments from Germany.[46] Otherwise, Dacke attempted to build on his support in those areas where it was weak, for example in Finnveden. It is also known that he paid another visit to Ture Trolle at Bergkvara; throughout the uprising it was normal for the rebels to descend on bailiffs and nobles to plunder and seize everything they needed.

Part of the royal army retired from the centre of the uprising and withdrew to Linköping. However, at this point there is no indication of the condition of the main force that was then down in Värend under the command of Germund Svensson. It would seem that they had ground to a halt, since otherwise there would have been information sent to the king about troop movements.

The rising was now so general that Gustavus Vasa found it necessary to make a temporary peace, ostensibly so that concord could again "grow and be fashioned".[47] The compromise is mentioned for the first time in a letter from the king on 5 October. In another letter of the same day, the commanders of the royal troops levied in Eastern Gothia were informed by the king that it seemed wise to "seize on some bargain or compromise with the Småland men".[48] The king allowed his commanding officers to begin negotiations with Dacke at Slätbacka in the parish of Skeda, and on 8 November an agreement was signed in Linköping.[49]

The rebel forces were promised an amnesty, while Dacke himself was not only to be pardoned; he would – if necessary – place his forces in the king's service and together with the royal bailiffs maintain law and order in the region. Together they would ensure that thieves and traitors received their just punishment. At the Linköping meeting, the Småland men handed over a letter listing the causes of the uprising, and the king promised to consider carefully what could be done to meet their demands. This agreement is one of the uprising's most important documents.[50] Since it has not survived in its original form, we have to compare a number of other sources that record what the peasants believed to be the greatest causes of concern. These can then be compared with a list of demands reproduced by Erik Jöransson Tegel in the late sixteenth and early seventeenth centuries.

L.-O. Larsson summarised all the demands that the peasants made between July and November and compared these with Tegel's list. The following tables thus reproduce both the peasants' demands made between May and November as they appeared in letters to the king, and the list of demands to be found in Tegel:

Common to all these complaints is an expression of the same grievance over which the peasants of Konga had protested at the very beginning of the uprising; they wanted a return to the old customs, to the times and conditions that had existed before all the novelties were introduced. They wanted a return to the old ways.[51] This list of complaints should thus be compared with the one supplied by Tegel. As will be seen, there are strong similarities between them.

We shall return to these demands later. For now, it suffices to note that they were directed in equal measure at the nobility and the Crown. Moreover, if we recall the number of noble manors that had been plundered and burned since the start of the uprising, it becomes even clearer that the uprising was directed not only against Gustavus Vasa's policies on taxation and the like, but also against the nobility's growing power at local and national level. There is a clear tendency in all the complaints to criticise the centralization of power, be it the power of the state or the local nobles. The way to express this opposition was for the peasants to cling to custom and the old laws.

Table 2. Complaints made between May and November 1542. Source: Larsson 1964, 38. Larsson's list is based on GVR 1542, 273 ff and 279 ff, and GVR 1543, 45 ff.

No.	Complaint	Place
1	Excessive and illegal taxation	Finnveden, Tjust
2	Unlawful demands made by the Crown and nobility	Småland
3	Raised manor rents and unreasonable demands placed on tenants during estate inspections	Småland
4	Lack of respect for freeholders from lords of the manor during estate rent inspections	Småland
5	Increased requirements to accommodate circuit and chief judges	Småland
6	Excessive fines imposed	Finnveden
7	Introduction of a tax on pannage	Tjust
8	Excessive demands for haulage	Småland
9	Complaints against bailiffs	Finnveden
10	Holding a cow annually for their masters against custom	Tjust
11	Taxation on water mills	Tjust
12	New settlements constructed too close to the old villages	Småland
13	Excessively harsh measures against the purchase of labour	Tjust, Småland

Table 3. Complaints according to Tegel. Source: Larsson 1964, 338 f.

No.	Complaints according to Tegel
1	Royal taxation and the nobles' levies had increased, together with excessive, unlawful taxes
2	The levies of fodder had increased, and fodder exacted unlawfully
3	Large manor rents were exacted, and it was often the case that for a small bribe the bailiff would enrol a poor man to be a soldier instead of a wealthy peasant
4	Increased requirements to accommodate judges on circuit
5	Excessively harsh bans on felling oak and beech forest, and excessive fines for the same
6	Complaints against the introduction of a tax on pannage
7	The bailiffs constantly forced them to a dalafärd (to work far from home)
8	Arbitrary behaviour and assaults by the bailiffs
9	They wanted to retain the arms that the bailiffs had taken from them
10	They condemned the plunder of the Church
11	Swedish mass should be celebrated in the customary form

The new truce: suspicions and preparations on both sides

Nils Dacke thus achieved what he had long sought: to negotiate with Gustavus Vasa about the concerns of himself and his brothers in arms. Gustavus Vasa, who twenty years before had swept to power in Sweden and marched in triumph into Stockholm as the true prince, had been forced to sit down with a poor peasant, a "murderer, whoremonger, and heretic" at that,[52] and his "rabble" to discuss terms under the threat of continued rebellion in the same manner as if two states were deciding on peace or war, if with less pomp and circumstance. So fragile was the power of the state; so strong, despite the events of the previous fifty years, were the community of peasants and their army.

Nils Dacke and his closest followers had taken over Kronoberg when the truce was proclaimed. There, in the middle of the uprising, he was based from November through to the New Year, and up until the point when the truce was broken. He was by no means idle in the meantime, for he continued with the measures begun before the truce came into effect. He strengthened his hold over the area and tried to ensure that it regained an even keel in law and order and fiscal matters. The chronicler Rasmus Ludvigsson gives a lengthy account of all his various efforts.[53] To begin with he announced the truce at a provincial assembly (S. *landsting*) in Växjö on 25 November, "proclaiming the peace according to the agreement made in Linköping between him and his followers on the one side and King Gustavus's soldiers on the other side". He underlined that it was to be an "enduring peace". In future, everything would be conducted according to the "old customs, at which the peasants were gladdened".

However, there were rifts in the rebel movement, and the divisions appeared clearly during the meeting in Växjö. One "part of Nils Dacke's followers" said that the deal with King Gustavus was made "in falsehood", in other words that they could not trust the king's word, nor if it came to that Dacke's either, and the uprising should continue as before. But "then Nils Dacke cried out to the peasants that they should promise him with raised hands that they would help each other as brothers, charged them on their lives to buy good, strong swords, and that they would have that year's taxes and levies to help them." The lords would not get a penny of the year's taxes; instead they would be used to arm the peasants. Even Dacke knew that the success they had enjoyed thus far depended on the peasant army and not on King Gustavus's benevolence. The truce would end one day, by which time the peasants must be better equipped than they had been when the truce began. Dacke was also waiting for a letter from the king, and for this reason announced:

> "When I receive it and it pleases me and is of service to us, then the oath will stand, but if it does not go as I would wish, then I know well the path that I will follow, namely war by land and sea."

Clearly he wanted to override the differences that existed amongst the peasants. It was now a question of holding the uprising together, of uniting the disparate wishes of those who had gathered in resistance to the king's policies. The hotheads had to be held in check so that the truce was not jeopardised, and the irresolute had to be infused with fresh courage. If the king and the nobles kept their word then the rebels would keep theirs, but if the King broke his promise, they could return to the "path" that they had trodden before: war by land and sea.

They also considered the state of law and order in the area at the Växjö assembly. They proclaimed a truce for the lords' estates, and announced that in future no one had the right to plunder and rob them at will. If anyone did so, then he must face punishment. Those who had only recently plundered noble estates had eight days from the day of the assembly in which Dacke would personally look at what had happened and decide what the right course of action was in the matter. On the same day as the *ting* was held – 25 November – Dacke received the king's letter confirming the truce.[54]

In the weeks after the assembly in Växjö, Nils Dacke travelled around the various hundreds to meet with the peasants across the whole area over which he now held sway. He placed his own men as bailiffs and other officers in all parts of the region. With the help of Rasmus Ludvigsson we can follow Dacke's journey through "Dackeland" in the winter of 1542–1543. On 2 December he was at a *ting* in Aringsås in the hundred of Allbo, where he placed Sven Månsson i Lekaryd as bailiff. A week later, on 9 December, he was in Ljungsåkra in the hundred of Kinnevald, where Erengisle Skräddare was made bailiff, and on 22 December he appeared at a *ting* in the hundred of Konga, where he made his brother-in-law Sven Gertorn bailiff. With the approach of Christmas he returned to Kronoberg, where he "drank ... his Yule".

Dacke also wrote a number of letters both to the king's supporters and to those closer to himself. Those he wrote to included Måns Johansson Natt och Dag, Jöran Eriksson, and Per Brahe about the letter of confirmation from the king that had arrived on the same day that Dacke had spoken at the provincial assembly in Växjö. In it the King had promised him free passage to Stockholm so he could pledge his allegiance to the king in person. Dacke and the other rebels had thought this insufficient, however, and had written again to the king. According to the chronicler, Dacke wanted to have part of Småland in fief "therewith he could be helped and hold 100 men there to protect Småland when the need arose, after their uttermost power and ability".[55] He argued his case in detail, and announced that he had been in contact with the Emperor[56] who had offered him the whole of Småland in fief if only Dacke and his men would help him bring down King Gustavus. But Dacke was a loyal Swede, and informed the king that he had declined the Emperor's offer.[57]

The correspondence between Dacke and the king continued throughout December, from which it is possible to gauge the depth of Dacke's suspicions about the king. In a later reply to the king's letter of confirmation, he said the king should bind himself "with his oath and on his royal honour" to Dacke in constant amity. If he did this, in return Dacke would for ever be his faithful servant and subject, and would risk life and limb in what was best for king and country.[58] However, it is scarcely credible that Dacke trusted Gustavus Vasa's promise that he would have free passage to Stockholm and arrive in the town in one piece. He therefore never risked such a move.

However, it does seem to have been true that he had entered into negotiations with Duke Albert of Mecklenburg, a direct descendant of the old King Albert of Sweden. A messenger came to Dacke's quarters while he was in Växjö to announce the truce, and they spoke in greatest secrecy, writes Rasmus Ludvigsson, about the future of the uprising and whether it was possible, if indeed desirable, to depose King Gustavus.[59] Unfortunately, on the return journey the duke's messenger was detected as he travelled through Denmark and executed. It appears, however, that if Dacke had so wished it, he could have had all possible help from the Duke of Mecklenburg. Admittedly, it would have been at a price in money and loyalty, but Dacke nevertheless seems to have thought this as nothing when set against achieving a final agreement with the king. There is no doubt that it was this last possibility that weighed on Dacke's mind. He wanted above all to achieve independence for Värend, and only if this proved impossible was he prepared to accept help from the king's foreign enemies in order to win.

During the truce the deep divisions within the leadership of the uprising surfaced once again. Måns Hane, who had earlier been made leader in Eastern Gothia, fell out with Nils Dacke. It is possible that the breach affected the outcome of the uprising. Rasmus Ludvigsson writes simply that Nils Dacke "had Måns Hane slain". Unsurprisingly, this provoked deep resentment amongst Måns Hane's friends and relations. At the same time, Ludvigsson remarks that Dacke had a number of prominent peasants imprisoned, enraging many of his followers.[60]

Dacke had written to the burghers of Ronneby to suggest free and friendly commerce between "Värendz land" and "their town" now that he had been reconciled with the king. They replied that they had written to their king for advice on how they should proceed, but meanwhile they wanted Dacke to ensure that the "forest bandits" of Värend ceased their "roguery and damage" against the peasants of Blekinge.[61] Dacke also appointed a peasant named Erik Larsson to be bailiff for the counties of Tjust and Tuna. Further, it is mentioned that he replaced the bailiffs in the hundreds of Östra, Västra, Norra Vedbo and Östbo.

On top of everything else, it seems to have been difficult to keep track of all the troops. Rasmus Ludvigsson records one such episode. On 29 November – in other words, five days after the agreement was made – "there arrived in Kind a party of Dacke's men 400 strong".[62] They sent out messages telling the peasants to rise against the royal troops, some 200 men, who were still in the area. The rising failed, however, and the peasants instead pledged allegiance to the king. The same Dacke men tried to call out the peasants in this area one month later, around New Year, with the same feeble result. All they managed to engineer was the plundering of a noble's manor.

Nor was Gustavus Vasa inactive. Admittedly, in the truce he had promised to keep strictly to the agreed terms, but that was no way to win a victory, and his priority was to mobilise as many troops as possible against Dacke's peasant army. Throughout the autumn he had given the Danish king to understand that it might be wise to send reinforcements; the uprising could spread into Denmark, after all. There were already signs of unrest in Blekinge. King Christian therefore sent a troop of soldiers "to help and assist against the rebellious Småland men".[63]

The war and the end

When the truce was finally broken, there was every indication that the uprising would soon end one way or another. From the letters discussed above, Nils Dacke clearly believed his position in Värend was strong at the turn of the year. He addressed his fellow princes in a manner befitting a regent, no less. It was as the protector of the Småland peasants that he envisaged his future. Gustavus Vasa had other plans. It does not appear for one moment to have occurred to the king that Nils Dacke should have his Värend. He took every possible step to stop Dacke in his tracks.

In the literature, opinion is divided on who broke the truce.[64] Some hold that Dacke had become so cocksure after the exchange with the Duke of Mecklenburg that he may have decided that a swift resumption of war was desirable.[65] L.-O. Larsson instead advances evidence from the sources that supports the idea that Dacke had no interest in a return to open conflict. After all, he had reached the point where he had obtained the king's letter confirming the truce. The next step was peace, not war. With a lasting peace, Dacke could begin to shape the new realm that he may have visualised at the beginning of 1543.

One must thus view Gustavus Vasa's agreement with Dacke as little more than a bid to win time.[66] The greatest fear of the king and his circle was that the uprising would spread to other provinces: the western parts of Småland had remained loyal to the king, as had Western Gothia and large parts of Eastern Gothia, and they were desperate to prevent the uprising from reaching these areas. Consequently, the king showed the peasants in these regions considerable favour. The king's chancery was transformed into an all-out propaganda ministry. All possible means of checking the rebels' advance were skilfully exploited. The king wrote in his letters to the peasants and nobles in other parts of the country that one could not trust Nils Dacke and the "*hönefreden*" [literally 'hens' peace' or 'fools' peace'] they had entered into.[67]

The king also called both the whole Council and the knights of the realm to a meeting in Örebro on 23 January 1543. The resolutions from this meeting have been preserved. The king did not claim that it was Dacke who had broken the truce; instead, he said it was Dacke's cooperation with their old enemy, Denmark, that had resulted in the king's decision to consider a resumption of arms.[68] In fact, the supposed collaboration with the arch enemy was based on a proposal that had been made long before, when Dacke had asked the Danish king if it were possible to engineer matters so that the peasants could retain their old privileges. Gustavus Vasa took this and inflated it as much as he was able.

Why did the king take this line? It seems that there was an element amongst the nobles who were prepared to enter into a more lasting settlement with Dacke, and it was essential for the king to win round the majority of nobles so that the royal army had their full support when it marched on Dacke. Among the decisions at the Örebro meeting they thus agreed plans for a new campaign. On 22 January the royal troops had gathered in Vadstena and Jönköping. Some were to occupy Finnveden and to pacify that part of Småland, while others were to make for the heart of Småland to consult with the peasants out in the hundreds. It was these manoeuvres that made Nils Dacke take up arms once again.[69]

Dacke's forces carried out some smaller operations, mainly designed to hamper the royal army's preparations. They struck a deal with the lord of Stegeborg, Svante Sture, after first having attacked and plundered his castle. They went on to blockade all the roads across Holaveden, the vast forest east of Lake Vättern that lay between Småland and Eastern Gothia. They also plundered their way across Eastern Gothia into the areas that were controlled by the royal army. Despite their efforts, the latter's preparations advanced nearly unhindered, and either on 10 March or shortly thereafter the royal troops marched off down through the hundreds of Kinda, Sevede, and Aspeland en route for Kalmar. Parishes the length of the march were pillaged and pressed to capitulate, but they remained defiant, and every parish in this area put up some form of resistance to the royal army.[70]

Dacke's forces were still slightly to the south. They had built a huge timber barricade in the parish of Högsby and manned it with men from several of the surrounding hundreds. Here they had planned to meet the royal army, but the latter had other plans, and proceeded to outflank Dacke's position. With a smaller force drawn from the men at Högsby,

Dacke succeeded in intercepting the royal army as it circled westwards, and met them in battle outside Virserum. Dacke was severely wounded in this clash that occurred at some point shortly before Easter 1543.[71]

The military operation Dacke and his men had set in train was designed more to delay than to prevent the royal army's advance. For this reason, their defeat cannot be depicted as massive. However, with Dacke wounded it seems that his significance as the leader of the uprising became all too apparent. Suddenly it became difficult for the rebels to agree on tactics and strategy. Many of the nearby hundreds came to an agreement with the royal troops. The hundreds of Östra and Västra, Södra Vedbo and Ydre, Norrvidinge and Uppvidinge were said by the chronicler Rasmus Ludvigsson to have capitulated.[72] After a successful march they were rejoined by the royal troops who had advanced from the west.

Thereafter the situation seems to have been quieter. At this juncture Dacke was hiding with peasants near the battlefield where he had been wounded. The calm did not prevail long, however, for after several weeks the conflict flared up again. Dacke's allies in Sevede, Handbörd, Ydre, and Södra Möre together with large numbers of the hundred's inhabitants swept into action again. L.-O. Larsson argues – despite the paucity of the sources – that Dacke lay behind this because he was surely on the mend.[73] By this time, however, the royal army had seized back the initiative, and the rebellion collapsed in short order. The royal troops hunted down the rebels wherever they were – as Gustavus Vasa had already determined should happen – and crushed them by force. Nils Dacke himself fled to the border region between Småland and Blekinge, where he was tracked down in the forest of Rödeby and shot dead.

With that the uprising ended and the reckoning could begin. The Småland peasants who had participated on the rebels' side were to pay dearly for their participation; the king was to use both executions and collective punishment.[74]

Understanding the Dacke War

Historians have attempted to explain the uprising in a number of fundamentally different ways. Some concentrate on the king's character and his somewhat drastic actions, but most numerous are those who seek their explanations in restrictions on the oxen trade or in other obstacles to trade that were said to have made it harder for peasants living along the border to maintain the links that they had long had with their peers in Denmark.[75] There are occasional references to the prevailing policy towards the Church as a reason for the uprising. It is said that the king's religious policy – not only the Bible and preaching in the vernacular and similar measures, but also the fact that the Crown laid brutal claim to the Church's estates and the treasures crucial to religious ceremonies – outraged the peasants so much that they rose to seize back what they had lost.[76] Finally, one common explanation is the increased pressure from taxation, partly because the peasants had been deprived of their customary rights to divide the tax burden amongst themselves, and partly because there was a dramatic increase in the amounts gathered. Taken together, these are said to have driven the peasants to rebel.[77]

Common to all these explanations is that they concentrate solely on political measures carried through by the Crown or the king, the peasants reacting to these measures and finding that they did not accord with custom and tradition. Yet these explanations all share the problem that they fragment the peasants' actions and beliefs; they make no attempt to understand the peasants' actions against a background of different ideas of the world or society, different views on the state and administration, different ways of deciding what was best for society.

It is easy to see Nils Dacke and King Gustavus as arch enemies, not least because Gustavus Vasa himself happily saw himself as the diametric opposite of Dacke: Dacke was only a peasant, and one who had whored and murdered at that; the king kept his word while Dacke broke his promises; the king was of the reformed faith, while Dacke was a heretic; the king stood for all that was new and improved, while Dacke stood for the bad old days; and so on. If the source material is taken as it stands, it would seem that the main difference lay between the king and new ideas on the one hand and the Småland men and old ideas on the other. Gottfrid Carlsson's opinion, based on just such a reading of the sources, is that the uprising was "a battle between old and new, in which Nils Dacke represented the old, while Gustavus Vasa was the man of the new age, of the new idea of the state."[78] Moreover, he continues, when it comes down to it, it was probably just as well that Dacke did not emerge victorious, especially bearing in mind "his risky foreign connections".[79] The inevitable result would have been "that Sweden would have come under foreign rule".[80]

If, however, one takes into account the tendentiousness that naturally exists in the royal letters and exhortations – the king had every interest in appearing to be the leading opponent of Dacke's rebel army – Gustavus Vasa pales as the antithesis of the uprising. It is just such a critical reading of the sources that L.-O. Larsson undertook, yet even he falls in the end for the conclusion that it was the Crown's increased fiscal pressure on the population along the border that made the uprising flare up where it did.[81] On the way to this conclusion, however, he also manages to analyse other aspects of the rising, for example "hostility towards the nobility". In contrast to earlier research, he suggests that "the hostile tone towards the nobility in the revolt has been considerably underestimated".[82] Complaints were directed just as much against the nobility as against the Crown, and the peasants' actions had a severe impact on the nobility.

Rasmus Ludvigsson used a significant phrase in writing about the truce with Gustavus Vasa, where it was agreed that all that was plundered "...the lords from the peasants or the peasants from the lords..." would be restored.[83] The uprising had shown that the lords could no longer continue taking from the peasants with increasing ruthlessness, and in time the truce forced the peasants to stop plundering the lords. And, of course, the lords included the king. This, then, was the contrast as it appeared at the start of the sixteenth century.

What then was the purpose of the uprising? To answer the question properly, we would need a source that reflects Dacke's and the other rebel leaders' more programmatic views. That they by no means formed a unified front has been seen from the course of events described above. On at least two occasions the disagreements between them broke out into the open. The first was in Växjö, when Dacke announced the agreed truce. A smaller number of the "multitude" called out that they believed neither the king nor Dacke, and that they wanted to continue the armed struggle against the lords. The other was when Måns Hane fell out with Dacke and was put to death as a result. On both occasions the uprising's 'programme' was a source of conflict, but we have no sources that can relay the different leaders' programmes directly to us. On the other hand, we do have the demands that reached the king and that he in his turn mentioned in those of his outgoing letters that survive. These will have to suffice.

At the outset, the uprising aimed to put a stop to Gustavus Vasa's and the lords' expansive domestic policy. All that was new – the Reformation, the new monarchy – only meant higher taxes and levies and less control over production. The 'list of demands' discussed above shows that such complaints against taxes and levies were frequent, yet it also reveals that the complaints were made about declining local or regional control over tax and levy rates. The new rates were 'unlawful'.[84]

The uprising had originally been intended to reinstate the old order, but the longer it continued, the more comprehensive its demands seem to have become. When Dacke celebrated Christmas at Kronoberg in 1542 there is evidence of other plans in train, more advanced than those previously seen. He wrote to the king – and informed his European contacts – that he looked forward to seeing Värend free, even if it was only as a royal fief. Fief or no, no royal troops would be found there, for Dacke's men alone would protect Småland. Furthermore, within the fief it would be Dacke who would levy the taxes, not the king. As few courtiers as possible would appear there, and order would be maintained with the help of Dacke's men. Clearly at this juncture, when everything seemed to be going his way, Dacke seems to have had a full-blown peasant kingdom in mind. Had he not negotiated with the king himself? Had the king not written to him personally, and on his honour tried to induce him to come to Stockholm? Yet Dacke, king of the peasants, did not trust the king of the nobles, and therefore stayed at home.

Geographical extent of the uprising

Clearly the uprising enjoyed far greater success than Gustavus Vasa had initially thought possible. Within a short time most of Småland and parts of Eastern Gothia had risen to join Dacke. Only a few hundreds in Finnveden thought it best to stay loyal to the King. With the help of L.-O. Larsson's topographical study of the spread of the uprising,[85] I will consider its different 'epicentres', basing my discussion on the letters of pardon that Gustavus Vasa dispatched to the *hundreds* and on the registers of fines imposed once the uprising had been defeated.

It was the south-eastern parishes of the hundred of Konga – Vissefjärda and Långasjö – together with the adjoining parishes in the hundred of Södra Möre that had formed "the original seat of the uprising".[86] By 20 July 1542, however, all the peasants in the hundred had sworn allegiance to Nils Dacke. The hundreds to the west – Kinnevald and Allbo – came into the uprising somewhat later, at some point between July and the end of August, and then only after pressure from Dacke's supporters persuaded the rest of the inhabitants of the hundreds to side with them. The peasants of the hundred to the north – Norrvidinge – joined Dacke towards the end of August, but their support seems to have been only half-hearted.[87] Finally, Uppvidinge – the final hundred in Värend – had already joined the uprising in July and remained loyal to Dacke for many of the skirmishes with the royal army. In the old region of Njudung there were two hundreds, Västra and Östra. The peasants of Östra joined Dacke in August 1542, and thereafter was reckoned one of the most steadfast for the remainder of the uprising; Västra had gone over to Dacke at the same time.

The rebels also had some success in the long, narrow province of Kalmar. The starting point was the hundred of Södra Möre, and Nils Dacke's home parish, Torsås, may be seen as the flashpoint of the uprising. Most of the peasants in the hundred joined the rebels, with the exception of those who lived close to the strongly fortified town of Kalmar that was never to fall into rebel hands. The peasants of the hundreds north of Möre – Handbörd, Stranda, Aspeland, and Sevede – joined the uprising around the beginning of September and remained loyal to Dacke to the end. Indeed, it was in these hundreds that the uprising was to flare up one last time before being stamped out for good. The inhabitants of the hundred of Tjust and the province of Tuna joined reluctantly, except for the episode when they attacked Stegeborg; only a few peasants are thought to have joined in willingly or to have stood by Dacke for the duration. Initially, the peasants of Södra Vedbo were not prepared to join him, but after some hesitation they went over to his side during the autumn.

In contrast, the peasants of neighbouring Norra Vedbo did not waver when at the beginning of October at the latest, and without undue pressure, they went over to Dacke. The hundreds of Kinda and Ydre had joined the rebels fairly early, at the beginning of September, and it was in Ydre that the royal troops were to meet with particularly stiff resistance in the final stages of the uprising. The peasants of the neighbouring hundreds of Tveta and Vista proved much more reluctant to join in. For much of the autumn nothing was heard of them, and only towards winter did they seem to have judged it wise to side with the rebels. Even then only a small number of the peasants in the hundred were anything approaching active in their support.

In Eastern Gothia a number of peasants in the south-western hundreds had joined the uprising as early as September. It was principally in the forested area that linked the hundreds of Lysings, Göstring, Vigfolka, and Valkbebo that Dacke was to find followers. Elsewhere, the island of Öland joined Dacke at some point in the late autumn of 1542. The peasants of Finnveden never seem to have been tempted to join the uprising, however; only a very small number of the peasants there took the rebels' part, and the vast majority decided – despite pressure – to swear allegiance to the king.[88]

Thus the uprising affected the whole of Småland, south-western parts of Eastern Gothia, and Öland. The most whole-hearted support came from the peasants of the woodland areas. The leaders of the uprising – Nils Dacke, Sven i Flaka, Tord 'the Knight', Måns Hane – either originated from or had fled to these heavily forested areas. Several 'epicentres' in particular emerge from the foregoing description: the adjoining hundreds of Uppvidinge, Östra and Västra showed strong support for the rebels' ideas; Handbörd, Stranda, Aspeland, and Sevede formed another area that showed many tendencies to resist the centralization of the king's and noble power during the uprising; equally, the hundred of Ydre remained loyal to the rebels throughout; and finally, the hundreds surrounding the impenetrable Holaveden forest were steadfast to the last.

Social range of the uprising

Another interesting issue is the different levels on which the uprising was driven forwards. The sources speak primarily of the traditional assemblies (S. *ting*), be they provincial or 'hundredal'. Both Gustavus Vasa and Nils Dacke mentioned and also used these assemblies. In this period the assemblies were not part of a fixed structure that could render them familiar or alien to one party or another; both sides in the Dacke uprising felt quite at home using them. However, during the revolt, it was certainly true that the royal party felt less certain in this forum than did the peasants. It was for this reason that the king's messengers did not venture to the assembly to read out the king's open letter in the initial stages of the uprising, and it was also why Gustavus Olsson met with no response when he came to Växjö to consult with the peasants. Both peasants and burghers quite simply avoided him. They were only interested in "making a bargain with him" if he could promise them a return to their old customs. As he found, it was impossible to address an empty arena.

There was one man, however, who believed himself to have just as much right to set foot in an assembly as any other during the uprising. This was Ture Trolle. When one of his brothers was murdered, he demanded at the *ting* that he, together with Dacke's men, should punish the "rabble of thieves" who had done the deed.[89] Yet it is equally evident from this episode that it was ultimately Nils Dacke who controlled this forum; it was Trolle who had to come to the assembly if he was to speak to the man who had the power to track down the culprits.

These examples can be multiplied, all demonstrating the significance of these traditional assemblies as a means of communication. They had a public nature that suited everyone, be they peasant, burgher, or lord. The public nature of the assembly can be seen as both communicative and representative;[90] the peasants communicated their concerns, and the lords 'represented' themselves.

Second only to the assemblies in terms of their importance in the sources, we find the idea of the region as a border area. For centuries peasants had struck bargains with other peasants; such deals could also embrace inhabitants either side of national borders. These agreements show that there were other forms of association that were more important than Crown and state.

The parish is also named on several occasions. However, it does not seem to have had the same importance as the hundred, emerging only when Nils Dacke and the other rebels were arming themselves and organising their defences. It was in this context that each parish was ordered to appoint four men, one per *fjärding* (quarter), to act as a 'contact' when Dacke wanted to send out messages quickly or to rally his supporters. In addition, following the Bergkvara truce he kept with him two men from every parish who could be dispatched rapidly with just such messages.

The parish also proved to be an important level for Gustavus Vasa's operations when the final phase of the conflict was reached. When the royal army had gathered in Linköping prior to its march on the Dacke strongholds in Småland, the king's captains called the peasants together parish by parish and asked them if they wanted to "come to terms, and ask again for mercy".[91] However, "the peasants did not give way ... by as much as three parishes", wrote the chronicler Rasmus Ludvigsson.[92] It was the same later when the waves of punishment and negotiations with the peasants in the assemblies began; a number of the collective punishments imposed took the parish as the basis for the allocation of liability.

The smallest social unit mentioned in the sources was the household or homestead. For example, after the truce the peasants were to make their way homewards, each to his own farm, where he was to equip himself with good weapons. Dacke promised not to levy any taxes on homesteads for this; instead the money collected in taxes over the year was to be used freely by the peasants to pay for their arms. Similarly, it was at this level that Gustavus Vasa operated when punishing the peasants who had taken part in the uprising. The punishments were imposed at the level of the household, even if action on two other levels – hundred and parish – was much more frequent. In certain cases fines were imposed on the household. This was especially the case when collective punishments were meted out.

Finally, it should be noted that the uprising – as it appears in the most detailed contemporary accounts – was a matter for men only. In the source material it is only men who are mentioned.[93]

Economy of the uprising

Here we can pose two simple questions: could the participants 'afford' to rebel; and what did they have to lose? The answers, in contrast, are anything but simple. By posing these questions, we have shifted focus somewhat from the immediate context of the uprising to the ideas held by the rebels themselves. These are extremely hard to identify, because they are not reported as such in the sources and can only be perceived indirectly from the sources left to us by the authorities.[94] That said, certain passages in the Rasmus Ludvigsson chronicle do shed some light on the matter. When the uprising began, the peasants were gathered at an assembly in Växjö, at a time at which the whole attempt could have foundered. Ludvigsson writes:

> "Meanwhile they wanted to settle down (S. *sittie stilli*); that at the same provincial assembly they would be promised that they could return to what was customary for all levies that they had been accustomed to pay ten or twelve years ago ... [and if] they could not enjoy that, then they would wager life and property for it."[95]

Thus for the best part of a decade so much had happened that the peasants were now prepared to take up arms to turn back the clock. They wanted to go back to a time before all the taxes were increased, when they still had control over how their production and the tax burden were divided amongst them. What was it then that most outraged the peasants? Returning to the chronicle, we find:

> "...King Gustavus heard that in Småland there was some ominous and strange talk amongst the common men about the account that the priests were to make for the tithes that were gathered into the church house each year, so that the priests were to demand such account more directly from the common men, and not to be content to write down how much and what each of them had carried into the church house, but asked and demanded that each should swear how much he had sown in his fields in the year and how much grain had come of it, and accordingly were they to demand the tithe and make their account."[96]

This passage reveals some key issues. It states that "each should swear" how much they had sown and harvested. A tenth of the sworn yield would go to the Church, or in fact, as was already actually the case, the Crown. It was not the quantities in themselves that the peasants were prepared to fight over; it was the ceremony associated with the tax. To force them to swear an oath that they had delivered up a tenth, and no less, of their crop inevitably removed their control over production. It was this control that they felt they had lost over the previous ten to twelve years, and that they now sought to take back, sword in hand if necessary.

Thus, they do not seem to have had very much to lose. Matters had already gone so far that in a very short time they felt they had lost control over their lives, and to win it back they were prepared to risk both life and property. Not all peasants reasoned in this way, of course, and for a number their principal concern was with their own lives and households. It was for this reason that the peasants in Finnveden did not want to join the rebels. They had probably also established good relations with the king and the lords of the vicinity. Whatever the case earlier, in the final phases of the uprising the peasants were clearly begging for their lives when they appealed to the king for mercy; then, if not before, they clearly had something to lose. For a time they had gambled with their lives when they attempted to force time and society to take several steps backwards under duress.

It is perhaps this that is most difficult to understand today. What were they thinking when they rallied to Dacke's side? Of themselves, their farms, households and families, their financial wellbeing, or their freedom? Or was it perhaps something else? To find the answers we must also understand the context in which such personal decisions were taken. Evidently we must look more closely at how individuals related to the collective as it was embodied in the *ting*, that most communal of assemblies.

All free men had access to these local assemblies as the representatives of their family and household. They were taken into the assembly by swearing an oath that placed them at the disposal of the community. However, the decision at an assembly that the hundred would join Nils Dacke had to be taken unanimously; it was not enough – as happened at the *ting* called in Finnveden – to attempt to talk the rest of a noisy assembly into going over to Dacke, as his supporters would then be isolated and would have to take on themselves the entire responsibility for the events that ensued. However, at those assemblies where they did reach a joint decision, they had understood that matters other than their own safety were at stake. The decisions of these assemblies referred instead to such things as justice and freedom.

Matters were different when we turn to royal rhetoric. Throughout the uprising it was the individual peasant who was the focus of royal eloquence, as when King Christian wrote to the Småland peasants to inform them that he too had joined with the Swedish king by sending troops to crush the revolt. He threatened them in the following words: if they did not come to their senses and submit, "then King Christian with King Gustavus and many of their friends, Christian lords and princes, would descend upon them and punish them, and they and their children and their children's children would never forget it".[97] The guilt lay heavily on each and every one of them, according to the king. So heavily, indeed, that even their grandchildren would rue the day.

For the king the most important relationship existed between himself and his subjects: between the monarch and each individual there was an invisible bond. In royal ideology, if this bond was broken then all his subjects were in extreme danger, for then they completely lacked protection. The peasants begged to differ. They sought protection in their communal assemblies. Jointly agreed decisions that did not leave any one man more responsible than the others afforded them protection against reprisals, and indeed anything else that could follow in the wake of a failed uprising. They also used a similar ploy when agreements were made between peasants: their names or marks were often put down in a ring, a ring that had no beginning and no end and in which there was no leader. Its individual elements were extremely difficult, if not impossible, to distinguish. It was in fact a closed circle, and everyone who had made his mark in the ring was equally important.

However, this union by no means excluded a king. A king, after all, could guarantee freedom and security, and it was for this reason that the rebels turned to the Sture family in an attempt to persuade one of the line to be commander of 'Dackeland'. Similarly, it was perhaps as such that Dacke came to see his own role; a peasant king who guaranteed peace and order in his part of the kingdom.

Chapter IV

Preludes and post-mortems

Had the 'revolutionary alternative' been preceded by anything in similar vein? Certainly Gustavus Vasa purported not to remember anything of the sort. On 5 August 1542, he wrote: "We are not aware, for what reason and out of what beginnings this has arisen and been undertaken, since have you brought to Us no requests or complaints, either last year in [the Chamber?] or since, as the good and old custom has been."[98] His surprise was feigned, however. He must have known that the peasants had been complaining bitterly in the years before the uprising,[99] and as soon as it broke out he wrote to many of his bailiffs instructing them not to press the peasants too hard, or else events would follow the same course for them as it had in Småland. On 6 July, for example, he informed Hans Skrivare and Jören Nilsson that he knew that they had been driving the peasants far too hard. His tone here is very different. Once the peasants have been impoverished, it follows "they have no other recourse, but are forced to quit house, home, wife, and children for the forest bandits, who are now in Småland, at no small annoyance, damage, and disadvantage to Us and the Realm".[100] On 19 July he wrote to the bailiff in Gästrikland and Hälsingland to the same effect, warning him that in these difficult times he should not tax the peasants with excessive fines, but rather act in a manner that will make them well-inclined towards both himself and the king.[101] Finally, by the time the assembly was held in Växjö, if not before, it should have been clear to him how great was the peasants' concern over the future.

How did the uprising come to be viewed in later years?[102] Not unexpectedly, it had a considerable influence during the century to come and was referred to on many different occasions. Here I shall only touch on one example. At the end of the 1590s, when the struggle for the crown between King Sigismund and Duke Charles had been underway for some time, one Peder Mickelsson was brought before the Stockholm high court charged with high treason. He came from the area around Virserum, where Dacke had had one of his key strongholds, and had earlier – first as a knight and then as a bailiff – been one of Sigismund's adherents. When Sigismund was forced to flee to Poland, Peder Mickelsson had followed him in the company of another man, a peasant and constable named Jon i Gavlö, who hailed from the region around the lake of Bolmen in Småland. They had remained in Poland for some time, where on several occasions – according to Peder's statement in court – Jon had spoken with Sigismund's sister Princess Anna, who had exclaimed during a conversation: "Do as Nils Dacke did! He fought for an unjust cause; nevertheless he raised such an uproar that my late grandfather King Gustavus was hard put to quell it. But now the matter is a just cause. If you need money for a new Dacke War, then you can seize the Crown's taxes in Småland and even tax the Småland bailiffs, priests, peasants, and the others who follow Duke Charles."[103] Admittedly, there was never any question of a new Dacke War, but it shows that it was still much in people's minds as a point of reference when new conflict loomed. The elite remained very much aware of the social forces that could be released in the event of a successful attempt to mobilise the entire population in a district.

The peasants had to pay dearly for the uprising, and it left deep scars on the afflicted communities. There was a fairly clear decision to use other means thereafter instead of rebellion. After the Dacke uprising, the Småland peasants only joined in noticeably smaller conflicts with the central authorities. Never again did they advance such far-reaching demands as Nils Dacke had done; in future their demands centred on the reduction of taxes and levies. They never challenged the king and the power of the state head on; instead they appealed to the king's goodness and mercy.

However, for several months there had been no avoiding the fact that Dacke was tantamount to a king in his own 'realm'. He behaved in the manner of all kings of his day. For him – a humble peasant from the woods of deepest Småland – it was not at all strange to act as a real prince, proclaiming his own realm, putting defences into place, replacing bailiffs, guaranteeing law and order, and so on. The legitimacy of the Vasa monarchy was by no means secure. In a very short time it had sunk in popularity. The peasants had looked back to the past and found there a better time and a better life. They also found a better man, Svante Sture, whom they wanted to see as their king. Yet they did not only look back; they looked forwards too. At a time of radical change – change for the worse, according to the peasants – they expressed a strong wish for an alternative future that was to survive the political ebb and flow at least until the seventeenth century.[104] Viewed in this light they were successful: the peasants saw that together they could form a powerful counterweight, and that for now they were taken to be a serious, even threatening, challenge. Of course, it also cost them a great deal, perhaps too much.

The contents of communalism: organisational principles, egalitarian and horizontal ideals

For many years historians have found many different ways to describe peasants and their ability to shape political events. At the one extreme we have the peasant as the apathetic victim of war and rulers alike, devoid of power to influence politics and justice.[105] At the other we have the peasant as embodiment par excellence, at least until the rise of the working class, of revolutionary potential, with an exclusive and almost impelling ability to push history forwards.[106]

In recent years, however, a different perspective has gained ground. The term communalism,[107] it has been argued, should be central to our understanding of peasants in older times. Before the rise of the strong, absolutist state, with its hierarchical structures, there were other principles of organisation at work in society that expressed a very different set of ideals and utopias than the state that we have come to know so well since its inception in the sixteenth century. The hierarchical order claimed that the needs of Creation and society were best met if all functions were divided between those who ruled and those who worked. Its opposite was the communalistic order that occasionally manifested itself openly, as in the European peasant republics of Switzerland, Friesland, and Dittmarsken, or in several different attempts to establish an alternative social order on northern soil. These medieval ideals and utopias were to survive into the new age, but as the absolute – and increasingly modern – state took over as the principle pattern of organisation, they were to fade away; they became increasingly utopian.

The distinctive features of the communalistic order were:[108]

1) a principally local and regional organisation of production, justice, religion, defence, and so on.

2) an egalitarian, horizontal ideal that grew in part out of feudal, vertical, medieval society.

3) an ideal that mainly found expression when the nobility lost their legitimacy as the defenders of law and order in the new kind of society.

4) a communal assembly and a *ting*. All free men had access to the communal assembly as the representatives of their family and household, admitted – often on oath – as full members with full voting rights. Well-nigh everyone had access to the *ting*, even if not all voices were equal. Men were more often heard than women, and so on. The assemblies and *ting* chose their own spokesmen and appointed panels of different kinds to see to the business of daily life.

5) the idea that a decision only won the force of law if it had been taken unanimously by those who were to be affected by it. This decentralising ideal often contrasted with the feudal, centralising ideal.

6) the idea that relations with the prince – the king – were regulated through a form of contract that none should break. If any party did break it, they risked losing all legitimacy.

These ideas were important elements in the peasants' world view.[109] How can we best present the peasants' view of the world? And how to differentiate it from, for example, the elites' world view during the later Middle Ages and the beginning of the early modern period? Before we tackle these issues, it is worthwhile concentrating on a particular period that is crucial to our understanding of the unease that manifested itself in society at the end of the Middle Ages and for a century thereafter. The period in question is the sixteenth century, and the historical process that I consider to be critical in this context is the rise of the absolute state.[110]

As prince, king and Crown became more influential, the 'feudal principle' of organisation lost its influence. Some historians, for example Perry Anderson, have argued that the feudal principle was transmuted into – or absorbed by – the absolute state.[111] During the fourteenth and fifteenth centuries, the medieval system of production had demonstrated its considerable limitations.[112] Strong forces were at work that repeatedly pointed out to kings and princes across Europe that the process that was underway would bring no good to anyone.

The Småland peasants in the south and west showed only slight regard for the growing national community of Sweden. Ultimately this was because for years they had developed an entirely different community of interests – economic, military, judicial – with the districts on the other side of the border. Värend, Finnveden, and the other 'small lands' (the literal translation of *Småland*) had become a hinterland for the trading towns of Blekinge and the ports of Denmark's eastern provinces. It was to these towns that they wanted to drive their oxen, not Stockholm. It was also this region that they wanted to defend from the growing threat posed by the national states; peasants were affected equally severely whether the constraints were imposed by Stockholm or Copenhagen. Moreover, they helped each other to keep law and order in the border country.

It was for these reasons that they had long concluded 'peasant peaces' (S. *bondefreder*, peace treaties concluded by the local peasants on both sides of the border).[113] One of the many peasant peaces in force from the end of the Middle Ages and into the sixteenth century stated that the peasants would certainly continue to pay taxes to their old lords, but that they would never follow their masters further than their own border. If they heard that an attack was being prepared, they would immediately inform their brothers on the other side of the border. Furthermore, they wanted to protect free trade across the border, and the freedom to bear arms.[114]

It was a horizontal structure that lay at the foundations of the peasant community. This is not to say that there were no differences – it was scarcely an equal society – but a decision did not come into force simply because it was taken by influential or wealthier forces within peasant society. Everyone who was affected by a decision had to be a party to it, for this was the only way it could win credibility and not be questioned. This pattern grew in part out of the feudal, vertical, medieval society that, when it was later confronted by different, alien ideas, became more defined in its contours, but it has also been seen to predate the feudal, hierarchical order.[115]

Per Nyström – in a work that has become a classic in Swedish historiography – wrote that the peasants experienced a tremendous alienation from the new ideals embodied in the legislation that evolved in the thirteenth and fourteenth centuries. Earlier, a legend had sprung up about the glossators who were said to have been active in Bologna in the eleventh century, and this myth reached Sweden in the thirteenth century. With the help of Roman law, these glossators had supposedly marginalised the customary law that until then had survived century after century without being written down. The opportunities this presented were seized upon by every prince in Europe during the thirteenth and fourteenth centuries. In a short time, one body of law after another was produced, examples being the *Sachsenspiegel* and *Schwabenspiegel* in Germany, and the *Tractatus de legibus* in England. Even in France many different bodies of law were to survive as *coutumiers* or *livres de pratique*. They had all come into existence in an environment moulded by the feudal upper class, and it was aristocratic interests that were stressed at the expense of those interests that had been the focus of customary law.[116]

This was mirrored by the loss by the nobility and the ruling elite of their legitimacy as the defenders of the peace. From that time on, an ever-current theme in assembly *(ting)* after assembly was this self-same relationship between written law and customary law,[117] and it was still not resolved by the sixteenth century. Thus Olaus Petri, for example, often commented on the importance of custom in the administration of justice:[118] he argued that "universal custom" should also be used as law, which not all lords of the day saw fit to do. This led to many injustices and much dissension.[119] Old customs were horizontal in their ideals, or, as Olaus Petri put it, identical crimes carried identical punishments. However, as he admitted, this had far from always been the case. Written law paid greater attention to whether the man who had committed the crime was rich or poor.[120]

The significance of the communal assembly was made clear in the foregoing description of the Dacke uprising. It was to the *ting* that the rebels turned to communicate with both the peasants and the central authorities.[121] It was only men who spoke at the assembly, as we have seen. On no occasion is the presence of a woman noted, which in itself is interesting. It perhaps says more about how those who produced the sources viewed women's participation in political life than about their actual involvement.

The king introduced many novelties to Småland, all of which were disliked by most of the peasants there. Whether it was the ban on hunting larger game, on felling beech and oak, or on purchasing land, all were prohibitions on behaviour that the peasants had long considered legitimate. Such bans paid no attention to the peasants' rights; they were only concerned with the Crown's rights. Similarly, the new policy on taxation was concerned only with the Crown's rights and not the peasants'. Deserted farms and new settlements were taxed as never before in a scramble for fresh sources of income for the state, and the Crown made ever greater claims on the ancient forests and common land. The purpose was to strengthen the Crown financially and politically, and correspondingly to undermine the peasants' freedom and communal order. And naturally the peasants themselves had no part in the decision; it was taken far above their heads.[122]

The relationship between the prince or king and the peasantry was regulated by a kind of contract that neither was meant to break. If one of the parties did so, they were threatened with the total loss of their legitimacy and left the other party free to act and liberated from the need to maintain their end of the bargain. The king promised to keep his part of the deal when he made his *Eriksgata*, or traditional progress through the realm, and the peasants in reply swore to their part. If either broke the contract, trouble would ensue, as is clearly evident in the initial stages of the Dacke uprising. The peasants wanted to hold an assembly in Växjö to discuss what they should do about the worsening conditions under which they had lived for the past decade or so. They put the demand – directed at the king – that if they "could return to what was customary for all levies" they would continue for a while with the loyalty and the men they had sworn to provide him with the last time they had met.[123]

This was repeated again and again throughout the uprising. When the king sent out letters to the peasants elsewhere in the realm, he was clearly keen to harp on this contract. For example, he thanked the peasants of the hundreds of Sunnerbo, Västbo, and Östbo – those who had not participated to a man in the uprising – for not making common cause with the Dacke rabble, and remaining the loyal subjects they should be, despite the difficult times. For this he promised personally to ensure that no injustices would be inflicted on the country in future.[124]

Once the contract had been completely broken – once the uprising was spreading without check, and many of the nobles had already lost both life and property – the path to a new contract appeared long and tortuous. Mistrust on both sides meant that shaping a new union would be taxing in the extreme, for it could never be revived in the same form as it had taken previously. Instead, in negotiations in the assembly after the uprising, the king gave ample proof of his almost Machiavellian concerns; those who refused to resign themselves to the new order were to be wiped from the face of the earth.[125]

The executions were many; terror was used as a weapon in crushing the final remnants of the uprising.[126] As the 'rightful lord' that despite all he seems to have thought himself, it was now high time to show just who was in charge.[127] He wielded his *jus vitae ac necis*, the power of life and death that according to Roman law was incumbent upon *patria potestas*. The king was meant to take possession of his subjects; not bargain with them in a public forum with a view to striking a balance between different interests.

But, before analysing further the peasant unrest in the Swedish realm we must turn west: first to Norway and then over the sea to Iceland.

NOTES

1 Ludvigsson 1905, 76. See also ibid., 75, where Nils Dacke tells the peasants that every man should make his way home and equip himself with good, strong weapons, and to help pay for them they should take that year's taxes. "The lords will get none this year."
2 See for example 'Styrilsi kununga och höfþinga', that drew for example on Egidius de Columna's 'De regimine principum' from the middle of the thirteenth century and contains rules for how a king could try to attain goodness.
3 3. See Larsson 2002 for a new 'portrait' of King Gustavus Vasa.
4 Larsson 1964, 22.
5 Here I have used L.-O. Larsson's approach. Several other ideas have also been raised in the discussion. See principally Härenstam 1947 and Carlsson 1948.
6 Suggested for example in Vejde 1931; Vejde 1943; Carlsson 1951.
7 Åberg 1960.
8 Larsson 1979; Larsson 1964.
9 On an empirical basis alone it is extremely difficult, as is demonstrated by the many suggestions. The decisive factor is rather the theoretical position one adopts; the perspective from which one views the issues.
10 It should be noted, however, that L.-O. Larsson has taken this idea the furthest. Taking a more local perspective, he has stressed the ambitions of the peasant army and Dacke himself in a way that has been absent from other works. See Larsson 1979; Larsson

1964. One typical formulation is: "Put simply, the Dacke feud was the last violent rebellion in our country between an expanding central authority and a decentralised peasant society that rallied to 'that which of old once was'." Larsson 1975, 120. It should be observed that there is a difference between this perspective derived from local politics and one based on the idea of 'communalism' discussed below.
11 See Larsson 1964, 291.
12 L.-O. Larsson argues that this was largely because at the outset Gustavus Vasa received insufficient and faulty information about the strength and character of the uprising, something of which he himself complained. See Larsson 1964, 294. Even if this were the case, it was still true that since January the king had known of the sensitive situation that had arisen in the province. At two *ting* in January – one in the hundred of Konga and one in Växjö – the peasants had expressed their discontent with royal policy. They were prepared to swear allegiance to the king if he promised that they could retain those customs that had been theirs since time immemorial.
13 GVR 1542, 84.
14 GVR 1542, 78 f.
15 Previously he had also written to Måns Johansson in Eastern Gothia.
16 In the king's words: "... according to what each and every man had sown in his field or how much pure grain he had gathered in." GVR 1542, 94.
17 In other words, the question of what taxation should be based upon.
18 See Larsson 1964, 293.
19 The following is based on Ludvigsson 1905.
20 The numbers are taken from Ludvigsson 1905. Naturally, they do not reflect exact figures, but they do give some indication of the trends.
21 L.-O. Larsson has arrived at a date for when this *ting* was held. See Larsson 1964, 295 and footnote 15.
22 Larsson 1964, 296.
23 Larsson 1964, 296.
24 Larsson 1964, 296.
25 In previous cross border agreements the common struggle against forest thieves had been an important element. However, it is absent from this letter. See Larsson 1964, 297; see also Johansson 1997, and the accompanying bibliography.
26 The figures for the peasant army show that Dacke could rapidly moblise large numbers of peasants from the hundreds around the town of Växjö.
27 Ludvigsson 1905, 65 f.
28 Ludvigsson 1905, 66.
29 Larsson 1964, 301.
30 Larsson 1964, 298.
31 L.-O. Larsson gives as the probable cause Dacke's need for support at a time when the military threat posed by the king had suddenly increased under the command of Gustavus Olsson. It is likely, however, that there was a different reason, as transpires later in the same letter. The Sture family had long been held in high regard in the villages: they had successfully led peasant armies, and had concluded a peace that had previously been to the peasants' advantage.
32 Ludvigsson 1905, 67.
33 Larsson 1964, 302; see also Larsson 2002, 8 ff.
34 Larsson 1964, 302 ff.
35 Ludvigsson 1905, 68.
36 Ludvigsson 1905, 68.
37 Rasmus Ludwigsson does not report the outcome, but considering his general line was favourable to the Crown, it seems safe to assume that Dacke joined with Ture Trolle to track down and punish the culprits, otherwise Ludvigsson would have taken this as further proof of the perfidy of the rebels.
38 Ludvigsson 1905, 69.
39 Ludvigsson 1905, 69.
40 Ludvigsson 1905, 70.

41 Ludvigsson 1905, 70.
42 For the Danish troops, see GVR 1542, 229. See also Larsson 1964, 307.
43 Larsson 1964, 308.
44 The identity of the latter has been much discussed. He had fled "to the woods" with some poor peasants because he feared the bailiff of Hov province. He was urged to turn back and was promised amnesty if he did so. He chose instead to continue with the uprising. See Larsson 1964, 309.
45 GVR 1542, 274.
46 Ludvigsson 1905, 72, 75.
47 GVR 1542, p.277. Åberg 1960, 110 f, writes that it was a sudden military defeat that forced the king to this compromise. L.-O. Larsson, however, has suggested that it was events over the previous two months that had led to the peace initiative. Larsson 1964, 313.
48 Larsson 1964, 278.
49 GVR 1542, 417.
50 It survives, however, only in the form given by Tegel. This reduces the usefulness of the list, as it does not exist in its original form, nor is it quoted or in any way accurately reported in the king's outgoing letters.
51 See Ludvigsson 1905, 67. See also Larsson 1964, 339. There are different views on how these references to old law should be interpreted, as discussed below.
52 See Ludvigsson 1905, 60.
53 Ludvigsson 1905, 75 ff. L.-O. Larsson argues that this account was based on "well-informed reports of developments in Småland during November and December". Larsson 1964, 314 footnote 1.
54 For a detailed account, see Ludvigsson 1905, 77 f.
55 Ludvigsson 1905, 76.
56 Carlsson 1962, 145. The report that Dacke had been in contact with the Emperor, Charles V, is in itself interesting. He had demonstrably corresponded with Duke Albert of Mecklenburg, who in turn said that he had communicated with the Emperor, but at the point when he claimed this it would seem he was lying. It was only shortly afterwards that the duke saw his opportunity to contact the emperor through Count Palatine Fredrick of Wittelsbach. Although he naturally knew nothing of what lay behind the duke's words, the whole episode serves to show Nils Dacke's awareness of contemporary high politics.
57 Ludvigsson 1905, 76.
58 Ludvigsson 1905, 81.
59 The messenger, Hans Plog, was dispatched by Duke Albert from his north German principality of Mecklenburg. The duke had given asylum to two exiled Swedes who had conspired against Gustavus Vasa during the *grevefejden*; the Bishop of Skara, Magnus Haraldsson, and one of Gustavus Vasa's most trusted servants in the central financial administration, Master Olof Bröms, had fled to a monastery outside the city of Rostock. It is probable that it was the latter who, at the duke's dictation, had written the letter – in Swedish – to Nils Dacke. See Carlsson 1962,142 .
60 Ludvigsson 1905, 77.
61 Ludvigsson 1905, 77.
62 Ludvigsson 1905, 80.
63 Ludvigsson 1905, 81.
64 Larsson 1964, 322.
65 Carlsson 1962.
66 Larsson 1964, 323.
67 For example, GVR 1542, 347.
68 The same observation was earlier made by L.-O. Larsson. Larsson 1964, 324. See also GVR 1543, 25 ff.
69 Chf. Larsson 1964, 325.
70 Larsson 1964, 328. Only a few parishes capitulated at this point.
71 L.-O. Larsson gives the date as 25 March 1543. Larsson 1964, 328.

72 Ludvigsson 1905, 85.
73 Larsson 1964, 330.
74 See for example Johansson 1997, 486, for a discussion of the immediate repercussions of the Dacke war.
75 Suggested by amongst others Vejde 1931; Vejde 1943; Carlsson 1951.
76 Suggested by Åberg 1960.
77 Suggested by Larsson 1979.
78 Carlsson 1962, 150.
79 Carlsson 1962, 150.
80 Carlsson 1962, 150.
81 See Larsson 1964, 348.
82 Larsson 1964, 343.
83 Ludvigsson 1905, 76. Normally he concentrates on the king's activities, but there are also many examples of expressions similar to this.
84 See the section 'The economic aspects of the uprising'.
85 See Larsson 1964, 333 ff.
86 Larsson 1964, 333.
87 Larsson 1964, 333. After the uprising, the king sent a letter of pardon to the peasants in the hundred, from which it is apparent that only a few had assisted the rebels.
88 This analysis is based on Larsson 1964, 333 ff, supplemented in an unsystematic manner by source material drawn from Kammararkivet, Småländska handlingar 1543.
89 Rasmus Ludwigsson does not give the outcome, but it seems reasonable to conclude that Dacke teamed up with Ture Trolle to track down and punish the culprit, otherwise the chronicler would have adduced it as a further example of Dacke's double-dealing.
90 Habermas, 1988; Arendt 1988; Österberg 1992; see also Aalto et al 2000.
91 Ludvigsson 1905, 84.
92 Ludvigsson 1905, 84.
93 Some research has been done in this area, but the principal sources give no support for the idea that women participated in the uprising. Theirs was probably a different role, taking care of the farm while the men were away, just as they had always done in time of war.
94 For the problems and possibilities inherent in this type of material, see Burke 1983a.
95 Ludvigsson 1905, 60.
96 Ludvigsson 1905, 61 ff.
97 Ludvigsson 1905, 74.
98 GVR 1542, 174.
99 The Småland peasants' appeal contains many of the points from Värend. See Mårtensson 1952.
100 GVR 1542, 78 f.
101 GVR 1542, 123.
102 I do not consider here the large number of myths which the Dacke uprising attracted, many of which have survived down to the present. L.-O. Larsson has discussed them in, for example, Larsson 1975.
103 The whole episode is taken from Carlsson 1962.
104 In the 1630s, Axel Oxenstierna noted with a shudder what could happen if the government did not discharge its duties adequately.
105 In older research in particular this was a standard view. See for example Sjöholm 1988, who never for a moment considered the peasants' role when the laws were written down or the national law code compiled. More recent research reflects a new variant on this. See for example Harrison 1997, in which he takes the line that fifteenth-century Swedish peasants learned over the course of fifty years that political violence paid off, and this was the reason for all the peasant rebellions. However, he argues against the peasants having any political order of their own to be preferred over that of the monarchy and high aristocracy.

106 See for example members of the historical association Folkets historia ('People's history'). See also Wallentin 1978. For Denmark, see for example Scocozza 1976.
107 A term taken from Blickle's work. See also for example Imsen 1994, who, however, uses the term heuristically.
108 Derived from Blickle's work, for example Blickle 1997. See also Axelsson and Cederholm 1997, one of the better expositions on the principles of peasant communalism in the Nordic area. See also a critique of the idea of communalism in Harnesk 1998.
109 For the peasants' world view during the medieval period see for example Gurevitj 1985. See also Österberg 1992.
110 I use the term both in Perry Anderson's more theoretical sense and as a more descriptive attempt to capture the character of the period. For the latter, see its usage by Erik Sparre, an aristocrat acutely aware of political rank, at the end of the sixteenth century when he remarked that "the saying, that hereditary kings should reign absolute, was not much heard in Sweden before".
111 Anderson 1980. For an overview of developments in the Nordic area, see Gustafsson elsewhere in this volume.
112 Anderson 1980.
113 Larsson 1975, 120. For peasant peace treaties, see Johansson 1997, and accompanying bibliography.
114 Johansson 1997, 485.
115 See for example Arendt 1988. For the decision process, see for example Aronsson 1992.
116 Nyström 1974. For an account of the transition to a centralised justice system, see also Westman 1908.
117 See also Brunner 1962.
118 Petri 1917.
119 In peasants' complaints before the Dacke uprising there were also demands that the fines for criminal convictions be reduced.
120 See also Nyström 1974, in which he writes of "the classbound views and values of the authors of the court books" that led them to apply different punishments to different men. See Nyström 1974, 71 ff. This theme is also addressed by Peter Blickle in Blickle 1986b.
121 See the section 'The social range of the uprising'.
122 Larsson 1975, 122. For the conflict between Crown and peasant see also Blickle's work: for example, Blickle 1981a.
123 Ludvigsson 1905, 60.
124 GVR 1542, 176f.
125 Johansson 1997, 486 f.
126 Johansson 1997, 486 f.
127 Larsson 1979, 106.

CHAPTER V

Resistance in the name of the law
Peasant politics in medieval and early modern Norway[1]

Magne Njåstad

At Easter 1578, the old bishop of Trondheim, Hans Gaas was on his deathbed. As his life was ebbing away, he heard the church bells ringing for a funeral and asked who was being buried. His servant explained that it was the bodies of Rolf Halvardsson and his four companions, who had been executed for rebellion four years earlier. Now their dead bodies had been removed from the gallows and were to be given a Christian burial. A high court of noblemen had quashed the judgement passed on them four years earlier and proclaimed their innocence. Instead, Ludvig Munk, the royal district governor (N. *lensherre*, the king's representative, holding the area as a fief) of Trondheim, was now found guilty of abusing his power. On hearing this, the old bishop responded that he could now die with peace in his heart, and he passed away shortly after.[2]

This story is illuminating for the subject of this study in several ways. It shows us that violent conflicts did occur between the common people and the central authorities, and that the rebels were severely punished. The riot led by Rolf Halvardsson was not the only riot in mid-sixteenth-century Norway, and the fate of the rioters was often similar to that of Rolf Halvardsson. The story also shows us that a legal assembly, whether a local assembly or a higher court, was considered the proper place to solve conflicts between the common people and the authorities. However, the key point here is that even the highest official could not feel safe when these conflicts went to trial. It also shows us that this was the way the common people felt it should be. The story has been handed down in both written and oral tradition, which should indicate that it reflects important values of the political culture of the people of late medieval and early modern Norway.

These aspects provide the three main themes of this chapter: the role of violent or illegal resistance, the role of legal assemblies and other legal ways of solving conflicts, and aspects of the political culture and rhetoric of the common people in sixteenth-century Norway.

Violent Norwegians?

First, we need to briefly examine the chronology of open peasant unrest in Norway. In this way we can focus on periods of more intense conflict between the central authorities and local communities. These periods can be characterised as waves of resistance, uprisings and rebellions.

In the pre-Reformation period, we can single out two periods of intense conflict between local communities and royal power. The first main period of unrest was in the 1420s and 1430s. Another period of violent peasant movements came around the turn of the century, loosely c. 1490–1520. A third period of serious conflict took place in the second part of the eighteenth century. The most important of these eighteenth-century conflicts were the 'War of the Strils' and other unrest in the 1760s, and the Lofthus uprising in the 1780s. In between these periods, there were a few scattered skirmishes, most notably in Telemark around 1540 and Trøndelag in the 1570s.

However, the seventeenth century and the first half of the eighteenth century would seem to constitute a period without any notable, open social conflicts. It is important to note here that we are in these cases dealing with conflicts that involve a certain level of violence. These are the events that we would traditionally label as 'peasant rebellions', or perhaps more accurately 'peasant uprisings'. These three or four waves of resistance raise two questions: 1) Why did they happen? and 2) Why did they not happen more often?

We shall look first at the first question. The events in the 1420s and 1430s are among the most debated cases of peasant unrest in Norway.[3] We can identify three phases of this unrest. First, we find peasant action against the local bailiffs (N. *fogds*, the local representatives of the district governor, N. *sysselmann*[4], who represented the Danish king in Norway) around 1424–1425 on both sides of the Oslo Fjord. Then there was the uprising in Østfold in 1436–1437, known as the revolt of Amund Sigurdsson Bolt. The uprising in lower Telemark on the west side of the Oslo Fjord in 1438 is often referred to as the uprising of Halvard Gråtopp. These three phases each have their own special characteristics.

The action in 1424–1425 was directed against the local representatives of the Crown. The peasants of Rakkestad in Østfold hounded the bailiff Herman Molteke out of the district. The next year they threatened to desert their homes if the bailiff was not replaced. The unrest on the other side of the fjord also seems to have been directed against the local administration in the Tunsberg area, but also at the general level of taxation. This unrest would seem to have died out by itself relatively quickly.

The uprising of Amund Sigurdsson was a more complex affair. The leadership of this uprising would seem to have been a mixture of gentry and wealthy commoners. The grievances and goals of the rebels were also more far-reaching than ten years earlier. The main target was still the local administration. However, we can also see the outline of a larger political agenda. The demands of the rebels concentrated on three points: 1) personal gains for the leader Amund Sigurdsson and security from punishment for the rest of the rebels, 2) a guarantee that positions in both the local administration and the Council of the Realm (N. *riksråd*) would be barred to foreigners and reserved exclusively for Norwegians, and 3) a demand for the lowering of taxes. The rebels were able to negotiate from a position of strength with the Council of the Realm in the summer of 1436, a position they lost during the following autumn. Even so, the final deal between the rebels and the Council of the Realm of February 1437 must be seen as at least a partial victory for the rebels. The main point seems to be that the Council of the Realm used the uprising to increase its own power versus King Eric of Pomerania.

The uprising of Halvard Gråtopp has traditionally been seen as a more 'pure' peasant revolt. This interpretation is based on the fact that either a smaller segment of the gentry or no gentry at all would seem to have been connected to the leadership of the uprising. Also, one of the acts by the rebels was to plunder the estate of Olav Bukk, a prominent member of the Council of the Realm. The leader of the uprising was a certain Halvard Gråtopp, who led a band of commoners on a march to Oslo. On the way, the band plundered the estates of Olav Bukk and the bailiff in Skien. However, they would seem to have lost their nerve and never attacked the city of Oslo or the castle of Akershus. The estate of the nobleman Sigurd Jonsson at Sudreim (Sørum) east of Oslo would, however, seem to have been attacked by another band of commoners. All in all, there seems to have been a more violent side to this uprising, both in the acts of the rebels themselves and in the way they were persecuted after their failure.[5]

The riots and uprisings briefly described here can be seen as resulting from the political and/or socioeconomic situation at the time. Traditionally, historians have emphasized the political aspect of the uprisings. They have been seen as a national reaction against the centralising ambitions of King Eric of Pomerania. The agitation against foreigners and the more independent role of the Norwegian Council of the Realm in the late 1430s have been interpreted in this vein.[6]

However, the conflicts have also been interpreted as an expression of social conflict. The riot of 1438 in particular has been seen as a 'purer' peasant movement directed against both local bailiffs and the aristocracy.[7] A third approach is to see the conflicts as a result of the growth of central authority. The rebels were an alliance of two groups: commoners oppressed by the growing tax burden and dissatisfied with the local administration recruited from outside the local communities, and elites of wealthy farmers and gentry. These groups were dissatisfied with the growing tax burden and were losing their local positions as foreigners were recruited as local representatives of the Crown.[8]

This approach partly overlaps Peter Reinholdson's main point in his study on Swedish late medieval rebellions or uprisings,[9] that the political conflicts of fifteenth-century Sweden were not rebellions but feuds. They were an integrated part of an established political culture, where the different strata and social groups countered each other in a system of mutual obligations. If one of the parties failed to meet their obligations, this constituted a legitimate reason for the other party to seek redress outside the law. A new aspect in the fifteenth and early sixteenth centuries was that the common people took an active part in this system, often in alliance with the nobility.

The interpretation Reinholdsson has presented of the stormy Swedish politics of the fifteenth century also illuminates the political conflicts of the 1430s in Norway, especially the 1436–1437 uprising.[10] We can see that, in return for lower taxes, the commoners allied with certain portions of the lower nobility in the struggle for control over local positions of power and against the policy of the Council of the Realm.

Perhaps the next wave of Norwegian riots can also be fitted into this same pattern. The riots and unrest in the first decades of the sixteenth century would seem to have been mostly conflicts against the regime of Christian II (viceroy 1507–1513, king 1513–1523). However, the beginning of this period of unrest lies in the 1490s, in several complaints from different parts of the country over greedy tax-collectors. In 1494, the district governor (N. *lensherre*) in Sunnmøre on the western coast and several of his servants were killed at a legal assembly, and in 1497 the bailiff at Romerike north of Oslo was killed while collecting taxes. The latter was bailiff for the nobleman Knut Alvsson, who was to lead an uprising himself a couple of years later. It seems that his uprising was partly motivated by a conflict with the leading nobleman Henrik Krummedike, who was King Hans' (r. 1481–1513) most trusted servant in Norway. Knut Alvsson sided with Swedish rebels against King Hans in 1498, and mobilised commoners to fight on his side. He was killed by Henrik Krummedike during the negotiations in 1502.

During the first decades of the sixteenth century, the focus of conflict shifted towards the confrontation with the regime of Christian II. The main actions here were the uprising in Hedemark in 1508 when Christian was viceroy of Norway, and the general violent unrest and riots along the west coast in connection with the heavy taxation in 1518–1520 in the last phase of Christian's rule. All in all, the riots of this period had an ambiguous profile – on the one hand there were the political manoeuvres of the nobleman Knut Alvsson with commoners as allies. On the other hand, there were the riots against bailiffs who were overstepping their authority – among them we find one of Knut Alvsson's own men. And finally, there were the riots aimed directly against the politics of Christian II, starting with the uprising in Hedemark in 1508 and the jailing of the bishop of Hamar, and ending with the tax riots in western Norway around 1520. If we follow Peter Reinholdson's interpretation, these riots foreshadow the rebellions of the 1540s in Sweden as purer peasant rebellions. The nobility were now less dependent on commoners as allies. Consequently, the commoners were less likely to succeed.

After a period of more than two hundred years without any significant peasant violence or open mass protest, unrest broke out again in the latter half of the eighteenth century. The tax riots of the 1760s and the uprising of the 1780s had a totally different character from the late-medieval uprisings presented above. They were mass movements on a scale quite different from the late-medieval uprisings. They were radical in the sense that they were directed not only against the local representatives, but also against the central authorities and their policies. In other words they were directed against the authorities as such, not just against abuses of authority.

The riots of the 1760s and 1770s were the result of stiffer taxation. Protests were massive along the west coast. The riots reached their height in the spring of 1765, when up to 2 000 people from the neighbouring districts around Bergen gathered in the city to express their protest. They attacked both the *amtmann* (the king's representative) and the bailiff in Bergen, and held them as hostages until their taxes were paid back. The riot in Bergen (known as the 'War of the Strils', as 'stril' was a degrading nickname for the population around Bergen) was not the first protest against the new taxes. However, it became an inspiration for commoners elsewhere. The protests against the new taxes never gained the same dimensions as in Bergen. Nevertheless, it would seem that, after Bergen, the threat of violence was enough for commoners along the coast to be able to negotiate over the size of their taxes or to refuse payment. The punishments meted out in the aftermath of the riot were not too harsh. Participants mainly had to pay back the money they had taken. A few of the leaders were sentenced to death, but later pardoned.[11]

The Lofthus uprising, named after the leader of the uprising, Christian Lofthus, had a different background, but exhibits some interesting parallels to events in Bergen. The main reason for the uprising was the dissatisfaction of the commoners over the sawmill privileges of the citizens of the towns along the southern coast of Norway. The usual dissatisfaction over taxation and the conduct of the local administrators were also contributory factors. What seems to have complicated the picture was a conflict between the citizens of the towns in the area and the owner of an iron mine and factory. The royal privileges he was given were in conflict with those of the towns. It seems that the commoners were able to use this conflict to their own ends.[12]

The similarity to the 'War of the Strils' was the scale of the uprising. According to the authorities, thousands of people were involved. The movement was a mixture of petitioning and riots, and it spread rapidly in the Arendal area. As in Bergen, the army was brought in to end the uprising, and the leaders were jailed. Summing up the new aspects of peasant unrest in the eighteenth century, we find the main differences in the magnitude of the unrest and the direction of aggression more directly against the politics of the state.[13]

All in all, this is not a picture of a violent and unruly society. We must instead turn our attention to other aspects of resistance.

Conflicts in the legal arenas

The main problem when analysing the conflicts between local communities and central authorities is not in identifying the reasons for these periods of open resistance, but rather in explaining why there was so little resistance compared to Continental Europe. We must see whether there were alternative ways of settling these conflicts. This takes us on to our second question: "Why did violent uprisings not occur more often?"

Günter Vogler and Steinar Imsen have proposed one explanation for the differences between German and Scandinavian peasant resistance and the question of why there was so little violence in Scandinavian peasant protests.[14] To put it simply, they explain the difference as being due to differing approaches to integrating and incorporating local communities within administrative structures. The dominating system of farming in the north, with family holdings in scattered households, differed from the German system of villages and the collectively organized aspects of village economy. Instead of the village, the scene of communal organisation in Scandinavia was the legal or judicial arena.

The local legal assembly (N. *ting*) with its jury (N. *nemd*) and peasant jurors and Crown commissions were important in solving quarrels before they came to the higher court. The importance of these legal structures was enhanced by the fact that the nobility took little part in them. There are many reasons for this, but the essential point is that geographical limitations and landownership structures prevented the development of large noble estates and thus hindered the development of noble jurisdiction over the peasantry.

The financial basis of the Scandinavian kingdoms in the high and late Middle Ages was also so weak that a high degree of cooperation with local legal and communal structures was inevitable. The solution was that the arenas of communal autonomy and organisation were integrated as the lowest level of Crown administration. There was a mutual dependency between the local communities and the central authorities in keeping the peace and ensuring effective operation of the system of justice. This system facilitated the solution of conflicts before they became too serious.

However, the fact that the administrative and legal structures of the Scandinavian kingdoms were of such a nature that violent resistance seldom occurred, does not mean there were no conflicts between local communities and the central authorities, whether Crown or Church. If we use the strong tradition of communal self-government to explain the lack of violent resistance in Norway, we must also look at the other side of the coin and ask if there were other ways in which the commoners acted politically when in conflict.

If we accept a rather broad definition of resistance, we may be able to see a political culture of a different kind. Let us define resistance as the legal or illegal means used collectively by peasants in conflicts with the central authorities to improve their own situation or avoid a worsening of it. The key words here are 'collective' and 'legal'. Stressing the collective aspect, we shall avoid taking account of individual attempts by peasants to better their situation. When including legal resistance, we must remember that much of the interaction between the state and local communities was based on the local legal structures. This broad definition of resistance is useful for capturing the whole process of discontent and conflict-solving, even where this did not lead to an uprising.

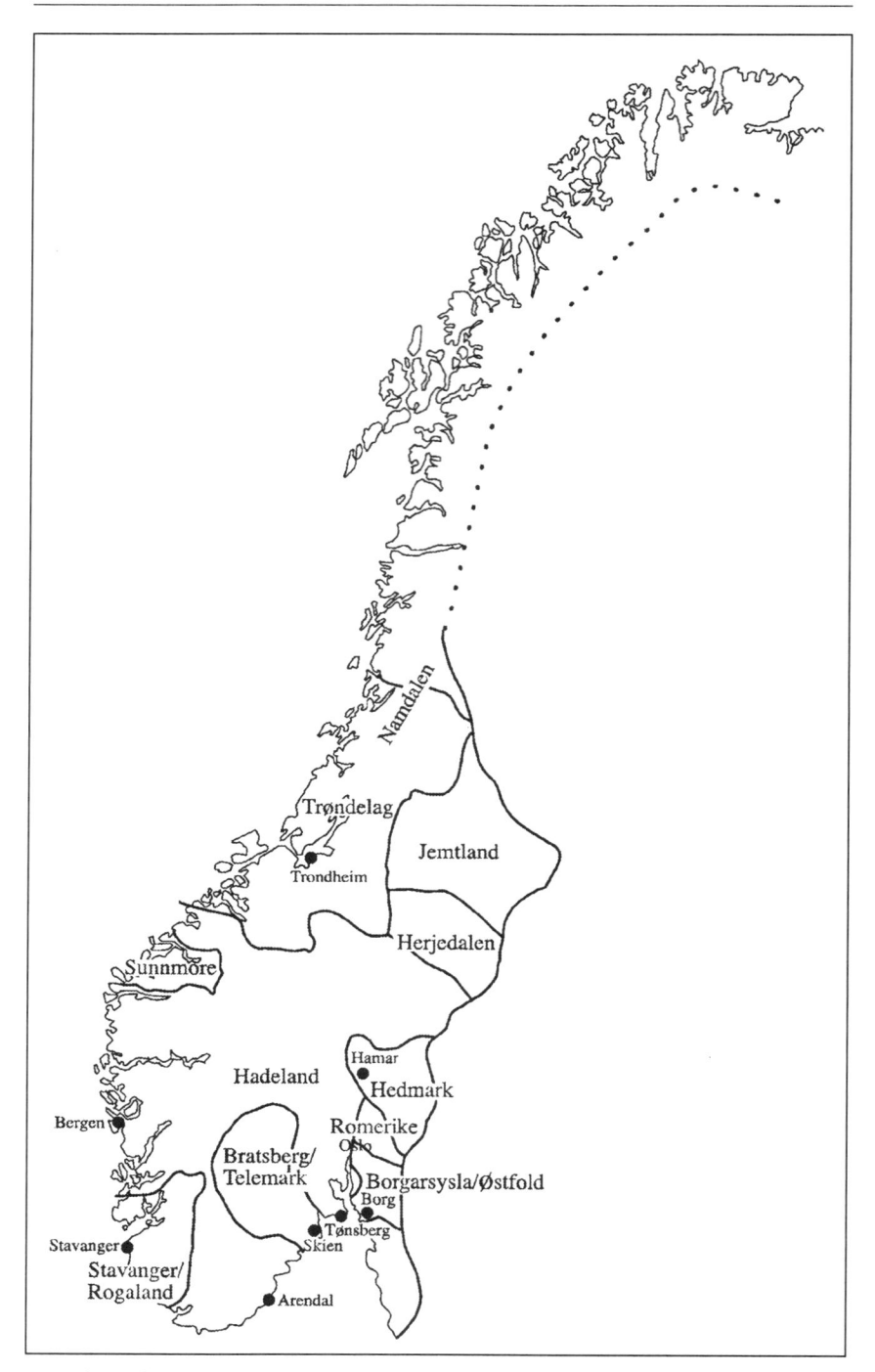

Map 4. Early modern Norway
Only provinces mentioned in the text are marked

If we apply this definition to rural Norway in the period 1300–1800, a new picture emerges. Certain parts of Norway were seething with unrest. The small riot in Trøndelag in 1573 is an example of one of the very few small, scattered, violent skirmishes we find in the decades after the Reformation. But this riot took place against a backdrop of almost 40 years of continued unrest in the region in the form of petitions, everyday resistance of different kinds, royal commissions looking into the local royal administration, and so on. It culminated in a series of spectacular trials where the commoners got the royal district governor (N. *lensherre*) thrown out of office and a number of bailiffs fined and jailed for abuse of power. It is a good example of the point that a lack of or a low level of violence and rebellion does not necessarily mean a lack of conflict and resistance.[15]

However, this system of interaction, cooperation between central authorities and local communities and the mutual acceptance of the legal system as a forum for solving conflicts was not stable and uniform. Norway had a relatively 'modern' codification of law for the whole kingdom from the thirteenth century onwards. Administration was by contemporary standards fairly streamlined. It is obvious that this must have collided with many local legal traditions, different social and economic structures, etc. This was to make the interaction and conflict between the central authorities and local communities differ from place to place and time to time.

Medieval local political cultures in conflict with the central authorities

Let us look at two examples to illustrate the factors that can explain local differences in conflicts. The examples are from the regions of Borgarsysla and Jemtland in the pre-Reformation period.

We have looked briefly at the riots and uprisings of the 1420s and 1430s, which took place mainly in Borgarsysla, modern day Østfold. If we look at Borgarsysla in a roughly 250-year perspective from 1300 to 1550, we can identify certain features that are characteristic of this area. Throughout the whole period the area would seem to have been a hotbed of violence and riots. There would seem to have been comparatively little resistance or conflict-solving within the legal system. Moreover, if we look at the conflicts that were brought to the legal assemblies, we find that they were often brought there at the initiative of the representative of the central authorities, especially the Church.

Conflicts between commoners and the Church were fairly common in this area. For instance, Øystein Tordsson, the priest in Eidsberg in the first decades of the fifteenth century, had a series of conflicts with the commoners in his area over ownership of land for a fifteen-year period around the turn of the century.[16] It is possible to see his actions as part of a Church strategy for retaining ownership to property where ownership rights had become obscured in the decades after the plague of 1349. In this sense, he was a local tool of Bishop Øystein Aslaksson of Oslo, who was the main architect of the restructuring and consolidation of the diocese's landed property in the 1380s and 1390s.[17]

Øystein Tordsson was the party to take the initiative in these cases. We can also note that Øystein and other priests were willing to pursue these cases to higher instances than the local legal assemblies, notably the bishop's officials or the ecclesial court in Oslo. An alternative proposition was for the officials to visit the area to judge these disputes.[18] The right of the Church to exercise legal jurisdiction in conflicts concerning its own landed property was a right it had been championing since the thirteenth century but had never fully gained.[19] This situation changed in the late fourteenth century. As part of the good working relationship between Queen Margaret and the Church (and especially the bishop of Oslo), the latter would seem to have expanded its judicial powers.[20]

Turning to the conflicts in the same area between commoners and the secular central authorities, we find a similar pattern. The legal assemblies played a role on conditions largely set by the authorities.[21] The partial distrust of the commoners towards the legal assemblies seems to be compensated by their willingness to go beyond the law. We have already seen that uprisings were more common in Borgarsysla than in other parts of the country. We can also see that everyday resistance such as refusing to pay taxes and dues was fairly common. In the 1370s, for instance, the king, the bishop, the clergy and the monastery at Varne all seem to have had serious problems in getting their taxes and land rent. We find this in several consecutive years.[22]

Summing up Borgarsysla, we can say that there was a tendency to go outside the law, to use extra-legal resistance both on a low level without violence and in violent uprisings. The conflicts seem to have been most severe with the king and representatives of the Crown. The legal system seems to have worked to the advantage of the central authorities, especially the Church.

Let us now take a look at a contrasting area in the same period, the region of Jemtland. In the 1320s and 1330s, the commoners repeatedly tore down the archiepiscopal salmon traps in the Indalselva river in Ragunda in eastern Jemtland and fished in his part of the river.[23] One hundred and fifty years later we find commoners violating the fishing rights of the local clergy in several lakes in south-eastern Jemtland.[24] The intervening century and a half repeatedly furnishes similar cases relating to fishing rights, forest rights and pasture rights.[25]

There would seem to have been a general culture of disrespect and everyday resistance in the form of violating the ownership rights of the Church. It also seems there was little the Church could do about it. Why was this? In the cases the Church brought to the legal court, the commoners justified their acts with reference to common rights, ancient rights or hunger. This clash between two ways of interpreting the situation is interesting. Even more interesting is the fact that the commoners stood a good chance of winning these cases. This is because they were brought before the local courts, where the commoners would be tried by their peers.

Something similar can be seen in the conflicts the commoners had with the secular power, the Crown. In the 1340s and 1350s there were a series of conflicts between the commoners and the district governor (N. *sysselmann*).[26] The focus of discontent was that the governor exhibited a mixture of greed and brutality in collecting taxes in the region. The forms of resistance were twofold. The commoners refused to pay taxes to the governor, Niklas Petersson. They did, however, pay their taxes, but seem to have collected them themselves, thus undermining Niklas Petersson's authority. They also repeatedly petitioned the king. They used the seal of the province on the petition to verify that the document represented the official collective opinion of the region as a whole. This was one of the peculiarities of Jemtland. It had a seal of the 'community' that signified a certain degree of autonomy.

Geographically, the petitioners represented all parts of Jemtland and also the neighbouring province of Herjedalen. The strategy of the district governor for freeing himself of the complaints was to question the petitioner's mandate. He asked if the seal had been used with the knowledge of the whole population. However he did not question the legitimacy of the communal organs that represented the whole of Jemtland in a conflict.

A different kind of conflict was to emerge a century later. A lot of farms that had been deserted in the century after the plague were slowly being reclaimed in the mid-fifteenth century for use as pasture instead of for growing cereals.[27] The bailiff of Jemtland represented the district governor (N. *lensherre*), who for 50 years was Queen Dorothea. He tried to claim royal ownership to these deserted farms. This would have meant the Crown had the right to land rent when the land was taken into use. This was contested by the commoners, who took the bailiff to court repeatedly to settle the right of ownership.[28] The Crown, represented by the bailiff, lost these cases.

In 1471, Queen Dorothea must have realised she could not resist the legal system of Jemtland, and surrendered her claim to royal ownership of the deserted farms.[29] Instead of land rent, she claimed that the farms should be taxed as regular privately owned farms. This was done without protest. Thus everyone was satisfied – the farmers got their land and the Queen got her income. This shows that the main aim for the commoners was not to evade economic dues, but to establish ownership of the land. The channel of influence they used was the local legal assemblies.

Summing up Jemtland, we notice that there was no open violent conflict between the commoners and the authorities. However, there were many conflicts on a non-violent level. These were often solved within a legal framework, and often to the advantage of the commoners.

Why this difference between Jemtland and Borgarsysla? We can pinpoint at least four factors that can possibly explain these differences:

1) Legal assemblies dominated by commoners.
2) Local social structures.
3) The local strength and power of the central authorities.
4) The economic importance of the areas.

Let us study these points one at a time, looking first at the legal sphere. There were marked differences between the legal systems in Jemtland and Østfold. The main contradiction lay at the level of the highest legal instance in the areas. In Jemtland, the central legal assembly was the *jamtmot*. This was a meeting for all free men taking place once a year. In theory, every free landowning man, which in reality meant almost every householder in Jemtland, could attend and be heard at this meeting. The *jamtmot* was clearly a remnant of an older system of law and order predating the incorporation of Jemtland into the Norwegian kingdom in the thirteenth century.

An attempt to introduce a representative legal assembly (N. *lagting*) resembling the system of the rest of the country as an intermediate court between the local judicial assembly and the Council of the Realm as the supreme court met only limited success in the late Middle Ages. This intermediate court began operating in the mid-fifteenth century in Jemtland. However, it was slow to gain the same importance as the *jamtmot*. The fact that the *jamtmot* was a meeting for all householders did not prevent the representatives of the Crown from trying to dominate it, with occasional success. In the conflicts of the 1340s, we can see that Niklas Petersson was able to muster support from the local members of the *hird* (men with personal loyalty to the king) and the clergy. But it seems clear that the legal assembly enjoyed a status as a forum constituting the local community of Jemtland. The royal officers had only a limited influence on it. It also seems that the supreme judge at the central legal assemblies (N. *lagman*) was not appointed by the king, but chosen by the local population.

In Borgarsysla, we find the 'normal' Norwegian system of representative intermediate courts (*lagtings*) as the highest local court. The highest judge in the region was appointed by the king, not by the inhabitants of the province, as in Jemtland. It would also seem that the legal structures of eastern Norway reflected a communal legal tradition to a lesser degree than those of the western provinces of Trøndelag and Jemtland. Instead of the central assembly, the judge was the main element.[30] There was therefore no central *lagting* meeting at fixed dates. Instead, the *lagman* was an ambulating supreme judge leading a court sometimes in Sarpsborg, sometimes in Tunsberg, Oslo or elsewhere.

The background of the lay jurors (N. *lagrettemenn*) is also important. A common characteristic of these persons – probably all over the country – was that they belonged to the social and economic elite of the local community.[31] Thus, when the legal assembly was used in a conflict with the central authorities it was represented by the 'best' men of the community. However, if there was a large degree of social stratification in the local community, the legal assembly would reflect this too.

This brings us to our second point (closely connected to the first), which concerns the social structures of the areas. In Borgarsysla, we find a fairly complex social structure resembling a 'European' system. There was a higher concentration of nobility and noble estates in the area than in other parts of the country. A great deal of wealth was concentrated in a few hands. On the other hand, there were a lot of tenants who owned little or none of the land they cultivated. In addition, much of the land was owned by the Crown or religious institutions, the monasteries of Varne and Hovedøen being the most important. The growing importance of the timber trade in the late fourteenth century must have paved the way for a new kind of economic elite.[32]

Jemtland in turn can be seen as a typical egalitarian society. This does not mean there was no social stratification, but the economic differences between the wealthiest and poorest farmers were not very great. Of equal importance was the almost total lack of nobility. There seems to be only one family that could be described as 'noble' in the sense of both being wealthy and having close ties to the royal houses of Norway or Sweden throughout the whole late Middle Ages. This was the Skåncke family of Hackås. But they very seldom engaged in local politics. Their stage was national. They generally intervened in Jemtland politics only in times of crisis, in the 1450s and 1520s.[33] To sum up, the relatively egalitarian structure of Jemtland must have given even more legitimacy to the legal system there, while the complex and non-egalitarian structures of Østfold must have worked the other way.

The local strength and power of the central authorities also played an important role in relations between their local representatives and the local community. The crucial issue here was the means the bailiff had at his disposal for exercising his power in the area. One of the most important factors was undoubtedly landownership. There was a considerable difference between a situation where the bailiff merely represented the king in court and as the royal tax-collector and one where the king was also a major landowner in the area whose dues and land rent were administered by his bailiff.

Other essential issues to be examined include how large an area the bailiff was expected to control, whether he had any assistants, whether he was able to find allies in the local population, and so on. It seems pretty clear that the representatives of the king or the Church had rather modest means for exercising power in Jemtland. In the fourteenth century, the king was represented by a district governor, who at times seems to have had a bailiff to assist him. In addition, we find one or two *hird*men, or noblemen loyal to the king. These disappear from the sources in the late fourteenth century. In the fifteenth century, the district governor (N. *sysselmann/lensherre*) was usually not present in Jemtland, but was represented by a bailiff. This meant that the king seldom had more than three or four immediate representatives in Jemtland. There was also little royal domain to support the district governor and bailiffs in the local community. They would therefore have to have made alliances with the local elite if they needed support. But as we have seen, the local elite usually united *against* the bailiff if there was a conflict.

The situation in Borgarsysla appears to have been very different. It would seem that the power base of the bailiffs and district governor was firmer in several ways. The area to be controlled was smaller, the whole of Østfold being about one ninth the size of Jemtland. Moreover, while Jemtland had only one bailiff, Østfold was divided into about 5–7 smaller districts. The proportion of royal and especially ecclesiastical property was somewhat higher than in Jemtland, but the main point was that the proportion of noble estates was very high for a Norwegian context.[34] The ties between the local elite and the representatives of the state would also seem generally to have been closer than in Jemtland.

We can use the bailiff Herman Molteke as an example. As we remember, he was hounded out of his district by angry commoners in 1424, and the commoners threatened to move away if he was not removed. Nevertheless, we find him in the same area a few years later, buying land and marrying into the lower nobility (actually with a cousin of Amund Sigurdsson Bolt, the leader of the 1436 uprising!). In this way, the borders between the state elites and the local elites, and also between royal domain and noble estates, could become blurred, a phenomenon Øystein Rian has pointed out as an important feature of the seventeenth century in other parts of the country.[35]

Moreover, the fiefs or districts in Østfold were rather small, and were often given as fiefs to noblemen who already had property in the area. The noble Galle family, for instance, held smaller fiefs in the area in combination with private estates in the late fifteenth and early sixteenth centuries. Thus, state and local power merged in this way, too. All these factors must have weakened the communal structures of the area. What makes this even more complicated is the leading role of local elites in the uprisings. It is tempting to assume that these persons belonged to those parts of the elite who were unable to profit from the ties to the central authorities. Perhaps this was the main reason for their rebellion.

Let us turn now to consider the last of our points, the economic importance of the area. If the economic importance of an area was great, the central authorities naturally used more resources in controlling it. Once again, we find a contrast between Borgarsysla and Jemtland. Borgarsysla had some of the best farm land in Norway, in addition to which the timber trade increased in importance in this area during the late Middle Ages.[36] Thus, Borgarsysla was interesting both as a producer of agricultural products and as a provider of goods that could be sold abroad. This made control of the area economically important to the central authorities. These things also made fiefs in the area interesting to the nobility.

Jemtland, in contrast, was not very interesting economically. Its main economic value was as a source of fine furs. The taxes from Jemtland were paid in furs: just some ermine skins per farm per year. The king would seem to have been content with this. With the exception of the 1340s, when King Magnus showed a certain interest in the region, we can find hardly any attempts to integrate Jemtland more closely into the kingdom in order to extract more wealth from it. Similarly, the Church could not expect very much from Jemtland. The concordat of 1303 between the king of Norway and the archbishop of Uppsala was very disadvantageous to the Church, which was to receive tithes only of cereals and dairy products, hardly the most economically interesting products in the area.[37] The Church attempted to compensate for this by gaining fishing rights in rivers and lakes. As we have seen, this resulted in conflict with the commoners over how to define the ownership of the common resources.

The triumph of the Crown in the post-Reformation period

The post-Reformation period offers a somewhat different picture. This was associated with two main factors. One was the confiscation of Church lands by the Crown in 1537, while the other was the centralising ambitions of the Oldenburg kings, especially from the times of Christian IV (r. 1596–1648) onwards.

The confiscation of Church properties and the integration of the clergy into the state machinery proved something of a mixed blessing to Crown. Before the Reformation, the Church owned as much as 40 per cent of all farmed land in Norway, while the royal domain constituted a mere 7 per cent (noble property accounted for c. 20 per cent, and the commoners' own property c. 33 per cent).[38] After the Reformation, a good part of the confiscated Church land was still administered by the local parishes. However, a large part of the property of the archbishop, the bishops and the monasteries was placed under the control of the district governors (N. *lensherrer*) and their bailiffs. This meant a tremendous expansion of the royal domain in certain areas. One of these was Trøndelag, which was the core of the archdiocese.

However, the king did not have effective control over the officials administering all this new wealth. During the first decades after the Reformation we find a series of conflicts between local communities and corrupt and abusive district governors and their bailiffs, although royal control over these officials did grow with time.

We can next look at four examples of the effects of increasing royal control on both local communities and local administration in the sixteenth and seventeenth centuries by analysing four different areas: the provinces (N. *len*) of Trøndelag, Jemtland (which we have already examined in the late Middle Ages), Bratsberg (present-day Telemark) and Stavanger (present-day Rogaland).

Trøndelag: controlling the local authorities

We have already mentioned the long period of unrest in Trøndelag connected to the district governor Ludvig Munk and several of his bailiffs. We shall now look at these conflicts in a little more detail.[39]

The discontent focused on two main themes: the growing tax burden and the corruption of officials. The growth in taxes began in the 1550s when the king attempted to revive the old duty of the *leidang*, a duty to build and keep warships. This attempt was met with massive protest and was therefore converted into an extraordinary monetary tax that was grudgingly accepted. In the following decades, other extraordinary taxes were regularly imposed and were regularly met with petitions. The coastal areas of Trøndelag were the most eager to protest. This can be explained by the fact that the coastal areas were also the most heavily taxed. It has been assumed that these areas were wealthier because of their income from the fishing trade. However, the price of fish fell rapidly during this period. This meant that an extra tax on fishing districts was felt to be unfair.

Conversion of old dues to certain religious institutions into a more regular tax after the Reformation also met with protest. The petitions on these matters were often examined by the Diet (N. *herredag*) or by an ambulating supreme court. The Diet examined the protests and unrest in Trøndelag in 1578, 1580 and 1597. The protests over new taxes went hand-in-hand with the complaints over the behaviour of the local officials. It seems that the bailiffs attempted to impose a wide range of new burdens for which there was no precedent, and which were not reported to the king. One example is the bailiff Hartvig Matssen, whose district was the northern coastal area of Namdalen. Matssen was extremely greedy and would seem to have had very little respect for law and order. What made his situation even more extreme was the fact that Namdalen as an area was quite similar to Jemtland. It was peripheral, egalitarian and was home to a large number of commoners who farmed their own land. The combination of this relatively autonomous and somewhat archaic society and the worst imaginable representative of the modern state led in 1597 to between ten and fifteen separate trials between the bailiff and the commoners of Namdalen.

The district governor himself was also the subject of grievances. He had imposed a large burden of labour service on the commoners living close to Trondheim. Those living in distant areas were subjected to mandatory provision of goods for the buildings at the governor's residence. These abuses would seem to have been rooted in the growing financial demands on the governor by the king. The districts were given to the governors as fiefs. However, they had to pay a certain sum of money per year to the royal treasury. During the last half of the sixteenth century, these royal demands grew. The governors tried to compensate for this loss of income by illegal means. This worked to a certain extent because of the weakness of royal control. It also fostered the growth of a patron-client system between the governors and the bailiffs. The bailiffs were extracting more taxes and duties than they should have, while the governor looked the other way. Perhaps they were sharing the profits. This led to the riot of 1573, when Hans Eriksson, a bailiff of Gauldalen, collected a lot of illegal fees and taxes. Although the commoners protested and later rioted, he could count on the support of the governor in using force to quell the rebellion.

The outcome of the commoners' actions was twofold. We have seen that they had a good chance of getting even with the local authorities. Governor and bailiffs were not above the law. But as a rule the commoners were not successful in their pursuit of lower taxes. Corrupt officials were sometimes forced out, but the new taxes remained in place. Ludvig Munk, for instance, was declared invalid to hold any royal office. He spent his last years in self-imposed exile on his estate in Denmark. Hartvig

Matssen was also removed from all duties and made to repay what he had wrongfully taken from the commoners. Another bailiff found guilty was Søren Sørensson in Jemtland. He would seem to have ended his days as an innkeeper in Bergen. Nevertheless, the new taxes stayed in place, and the growth of taxes continued at an even more rapid pace during the next century.

Jemtland: controlling the peripheries[40]

Jemtland represented a growing problem for the Danish-Norwegian monarchy in the mid-sixteenth century. Much of the problem was connected with the semi-autonomous status of the region outlined above for the late Middle Ages. After the final break-up of the Kalmar Union in the first half of the sixteenth century, the Scandinavian kingdoms embarked on a period of fierce competition for supremacy that lasted 150 years. This meant increased importance for the border territories between the kingdoms of Denmark-Norway and Sweden. Jemtland held a particularly crucial position here, because the province was still clerically under the Swedish diocese of Uppsala. This represented a more acute problem now than in the pre-Reformation period, because the Swedish Church was also now under royal control. It would seem that King Gustavus Vasa used the priest of the main church in Jemtland, Erik Andersson from Oviken, as his tool to gain as much influence in the province as possible.[41]

The problems created by this dual obedience to or relationship with both the Swedish and Norwegian kings were settled after the Nordic Seven-Year War of 1563–1570. In the Treaty of Stettin in 1570, one of the concessions given to Denmark-Norway was the transfer of Jemtland to the Norwegian diocese of Trondheim, thus bringing it under Norwegian jurisdiction in religious matters as well as secular. This was the starting point for an intensive policy of integration, with the institutions that had expressed the relatively autonomous status of Jemtland being curbed one after the other over the next 75 years.

The first phase of integration was rather relaxed and met only slight opposition. The main goal of the king in the first few decades after 1570 was to 'nationalise' the Church by replacing Swedish priests with Danes and Norwegians. Otherwise, things were left pretty much as they were. This changed drastically after the next Nordic war in 1611–1613, when Jemtland was occupied by Swedish troops. After the peace treaty of 1613, Christian IV initiated a more active integration policy in the area. The first step was a confiscation of all land owned by commoners who had sworn allegiance to the king of Sweden during the occupation. Almost everyone in the area was affected, and the confiscation gave the state a power base in the area such as it had never had before. This power was used in implementing the next steps of an intensive policy of integration.

The second step was to increase the number of royal officials in the territory. However, they were also put under more intensive royal control. The most important change here was the appointment of scribes (N. *skriver*) both for the Church and the local courts, royal appointment of the bailiff and judge (N. *lagmann*) and the introduction of army officers. This was followed by a policy of imposing military duties and obligations on the population. Another aspect of the integration policy was to curb legal institutions that did not fit into the concept of a centralized state. Important decisions were the revoking of the provincial seal and abolition of a local 'high court' of 24 men. Finally, an even greater tax rise was introduced in Jemtland than for the rest of the country. This was based on the knowledge the king and his representatives had gained on the resources of the territory during the confiscations of 1613.

This policy of integration was of course not accepted without protest in Jemtland. Espen Andresen has analysed the reactions of the inhabitants of the area to this policy. He points to an interesting dialectic between state and commoners. Every step by the state towards a closer integration of Jemtland into the Danish-Norwegian kingdom would meet with protest, usually in the form of petitions. The king would then take a few steps back and modify the measures taken. For example, when the communal seal was revoked in 1614, it became one of the subjects of the many petitions and supplications of the following years. In 1636, the province was given back the right to carry its own seal, but on more restricted terms than before. The office of local judge (*lagmann*) also underwent a similar development. In 1597, Jemtland lost its separate judge, who had been beyond the control of the central authorities of the state. Instead, they now shared a royal judge with Trondheim. In the 1620s, the inhabitants of Jemtland petitioned to get their judge back. In 1630 a separate judge for Jemtland was duly appointed, but this time solely on royal terms similar to the rest of Norway. The *lagmann* as a representative of the province was now a thing of the past. What we can observe here is, therefore, a policy that can be summed up in the proverbial "two steps forward, one step back". This policy was so successful that by 1645, when Jemtland was ceded to Sweden, the territory was well on the way to becoming a normal province just like any other part of the Danish-Norwegian state.

Bratsberg: controlling the finances[42]

Bratsberg (present-day Telemark) is an area stretching from the coast southwest of Oslo to the mountains dividing eastern and western Norway. The region contained a large variety of local economic and social structures. Certain areas of upper Telemark were economically poor and socially egalitarian communities. They had traditionally been beyond both the reach and the interest of the central authorities. The coastal areas and lower Telemark were economically more important, both as agricultural producers and as producers of the new source of wealth: timber. How did this diverse region react to the royal demands for higher taxes and increased control by the central authorities over the local communities through the presence of a larger number of officials?

Øystein Rian has analysed these processes and made some very interesting observations. We shall look first at the 'classical' reasons for peasant revolts: higher taxes. The general level of taxes in Bratsberg were raised about 900 per cent during the seventeenth century. The response to this was low level resistance, petitions and (perhaps surprisingly) sabotage against the tax-collectors! Let us look at some examples. First we shall investigate the petitions. In the early 1630s, heavy taxes were imposed on the timber resources of the commoners. Collection of this tax was not very successful after the first couple of years. The commoners petitioned and argued that their forests were being devastated by overly intensive lumbering. By the 1640s, the more or less annual demands of the king for the timber tax and the refusal by the commoners to pay up accompanied by petitions had become an empty ritual. The whole attempt to tax the forests was quietly abandoned.

Around the middle of the century some attempts were made to rationalize the taxing of the commoners by tying the taxes to the wealth of the individual farms. Attempts in the 1640s and 1660s to map these resources on a national scale were fairly successful. This success was, however, to some degree negated by the farmers' efforts to have their farms revalued at a lower value in an attempt to avoid the tax. In Bratsberg, this seems to have been done systematically in an alliance of the commoners and bailiffs. The bailiff who was to estimate the value of the farms reported them as smaller than they actually were. The farmer and the bailiff shared the saved taxes between them.

A similar strategy was used throughout the seventeenth century to solicit tax exemptions on the grounds of poverty. The farmer paid the bailiff a small sum and was officially exempt due to poverty. There were some attempts by the central authorities to get control of this practice. For instance, the exemptions on the grounds of poverty were to be confirmed by sworn witnesses. This relationship between the commoners and the bailiffs was not always harmonious and to their mutual advantage. The bailiffs in particular were pressured by the district governor or the authorities in Copenhagen to collect delayed taxes or arrears. The bailiff would otherwise face dismissal. At these times the methods used by the bailiff could get out of hand, which would in turn to lead to more petitions.

This situation seems to have been behind the government action of 1661. A new official, the *fiskal*, was introduced to oversee the work of the bailiffs. In Bratsberg he was initially to supervise the commoners, because the bailiffs had complained over the unwillingness of the peasants to give correct information on their properties in 1660. These complaints were probably an attempt by the bailiffs to clear themselves of accusations of dishonesty. Introduction of this new official caused massive protests, not from the commoners, but from the bailiffs and royal scribes (N. *sorenskriver*, a scribe appointed to assist the local legal assemblies) in Bratsberg. The reason was probably the same: an attempt to avoid accusations of dishonesty.

It would seem the work of the *fiskal* gave the commoners reason to delay payment of taxes and intensify their protests against the bailiffs and other administrators. The conflict even went so far that the *fiskal* in Bratsberg was taken under arrest to stand before a royal commission investigating his acts in his duties. However, he was able to escape and to hide among the commoners of the area. It turned out later that the scribe who had raised the action against the *fiskal* had personal reasons to avoid investigation of the *fiskal*, and his action rebounded against himself. Both the *fiskal* and the scribe were summoned to Copenhagen for further investigation. It seems that the scribe lost favour with the authorities. The rebelliousness of the Bratsberg commoners did not have any negative consequences for them.

By the late seventeenth century, the lenient policy gave way to a more severe approach. The new, centralist and autocratic rule from Copenhagen led to more intensive local administration with the primary job of collecting the ever-increasing taxes. Among the new means employed for tax-collecting was the use of soldiers. If a farmer was late in paying or refused to pay he would have to open his home to quarter soldiers. On the other hand, Rian has concluded that one of the reasons why it was possible to increase the level of taxes to such an extent was that the controls over the tax-collectors were also becoming more efficient.[43]

Rogaland: draft-dodging, a case of everyday resistance

The main focus so far has been on violent resistance or conflict-solving through legal channels. But we have seen that there was a close connection between conflict-solving in the legal spheres and everyday resistance. We can loosely describe everyday resistance as resistance on a low level and of a mostly passive nature. A more precise definition is given by Jørn Sandnes, who has proposed a typology of everyday resistance, where the focus is on five different aspects of resistance:[44]

1) Failure to respect a court and resistance against Crown obligations (not respecting sentences, not showing up for trial, etc).
2) Tax evasion (paying late, paying in low-quality goods, etc).
3) Resisting imposed duties (not taking part in work duties such as transporting officials, maintaining the roads, etc).
4) Verbal resistance (creating disturbances in crowds such as at the local court – *ting* – or in church).
5) Illegal economic activities (i.e. failure to respect royal trade privileges, etc).

We have touched upon resistance of this kind in our analysis of late-medieval resistance in Jemtland against property claims by the Church, and we have seen examples of tax evasion as a form of resistance throughout the whole period.

We can see that the effort to trace everyday resistance faces a serious difficulty from the scarcity of sources. Most of these activities did not leave any trace. We can trace this strategy almost solely through royal decrees on taxation and scattered court sessions dealing with such crimes as breaches of restrictions on hunting and fishing rights. It is highly probable that these cases represent only the tip of the iceberg. It is almost impossible to get a clear picture of how common and how serious these breaches were.

One case of everyday resistance which has been given recent attention concerns the military conscription of peasants and their strategies to avoid it. We shall now take a closer look at this form of resistance.

In order to analyse this avoidance, we must first take a look at the changes in the military duties of the commoners during the previous period. In the Middle Ages, the king of Norway depended on a force of commoners. They were obliged to man ships and aid the king when the country was under attack. This service was called the *leidang*. The country was divided into about 250 districts (*skipreide*), each of which had to man a ship. During the late Middle Ages this duty was converted into a tax. The last time the *leidang* fleet was used was in 1429. Attempts to reintroduce a modified *leidang* fleet in the 1550s were unsuccessful. However, there was some conscription of soldiers and sailors for the Danish-Norwegian fleet in the sixteenth century. This conscription was not very popular, and neither was the duty to sell food and other necessities to the navy on low, fixed prices. These measures often led to desertion and sabotage.[45]

Norwegian commoners still had a duty to have weapons ready and to defend their country if it was attacked by an enemy. This happened in both the Nordic Seven-Year War in the 1560s and the Kalmar War of 1611–1613. On both occasions the commoners turned out to be an unruly and undependable army who had little interest in leaving their homes to fight the enemy. Lacking military training, they were more or less unsuited for use as soldiers from a military point of view. In 1611, the Norwegian attack on Sweden had to be abandoned as a result of mass desertion.

The intensified warfare of the late sixteenth and seventeenth centuries led to increased demand for disciplined soldiers. Attempts were made during the first decades after the Kalmar War to create a modern army based on conscript soldiers with basic training. This was attempted in both 1614 and 1628, but was not actually realized until the 1640s. Now a permanent army structure was introduced based on paid officers and conscript soldiers recruited from a special unit called the *legd* consisting of a certain number of farms who had to provide one soldier. The introduction of a standing army coincided with the most intense period of warfare, with four wars between Denmark-Norway and Sweden between 1643 and 1679. How did the local communities react to this development?

Runar Mathisen has studied the reactions of the commoners to the conscription in Stavanger province (present-day Rogaland) during the first two decades after 1640.[46] He has pointed to several different strategies by the commoners to avoid conscription: obstructing the process of conscription, running away from service and bribing themselves out of service. A fourth element was also added when the number of conscripts was increased in the late 1650s: alliances with the local officials.

Obstructing the process of conscription could take several forms. The tricks used by the recruitment units were to send a mentally or physically disabled man, or men who were already in the army. Another quite drastic way of avoiding service was to mutilate oneself so as to be unfit for service. The most usual way, however, was simply not to show up for training.

Running away seems to have been simply an individual decision rather than an organized means of obstructing conscription. While trials for failure to show up for military service would seem to a certain degree to have been conducted as mass trials, trials for desertion focused on individuals. Desertion would seem to have been less common probably due to the harsher punishments. Bribing local officials in order to avoid military service is of course more difficult to trace, because it would have required close oversight of the local officials to bring it to light. Nevertheless, Mathisen manages to show that this did occur rather frequently.

The last point, alliance with local officials, was restricted to the periods of most intense conscription. The officials were dependent on having a stable workforce in their districts to run the farms and pay the taxes. It would seem that the wars of the late 1650s required so many soldiers that they began to seriously damage the economy of the region and the cultivation of the officials' farms as well. It would also seem that this was not a phenomenon limited to the mid-seventeenth century. A very similar picture emerges 50 years later in the same area, this time in connection with the Great Northern War.[47]

In general, it would seem there were several reasons for the resistance to military conscription:

1) There was a collision with old, established customs. The old *leidang* and duty of defence were duties of self-defence. Being shipped away to fight a war in another part of the country or abroad was not traditionally accepted.
2) Therefore the commoners did not have a patriotic identity with the larger domain of the kingdom. This was especially the case in the wars of the 1560s and early 1600s. We have seen that the Jemtlanders in 1611 had no objection to swearing allegiance to the king of Sweden rather than fight against the Swedish soldiers.
3) Military conscription presented a serious economic threat. Providing a soldier for war would usually mean permanent loss of his labour.

In summing up, we can say that military obligations in peacetime or in distant parts of the country were seen as a breach of the military duties the common people were willing to fulfil. Consequently, it was seen as legitimate for the commoners to break the law in order to avoid conscription.

The cases of Trøndelag and Bratsberg show a number of common traits. Crown representatives were sometimes pocketing more than their share of taxes, fines and land rents. As a counter-strategy, the commoners exercised their right of complaint directly to the king. From the late sixteenth century a third element was added: the royal policy of examining complaints in order to get a firmer grip over local Crown representatives.

This royal policy of tightening the grip on local administration was somewhat sporadic in the late sixteenth century, but became more organized later on. The main tools for discovering and investigating misconduct were complaints from the commoners and ambulating sessions of the Diet (N. *riksråd, herredag*). Royal commissions were a third element added to this system at the beginning of the seventeenth century.

As we have seen, complaints direct to the king were not uncommon in the late Middle Ages. Direct access for subjects to the king was an important feature of the Nordic political culture, especially in Norway and Finland. However, there would seem to have been a tendency for increased petitioning from the sixteenth century onwards. This cannot be attributed solely to more substantial source material. An important element here is the appointment of royal scribes to assist the local courts, or *ting,* made mandatory by law in 1591. Over time, the scribe would seem to have acquired a wider range of duties than those originally prescribed. Among these were the duty of helping commoners write their petitions. By the 1630s, this was formalized in a royal decree.[48] The motivation was partly to reduce the number of petitions, but also to provide formalized and secure channels for communicating grievances.

The Norwegian Council of the Realm disappeared after the Reformation and subordination of Norway to Denmark. The role of the Council as a supreme court was replaced by the *herredag*. This was a section of the joint Danish-Norwegian Council that was vested with powers to investigate and pronounce judgement on complicated legal cases. It also investigated complaints against dishonourable district governors or bailiffs. As we saw above, it was one of these sessions in 1578 that restored the honour of the executed rioters. A similar session deposed the district governor Ludvig Munk in 1597. In the second half of the sixteenth century, these ambulating sessions were irregular and sporadic, but by the late 1590s they visited Norway every third year as a more or less regular supreme court.

Ad hoc commissions became an increasingly important tool of control under Christian IV. As the *herredag* became a regular supreme court, the commissions would look into matters that required extraordinary attention. They worked usually in restricted fields, mostly in connection with the organisation of administration and taxes.[49] However, in certain cases the duties of a commission would be more far-reaching and result in more thorough reforms. The primary example of this was the *Bjelkekommisjon*, named after the chancellor Jens Bjelke. This commission, consisting of Jens Bjelke and two assistants, travelled the entire coast of Norway from Telemark to Trondheim and listened to grievances concerning local administration and tax burdens. This commission's work resulted in large-scale reform of local administration in the 1630s and far-reaching legal reforms that initiated the process leading to a new national law for Norway in 1687.[50]

This policy had a number of results. The commoners and central authorities had common interests in developing tools to control the local administration. Formalising the petitions and ensuring direct access to the king meant that the king was able to use the commoners' discontent to get a firmer grip on the lower levels of administration. After a period of several decades from the late fifteenth century when the Crown had been unable to guarantee law and order, the resulting return to more stable conditions increased the legitimacy of the central authorities and also made it easier to impose greater burdens on the subjects. A 150-year period from the late sixteenth century onwards saw a rise in taxes to previously unknown levels.[51] In addition to taxes, there was also the additional burden of military service. That this policy was implemented without much violent resistance suggests the subjects of the Crown were perhaps willing to pay a fairly heavy price for law and order. The increased royal income combined with the growing control over local administration also meant that the central authorities were better equipped than before to create a more uniform administration for the whole country. This meant that local traditions and cultures played a smaller role than before, which in the long run could perhaps alienate the local communities from the central authorities.

What these examples reveal is that the 'communalistic order', as an explanation for the lack of violent conflicts between local communities and the central authorities, was a complex system of mutual obligations, depending on the balancing of several factors. If this balance was disrupted in one way or another, the local communities would feel the central authorities were not meeting their obligations. Concretely, this would normally mean that the representative of the central authorities felt there was room to abuse his position for personal gain, and the King or Church were unable to protect the commoners from such predation. Alternatively, at certain times the king or Church would as a matter of policy seek to disrupt this balance in their own favour without giving anything in return, by, for instance, imposing military duties. This would also be met with resistance.

The eighteenth century – subordination or consensus?

As we have seen, the riots of the late eighteenth century seem to represent something new. Gustav Sætra has analysed these revolts. His conclusion is that they represented a growing danger to the foundations of the twin kingdom of Denmark-Norway.[52] He points to the magnitude of the revolts, the rapid spread of the movement and the proto-nationalistic speech of some of the leaders. Sometimes the local administration was on the side of the commoners. There are some similarities between the riots around 1500 and the late eighteenth century in the intensity of the riots and the direct attacks on royal power. But it is also important to note essential differences. Most of all, the riots of the eighteenth century took place in a bureaucratic, ordered and absolute state.

Against what background should we attempt to explain these uprisings? In general, we can say that too little research has been done on conflicts and conflict-solving on the lower levels of society in this period. The large uprisings have overshadowed the other smaller conflicts between the local communities and the central authorities. However, it is possible to sketch in two competing interpretations on the role of the local legal structures of the eighteenth century.

One explanation focuses on the increasing power of control on the part of the state. While the balance between local communities and the central authorities was threatened around 1500, it was restored and strengthened under Frederic II and especially under the legal reforms of Christian IV. However, the development towards an absolutist, bureaucratic state marginalised the local communities in the long run. One example of this is the local legal assemblies, where the element of local peasant control was gradually weakened while the power of the royally appointed scribe grew until he became the sole judge at the assembly. Hilde Sandvik has characterized the development of the local legal assemblies as a change from a forum of interaction to a forum of subordination.[53] The closing of the channels of interaction in combination with the growth of the tax burden may have produced a political climate conducive to the large scale revolts of the 1760s and 1780s.

This provides an interesting opportunity for comparison with the theory of *Verrechtligung*, the juridification of conflicts. The concept of *Verrechtligung* has mainly been used in explaining the decline of riots and revolts in Germany and the Habsburg empire in the seventeenth and eighteenth centuries.[54] Winfried Schulze has pointed to the impact of the Great German Peasants War of 1525 as explaining the strengthening role of the legal system in solving conflicts. The authorities would go to great lengths to avoid this type of uprising in the future.[55] The decline in peasant rebellions in the late seventeenth and eighteenth centuries must also be seen in connection with the growth of royal/imperial juridical power. The strengthening of royal jurisdiction meant the weakening of noble jurisdiction. The peasantry felt that royal jurisdiction was 'fairer'. It did not represent the interests of the landlords to the same degree as noble jurisdiction.

If we apply this model to the Norwegian society of the late seventeenth and eighteenth centuries, we find a peculiar feature. The strengthening of royal jurisdiction did not marginalise the landed aristocracy holding legal rights over their peasants. The actual 'losers' were the commoners. This can explain the paradoxical situation that stronger royal jurisdiction led to less peasant uprisings in Germany and the Habsburg empire but to a growing number and ever wider peasant uprisings in Norway. In this context the 'War of the Strils' and the Lofthus uprising can be seen as explosions that were just waiting to happen. In a kettle where there is no way to let off steam, explosion is inevitable. In a society with few or no channels for the populace to air their grievances or to influence decision-makers, violent reactions are a realistic option.

There are certain weaknesses with this analysis that nevertheless point the way towards another explanation. The crucial point is whether the commoners really lost control over the local courts. It would seem that to some extent this was not the case. Even though the royal scribe became a judge at the local assizes (N. *ting*), he had to lead the court session in cooperation with a given number of lay jurors (N. *lagrettemenn*). These had traditionally represented the local elite and, even though they were partly only assisting the royal scribe, they gave authority to the decisions. During the eighteenth century the lay jurors were recruited from a broader group of the population than earlier, giving greater representativeness to the local assizes. It was important to reach a certain degree of consensus in the court session. Otherwise the lay jurors would be able to sabotage the decisions in one way or another with the weight of the local community behind them. In the area of the rebelling 'stril' commoners, Atle Døssland has shown that this was done in several ways. One way was to refuse to sign the court decisions. Another was to try to settle matters outside court with the lay jurors as go-betweens. One way of obstructing the royal scribe's work was for the lay jurors to simply not show up in court. It is also obvious that the sheer number of commoners present at the local assize would discourage the royal scribe and bailiff from provoking the community. If they did, the situation could easily get out of hand.[56]

Another point, as we saw in seventeenth century Bratsberg, was the use of sworn witnesses to confirm poverty in disputes over taxation. Originally introduced to hinder tax evasion, the practice could easily be transformed into a tool for internal solidarity in the local communities. If levels of taxation were raised too high, the over-taxed farmers could become a burden on the local communities. To avoid this, the community would readily protect its members from taxation by attesting to their poverty.[57] Yet another aspect of the eighteenth century local assize was its use as a forum for commoners to settle disputes by discussion. The case would then be withdrawn before judgement was pronounced. This way the parties to the case could avoid paying fines for what the authorities obviously viewed as crimes. The royal scribe and bailiff would then be impotent bystanders to the real settling of disputes. Thus, the assize was an institution that functioned on several levels, and the authorities could not control or even understand all of these.[58]

The last difficult point in this explanation is that the role of supplications directly to the king was undiminished. The role of supplications was regulated in the national law of 1687 and later additions. They still played an important role as a basis for decision-making by the central authorities, for perhaps even longer than in the seventeenth century.[59]

These examples perhaps indicate that the commoners' influence on legal processes was undiminished. The uprisings of the 1760s and 1780s can then be seen rather as extraordinary happenings, provoked by special circumstances, primarily extra taxes in the 1760s and local economic structures in the Arendal region in the 1780s.

Law, custom and resistance

Our final point concerns the rhetoric of the commoners in conflict. How did they argue, and what values did they appeal to? We can fairly easily sum up the answer in a single concept: respect for law and customs. Any disagreement with the authorities would be seen in the light of old law, old custom, St. Olav's law, and so on. Not only did the commoners refer to some abstract law or the spirit of the law, but quite often they would show a surprising knowledge of the concrete letter of the law. In legal cases between commoners and local representatives of the central authorities in the late sixteenth century, we can find the farmers quoting or referring quite fluently to paragraphs from the thirteenth century national law, which was often more than could be said of their opponents.

The reason for this one-sided form of argumentation is simple: it worked. With few exceptions, it was in the interest of both the central authorities and the local community that no one was above the law. We saw in the case of Rolf Halvardsson that no official was too high or too noble to be spared once the whole machinery of justice was deployed against him. Another point of interest here is that the rebuilding and strengthening of the legal system in the sixteenth and seventeenth centuries coincided with a massive rise in taxes for the populace, a rise that may have met with some protest, but did not stimulate uprisings. We could say that higher taxes and the restoration of law and order were two sides of the same coin, and that the taxes were a price that the people were willing to pay – up to a certain point.

Thus, there is a surprising lack of the religious rhetoric of resistance current in late-medieval Norway. Looking at European peasant resistance, there was a long tradition of arguing in religious terms – the law of God versus the law of man, millenarianism and eschatologism, etc. This was very evident in the Reformation period, but it was an important element throughout the whole of the late Middle Ages and the early modern period.[60] This was not the case in Norway.[61] We can hardly find any religious rhetoric at all, not even from the sixteenth century. This was so despite the fact there seems to have been some uneasiness about the Reformation among the common people. An example is the uprising in Telemark around 1540. It would seem that this was in part a religious riot. The aggression was directed at a party of German mine workers at a newly opened mine. The conflicts were over labour service, but it also seems to have been a major source of provocation that the workers were ardent Protestants. This seems to have fired a general scepticism towards the Reformation, even though this was communicated only indirectly.[62]

And to conclude with a return to our dying bishop: in the case of Hans Gaas, too, the moral of the story was that the bishop's satisfaction was not solely that God's will had been done, but also that the law of man had prevented injustice.

NOTES

1 Early drafts of this article have been presented to the *Doktorandekolloqvium* in the Department of History, University of Bern in December 1999 and the *Instituttseminar* in the Department of History, Norwegian University of Science and Technology in Trondheim in April 2000. I am grateful for helpful comments made on these occasions. I also wish to thank the foundation *Arkitekt Eugen Nielsens stiftelse*, which granted additional funding for this work, the Norwegian Historical Association (HIFO), and the foundation *Landsprost Erik Andersson i Ovikens minnesfond*, which provided me with a travel grant for the 1999 *kolloqvium* in Bern.
2 Koht 1926, 87; Lysaker 1987, 48–77.
3 For the historiography see Kirkeby 1995, Bjørkvik 1996 and Imsen 1997.

Chapter V

4 4 The *sysselmann* was an administrative district governor in medieval and late medieval Norway. From the fifteenth century onwards the provinces were given as fiefs and their governors were known as *lensherre*. Both *sysselmann* and *lensherre* are translated here as 'district governor'. The original form is mentioned in brackets.
5 Kirkeby 1995.
6 Johnsen 1919, 170–174. Koht 1926, 29–37.
7 Koht 1926, 29–37. Halvdan Koht stresses that the aims of the peasants were a bettering of social conditions, while the aims of the noble leadership in 1436–1437 were of a more 'nationalistic' character.
8 Imsen 1997, 60–74.
9 Reinholdsson 1998.
10 Yves-Marie Bercé has made much of the same point in a work on European peasant rebellions and violence. He sees violence and resistance as a natural way of expressing discontent when central authority cannot meet its obligations towards local communities. Bercé 1987.
11 Døssland 1998, 168–174.
12 Såghus 2000.
13 Sætra 1998.
14 Imsen and Vogler 1997, 5–43.
15 Njåstad 1994.
16 DN V: 420, 421, DN VII: 336, DN III: 579, DN VIII: 251, DN VII: 348.
17 Ringstad 1994.
18 DN II: 501, DN IV: 716, 420, 421, Possibly DN IV: 822, DN V: 553, DN II: 769, DN II: 947.
19 Seip 1942.
20 Haug 1997, 343–363.
21 DN IX: 196, DN II: 614, 624, DN I: 616.
22 DN II: 417, 418, 430.
23 JHD I: 29, 31, 35, 39, 40, JHD S: 1332:A.
24 JHD II: 209, 245.
25 JHD I: 281, JHD II: 161, 169, JHD S: 1380:A, 1395:A, 1408:A.
26 JHD I: 65, 67, 68, 77, 79.
27 Salvesen 1979.
28 JHD I: 286, JHD II: 20, 27, 46, JHD S: 1452:A, 1473:B.
29 JHD II: 83.
30 KLNM: 'Lagting'.
31 Imsen 1990, 143–149.
32 Bugge 1925.
33 Ahnlund 1948, 301–331, 573–604.
34 Bjørkvik and Holmsen 1954.
35 Rian 1990.
36 Bugge 1925.
37 JHD I: 12.
38 Moseng et al 1999, 225–233.
39 The following is based on Njåstad 1994 and Njåstad 1997.
40 The following is based on Andresen 1997.
41 Wangby 1975.
42 The following is based on Rian 1997.
43 Rian 1997, 218.
44 Sandnes 1990.
45 Njåstad 1994, 62, 66–67.
46 Mathisen 1998.
47 Lode 1978, 58–60.
48 Supphellen 1978.
49 Imsen 1982.
50 Nissen 1996.

51 How large this increase was has been an important topic for discussion among Norwegian historians. A good introduction to the debate is Rian 1992.
52 Sætra 1998.
53 Sandvik 1992.
54 Schulze 1980, 1983.
55 Schulze 1982, 294.
56 Døssland 1998, 113–132.
57 Tretvik 2000.
58 Sandmo 1992.
59 Supphellen 1978.
60 Günter Franz pointed out the two concepts of *alte Recht* and *Göttliche Recht* as the two main points of peasant rhetoric in his 1933 classic *Der deutsche Bauernkrieg*.
61 A very important exception is the Sami population in the nineteenth century. The teachings of the priest Lars Levi Læstadius in northern Sweden instigated a separate interpretation of Christianity among the Sami of Sweden and Norway. This fostered a separate religious identity within the framework of the Church, and a Christian rhetoric of resistance in conflicts with the secular *and* religious authorities of the Swedish and Norwegian states. The most obvious example of this is the Kautokeino uprising of 1851–1852.
62 Telnes 1991.

CHAPTER VI

Peasant unrest in Iceland

Árni Daníel Júlíusson

In the early 1200s the West Fjord peninsula was split between the followers or *thingmenn* of two leaders.[1] The followers of Sturla Sighvatsson lived on the south and west sides of the peninsula, while the *thingmenn* of the Vatnsfirðingar family (or clan) lived in the east around the Ísafjarðarjúp fjord. In the autumn of 1230 the Vatnsfirðingar attempted to take over the whole area. They demanded tax from both their own *thingmenn* and the *thingmenn* of Sturla Sighvatsson, and followed this up with a show of arms in the whole area. The *thingmenn* of Sturla Sighvatsson complained to him about this illegal taxation and the attempt of the Vatnsfirðingar to gain influence over Sturla's area. Sturla reacted by killing two brothers from the Vatnsfirðingar family.

The famous writer Snorri Sturluson, the author of the *Heimskringla*, was involved in the conflict. He supported the Vatnsfirðingar against Sturla Sighvatsson. He sent his son Óraekja to the manor of Vatnsfirðingar, Vatnsfjörður in Ìsafjarðarjúp, to join the fight against Sturla. Óraekja collected a large group of men in Vatnsfjörður. This army naturally required large amounts of food and other provisions. In order to obtain these, Óraekja's steward, Björn, went around the Ìsafjarðarjúp and stole provisions from the farmers of the area. As we have seen, the *thingmenn* in the area were supporters of Vatnsfirðingar, but this does not seem to have hindered the robbers. Later Björn also went to the south of the West Fjords, to Breiðafjörður. There he demanded food and animals from the peasants. If they refused, he robbed them. He did this to supply the large armed group of Óraekja at the Vatnsfjörður manor. One farmer, Einar Hollur, was killed because he refused to sell food to Björn.

In the autumn of 1235, Óraekja himself travelled to the West Fjords and acquired provisions forcefully from the peasantry. He took the farms of the manorial estate of Hagi (probably 10–15 farms) from the priest Haukur, and also took Hagi manor itself. After this the peasantry in the area seem to have accepted the dominion of Óraekja, because it is told that no force was used to resist the acts of Óraekja's men at Vatnsfjörður, although he taxed all the farmers in the area. Later the people in the area supported him when he needed an army to fight Sturla, even though he and his servant had taxed and even robbed them. He then raised an army

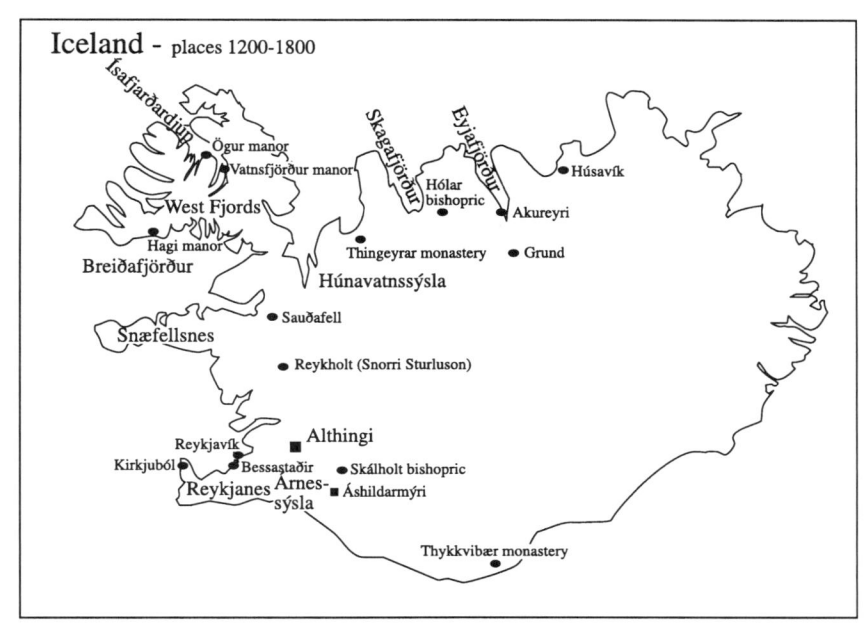

Map 5. Medieval and early modern Iceland

of 720 men from the West Fjords, probably mostly from Ìsafjarðardjúp, and went south to Sauðafell in Dalir, where Sturla Sighvatsson resided.

This account is from the *Íslendinga bók* by Sturla Thórðarson. It is taken here as a point of departure into the social conflicts of Iceland in the period 1300–1800. The reality it describes is at once both complex and straightforward. On the one hand it shows how a chieftain had to rely on the peasantry and their food production for provisioning his band of followers. On the other it shows how the peasants were ready to support a chieftain who had proved himself worthy of support. This was the case even where it could be said that Óraekja had proved this precisely by plundering the peasantry. The events show clearly how important the surplus production of the peasantry was in the political and military conflicts in medieval Iceland. It was the basis of political and military power. Without provisions, a chieftain was unable to maintain an army to defend and/or increase his power.

It is also clear that the peasantry needed the protection of a strong chieftain to secure peace, which was essential to production on the farms. This was the real reason behind the peasantry supporting chieftains like Óraekja.

Rebellion, unrest and conflict

Peasant rebellion in its 'traditional' form with burned manors and slaughtered nobility has never occurred in Iceland. There were rebellions like the one in 1301–1320 initiated by the aristocracy against the power of the

Norwegian king. The aristocracy had the support of the peasantry in this rebellion. However, it is important to underline the fact that the peasantry never rose in violent rebellion on its own account.

So why write about peasant rebellions in a country where they never happened? There are at least two reasons for this. Firstly, there were indeed several rebellions in Iceland, and, secondly, some of these bear quite similar characteristics to the events that have usually been described as peasant rebellions in other countries. Thus, if the Icelandic rebellions were not actually peasant rebellions, it would follow that the others were not either. This could be described as a sort of deconstruction of the concept of peasant rebellion used in historical literature.

On the other hand, unrest was fairly common in Icelandic society and among the peasantry, both petty unrest and unrest on a larger scale. The Icelandic society of the period was not a society of equality, and the history of peasant unrest is a good way of showing this. However, to be able to understand the kinds of conflict that occurred in Iceland at this time, we must first study the structures indicated by the story outlined above. This is essential to understanding the social conflicts in Iceland before the 1550s, and to comprehending why they changed in nature after that time.

The Sturlungar era

The society of the Icelandic free state has been subject to a great number of different interpretations during the last two or three centuries by intellectuals in the Western world and others. Its political assembly, the *Althing*, has been called the world's first parliament. It has recently been pointed out as a possible model for an 'anarchistic' free market society. In Icelandic nationalist ideology it is sometimes seen as a golden age which was regained in the new Icelandic republic. These countless modern myths and readings of the ancient Icelandic 'free state' could form an independent field of study in themselves. A common trait in most of the versions until the beginning of the 1980s was to interpret the change in 1262, when Iceland became part of Norway, as a qualitative leap from a golden age into social desolation. There have been growing doubts about this since, for example in the works of the German literary historian Jürg Gläuser.[2] Let us put these doubts to one side for a moment and take a look at how historians have traditionally constructed the picture of this social catastrophe; the fall from grace, from a kind of social Garden of Eden where the virtues of manliness and honour still reigned unsullied in this small corner of the world before darkness fell.

Until the twelfth century, according to legend and the law of Grágás (an Icelandic law codex from the thirteenth century), political power lay in the hands of *godar*, which according to the same legends numbered 36–39. The political units they controlled were called *godord*. Nothing is known for certain about this, but there has been a great deal of guesswork. In the twelfth century there began a concentration of power in the free state. A few families took control of all the *godords*. This process began in the south, with the Haukdælir family taking power in the Árnesthing area. A little later the Oddaverjar took power in Rangárthing. The family of Ásbirningar did the same in Skagafjörður, and the Svínfellingar took the eastern parts of the island under their strong influence.

In the early thirteenth century, the Sturlungar family began to claim power in the west and parts of the north which were still the domain of *godar*. The Sturlungar were skilled in politics and soon took control of this area. The core of the family comprised three brothers, sons of Sturla Thórðarson in Hvammur. They were Snorri Sturluson in Reykholt, Sighvatur Sturluson in Grund in Eyjafjörður and Thórdur Sturluson in Snæfellsnes. They also had sons who took part in the struggle. However, the fight for power touched the family on the inside too.

In 1238, Sturla, the son of Sighvatur, attempted with the support of the Norwegian king to seize control of the whole country. He took all the areas governed by the Sturlungar in the west and north and gathered armies there. Two old families, the Ásbirningar and Haukdælir, allied with some others against him and defeated him in battle at Örlygsstadir in Skagafjörður. This was one of the most important events of the Sturlungar era in Iceland and has been interpreted as a period of civil war lasting from about 1220 to 1262. In this war, various factions and individuals made alliances, some but not all of them based upon the old families, and each in turn seeking alliance with the king of Norway. According to this interpretation the old 'democratic free state' system disappeared totally during the thirteenth century.

The main problem with this interpretation is that there is no historical evidence for such a period of democracy. The history of the 'free state', as far as can be determined by conventional historical scrutiny, seems to be dominated by a few chieftains fighting each other in large alliances stretching across large areas, exactly like in the Sturlung wars. The change in political and military history after 1262 seems to have been minimal. Politics were still dominated by a few quarrelling families or alliances. However, the formal position of Norwegian royal power was different after 1262, and this certainly led to some changes. There were now formal representatives of the king (who could be pursued and killed, and many of them were).

The power of the Sturlungar family was clearly not based solely on the political power of the *godord*. The foundations of their power rested on the ownership of land, manors and manorial estates. All of the families in power in the early thirteenth century owned several manors. At least three of the manors of the Sturlungar family had outlying rented farms connected to manors forming a system of manorial estates.[3]

There are no surviving conventional rent lists or lists of farms in this period with the exception of Church estates. For example, there are lists from the monastery of Thykkvibær in Vestur-Skaftafellssysla on the land rents the peasant farms paid to the monastery, and lists of the farms the monastery owned, probably in 1218.[4] There is also another list from 1220 of the cattle the peasants had rented from the monastery of Thingeyrar.[5]

These lists suggest, with the aforementioned information on the property of the chieftains, that the basic characteristics of medieval land owning relations already existed long before the collapse of the 'free state'. One of the nationalistic myths about the 'free state' is that it was a society of freeholder farmers who owned their own farms. The historical evidence gives very scant support for this supposition. Be that as it may, if the 'free state' of freeholder peasants ever existed, it had vanished long before the twelfth century.

Historical evidence on landownership becomes increasingly plentiful during the fouteenth and fifteenth centuries. However, there are no surviving property lists of the chieftains from the period before the fifteenth century. Until then the preserved material is mostly on Church property, which is often very good and detailed. On the whole the evidence for the political and economic history of Iceland from the eleventh to the fifteenth century does not point to any special rupture after or with the fall of the free state.[6]

Conflict in the Sturlunga

The conflicts of the twelfth and thirteenth centuries led to numerous battles and atrocities. Civil war in Iceland in this period was undoubtedly a form of peasant unrest, if only in the sense that, although under the control of several chieftains, the peasantry was the main protagonist. How was this unrest organized? What kind of social patterns can be traced in the course of the conflict? And was there any fundamental change in the situation after 1262?

The source material is very special and the problems with interpretation exceptional. The Sturlunga saga, one of the famous Icelandic sagas, is a narrative containing a wealth of information on most aspects of life in this period. However, it is defective in the description of economic matters, as it does not absolutely or unambiguously declare that the chieftains of the families in power were also landowners and manorial lords, although this can be inferred from the text. All in all, the saga is unsurpassed in its description of conflict and the social dynamics of conflict.

A most peculiar aspect of the conflict was the active participation of a large section of the peasantry. In the aforementioned battle of Örlygsstadir there were at least one thousand participants on each side collected from the whole countryside.[7] The farmers of Ìsafjarðardjup rose to fight aside the chieftain although he had just taxed them heavily. There are also other references to this double role of the peasantry in the conflicts.

How can we analyse social conflict in Iceland in the period 1100–1550? There were numerous conflicts, but formally they were wars between different chieftains and their followers. One key to understanding the problem is to realise that the culture of the medieval elites was very violent. The need for protection was therefore exceptionally important. Peace was essential for successful agriculture. War led to rape, pillage and arson. Animals were stolen or killed and eaten. This did not facilitate successful agriculture. The peasantry therefore tended to support those who could secure the peace. This meant that powerful chieftains with the means to make peace were in favour even in a society which, according to the legend, was formed by individuals that had fled the strengthening of royal power.

The culture of the period, however, placed limits on the powers of the chieftains. Power was associated with the person of the chieftain, and a large part of it would die with him, even if members of the same family, sons or relatives, would often take his place. Rules of inheritance tended to disperse power which had been gathered into one pair of hands. The conflicts therefore tended to reproduce themselves in endless cycles. The only power in Iceland before 1262 which could in theory prevent this was the Church. Ecclesiastical property was not subject to inheritance rules and therefore could not in principle be alienated. After 1262, royal power also became a potential stabilising factor in society. However, the Crown did not manage to gain any substantial property, or perhaps was not interested in doing so. This is not at all clear. Be that as it may, the Church was the only force to compete in the sociopolitical system with the chieftains right down to 1550. And this competition between partners was a tough battle.

On the surface, the conflicts of the twelfth and thirteenth centuries were mostly political, being directly concerned with the rule of certain areas. In contrast, the conflicts of the fourteenth to sixteenth centuries were more socioeconomic in nature. They concerned control over landed property, manors, animal husbandry and manpower. However, these were just as violent and disruptive for agriculture as the earlier conflicts had been. And the conflicts in the twelfth and thirteenth centuries were in fact more or less similarly motivated. It is often said that power in a medieval society came from the ownership of land. However, this is somewhat misleading. The ownership of land was closely intertwined with the leadership of men. Ownership of manorial estates and landed properties meant nothing without the loyalty of the peasantry on the farms of the estate. The social hegemony of the period was based on the peasantry feeling the need for protection from the lord, whether this need was real or imagined.

Conflicts between the peasantry and chieftains in the Sturlunga

The latent conflict between the peasantry and the chieftains was for a long time kept in check by the peasant's need for protection. However, there are also clear examples of conflict between the local elites and the peasantry within the 'free state' society. The unequal social relations were formalized in both law and culture. This difference in status is also reflected in the sagas.

There are as great dangers in applying the nineteenth and twentieth century concept of 'class conflict' to the Icelandic 'free state' society as there are in seeing in it the cause of Icelandic nationalism. This must be kept in mind. However, a situation in which just a few chieftains and ecclesiastical institutions owned most of the land and controlled the politics and culture of the country, and where most of the population were peasants living on farms and paying land rent to the few owners, must surely bear the seeds of conflict in itself. This was the situation in Iceland from the eleventh to the sixteenth centuries (and thereafter in part right through to the nineteenth century). The official cultural focus of social conflict did not, however, shift from feuds to polarized conflicts between social groupings until after the mid-sixteenth century.

During the Middle Ages, probably in the fourteenth century, the cultural landscape of Iceland became fully formed. After that, new forms of habitation did not appear until the eighteenth century. Sources from the fourteenth century and earlier reveal a landscape very similar to that encountered at the end of the seventeenth century. About half the land was in agricultural use. The rest was mostly sand, lava, desert or glaciers, unsuitable for farming. The half of the island in productive use can be further divided into two distinct land types. The lowland plains and valleys were fertile and dotted with farms, while the highland areas were used mainly for grazing sheep when used for production at all.

The Icelandic landscape was characterized by an absence of villages. A typical Icelandic farm stood alone in the landscape. It was often 100–500 hectares in size. About 2–4 hectares of these were hedged in and manured as hayfield.[8] Hay was also mown from the outfields. Many farms had shelters where the cows and sheep were kept during the summer and milked, and the milk used to make dairy products. It would seem that an average farm such as this in the Middle Ages would have had 4–6 cows, some calves, about 20–30 sheep and some wethers.[9]

In the south, primarily along the coast, there were a number of tenant farms and Church farms with sub-tenancies.[10] These sub-tenancies were connected to fisheries and the sub-tenants often had only a few animals and perhaps a cow. The main tenant was well placed to control the labour power of the sub-tenants. For example, the sub-tenants had to perform work on fishing boats. However, the sources contain no mention of day labour on ordinary peasant family farms before the late fifteenth or early sixteenth centuries. Neither is there any mention of rent service by the sub-tenants. According to the *Jónsbók* law codex from 1281, a peasant on a rented farm had full legal rights. Among other things, this meant that peasants had full rights to trade with foreign merchants in the trading places along the coast.

The position of a peasant on a family farm was relatively strong. It must have been rather difficult to control numerous peasant farms in a relatively inaccessible and sparsely populated terrain. Acceptance by the farming population must have been essential to the official ideology. However, as mentioned above, the farms were vulnerable to attack. The peasants must therefore always have taken the threat of violent attack into account.

Communication was maintained by horse, and almost every peasant had at least one horse. There was no difference in this respect between the peasantry and the elite. The difference lay in the size of the farms. The largest manors of the elite had maybe 50–100 people living on them, with about 40 cows and 200 sheep. Such a manor was always a powerful military, political, economic and social unit.

'Patriotic' unrest and rebellion in the late Middle Ages, 1300–1550

Unrest 1301–1320

Social conflict in late medieval Iceland had several facets. The most important of these were the existence of patron-client hierarchies and the institution of the feud. This structure forced the peasants and the chieftains to stand together. The patron-client hierarchy was the basic functional unit in the exercise of power at local level. Conflict could take several forms. Sometimes the Crown's action, legal or otherwise, caused a reaction by local powers in the form of a rebellion or a feud. In another case two local powers would fight each other. There were also chieftains fighting against foreign enclaves of merchants who were hiring local hands.

During the fifteenth century a new kind of conflict emerged. The peasantry and the Crown banded together against the lawlessness and autonomy of the local powers. This new development seems to anticipate the diminishing of the medieval principles of social organisation and medieval political culture in the sixteenth century. There was something of a change in the relationship between the Crown and local patron-client hierarchies, at least in the manner in which the local power presented itself.

In 1280–1281, a royal official by the name of Lodinn Leppur was sent to Iceland by the Norwegian royal council to persuade the Icelanders to accept the king's law codex, the *Jónsbók*. At the *Althing* of 1281, he rejected the appeals the Icelanders had made for changes in the codex. According to Bishop Árni's saga, he was very angry because the Icelandic leaders had assumed to themselves the right to set law in the country, which was the right of the king alone. If they were absolutely sure they wanted to change the law he was presenting to them, they should first accept the codex and then appeal to the king over the points they wanted to change.[11] The Icelanders appear to have done nothing.

Twenty-one years later the king sent four men, all from Norway, to Iceland. They were to rule the country on his behalf. At the *Althing* of 1302, the Icelanders rejected these men. Two new articles were added to the agreement from 1262 in which the Norwegian king had been accepted as head of the country. These articles were that 1) the king should not have the right to order Icelandic men to come to the court in Norway, and 2) all the administrative offices in the country, except the top one, should be in the hands of the old *godar* families, meaning those families that had delivered the *godord* to the king in 1262.[12]

The King was not of a mind to give in to the Icelanders. He sent three of the four men back to Iceland with the same mission. One result was that the people of western and northern Iceland refused to arrive to the *Althing* in 1304 and 1305, instead holding their own meetings at home. In 1305, one of these three royal envoys, Krók-Álfur Bassason, was instructed to impose an extra tax on Icelanders because the king was at war and in need of money. This was rejected at a local assembly in Hegranes in Skagafjörður. Krók-Álfur was attacked by the mob. He died shortly thereafter, either of wounds or on his sick bed.

In 1306, the Icelanders came to the *Althing* from all parts of the country. They rejected all extra taxes and pointed to the agreement from 1262. All members of the *Althing* (except those representatives of the king's court and those who were under the king's fief, the *handgengnir menn*) signed a letter to the king. This letter was called *Almúgans samthykkt*, the agreement of the common men. It is important to emphasize the meaning of 'common men' in this context. In the words of Björn Thorsteinsson, this was an agreement between *stórbændur*, literally 'big farmers'. This meant all landowners and powerful men attending the *Althing* except those who had directly sworn allegiance to the king's court. The difference between the two groups is of no great importance, as the agreement supported an earlier agreement, the one from 1302, where all offices had been demanded for the Icelandic elite. In this letter the Icelanders rejected all new taxes. The king had no option but to accept this.[13]

The protests against the Crown's demands continued. In 1314, the king ordered Icelanders to come to the *Althing*, but they stayed away. Finally, in 1320, the king and the Icelanders seem to have come to an agreement and the peace between the two was restored for a while. The king could not fill Icelandic offices with Norwegians, nor had he the right to impose extra taxes on the Icelanders. On the other hand, he was entitled to decide which of the Icelandic chieftains was to rule the island.

The conflict can also be seen in a larger context, as part of a struggle between royal power and the high aristocracies in Norway and Iceland. King Håkon gave a new law in 1302 to prevent abuses by strongly placed members of the royal court. In the same year, one of these men, Auðunn Hugleiksson, was imprisoned and then hanged, apparently for corruption and treason. Auðunn is in one source called Earl of Iceland. Herr Bjarni Loðinsson was also imprisoned for similar offences. There were two things the king wanted to prevent: the court aristocracy weakening royal power by taking for themselves some of its authority or resources, and the court aristocracy and others in power abusing the common people. Abuses included collecting fines in an unlawful manner, accepting bribes, burdening the common people with unlawful taxation and refusing to attend court to answer for these acts.[14]

This law was made for the whole Norwegian realm. Although not entirely successful, it nevertheless showed that the classical conflict pattern of the Middle Ages, Crown versus high aristocracy, also touched Norway. No complaints over abuses by Icelandic officials would seem to have reached the king at this time. No Icelandic high aristocrats were arrested or executed. The politics of Iceland, as described in the annals for the early fourteenth century, would seem to indicate a fairly high degree of Icelandic solidarity against the demands of the Crown. This is to some extent reminiscent of the situation in the seventeenth century.

The battle of Grund in 1361 and other conflicts of the late seventeenth century

In 1354, changes were made in the manner in which taxes were collected in Iceland. The holder of the office of *hirdstjóri* (a kind of governor) was now to pay the king an advance payment for the office. During his period in office he would then try to extract as much income as possible from the country.[15] Norway had just come through the plague and lost 2/3 of her population, according to an Icelandic annal written at the time.[16] The Crown seems to have sought cheaper ways of governing, and this was one of the results. The Icelanders, however, were unsatisfied with this state of affairs, as the system led to higher taxes. This eventually led to conflict.

The first conflict took place in 1359, when Jón Skráveifa, the king's *hirdstjóri*, attempted to collect taxes in northern Iceland. Four hundred men from northern Iceland congregated at Thverá in Húnathing and prevented further tax-gathering. The second battle was a result of the attempts of a Norwegian, Smidur Andrésson to collect taxes in alliance with Jón Skráveifa. Smidur had purchased the office of *hirdstjóri* for the year 1360. He came to Iceland that year and went north with Jón Skráveifa and thirty men. On July 7, 1361 they reached the manor of Grund in Eyjafjörður and went to sleep. In the morning they were attacked by men from the surrounding countryside. Smidur, Jón and seven others were killed. This put an end to the attempts to subdue the northern Icelanders.[17]

In 1375, the Icelanders agreed to a document called *Skálholtssamthykkt*, in which they declared their rights against the Crown. This once again underlined the articles from 1306 about officeholders being from the old Icelandic families and the king having no right to order the Icelanders to come to Norway for trial. Of the new demands, the most important was that the 'lawmen' (I. *lögmenn*), the two highest officials of the *Althing*, should be elected by Icelanders and not appointed by the King. They also demanded a change in the system of paying taxes to the king. They wanted an end to the system whereby Crown officials' payment for their office served as the tax from Iceland, wanting them instead to keep an account of the actual taxes gathered. Such a system was not introduced until much later.[18]

In 1398, a man by the name of Páll Gaddur Guðmundsson was captured in the south of Iceland and taken to Húnavatnssýsla, where he was tried and executed for his crimes. He seems to have been a well-known troublemaker, but also possibly an official of the Crown, a *syslumadur* (sheriff). In 1400 a *syslumadur* by the name of Gunnlaugur Magnússon was killed in Reykholt. Gunnlaugur was accused of attacking some men referred to as *bændur* (a title signifying a high social status in late-medieval Icelandic society) with violence and 'oppressive behaviour'. A year before he had also killed Jón Afbragd, a man in a high position.[19]

It is possible that the primary cause for these events had little or nothing to do with the fact that they were officials. Feuds of a wholly unrelated kind may have been behind the events, the officials being killed not because they were officials, but because they were parties to a feud. It is also possible that Gunnlaugur abused his power as an official to attack his enemies or had made the mistake of enriching himself at the cost of other rich men who were powerful enough to be able to take revenge.

The drowning of a bishop and other events of the fifteenth century

Around 1400, the ties between Iceland and Norway became weaker when Englishmen began sailing to Iceland to trade and fish. Royal power was on the wane in Norway. The three states of Scandinavia were united under one king in the Kalmar Union of 1397. The centre of the Kalmar Union was in Copenhagen, whereas during the Norwegian reign it had been in Bergen or Trondheim. Iceland was for a while outside the sphere of Scandinavian influence in many important matters. The English gained a great deal of influence in Iceland during the years 1420–1450. The clash between the Danish Crown and the English was the root reason behind the killing of bishop Jón Gerreksson. Jón represented Danish royal power and had attempted to strengthen Danish or Scandinavian influence in Iceland. He was the bishop in Skálholt in the south, while the bishop in Hólar in the north was an Englishman.

Jón Gerreksson was attacked by two of the most powerful chieftains in northern Iceland, Thorvardur Loftsson in Mödruvellir in Eyjafjörður and Teitur Gunnlaugsson from Skagafjörður, and drowned in the river Brúará, close to the bishopric of Skálholt. Most of his retinue, or *sveinalid*, who were Danish or Icelandic soldiers, were killed. However, some escaped on a ship to Denmark. Teitur was awarded the status of lawman by the *Althing* shortly thereafter and was never charged with the bishop's murder.[20]

In the fifteenth century, several chieftains behaved in a violent and reckless way when riding through the country with their soldiers, or *sveinalid*. One such event was the tour of Gudmundur through the district of Húnavatnssýsla in 1427. Gudmundur attacked and robbed the farmers in Húnavatnssýsla, where he was *syslumadur*. This act was eventually punished much later by the Crown; at the trial, all Gudmundur's 170 farms and six manors were confiscated. The Crown was in this instance aided by other rich landowners and chieftains, Björn Thorleifsson and his brother Einar. They forced Gudmundur to sail to the king in Copenhagen for trial. Nothing was heard of Gudmundur again, and it is not known what happened to him. Björn Thorleifsson subsequently became by far the richest man in the country. He was himself killed by the English in 1467.[21]

In 1442 the following statute was issued in Norway and Iceland by the Union king, Christopher of Bavaria:

> "In like manner We forbid all and especially Our bailiffs and officials that none of them or their servants should keep or give shelter... ...especially to thieves, robbers, violators of churches, rapists or others like them, and they are not to keep any who has lost his right to peace in Denmark."[22]

This statute reflects not only earlier unrest in the Kalmar Union in the 1430s, but also clearly reflects the tendency of powerful local leaders to rule their areas like sovereign princes and protect those of their liking, and the attempts of the Crown to prevent this.

In 1450, the Crown imposed a new law on Iceland which dealt with similar matters. This was called the *Lönguréttarbót*.[23] It contained several sections. The first threatened those royal officials who did not do their duty in taking care of cases that were brought to them by "the weak and powerless". The second section forbade all unethical and rebellious behaviour, disagreements, unruliness, thievery, robbery and other kinds of violence which had been current in Iceland for a while. This section focused especially on the violent marauding on horses through the country referred to above, which had caused great damage to the king's subjects and all the common people of Iceland. The third section forbade the illegal seizure of any man's rightful property or manors. The fourth forbade the mightiest men in the island from riding around with more than eight armed men if they were not defending their property. The next most powerful could be accompanied by five men, and the others by three. The common peasant was told to do what he was supposed to do, without further definition.

Section six of the 1450 law applied the same rules to the abbots of the cloisters and to the rich priests. They were also forbidden from riding with more than five or three men, respectively. The seventh section forbade men of power, except the *hirdstjóri* and the bishops, from taking servants (*búsveinar*) to themselves other than those who lived on the farms on their own landed properties. This clearly indicates the connection between the ownership of property and control over men and is as such a sign of the 'feudal order'. The fourteenth section forbade chieftains from taking as armed escorts and daily servants those who could just as well stay at home with their wives, cultivate their farms and tend to their animals. This recruitment of armed retinues seems to have been regarded as a prime cause of the desertion of farms on Iceland of which the king had heard (and which was actually caused primarily by the plague). The king believed this desertion of farms was costing him tax revenues. Even worse was that the men involved were following the violent chieftains who were causing so much trouble for the common people. The situation described in the document relates to the period before 1450, when the Crown had little power or ability to control events on Iceland.

In 1496 the *Áshildarmýrarsamthykkt* [24], or *Árnesingaskrá* repeated many of the accusations against the officials of causing anarchy, unruliness and fear with their behaviour. Here the common people of Árnesthing, under the leadership of twelve of the foremost farmers, agreed to put an end to this violence by founding an organisation to defend the area. In each community two farmers were to be responsible for defence and upholding the agreement. This document has been used as an example of proto-nationalism or proto-patriotism because of the demand that the landlord (the king's representative) of Árnessýsla should be Icelandic and not foreign. However, the primary aim of this demand was to have the local administration in local hands. The point was not opposition merely to those who were not Icelanders, but also to those who came from other parts of the island (*utansveitarmenn*). The document forbade the local farmers from taking as a lord a man who lived outside the county (*Árnesthing*), even if the farmer lived on a farm that although situated inside the county was owned by a man who lived outside it.

The later history of this organisation is not known, but what we know from this document fits nicely with an interpretation that sees the organisation as a sign of a growing will on behalf of the common people to put an end to the violent behaviour of chieftains and their armed followers. This would seem to have been a very serious social problem in Iceland at this time. There would also appear to have been a wish to limit the power of the landowning elite. This elite was seemingly organised in its own equivalents of small, informal power areas, each with its own army that did not follow the laws of the kingdom any more than the leaders thought necessary. This situation appears rather different in nature from the events of the fourteenth century, when the common people would seem to have supported the local chiefs or at least did not actively oppose them in their struggle against the consolidating royal power. During the fifteenth century, the common people were pulling in the opposite direction.

Bishops against the king, the Reformation war

The next century split the Kalmar Union, and Iceland was left under the Crown of Denmark-Norway. This period saw the emergence of two strong leaders in Iceland. These were Roman Catholic bishops, the last in Iceland, Ögmundur Pálsson in Skálholt and Jón Arason in Hólar. They both ruled their bishoprics from about 1520. Ögmundur was set aside in 1539, and Jón Arason was decapitated in 1550. At the beginning of their period they were at odds with each other. At one point they both brought to the *Althing* over a thousand armed men, but in 1527 they came to an agreement, and there was peace between them after that.[25]

By 1537 the period of civil wars in Denmark had ended and it was time to bring the Reformation to the outlying provinces of the realm. This led to war in Iceland. The first violent act was the pillaging of the monastery in Videy in 1539. Both Danes and Icelanders were involved. A group of learned Icelanders under Lutheran influence had studied together in Skálholt school. They had probably discussed the need to introduce Lutheranism to Iceland. One of them was Gissur Einarsson, who in 1540–1542 became a bishop when the Danes arrested the Catholic bishop, Ögmundur Pálsson. Gissur was able to negotiate a very favourable deal with the king. Some of its principles remained in force even after his death. One of these was the independent status of the Icelandic bishops. This was quite a different arrangement from that pertaining in Denmark and Norway.

The Danes were unable to arrest Jón Arason at the diocese of Hólar in the north, but did not pursue him while Gissur was alive. Part of the deal Gissur had negotiated was probably that Jón should be left in peace. Gissur died suddenly in 1548, and Jón Arason saw it as his duty to take the Skálholt bishopric back under Catholic control. This of course constituted direct rebellion against the Crown. The Danes prepared an armed naval expedition to Iceland to defeat Arason. On reaching Iceland in 1551 they heard that the Icelandic enemies of Jón had arrested him during the autumn and decapitated him in Skálholt with two of his sons. They had not dared keep him in prison for fear he would become a martyr. But he still became a Catholic martyr and some of his followers (*sveinalid*) took revenge by killing fourteen Danes in Kirkjuból. Among those killed was Christian Schriver, who was at the time the Crown bailiff in Iceland.[26]

On one side, the social forces at play in the Icelandic Reformation war were the old kind of patron-client hierarchy, here under the name of the Skálholt and Hólar episcopal sees. These two bishops inherited an unusually strong position, the Church having strengthened its power enormously during the period 1500–1520. On the other side stood the Crown and some of the Icelandic lay landowners, the chieftains. In 1513 a group of chieftains under the leadership of Jón Sigmundsson and Björn Gudnason protested against the power of the Church in the Leidarhólmsskrá.[27] The conflict arose from the enormous number of farms the Church had acquired, thereby restricting the opportunities of the lay land owners. The local chiefs were natural allies for the royal power against the power of the Catholic bishops. Thus, the forces on each side were strong, and the conflict was intense. We should note that this was the last great conflict of the old kind where feudal relationships of loyalty played a decisive role. It was the last breath of the medieval political culture of conflict in Iceland.

In essence, then, this conflict was very similar to many late medieval conflicts. The Crown had Icelandic allies fighting against strong Icelandic leaders. In the Reformation struggle, the Crown with its Icelandic allies clearly had the upper hand, whereas the reverse had often been true in the Middle Ages, for example in the battle of Grund in 1361. The result was the decisive downfall of the old political culture, and this was underlined in the confiscation of arms in 1575.[28] According to one source, the Danes ordered the confiscation of all the arms in Iceland. There are numerous accounts of armed forces following chieftains after this, for example Magnús Prúdi Jónsson in Ögur. However, never again was there to be armed conflict between chieftains or other powers internally in Iceland. The turnaround in the culture of violence is also reflected in the immediate fall in the number of homicides after the 1550s. These came down from about 30 in the period 1475–1550 (one every two years) to five in 1550–1625 (one every 15 years).[29]

The events of the Reformation war resulted in a 'social revolution' in Iceland. This represented a big step in a positive direction for the common people, with an increase in social peace and security. In essence, the demands of the *Áshildarmýrarsamthykkt* from 1496 were now fulfilled about fifty years later. For the first time, the Crown now had the means to intervene actively in the functioning of society to fulfil the promises of King Håkon from 1302 and *Lönguréttarbót* from 1450. The royal power now extended a protective hand over all its subjects, upholding the rule of law and preventing at least the grossest kinds of abuse of power by royal officials and other powerful men.

Chapter VI

Conflicts between peasants and elites 1300–1550

Conflicts over cow rent in the late Middle Ages

The land in Iceland was almost totally owned by the local chieftains and the Church. These also owned a lot of cattle and sheep, in many cases more than they could take care of themselves. So began the practice of leasing animals to tenants. The Sturlunga saga contains an account of the slaying of the farmer Thórdur at Fagriskógur in Eyjafjörður. Thórdur had rented a cow from the chieftain Gudmundur Dyri. Gudmundur decided that he had another use for this cow and sent two of his men to Thórdur to get the cow back. However, Thórdur had killed the animal and tried to offer another instead. His offer was rejected, and Gudmundur's men killed him.[30]

The Sturlunga saga also contains other stories about the conflicts between chieftains and farmers. Snorri Sturluson, the chieftain in Reykholt, used horses for transporting timber from Skagafjörður to Reykholt. The factor of Reykholt, Valgardur Styrmisson went to Eskiholt farm, the home of the farmer Halldór. Valgardur asked for horses, but Halldór refused to give them. Valgardur threatened him with a javelin and took a horse without permission. The saga tells that Halldór went after Valgardur and killed him.[31]

In another story, the chieftain Björn Sæmundsson of the Oddaverjar family asked the farmer Jón Kráksson at Egilsstadir for food and shelter for himself and his men. Jón refused, but Björn took the food anyway. Then Jón killed one of Björn's men, Vigfús Kálfsson, and fled to Sighvatur Sturluson, who was a chieftain of the Sturlungar family. Sighvatur helped Jón out of the country. Björn took revenge by hewing the legs from Jón's brother Haflidi.[32]

These three stories describe three of the most common types of medieval conflict between tenants and landlords. There was the conflict over rented cattle and sheep, the conflict on loaning horses and the conflict on housing and feeding chieftains and their entourages. A fourth pattern of conflict, disputes over the duties of the tenants to row the landowners' boats and mow their hay fields, are documented in sources from the late fifteenth and early sixteenth centuries. The fifth pattern of medieval conflict was the refusal of farmers to utilise traditional resources, especially grazing in the highlands. This occurred after outbreaks of the plague, because the farmers then had no need to put their animals to graze in the highlands. Landowners were used to deriving income from this use of their property and demanded that the farmers act according to tradition.

Conflicts over rented cattle and sheep were a constant problem due to the nature of Icelandic agriculture. It was very difficult for the landowners to control the way their rented animals were treated because of the distances and large numbers of cattle and sheep involved. The problem was especially acute after periods of bad weather, for example in 1504 after the harsh winter. A lot of animals had died and many farmers had lost their rented cattle. The farmers were ordered in court to pay the landowners the value of the dead cattle. They were to give all living animals on their farms to the landowners in place of the dead rented ones. They were also forced to promise to serve the landowners who had owned the animals that had died.[33] Landowners were not pleased if farmers rented cattle from someone other than the owner of the farm. They even tried to close off this possibility with court decisions.

Conflicts over duties

The manors needed large numbers of horses for transport, as described in the story of the death of Snorri Sturluson's factor. In 1492, a similar case arose in the Skálholt episcopal see.[34] Three farmers were sentenced for refusal to lend horses for transporting fish from Grindavík on the south side of Reykjanes to the ports on the north side. They were forced onto their knees before bishop Stefán Jónsson in the cathedral at Skálholt, where they received their sentence. All tenants, the bishop said, who had the duty to lend horses according to the terms of their tenancy also had the duty to find the horses. If they did not own any, the reason these three had used as an excuse, they were to rent horses from those who did.

In 1511, the tenant Einar Þórðarson on one of Skálholt's farms was taken to court for refusing to row the bishopric's boats during the fishing season. The factor of Skálholt had declared at the annual meeting of all the see's tenants that they were all to row the Skálholt see's boats.[35] It is not clear if this had been the practice before, but it was to be from then on right through to the nineteenth century.

Duties of the kind where tenants were to row the landowner's boats are never mentioned in manorial farm lists from the fourteenth or fifteenth centuries. However, they begin to appear in the sources from the sixteenth century. It is possible that the reason for the conflict at the beginning of the sixteenth century was a lack of manpower in the fisheries that the bishops tried to compensate for by forcing their tenants to row the Skálholt see's boats.

Consequences of the plague in the fifteenth century

As mentioned above, the epidemics of the plague in the fifteenth century led to conflicts over grazing in the highlands. This was an ongoing conflict throughout the sixteenth century. It would seem the landowners were never able to permanently force the farmers to graze their animals in the highlands. Highland grazing was reintroduced again later when the population recovered and there was no longer enough room for grazing in the lowlands. Of course, it was a relief for the farmers not to have to take their sheep far inland in the spring and then collect them again in the autumn, which was hard work.[36]

There were also other positive consequences for the peasantry who survived the plagues. Land rents fell dramatically and a great number of good farms became available for farming. Those who had had poor farms, or none at all, now had an opportunity to rent a good farm. After the plague of 1494, the annals record that many poor families from the West Fjords moved to northern Iceland. This later outbreak of the plague that visited terrible consequences on the rest of the country did not reach the West Fjords. This led to many areas in northern Iceland being rebuilt by people from the West Fjords, traditionally a rather poor farming area, and these people probably became better off as a result.

It is quite clear the potential existed for conflict between the peasantry and landlords. Sometimes it also led to court cases. However, late-medieval political culture did not focus on the conflict between landowners and tenants, but on the conflict between rival hierarchies of chieftains and their men. This was to change completely after the Reformation.

The 'patriotic' struggle for rights 1550–1800

The struggle against the trading monopoly

For a while in the fifteenth century, the English became the main trading partners of the Icelanders. It would seem they were welcomed at first. However, from the 1430s onwards complaints began to be heard over their presence in Iceland. In 1480, a complaint was sent to the king in Copenhagen. Common people from the whole country (according to the document) complained about the improper tradition of foreign merchants living in Iceland all year round. They were said to keep houses and farms by the sea and seduce Icelandic servants to work for them. Because of this the Icelandic farmers/landowners (*bændur*) could not get servants/peasants to work on their farms. According to the complaint, these merchants also sold useless things to the Icelanders. And they took dried fish, butter, meat and woollen cloth at disadvantageous prices for the Icelanders.[37]

In 1490, the Crown responded. In a document called *Píningsdómur*, Didrik Pining, who was the *höfudsmadur* or *hirdstjóri* in Iceland at the time, forbade English and German merchants from staying in Iceland over the winter. They were also denied the right to employ Icelanders. This ban was not immediately enforceable, but it proved to be the long-term policy of the Crown to take the ban seriously.[38]

At the same time, limitations were imposed on the specialised fishermen whose existence had been specifically permitted by the Crown from the fourteenth century onwards without restrictions.[39] In the fourteenth century, the authorities repeatedly banned people from living as fishermen by the sea if they did not possess a specific sum of money, the equivalent to the price of three or five cows. The main argument for these limitations was the lack of agricultural labourers. Fisheries as such were not forbidden, indeed they were one of the mainstays of the peasant economy of Iceland. However, the combination of foreign merchants staying on the island all the year round and Icelandic fishermen, perhaps under the protection of foreigners, seems to have been anathema to the Icelandic authorities.

The reaction of the government to the activities of the English and Germans is very interesting. The Icelandic authorities and the Danish Crown forbade foreign enclaves on Icelandic territory. About the same time, the German merchants in the Norwegian town of Bergen began to lose their position to a new group of Danish-Norwegian merchants. Unlike Norway, Iceland had no towns. Among the Scandinavian towns, Bergen was the traditional trading partner of Iceland. However, it was not Bergen that benefited from the government's new Icelandic trading policies. The winners were the towns of Copenhagen, Malmö and Helsingör.

Englishmen sailed all the seas of the world from the sixteenth century onwards. They established commercial enclaves in many places and gradually built up the British Empire. During the sixteenth century, however, they lost the position they had held in Iceland from about 1400. They kept on sailing the Icelandic waters for fish, but lost all the positions they had gained on land. At first the German Hansa merchants, especially from Hamburg, Bremen and Lübeck, took over this trade. Later, Danish merchants also became involved, and even some Icelanders. During the Reformation war in 1547, the Danes confiscated all the fishing boats owned by Hamburg merchants in the southwest of Iceland. This was probably because the merchants had sided with bishop Jón Arason against the Crown.

From the 1550s to 1602 the Danish Crown held a tight grip over Icelandic trade. It issued letters giving certain merchants use of certain harbours or trading places in Iceland. There was only one merchant allowed per harbour, and they were not allowed to stay in Iceland over the winter. In this way the demands of Icelanders from 1480 were finally met, but the Icelanders themselves were not satisfied. The price of their primary export product, fish, began to fall during the latter part of the sixteenth century, while merchants stopped sailing to some ports in the north and east of Iceland, especially those where fish could not be bought.

Perhaps to meet the complaints of the Icelanders, and perhaps also to be able to control the trade more closely, the king decided in 1602 to establish a trading monopoly with Iceland. Only merchants from the three Danish cities mentioned above – Copenhagen, Malmö and Helsingör – were allowed to conduct trade with Iceland. Another aim of this move was to strengthen the power of the Danish Crown against its traditional enemy, the Hansa cities. However, if the intention was to pacify the Icelanders and keep them satisfied with the trade, the policy was a singular failure. The result was quite the opposite. Now, in a reversal of the politics pursued in the late fifteenth century, the Icelanders began to use the presence of the English fishing fleet in Icelandic waters to pressurise the Danes.

All through the seventeenth and eighteenth centuries, Icelandic protests and complaints on the trading monopoly rained down on the tables of the state bureaucrats in Copenhagen.[40] There were violent confrontations in the ports between the Icelanders and the Danish merchants or their servants. This happened despite the Danes taking great care and never staying in Iceland during the winter. Danish merchants were even killed on several occasions, as were Icelanders. Icelandic farmers from

Thingeyjarsýsla went so far as to demand the abolition of the trading monopoly, proposing the introduction of free trade in a document hailing the coronation of Frederic III of Denmark in 1649.[41]

What was the nature of Icelandic dissatisfaction with the trading monopoly? What groups were involved and who protested? The causes of discontent during the seventeenth century can be simplified into three categories:

1) The lack of merchandise and the paucity of sailing.
2) The rising prices of the foreign products.
3) The trading monopoly itself. Icelanders wanted to trade with the English and Germans as well as the Danes.

These three causes reflect the situation in the seventeenth century. In the eighteenth century, the Danes themselves began to blame the monopoly for the stagnation in Iceland. After 1750, several revolutionary novelties were introduced to pull Iceland out of its supposed stagnation. It was decided that towns must be founded to allow merchants to live on the island all the year round. The trading monopoly was finally abolished altogether in 1787.

Discontent with the monopoly came from all social groups and was significant from the outset. The reaction or unrest of Icelanders in the period 1602–1631 is reminiscent of the unrest in Iceland in 1301–1320 when the king of Norway was attempting to strengthen the power of the Crown.

In 1604, the *Althing* brought forward a complaint over the high prices of Danish merchants, and a supplication on this matter was sent to the king.[42] In 1613, about 300 farmers from Thingeyjarsýsla complained because of high prices. Another reason for their complaint was that no merchants had sailed to their harbour, Húsavík, for 30 years. They were forced to trade in Akureyri in Eyjafjörður. But the problem here was that the only ship that came each year to that port also had to serve the 300 farmers from Eyjafjörður. The trading monopoly was in fact not to blame for this. According to the document[43] there had been no sailing to Húsavík since long before the establishment of the trading monopoly. The king took the complaints seriously and took care that a ship sailed again to Húsavík each year. So, in this case the trading monopoly was actually a blessing.

By 1615, the Icelanders had become tired of useless complaints to the king and decided to take matters into their own hands. The first to do so was the sheriff and chieftain Ari Magnússon in Ögur in the West Fjords. The people of Ìsafjarðardjúp had complained about the Danish merchants in Ìsafjörður. They claimed the law had been broken, the merchants had cheated the poor common people, and the imported grain was of bad quality. The price of fish had been pushed very low, much lower than before. If the common people complained, they said, the merchants answered with contemptuous words. Only one small ship came to trade with more than 350 farmers from Ìsafjarðarsysla and many more farmers from other areas. The common people were forbidden to trade with the captain and men of the ship, and totally forbidden to trade with the English. The protest was not made by the common people alone, as six priests were also involved.[44]

The sheriff Ari Magnússon appointed a court to deal with the complaints. The verdict addressed the main problem: it was forbidden to raise the prices of foreign goods. The common people were forbidden to trade with merchants demanding the new, higher prices. It was decided that the only solution to the problem was a new price list, favourable to the Icelanders. After this verdict, Ari Magnússon set a new price list. However, the list did not fully restore the low prices of the sixteenth century. In actual fact, Ari accepted a considerable rise in the prices of foreign goods.

There was also unrest in Rangárthing and Bardastrandasysla, where Björn Magnússon, Ari's brother, was sheriff.[45] In 1617, the merchants complained to the king about the actions of the Icelanders. The king decided that the *höfudsmadur* or *lensman* (the top official of the king in Iceland) should meet the most important men of Iceland and try to find a solution that could satisfy both merchants and Icelanders.

In 1618, two Danish officials were sent to Iceland. Their mission was to put the country in order. They were to investigate several issues, including the complaints over the trading monopoly. In a letter of the king from 1619 the *lensman* or *höfudsmadur* was ordered to place the merchants under tight control so that they did not offend the Icelanders. This represented an attempt to halt the flow of complaints from Iceland. Four men were sent from Iceland to Denmark to negotiate with the Crown. The negotiations resulted in a compromise, and neither the Danish merchants nor the Icelanders were fully satisfied.[46]

The underlying problem was the rising price of grain. This rose steadily in the period 1611–1630. In 1631, the merchants complained about the low price they got in Iceland for grain and demanded a price rise. The king accepted their demands. When a proclamation on the higher prices for grain was published at the *Althing* in summer 1631, it immediately stimulated a great deal of protest at the *Althing* itself. The *Althing* wrote a letter of protest to the king over the price rise. This told the king that the weather had been extremely bad and people were dying from hunger all over the country. In addition to this, it claimed the merchants had broken the price list from 1619 several times.[47]

The king answered the protests with a new proclamation. He took back the new higher prices and ruled that the Icelanders should cease trading with the English. This set the status quo for the next 50 years, with prices remaining unchanged over this period. The Danish merchants did not like this and tried to evade the ruling, with varying results. A new price list was set in 1684, which again caused many protests in Iceland. The protests were also successful again, a new lower price list being issued in 1702. Some of the prices even returned to the levels in the list from 1619. These prices remained stable for 74 years, until 1776.

Besides this main conflict over prices, there were also several other reasons for conflicts between the Icelanders and the Danish merchants.

Often the result was death. A quarrel over trade led in 1670 to a Dane killing an Icelander with a gun in the port of Djúpavogur in eastern Iceland. Ten years later an Icelander, Jón Thorsteinsson, quarrelled with a Danish merchant in Skutulsfjarðareyri (Ìsafjömður) and killed him. In 1682, Jón Eggertsson and a group of men attacked a Danish merchant and his men in Akureyri. They hit, kicked and threatened the merchant. In 1698, a merchant in Akureyri complained because the common people had been drunk and contentious. In 1700–1706, there were once again several conflicts between the merchants and Icelanders in Akureyri and Húsavík.

After 1750 the Icelanders got more support from the Crown in their quarrels with the monopoly traders. In 1768, the common people of Reykjavík and Seltjarnarnes demanded the removal from office of the merchant of Hólmur (Reykjavík), Ari Guðmundsson, who was very unpopular, despite being himself an Icelander.[48] He remained in office, but was reprimanded by the authorities.

The unrest around the trading monopoly is hard to categorize. In some respects it is reminiscent of the fourteenth century opposition to the strengthening grip of the Crown. However, viewed from the other side it points forwards to the nineteenth century, when Icelandic peasant cooperatives took control of the trade. Perhaps it can be merely seen as a pragmatic reaction to the bad trading practices of the Danes. It should be noted that the trading monopoly did not in any way alter the socioeconomic situation in Iceland. It did not intervene in the structure of Icelandic society. In this way it fulfilled the policy declaration of 1490, the *Píningsdómur*. The existence of English or German enclaves with merchants living there the year round would probably have had a greater impact.

Taxes

Icelanders had already in the early fourteenth century refused to pay extra taxes to help the king of Norway fight a war. In the seventeenth century, there were several attempts to introduce new taxes in Iceland. Icelanders averted this in the same way they had reacted to the trading monopoly. Now they expressed their protests through letters and supplications to the king. The resistance was organised by top level officials and in the *Althing*. The attempts of the Crown to collect extra payments from Iceland and the results thereof can be presented as follows:

- In 1625, the king of Denmark asked the *Althing* to agree to an extra tax because the Danes had been at war in Germany and needed money to pay the high costs. The *Althing* refused to pay anything, because the state of the country was such that nothing could be paid. It was a poor, cold, desolate, barren country, the *Althing* complained. An extra tax would only contribute to a complete collapse of an already shaky economy.[49]
- In 1638, a second attempt was made to get the Icelanders to pay extra taxes. This time the Icelanders protested, but still paid the tax.[50]

- In 1662, the Icelanders were asked by the Danish *lensman* to pay for a permanent defence ship in Iceland. This they completely refused to do at the *Althing* in 1663.[51]
- In 1667, Henrik Bjelke organized the building of a fortress at Bessastaðir, the seat of the Danish government in Iceland. In the winter of 1667–1668, Bjelke wrote a letter to all *sýslumenn* in Iceland, ordering a tax to be paid so this fortress could be built. The tax amounted to 1,500 or 1,600 Danish thalers, and the peasants in the vicinity of Bessastaðir were ordered to build the fortress without compensation.[52]
- In 1679, Icelanders were again asked to pay extra tax. After protests and complaints the king agreed to lower the tax by half.[53]
- In 1695, Icelanders were asked to contribute men to the Danish army. This was called *mannsskattur* or 'man tax', and the result was that 30 Icelanders were sent to Denmark to do service in the Danish army. This was tried again in 1697, but now the Icelanders refused, because there was a lack of men.[54]

If this list is compared with the simultaneous extra taxes in Norway, it is evident that the Icelanders were successful in rejecting the attempts of the Crown to impose extra taxes.[55] All in all, Icelandic political organisation in the seventeenth century was comparatively effective in countering the effects of the strengthening power of the Crown, just as it had been in the fourteenth century. This was especially true in the field of trade and taxes. Even so, the strengthened central power soon began to make itself felt in numerous ways. There were considerable changes in political culture from 1550, especially in the level of violence, and probably also in the prestige of the *Althing*, the local assemblies and the sheriffs. These institutions became the focus of resistance against central power.

Conflict between the peasants and the elite 1550–1800

Rents 1550–1800

Was there conflict between Icelandic peasants and the Icelandic landowning elite in the early modern period? In contrast to the relatively well-known conflict over the trading monopoly, the conflict between the peasantry and the landowning elite has received little attention. Primary sources from the sixteenth and fourteenth centuries show that there certainly was conflict, and they also indicate the two main reasons for this conflict. These were 1) the demands of the elite for the goods produced by the peasantry (the level of taxes, rents and other burdens) and 2) the duty of peasants to work for the estates for nothing. The sources show considerable unrest, enough to leave clear evidence in the court books.

However, there were no dramatic revolts, except perhaps for the fall of bishop Jón Vigfússon in the Hólar bishopric around 1690. An important contribution was made to his fall by the accusations of the farmers in the region of Fljót, who complained that the bishop had exploited them very brutally. However, apparently the real movers behind the sacking of the bishop were some clerics in the north who had never been satisfied with him and wanted him replaced.

It is important to emphasize that the general drift of the period was in some respects favourable to the peasantry, and this applies especially to the development of rents. The basic land rent fell dramatically in the period 1402–1500. The sources show that rents fell by as much as 54 per cent on some estates during this period, and the reduction in most places was around 50 per cent. The decrease in the number of rented cattle was less dramatic and would seem to have followed the ups and downs of economic life during the sixteenth and seventeenth centuries more closely than the value of the land rent.[56]

In the period 1500–1700 there was probably considerable growth in the need for land as the population recovered in the aftermath of the plague. Sources covering the second half of the seventeenth century show a clear growth in the number of farms. Despite this, there was no increase in land rents during the period. Research on cattle rents would probably show a closer relationship between rent levels and population growth. There was certainly pressure from the landowners to raise the rents. In 1634, the farmers in Árnessýsla complained, or someone complained on their behalf, that the landowners of the Skálholt bishopric were trying to press them to feed more cattle and take in more rented cattle than the figure recorded in the rent book.[57] The *lensman* in Iceland, Pros Mundt by name, was ordered to see to it that this did not happen and to take care that the number of rented animals stayed the same as it had been since the dawn of time (sic). This was probably related to Crown nervousness over the growing strength of the bishops. In 1611, the bishop in Skálholt, Oddur Einarsson, was accused by the Danish officials at Bessastaðir of having oppressed the estate tenants of Skálholt.[58] According to his own letter in which he tried to defend himself, he was accused of having oppressed and exploited the tenants with new and unbearable rents and for wrongfully taking things from the peasants.

Conflict or tension between the bishopric and other parts of society was probably partly the heritage of the Reformation. Earlier, in 1593, the bishop had tried to forbid the tenants paying a tax of five ells of wool to the lawman Jón Jónsson, who was to sail to Copenhagen to discuss Icelandic affairs with the king.[59] The tension between the parties is clear. In 1602, the bishop complained that the landowners forbade their tenants paying old tolls and taxes to the Church on the excuse that these payments were a remnant of the old Catholicism and should not be allowed in the Reformed Church.[60] He himself accused the landowners of exploiting their own tenants without mercy. The Crown was on the side of the lay landowners and peasants against the Church, which it might have regarded as a threat to its own interests.

Be that as it may, the Crown certainly did not support those landowners who tried to raise rents. In some cases, the Crown also opposed those who tried to burden tenants with fishing duties. The argument was that this led to neglect of the rented cattle. On the other hand, there were also cases where the Crown supported the manorial estates against their tenants in quarrels over the latter's duties. For example, the tenants of Thykkvibær monastery refused to lend horses or pay fishing duties. They also did not want to row the ships of their landlord, but it was pointed out at the *Althing* that this was something that, as tenants, they could not refuse.[61]

Around 1700, the tenants on farms owned by the Crown in the southwest parts of the island were instructed by court order to perform fishing duties for the state.[62] This amounted to a considerable increase in their land rent, which would seem to conflict with the former Crown policy of not raising rents in Iceland. The decision was reversed by other authorities shortly after.

It is clear that, officially, the rent on the farms under the Crown manors in Iceland did not rise at all between 1597 and 1660. The books on these manors all show the same rent, the same number of farms and so on during this period. However, they appear to be copies of one another, and it must be doubted if they present the real situation.[63]

After 1707–1709, the land rent fell again, by an average of 18,4 per cent.[64] This was directly related to the decline in the population as a result of a smallpox epidemic. About 25–33 per cent of the population had died, and the demand for farms plummeted. The system of land rent would seem to have been twofold. The rent fell considerably because of the catastrophic epidemic and the resulting losses in population. On the other hand, the Crown would seem to have prevented rent rises in better economic times and during periods of population pressure, at least on the Crown's own farms. This strange state of affairs was clearly favourable to the peasantry. However, the peasants always complained bitterly about the heavy burdens they had to bear.

Cattle rents, duties and taxes

The most common reason for the peasantry to complain, or at least the most common conflict between peasantry and landowners in Iceland, was the cattle rents. The owners of large manors, for example Skálholt, often tried to prevent farmers renting cattle from anyone other than themselves. There were three categories of cattle and sheep on the farms under Skálholt manor. First were the cattle and sheep the farmers owned themselves. Then there were the rented cattle and sheep owned by the lord of the manor. And finally, there were the rented cattle and sheep owned by other owners.

The winter of 1641 was hard, there was a shortage of fodder, and in the spring it was clear that something had to be done.[65] Some animals were slaughtered to increase the chances of survival for the remainder. A local assembly in Vatnsleysa in Biskupstungur decided on the 20 March that the rented cattle that were not owned by their own landlord should be sent to their real owners. The decision stated that if the owners would not respond or accept the cattle, the farmers had the right to kill the animals rather than risking the death of others due to the famine.

There were many similar cases, for example in 1648 on the farms of Hólar bishopric. These were often connected to bad weather. The situation was also grave following the harsh winter of 1601. In 1605, the lawman Jón Jónsson asked for a ruling on the problem.[66] Should the farmers be responsible for the rented cattle that had died that winter? The court said yes. The farmers were ordered to hand their own cattle over to the landowners in payment for the rented cattle that had died during the winter. If the farmers did not own any cattle, any other animals or valuables they owned could be confiscated. Thus the elite secured its interests at the expense of the farmers.

Farmers in Skagafjörður responded in at least two cases by killing their own cattle instead of letting the landowners take them.[67] In 1591, a farmer who had lost two rented cows was sentenced to work for the man who had owned the cattle. However, two thirds of the produce of his work was to go to the upkeep of his children.[68]

The cattle rent conflict was an ongoing and inbuilt conflict in the agricultural system of Iceland. The same can also be said of the conflict over duties. In 1588, a tenant called Jón Thorvaldsson in Gardsvík refused to row the boat of the priest Stephan despite the fact that this had been a condition of the agreement whereby Stephan had rented the farm to Jón. Jón was subsequently sentenced to leave the farm.[69] In 1632, the tenants on the estate of Kirkjubæjarklaustur were reminded, under threat of punishment, to uphold the duties and rents they were supposed to pay.[70] Besides cattle rent and land rent, this included the duty to lend a man to the boat of the manor during the fishing season, to lend a man to mow hay during the harvest season, and to lend horses to serve the manor's transport needs.

Another conflict in the early seventeenth century was that of the landowners trying to secure peasants for their farms. In one case a peasant was accused of breaking a contract with the landowner. He had promised to be a tenant on the farm of this landowner for his lifetime, but had broken his promise. Sometimes the landowners were accused of the exact opposite, of chasing farmers away from their farms for no reason.

The Icelandic peasantry were none too pleased with all the tithes and taxes they had to pay to the Church and the Crown. On some occasions they protested. As mentioned above, the country was a separate tax area for the extra taxes the Crown sometimes tried to impose and which were most often refused by the *Althing*. Here it was the Icelandic common people against the Icelandic authorities. There was the case of the farmers in Thingeyjarsýsla. In 1582, they complained that they could not pay their tithes in woollen cloth because of the lack of sheep and wool. It is not clear what caused this, whether it was bad weather or some sheep disease. There was disagreement between the sheriff and the commons over the price of wool. The problem was that two or three hundred people were wandering nearly naked because of the lack of wool and the harsh policies of the authorities in demanding the tithes in wool.[71]

In another case in 1608, four farms in the West Fjords refused to pay any tithes at all. This must have been part of a larger problem, because the bishop, Oddur Einarsson did not get the tithes he was supposed to get from many parts of the country. Everything had been tried – letters, messages by word of mouth and so on – but nothing could induce the peasants to pay up.[72]

Conflicts in the period 1680–1710

The years between 1680 and 1707 were a period of unrest. There was the fall of bishop Jón Vigfússon in the north, there were hunger uprisings all over the country around 1700, and in 1705–1706 the sheriff and landowner Laurits Gottrup and the farmers of Húnavatnssýsla were in conflict over land rent and other related issues. In 1702, the official Sveinn Torfason in Munkathverá was accused of being too demanding regarding land rents. People felt at the time that there was pressure on resources, the population was unusually high and there was a period of bad weather and bad fishing in 1685–1702. After the smallpox epidemic of 1707–1709, the pressure on resources was relieved, and the period 1710–1750 was relatively peaceful in comparison with the 30 years between 1680 and 1710.

In 1684, Jón Vigfússon was ordained bishop in Hólar. He had lived in Leirá in Borgarfjarðarsýsla in the south and had been sheriff there. Ten of the foremost priests in the north banded together against him, wanting one of their own number to get the post instead. In 1688, Jón was accused of having forced the tenants of Hólar bishopric in Fljót to sell half of their ship to the Hólar estate, of having burdened the peasants with higher cattle rents than was customary, of having burdened them with having to feed more lambs than usual for the estate, and several other crimes. All this was written down, both clerics and lay people signed their names to it, and the letter was sent to the king. Jón was also accused of trading with foreign nations and enriching himself with the sale of tobacco. Jón fled to Copenhagen in 1689, but got no assistance from the royal court, and died in 1690, before the court decision on his case in Iceland.[73]

In the period 1695–1702 the weather was very bad and cold, and this made agriculture very difficult. It had been bad since 1685, but now it deteriorated even further, and fish also stopped coming to the traditional fishing grounds for a while. People got desperate. In the winter of 1697–1698 there was unrest due to thefts and robberies, chests and houses were broken into and sheep stolen from houses. Sheep were stolen even if kept inside people's homes; they were sometimes killed on the spot and sometimes driven away. In 1699, three of the worst thieves were caught and hanged. In 1701, 20 thieves were punished in Árnessýsla, and the following year three were hanged in Gullbringusysla and four others elsewhere in the south and west of Iceland.[74]

In 1705–1706, Laurits Gottrup accused several tenants on royal farms in Húnavatnssýsla of not fully paying their land rent. Behind this were two men, Árni Magnússon and Páll Vidalin, who in this period were given widespread powers in Iceland in the name of the king. As representatives of the Crown, they supported the farmers in Húnavatnssýsla against the local landlord, Gottrup. The funny thing was that the representatives of the Crown were Icelanders in nationality, but represented state power in a very modern way, while Laurits Gottrup was a Dane, but conducted his life and affairs as far as he possibly could in the manner of the old Icelandic chieftains. He had among other things the largest manor in Iceland, other than the bishoprics, in Thingeyrar. In 1706, Árni Magnússon accused the *amtmand*, as the top Crown official was called at the time, of abusing the rights he had as an official to stay at the houses of farmers. The *amtmand* was also a Dane.[75]

The late eighteenth century

In many ways the latter half of the eighteenth century marked a watershed in Icelandic history. In 1765 and 1766, Danish merchants were allowed to settle in Icelandic fishing villages. This was the first time the Icelandic authorities had allowed foreign merchants to settle peacefully and without restrictions in Iceland, and it meant the beginning of the end of the old Icelandic peasant society.

In 1752, a large industrial project involving the processing of wool was launched in Reykjavík. This was the real beginning of the town of Reykjavík, which had hitherto only been one of several hundred small manors in the countryside, but also a trading place without permanent settlement. The project was supported by the Danish authorities with large sums of money, and even if it was not entirely successful it launched Reykjavík on the road to becoming the capital of Iceland. In 1770, a stone prison was built in Reykjavík, and in 1785 the bishopric of Skálholt was moved there. Later the Hólar bishopric was also moved there and combined with the other bishopric, making Iceland one bishopric for the first time since 1106.

The Danes had become very concerned about their northerly island, which did not seem to be thriving. A commission was established in 1770 to inspect the situation on behalf of the government, and it carried out extensive research. It received scores of letters from all over the country and from all sorts of people about the state of the country. The letters from the peasantry reveal a similar pattern as the one we have seen above: conflicts between landowners and peasantry over cattle rent, duties and similar issues.[76] The commission also researched the situation of the trading monopoly and received numerous complaints from the common people along with the opinion of the officials. This was part of the process that eventually led to the introduction of more liberal trading in Iceland in 1788.

In 1795–1797, a wave of unrest swept through the country. In many ways the unrest bore the characteristics of a peasant rebellion, and it was clearly inspired by the French Revolution and the wave of revolution in Europe at the time. Peasants rebelled in ports against the merchants and the *Althing* agreed to an extremely aggressive text on trade matters directed to the king and named the *Almenna bænaskráin*, meaning the

'Pleas of the Common People'.[77] This was perhaps surprising, because, as mentioned above, the trading monopoly had been relaxed in 1788. But the peasantry and Icelanders in general soon became dissatisfied with how the authorities managed the new free trade arrangements, and the explosion of unrest in 1795–1797 was a result of this. It was at once reminiscent of the early seventeenth century, when Icelanders had fought the trading monopoly, while also representing a new departure pointing towards the future. Eventually, in the 1880s and into the 1920s, the peasantry and the new Icelandic trading class would push the Danish merchants entirely out of trading in Iceland, and the island would become independent.

Meanwhile, around 1800, the Danish authorities were changing the nature of Icelandic peasant society. This was done through the large-scale sale of Church property. In two major stages, the farms of Skálholt bishopric were sold in 1785, and the farms of Hólar in 1802. Many peasants bought the farms they rented, but the sale also eventually made many landowners rich. A large part of the Church property ended up in the hands of rich landowners. The nineteenth century saw a blooming of the landowning class in Iceland, the last such period. Large landowners ruled in, for example, Eyjafjörður and Skagafjörður, and in southern Iceland.[78]

At the same time, many more peasants owned their farms in the nineteenth century than before. The situation had already begun to change in the eighteenth century. A land register from 1762 shows a considerable rise in the number of farmers who owned their own farms compared to the seventeenth or early eighteenth centuries.[79] It changed further with the sale of the lands of the bishoprics, but still by the mid-nineteenth century only about 25 per cent of peasants owned their own farms. This is very different from Denmark, Norway or Sweden, where owner-occupation was much more widespread at this time, but it was a process of change that could not be halted.

Peasant unrest and rebellions: a useful idea in the history of Iceland?

The difference between peasant unrest and unrest with the participation of the peasantry is very important for Iceland and some other countries, including Sweden. Unrest with peasant participation is seen at every turn in the history of Iceland, while the peasantry as a class does not become an idea in Icelandic politics until after 1550. This is brought about by the intervention of state power, which takes it upon itself to protect the peasantry against the tyranny of local landlords.

In his book from 1998, Peter Reinholdsson put forward a theory, or idea, about the nature of peasant unrest in Sweden in the late Middle Ages.[80] Reinholdsson argues that the vocabulary of class conflict cannot be used to explain the unrest in Sweden in this period; rather these conflicts must be seen as part of an established political culture based on the concepts of law, mutual obligations and feuds as a legitimate form of solving conflicts not solved by law. In the 15th and sixteenth centuries, the peasantry appeared on the Swedish political scene as a distinct group; it was, so to speak, invented. This is a new and interesting interpretation of the history of these uprisings.

Can the warfare and conflicts of the Icelanders in the period 1100–1550 be classified in the same way? The terms used by Reinholdsson for Sweden fit very well in the Icelandic context. The analysis of narrative and conflict in the Sagas by many literary historians has led to very similar conclusions. The analysis of conflict in late medieval Iceland reveals the same pattern of feud,[81] with the exception that the peasant class is not conceptualised or articulated until after 1550. It does not appear on the political scene in the fifteenth century in the same way as in Sweden. It is with the Danish intervention in Iceland at the Reformation that the idea of a class of peasantry in need of special legal protection from the state appears. This was a very influential idea in the whole of Danish policy in Iceland between the sixteenth and eighteenth centuries.

We must now ask if it is at all useful to analyse Icelandic society in the period 1300–1800 in terms of social conflict, because it does not exhibit very dramatic conflicts. The answer must be in the affirmative. Our survey has revealed two main forms of conflict, related to two different forms of social relationship. On the one hand there is the conflict between the Crown on one side and Icelandic society in general on the other. Here, Iceland appears as a local area or province subject to the taxation and administration of a royal central power, either the Norwegian Crown or the Danish-Norwegian Crown. Trade and taxes are regulated by the Crown, and this leads to conflicts with the local elite, and sometimes the whole local population in Iceland. This conflict has a similar style or appearance throughout the whole period 1300–1800. There was, however, a change in the intensity of conflict over trade after the establishment of the trading monopoly in 1602.

On the other hand, there is the conflict between landowners, or the Icelandic elite, on one side and the peasantry, or those who produce food from the land, on the other. The elite owned almost all the land, and the peasants were tenants. There was conflict between the peasantry and the elite over land rents, cow rents and the like throughout the period 1300–1800. After 1550, the state intervened on the side of the peasantry. According to the state, the relationship between the peasantry and the elite should be subject to the rule of law. The state now took it upon itself to protect the peasantry, whereas before 1550 their protection had been in the hands of a social system of feud, chieftains, patron-client hierarchies and local wars. This was a very ineffective and at most times counterproductive system, and also violent, and the rule of the state after 1550 represented a major step forward for the peasantry.

NOTES

1. Sturlunga saga 1988, 329–375. *Thingmenn* were followers of *godar*. Every farmer had to choose a *godi* as a protector.
2. Gläuser 1983.
3. These were the Hagi in Barðaströnd, Brjánslækur in Barðaströnd and Staðarhóll in Saurbær. Sturlunga saga. 1988, 187, 371, 433.
4. Diplomatarium Islandicum I, 396.
5. Diplomatarium Islandicum I, 396–401.
6. For further reading on this idea see Júlíusson 1997a, 57–69.
7. Íslenskur söguatlas 1. 1989, 99.
8. Thoroddsen 1919–1922, 97; Júlíusson 1997b, 197.
9. There are not many references to the number of animals on farms in the Middle Ages but there are some. See e.g. Diplomatarium Islandicum III, 627. For a general discussion and reconstruction see Júlíusson 1997b, 193–207.
10. Most farms in Iceland were owned by the elite, as already mentioned, and rented out. They were thus tenancies. On these tenancies there were in many cases sub-tenancies, a situation well known in England. In Iceland these sub-tenancies were called *hjáleigur*.
11. Helle 1995, 208.
12. Laxness 1987, 155.
13. Thorsteinsson 1980, 187–194; Kristinsson 1998.
14. Helle 1995, 209–210.
15. Kristinsson 1998, 141.
16. The number of inhabited farms in Norway was about 60 000–70 000 before 1350. This number may have fallen to about 30 000–40 000 after the plague, and later fell even lower, but the number of Icelandic farms in the fourteenth century may have been about 10 000. These are rough estimates, but they indicate the approximate tax base in each case, until the plague reached Iceland in 1402.
17. Storm 1888, 225–226.
18. Diplomatarium Islandicum II, 355–357.
19. Storm 1888, 285.
20. Thorsteinsson 1980, 254–255; Storm 1888, 295.
21. Thorsteinsson 1980, 259–261.
22. "Item biwde wi eder alle og serdelis wore fogutte oc oc [sic] æmbesmen at engen then anners wartnade eller thiænere holder eller forsware ... oc sierdelis tiwfe, røfuere, kirkebriter, waltaghere oc andre thelige jcke scal oc nogher herj riket holde nogurn then som fretloos er giord i danmark..." Diplomatarium Islandicum V, 15.
23. Diplomatarium Islandicum V, 63.
24. Diplomatarium Islandicum VII, 321–323.
25. Íslenskur söguatlas 1. 1989, 150.
26. Storm 1888, 375.
27. Diplomatarium Islandicum VIII, 429–452.
28. Jóhannesson 1968.
29. Diplomatarium Islandicum 1475–1570; *Althingisbækur* 1570–1625.
30. Sturlunga saga 1988, 171.
31. Sturlunga saga 1988, 349.
32. Sturlunga saga 1988, 350.
33. Diplomatarium Islandicum VII, 725.

Chapter VI

34 Diplomatarium Islandicum VII, 152–153.
35 Diplomatarium Islandicum VIII, 362.
36 Diplomatarium Islandicum VII, 559–560, 814.
37 Diplomatarium Islandicum VI, 281–285.
38 Diplomatarium Islandicum VI, 702–704.
39 Diplomatarium Islandicum II, 859.
40 Aðils 1919, 131–178, 515–545.
41 Skjöl um hylling Íslendinga 1649 við Friðrik konung thriðja 1914, 56.
42 Althingisbækur 3, 342–344.
43 Althingisbækur 4, 189–191.
44 Althingisbækur 4, 274–281; Aðils 1919, 87.
45 Aðils 1919, 87.
46 Althingisbækur 4, 485.
47 Althingisbækur 5, 213–218.
48 Aðils 1919, 241.
49 Björnsson 2000.
50 Björnsson 2000.
51 Althingisbækur VII, 25–26.
52 Íslenskir annálar 1400–1800 II, 446, 494, Íslenskir annálar 1400–1800 III, 143, 148.
53 Björnsson 2000, Althingisbækur 7, 484–486.
54 Lovsamling for Island I, 542.
55 Rian 1995.
56 Lárusson 1967; Júlíusson 1997b.
57 Kanc. brevb. 5.4.1634, 578; Kanc. brevb. 29.4.1635, 144.
58 Althingisbækur 4, 168.
59 Althingisbækur 2, 383.
60 Althingisbækur 4, 223.
61 Althingisbækur 5, 17.
62 Árbækur Espólíns VIII 1829, 48; Ísl. annáolar 3, 381.
63 Thjóðskjalasafn (Icelandic National Archives): Rtk. Lénsreikningar 1597–1660.
64 Lárusson 1967, 54.
65 Þjóðskjalasafn.: JÞ XIII, AM 258 4to Bréfabók Skálholtsstóls m. hendi Hákonar Ormssonar 1643.
66 Þjóðskjalasafn.: JÞ XIII, Uppsalasafn R 713 bl. 127, 27.8.1605 á Sveinsstöðum.
67 Þjóðskjalasafn.: JÞ XIII, IBfél. 125 A 4to bl. 165a–169b. 30.11.1615 á Seylu.
68 Þjóðskjalasafn.: JÞ XIII AM 197 4to b. 19a–b, 12.5.1591 á Reyðarvatni.
69 Þjóðskjalasafn.: JÞ XIII Ny kgl. saml. 1945 4to bl. 323a–b.
70 Þjóðskjalasafn.: JÞ XIII AM Apogr. 3040. 8.6.1632 á Bessastöðum.
71 Althingisbækur 2. bindi p. 11. Helgastaðadómur Vigfúsar sýslumanns Thorsteinssonar um tíundargjald.
72 Þjóðskjalasafn: AM 253 4to bl. 158–159.
73 Árbækur Espólíns VIII 1829, 30.
74 Árbækur Espólíns VIII 1829, 66, 73, 78.
75 Árbækur Espólíns VIII 1829, 99.
76 Gustafsson 1985, 131–149.
77 Íslenskur söguatlas 2. 1992, 54–55.
78 Íslenskur söguatlas 2. 1992, 52–53.
79 Íslenskur söguatlas 2. 1992, 22–23; Þjskjs.: Manntalið 1762, Norðuramt.
80 Reinholdsson 1998.
81 Júlíusson 1997b, 313–379.

CHAPTER VII

The changing face of peasant unrest in early modern Finland

Kimmo Katajala

We have come a long way from medieval times to the end of the early modern period, from the mountains and fjords of Norway to the plains and grassy hills of Iceland. It is now time to return to the Swedish realm in the reign of Gustavus Vasa, the period in which the transition from the late medieval to the early modern has traditionally been located. The Dacke War of 1542 was the last large-scale peasant uprising in the western half of the Swedish realm. In the present chapter, the focus shifts to the eastern part of the realm, to Finland. And Finland did indeed see a good deal of tumult and unrest during the sixteenth and seventeenth centuries. At the end of the sixteenth century there was the Club War, the largest armed peasant uprising ever in Finland. This would seem to suggest it is reasonable to consider the question of peasant revolts from a 'Finnish' perspective, too. Yet, as we shall see, Finland and the unrest there were closely tied to the political culture produced by early modern power in Sweden.

The state enters local society: the unrest in Karelia 1551–1553

As we saw in chapter IV, the reign of Gustavus Vasa was by no means a period of calm in Sweden. The Dacke War was preceded by many smaller disturbances having both political but also religious content. In contrast to Germany, the Reformation came to Sweden from above, as a command of the Crown. For Gustavus Vasa, the Reformation was perhaps merely a fiscal rather than a religious matter. Much of the Church's property, in land and goods, was confiscated by the Crown. This was one of a number of factors that annoyed many of the peasants in the parishes.

The way the Reformation was carried out shows us clearly how strongly the new rule of Gustavus Vasa was able to penetrate local peasant society. And it did so on the other levels of government as well. This could not pass off without any discontent among the peasants. One expression of this discontent was the disturbances that occurred in the easternmost corner of Finland near the castle and town of Viipuri in 1551–1553. The events began in late summer 1551, when three men from the parish of Lappee arrived in Stockholm to deliver a written complaint to the king.[1]

The complaint presented a long list of abuses of the peasants by the local judge, Bertil Jönsson. King Gustavus listened to the complainants, gave them a letter of safe conduct, and sent them home with the instruction to return next spring with the judge.[2] This actually happened! The peasants and the judge from the remotest corner of the realm stood in front of the king in early summer 1552. The peasants now presented new complaints, this time also concerning the Crown bailiff, Bertil Jörensson.

The peasants complained that the judge had taken more and new goods for his salary. He had taken more than the customary amounts of grain, dried fish, hemp, hare skins, sheep and iron. They also complained that their obligation of providing carriage for travelling Crown officials had become an unbearable burden. They claimed that the judge used the peasants for this task more than did the whole castle of Viipuri. He had built a manor and enlarged its area by evicting seven Crown peasants from their holdings. He had also appropriated for himself a large part of the common fishing waters and twenty-four islands. A peasant who had fished in these waters had forfeited his nets, seines and fish traps. They also claimed that travellers could no longer have a jug of beer to quench their thirst because the judge had imposed such a severe fine on the innkeeper.

However, the most serious complaint was that the judge held sessions of the local court four times a year, although in other parts of Finland there were only two sessions a year. Moreover, the court sessions were not opened on the day they were announced, but three or four days later. This was most irritating for the peasants, who were in a hurry to get to work. During these days they also had to feed the judge, the bailiff, and the dozens of soldiers who accompanied them. Their horses had to be fed, too. The bailiff had also increased the taxes, taken taxes for his own purposes and demanded four extra statutory labour days for Viipuri Castle, claimed the peasants.[3]

The bailiff was not present and therefore could not defend himself in front of the king. But the judge, Bertil Jönsson was present. He denied all abuses: he had not increased the payments for his salary and had never forbidden the sale of beer. Drunken innkeepers often raged around with their knives, and this was the reason for the fines. His manor was situated at the crossing of the roads between the castles of Hämeenlinna, Savonlinna and Viipuri. This was why high Crown officials often visited his manor, and these visitors had to be carried forwards. It was not his fault.

According to the judge, the quarrel over the common fishing waters was a total invention of the peasants. He had not taken any waters for himself, but simply enjoyed the common waters. He had legally purchased two of the islands the peasants complained about, and two others belonged under his manor. The peasant who had complained about his nets and fish traps had intentionally fished just around the judge's traps. However, all the property the judge's hands had taken from the peasant had been returned to him after a few days. No peasant had been evicted to enlarge the manor. Some peasants had left their houses willingly, and some had sold their holdings to him. The days before the opening of the court sessions were spent in collecting tax arrears and the poll tax. According to the judge, it would otherwise be pointless attempting to get anything out of the peasants.[4]

The judge was well aware of the truth of the old proverb "attack is the best form of defence". After explaining all the alleged abuses as best he could, he registered his own complaints about the peasants of Lappee parish. The peasants in the hundreds of Lappee and Äyräpää had stopped holding the court sessions in spring and autumn. The court sessions were held only in winter and summer, as in other parts of Finland. Much of the Crown's taxes were left unpaid. The peasants had paid nothing for the judge and the parson. During the court session, the judge's horse had been beaten with clubs and driven from its feeding. The church bench of the judge's wife was smashed into a hundred pieces during the Christmas service and insulting words were thrown at her in public. The hatred and threat was clear for all to see. The complainants had driven in their sledge around the parish and instigated the peasants to withhold their taxes, while collecting grain, butter and fish for themselves.[5]

In autumn 1552, the bailiff Bertil Jörensson travelled with his accounts to Stockholm. It is evident that while there he had an opportunity to strongly influence the opinion of the king. This we can see from the letter King Gustavus sent to the Lappee peasants on 12 December 1552. At the very beginning of his letter the king reproaches the peasants for intervening in matters that did not concern them. According to the king, the old local custom of holding four court sessions a year was useful. There was therefore no need to change this practice. The food supplies collected for feeding the judge, the bailiff and their entourage were Crown taxes. The peasants had nothing to do with these goods. If something was left over it was to be carried to Viipuri Castle for maintaining the military garrison. What was taken for the Crown was Crown property and the peasants had no business interfering.[6]

The king now branded the complainants traitors who had just collected the goods from other peasants for their own needs. When travelling around the parish they had instigated other peasants to be recalcitrant towards the king's servants. A peasant named Maunu Nyrhi, who had risen to become leader of the mutinous peasants, had even threatened with an axe a peasant who had been willing to pay his taxes. He had also prevented the bailiff from collecting the tax arrears. The king considered this intolerable. Every peasant who had any sense understood that he could not secure their safety from the enemy without funds: "And you must know that We are your true Master and authority, for We are ruling you, you do not rule Us. So We order you not to make your own government or order for yourself, but let Us rule."[7]

There are several interesting points in this letter. Firstly, we can clearly see how the speech and views of the bailiff Bertil Jörensson are reflected in the contents of the king's letter. The bailiff must have been the king's main informant on the events in distant Lappee parish. Secondly, we can see that Gustavus Vasa still defended his right to the taxes in medieval 'feudal' terms. The king secured security and peace. For this service the peasants were obliged to pay taxes. The third point is that the king was now an absolute ruler in his territory. No other governments or rules were accepted. As a natural consequence of this, Gustavus believed the leaders of the 'troublemakers' should be punished.

The letter was sent to the master of Savonlinna Castle, Gustavus Fincke and to the *lagman* (a judge of higher rank) of southern Finland, Henrik Classon Horn. The court investigating the unrest apparently sat in spring 1553. At ordinary court sessions there were twelve lay jurors, but now 24 men sat on the jury. A lot of people had arrived at the court from the neighbouring parishes, and even from more remote areas. They had come to see if the Lappee peasants would succeed in their demands for lower taxes. If they did, the other peasants would follow their example.[8]

The king's letter was read aloud to the commons. Maunu Nyrhi then stood up and shouted loudly that they would in no way accept four court sessions a year. Two were enough, as in other parts of the country. The people in the assembly concurred with Nyrhi's opinion. When the *lagman* asked if the peasants would obey Nyrhi or the king's orders, one of the lay jurors, Ingi Multiainen stood up. He said several times that two courts in a year were enough, they could not accept more. According to the *lagman* these men had openly opposed the king's orders and instigated the commons at the court against the king's proclamation. They were therefore immediately arrested and sentenced to death for insurrection and disobedience. The commons formed a crowd and tried to free those convicted, but the execution was carried out immediately. This bloody affair calmed the disorder in the court. The commons begged for mercy and promised to obey all the king's orders.[9] The Lappee uprising was over.

This rather modest disturbance presents a good example of the new situation the Swedish peasantry were facing in the first half of the sixteenth century. The newly constructed organisation for collecting the taxes was more effective than before. The new order did not please all the peasants. Crown officials were increasing in number, and their drive to exploit local natural resources was striking against the interests of peasant society. Supplying the bailiff and the judge at the court sessions had previously been the direct responsibility of the peasants. Now a tax was collected to cover this obligation. After the court sessions, the remainder was transported to Viipuri and no longer used to meet the common needs of the peasants. It has been calculated that the taxes raised in Finland increased about 30 per cent during these decades.[10] There was widespread discontent.

We can also compare the Lappee revolt with the revolts and peasant wars which took place on the Continent during the sixteenth century. First of all, there is an enormous difference in the scale of the disturbances. The European revolts were large-scale violent events often involving tens of thousands of people. The events in Lappee were a modest tax strike by perhaps a few hundred peasants with violence of mostly a symbolic nature. The role of the Reformation was also the opposite, especially if we consider the revolts and peasant movements in the German areas of the Holy Roman Empire. The Lutheran Reformation was one of the central forces motivating the peasantry in early sixteenth-century Europe.[11] In Lappee, by contrast we catch just a glimpse of the Counter-Reformation in the accusations of the peasants against the judge who had confiscated the properties of the parish for himself.

However, we can see an important similarity between the scenes of European unrest and the Lappee revolt. One of the most important motivating forces in the German Peasant War of 1525 was the competition over natural resources. The forests, meadows and waters were taken for the private property of the lords. The commons were forbidden to hunt, fish and collect firewood from these properties that had earlier been in the common use of peasant society. The resulting severe discontent can be clearly seen in the well-known 'Twelve Articles', the programme declared by the German peasants during the Peasant War.[12] The enclosure movement caused strife in England from the sixteenth century onwards. The meadows used by the commons were enclosed by the gentry with hedges for their sheep. Disputes over the common usage of land and forests were the prime cause of the English revolts of the period. One example of this was Kett's rebellion in 1549.[13]

The disputes over fishing and the use of meadows and holdings near the judge's manor in Lappee were an integral part of the complaints the peasants brought to the king. The organisation of the early modern state as it took shape reached into the local sphere with a new intensity and began to come into conflict with the customary rights of the peasants to use the local natural resources. In continental Europe, the lords took control of the wealth of local society. In sixteenth-century Sweden, the new status of the local Crown officials resulted in peasant protests with similar backgrounds to the European revolts.

Bitter fruits of the 25-year war: the Club War of 1595–1596

Gustavus I died in 1560. The Diet of 1544 had declared that the crown of Sweden was from now on hereditary, the king was no longer to be elected. Gustavus Vasa had four sons: Eric, John, Magnus (who was mentally ill) and Charles. The eldest son reigned as Eric XIV until 1568, when he was overthrown by his brother John. In 1562, John had married Catharina Jagellonica, sister of the king of Poland. Their son Sigismund ascended the Polish throne in 1587. However, long before this – in 1570 – a war had broken out between Sweden and Russia.

The battles took place mostly on the borderlands of the Russian and Swedish realms, yet the effects of the war touched the whole area of Finnish territory in many ways. An essential component of contemporary warfare was the activity of peasant guerrillas. Groups of armed peasants from both sides made long-range attacks over the border. Villagers were robbed, tortured and raped, their houses burned. However, this was not enough. Warfare also required a lot of money and food, and the troops had to be billeted. Most taxes for the war were collected from the Finnish half of the realm. In the middle of the sixteenth century about 25–30 per cent of the realm's taxes were collected from Finland. During the war this proportion grew as high as around 60 per cent. The total number of Swedish troops in Finland rose to 17 000. Only about 6 000 of these were Finns. More than 10 000 were brought in from Sweden or were German, Dutch or Scottish mercenaries.[14]

The troops were not at the frontier all the year round. Autumn and spring were periods when warfare was almost impossible on land and the troops were billeted in the villages. A tax called *borgläger* was collected for maintaining the soldiers who were accommodated amongst the peasants. This system was also in use during the armistices in 1573–1577, 1583–1590 and 1592–1595. The *borgläger* – money, foodstuffs and hay for the horses – was initially collected by the Crown sheriff (S. *länsman*, rural civil officer taking care of police and administrative matters) and then distributed to the military. This system was changed in 1574. From then on the soldiers had the right to collect the *borgläger* themselves straight from the peasants.[15]

This led immediately to complaints from the peasants of abuses by the soldiers. It also led to a violent response by the peasants. The peasants complained that the soldiers robbed them, took their property, raped their wives and daughters and burned the houses of those who did not want to submit to their demands. John III tried to prevent this high-handed behaviour, but his letters to the military officers had little influence.[16] The action by the Crown was ineffective. Some special courts were set up to investigate the alleged abuses. However, this achieved little for the peasants. It is therefore no wonder that they rose up in violence. In some parishes in southwest Finland the peasants captured groups of soldiers. Their horses were beaten to death and the soldiers themselves were driven in shame out of the village.[17]

During the first armistice, the peasants took violent action against the military over almost the entire Finnish territory. The resumption of hostilities and the return of the soldiers to the frontier led to a break in the peasant resistance. When the new truce of 1583 brought the soldiers back to the peasant villages, the events of the earlier armistice were repeated. The peasantry complained about the abuses, and when nothing was done they rose up again in localised violence against the soldiers. The 25-year war ended in the Treaty of Teusina in 1595 and the redrawing of the border farther to the east. However, if we were to suppose that everything was to be fine with the restoration of peace, we would be seriously mistaken. Just a year and a half after the peace treaty the greatest peasant revolt on Finnish territory, the Club War, was raging in most corners of Finland.

Yet, before turning to the events of the Club War we must briefly discuss what had been happening in Swedish politics during the last decades of the sixteenth century. The son of the late King John III, Sigismund (king of Poland as Zygmunt III) had ascended the Swedish throne in 1594. Meanwhile Charles, Duke of Södermanland, the youngest son of the late Gustavus Vasa, had grown to manhood and begun to seek the Crown. Conflict between Sigismund and his uncle Charles was already evident in the early 1590s. Duke Charles enjoyed a rather strong position in Sweden.

Sigismund retained his residence in Poland but had as his most loyal supporter Claus Fleming, the commander of the Finnish troops.

The system of *borgläger* did not originally extend to Ostrobothnia. The peasantry there traditionally took care of the defence of the area themselves. They were therefore not obliged to billet the troops with *borgläger* payments. Many wealthy peasants of Ostrobothnia had equipped a horseman for the king's troops. In return, they were excused most taxes and were given the right to collect the *borgläger* payment. This irritated a lot of the neighbouring peasants, who now had to pay more taxes and also bear the *borgläger*. During the armistice these horsemen served as ordinary farm hands for their masters, who also enjoyed the *borgläger*. This was very profitable for the masters. The other peasants called these horsemen 'muck riders', because they led their horses in front of a sledge full of muck instead of riding in the war as intended.[18]

Complaints about the *borgläger* were already being sent from Ostrobothnia to John III in the early 1590s. The king issued an order in July 1592 releasing the Ostrobothnians from paying it.[19] However, the king died in November of the same year. An armistice was agreed with the Russians in January 1593, and the solders returned from the front. The events of the earlier armistices were now repeated. Complaints over abuses by the soldiers began immediately. There were rumours from the countryside about soldiers being killed in the dead of night.[20] The order of the late king had no meaning in Ostrobothnia, the *borgläger* being collected regardless.

The first traces of violent resistance began to occur. Two separate groups of about 30–40 peasants armed with clubs roamed around Ostrobothnia and tried to prevent collection of the taxes. The arrival of the military made these groups disperse, but the leaders were captured. One received a hefty fine, another was arrested and taken to the jail in Oulu Castle.[21] The Treaty of Teusina in 1595 did not change the situation in Finland. Claus Fleming did not demobilise the troops. The conflict between Duke Charles and King Sigismund was now an open breach. Claus Fleming was now afraid of a possible military attack on Finland by Duke Charles. This was the main reason the soldiers were kept billeted on the peasants in the villages.[22]

The peasants were in difficulties. The hard burden of taxation was pressing heavily upon them, the soldiers collected their *borgläger* and 1595 brought a total crop failure. Where could they turn for help? It would seem clear the peasantry were able to assess the political situation. They must have been aware of the conflict between the duke and the king. They knew also they could expect no help from Claus Fleming, who himself had ordered the military into the *borgläger*. The Finnish peasantry chose the side of the duke. Numerous delegates were sent with complaints to the Diet held in Söderköping in 1595. This activity was well organised. Hans Fordell, a burgher from Ostrobothnia, maintained a kind of office where the complaints were written in the necessary official style. The seal of Ostrobothnia was put under these documents. The complaints about the *borgläger* and abuses by Fleming and his men were well suited to the plans of Duke Charles. It would seem he supported the peasant action behind the scenes. The peasant complaints were a suitable weapon for Charles to use to persuade the Council of the Realm to act against Claus Fleming. However, the Diet refused to give permission to Charles to suppress Claus Fleming with military power.[23]

The discontent in Finland got worse, and there were violent episodes. The men of Rautalampi parish in the province of Savonia rose against the soldiers on Christmas night 1595. The peasants attacked a house where a group of soldiers, recruited from Uppland in Sweden proper, were sleeping. Four of them were killed immediately. The rest were captured and taken to the frozen lake where they were pushed under the ice. January 1596 began with a large number of armed peasants streaming southwards from Savonia robbing the soldiers they met en route and seizing the *borgläger* that had been collected. Claus Fleming sent a troop of cavalrymen to meet this improvised peasant army. Before these troops arrived, the peasant army dispersed into the forests and no battle took place. Five leaders of the mutiny were arrested and executed. Part of the punishment was that the soldiers raped and looted the villages involved in the revolt.[24]

These events were repeated almost simultaneously in southern Ostrobothnia. The leader of the peasant group that evicted the soldiers and seized back the goods that had been taken as *borgläger* was Jaakko Ilkka. Claus Fleming sent troops to intercept them, but the peasants vanished into the forests. Jaakko Ilkka was arrested and taken to prison in Turku Castle.[25] It seemed to the peasants that nothing could help their cause. Complaints in the Diet had no effect. The local violence had simply made matters worse. Another delegation was sent to Duke Charles in November 1596. Charles could not give straight promises to the Finnish peasants, but his words to them have been considered the opening shot of the Club War: "I cannot give you any other advice than to gain the peace with your own hands. Your number is so large that you can surely defeat the soldiers. If there is no other way, use sticks from the fences and clubs. You defend yourselves on land. I shall guard the sea."[26]

Charles' words soon reached Ostrobothnia. At the end of November a group of peasants attacked the soldiers. One was killed, some were arrested and tortured, and the others fled. Jaakko Ilkka had escaped from prison in Turku and as if by miracle arrived in Ostrobothnia that had just burst into flames of rebellion. He was elected leader of the peasant army. A man from each house was taken for the rebel troops. Soon more than a thousand men were assembled. The peasant army was divided into three detachments. The task of the first was to march southwards down the west coast to the town of Turku. The main group approached the same target through the inland forests under the lead of Jaakko Ilkka. The third detachment set off for the province of Savonia with the aim of recruiting more men and then rejoining the main force.

Claus Fleming was well informed on all this. He sent military detachments to meet all three detachments of peasant troops. The first peasant detachment met Fleming's soldiers at Ulvila, where something odd took place. The peasants offered their leadership to Axel Kurki, the head of Fleming's detachment. Kurki refused, attacked the peasants and defeated them easily. The main force arrived in Nokia at Christmas 1596. There this peasant army of about 2 500 men met Fleming's troops, about 3 000 in number. A few canon shots sufficed to cause confusion among the peasants. Some of them wanted to fight, while others began their escape. The result was a total rout. The peasants running on foot through thick snow were an easy target for the armoured soldiers on horseback. About 500 were killed in the forests. The leaders were captured in Ostrobothnia and publicly executed.

The third peasant detachment was successful in recruiting men from Savonia. They met Fleming's soldiers at Nyystölä village in Padasjoki parish. The resistance was initially successful because the peasants had good shelter from the buildings of the village. The leader of Fleming's troops, Ivar Tavast, promised free passage for the peasants if they would lay down their arms. The peasants swallowed the bait. Immediately they laid down their arms they were massacred. About four hundred peasants were slaughtered on the open field.

The province of Savonia acted out its own drama on the fringes of the Club War. News of the uprising in Ostrobothnia had reached this eastern corner of the realm and groups of men rose here, too, with clubs in hand. The rebellious peasants of Savonia sent a message to Gödick Fincke, the bailiff of Savonlinna Castle, asking him to take military command of the rebels. He naturally refused. The hands of the messengers were chopped off and they were sent bleeding home. Soldiers from the castles of Savonlinna and Viipuri defeated the Savonian rebels in several battles.

However, the Club War was not yet over. Although the peasants of southern Ostrobothnia and Savonia had been suppressed, the northern parts of Ostrobothnia now rose up. Soon about 3 000–4 000 peasants were in arms. The soldiers were again beaten and driven from the area. Claus Fleming met this peasant army near the village of Kurikka. The peasants attempted a surprise attack on the soldiers under cover of darkness, but were unsuccessful. During the battle many of the peasants were killed. About five hundred were taken to Kyrö village, where they were whipped and an oath of allegiance extracted from them; they were then set free. The rebellious territories were looted again. The Club War claimed about 2 500–3 000 victims, almost all of them peasants. The memory of this tragedy has lasted through the centuries. So it is no wonder this event has occasionally been the focus of heated debate among Finnish historians.

There has nevertheless been unanimity on one issue: one of the main reasons for the peasant discontent was the *borgläger*. However, this begs the question of whether this was a good enough reason for hundreds and thousands of peasants to take up arms and attack the military? Heikki Ylikangas has underlined the importance of the conflict between the peasantry and the rising nobility as the prime mover of the Club War. The nobility and the soldiers in their troops used the poor peasants at will. Collecting the *borgläger* was just one suitable tool for this looting.[27] Another view has stressed the serious economic losses of the peasantry due

Chapter VII

to their serving as guerrillas during the war, the high taxes, the *borgläger*, abuses by the soldiers and crop failure. This all brought the peasantry into such a desperate situation that they took up arms and tried to pressure Fleming with violence.

These factors were all clearly present. There was immense bitterness between those who could benefit from the *borgläger* and the peasants generally. All the losses the peasantry suffered during the 1590s simply exacerbated the situation. However, could we perhaps ponder the Club War from the perspectives we have presented earlier in this book? On what basis was the war organised? Did the peasants take part in politics? What kind of political culture do their acts in the Club War imply?

But first a question: why did the Club War begin in Ostrobothnia and not in any other province? As I see it, we can identify three main reasons for this. Firstly, the obligation to pay the *borgläger* was felt as an exceptionally severe injustice in this area, where territorial defence was traditionally organised by the peasants themselves. If there was no military to defend the Ostrobothnians, why should they pay taxes and *borgläger* for them?

Secondly, trade played an important role as a source of livelihood in the area. Mercantilist laws forbade trading in the countryside. However, in Ostrobothnia many wealthy peasants traded in tar, grain and other goods. As John Maarbjerg has pointed out, the export prices of the wares produced in the area had been in a long process of decline since the 1570s.[28] The economics of the area was in serious trouble. Many leaders of the rebels were or had formerly been traders. Many of them were in important positions in local society. They were or had been sheriffs (*lensmen*) or 'quartermen' who took care of collecting the taxes in their 'quarter' of the parish. These offices were at this time poised on the watershed between the medieval and modern systems. They were elected by the peasants but represented the authority of the Crown in their parish. They were almost always recruited from the wealthiest peasants in the parish, often traders. These occupations – trade and public offices – had provided the skills, experience and tools necessary for initially leading the resistance with complaints and later organising the violent uprising.

Thirdly, the rebellious area was situated far from Turku, the political centre of the Finnish territory. The remote military citadels could not extend their immediate influence over the province. The Ostrobothnians there had room to rise up. In contrast, there was great discontent in southwest Finland, but no violent protests were possible after 1595. Claus Fleming held this part of Finland in a firm grip. Any sign of resistance was severely punished. He made it known that anyone going over the sea to Stockholm to complain to Duke Charles would face sentence of death. Despite this threat, 39 peasants from different parts of southern Finland succeeded in taking their complaint to the duke. There they promised to be faithful to him "as long as our blood is warm in our hearts".[29]

As mentioned above, the peasants were indeed involved in politics. Because there was no hope of help from the side of Sigismund or Fleming, they chose the side of Duke Charles. Allying with a mighty lord was the only way for them to achieve results in the political culture they were living in. Alliance with the Finnish peasants suited the duke's plans very well. As the protector of these poor peasants he could act like a king and present himself as the guarantor of the Lutheran faith in Sweden against the Roman Catholic Sigismund, while at the same time calculating that the unrest in Finland would undermine the strength of Fleming, Sigismund's right hand. The interests of these two were tightly interwoven. The Finnish peasants promised their allegiance to the duke, and Charles exhibited great interest in helping them. He even tried to persuade the Diet to allow him to suppress Fleming with military power, but this was denied. The encouraging words he gave to the peasants from Ostrobothnia cost him nothing.

We can see here important traces of the late medieval political culture introduced in chapter III of this book. The peasants viewed the protests and the uprising as 'legal' because the king was not protecting them against the 'looting' soldiers. He, or his servant, were demanding *borgläger* from peasants who traditionally defended their province themselves. According to the medieval mindset the peasants still had, this was totally unjust. To get power behind their demands, the rebellious Finnish peasants allied with Duke Charles, the pretender to the throne. They were close to achieving a military alliance similar to the late medieval alliances between the Swedish peasants and the nobility. However, this never happened. Times had changed, and the result was the total defeat of the peasants.

The peasantry and the emergence of the Swedish state

Claus Fleming never returned to Turku from Ostrobothnia, dying on his way home in April 1597. However, in autumn Duke Charles sailed with troops to Finland and conquered the castle. The conflict between the duke and the king was resolved in battle at the River Stånge in September 1598. Charles succeeded in defeating Sigismund's Polish-Swedish troops who had entered the country. The following year the Diet proclaimed Charles ruler of Sweden. Sigismund and his descendants were portrayed as Catholic traitors who had lost all their rights to the Crown. A bloody drama was then acted out. Charles conquered the Finnish territory from Sigismund's supporters. As the castles and towns were taken, the leading 'Sigismundians' were without exception executed. Around fifty members of the Finnish nobility lost their heads in Turku Castle. This bloodbath was repeated in Sweden, if on a much smaller scale. Duke Charles used the title of king for the first time in 1604 and was crowned Charles IX in 1607.

The warfare between Sweden and Poland endured in the Baltic throughout the years 1600–1610. Both realms were simultaneously involved in the heated hereditary disputes in Russia. Although the Polish candidate was appointed to the throne of Russia, Charles took revenge by conquering the town of Korela (S. *Keksholm*, F. *Käkisalmi*) in Karelia. He could not, however, enjoy this victory for long, as he died in 1611. His successor, Gustavus II Adolph was only seventeen.

A young king on the Swedish throne tempted the Danes into starting a war with Sweden. Against all the odds, this war of 1611–1613 resulted in victory for the Swedes. The political machinations that Charles IX had begun in Russia came to nothing, but Gustavus II Adolph enjoyed considerable military successes on the eastern front. The westernmost corner of Russia, the Uezd of Korela in Karelia (which the Swedes had begun to refer to as the province of Käkisalmi) and the province of Ingria, was ceded to Sweden in the Treaty of Stolbova in 1617. Sweden had grown into one of the great powers of Europe. So it is no surprise that Sweden and Gustavus II Adolph became involved in the Thirty Years War in 1630.

All this warfare, conquest, billeting of troops, paying the soldiers and officers, and so on was possible only with an effective machinery of state. During the opening decades of the seventeenth century Sweden developed one of the most effective European bureaucracies. Central government was reorganized. Quasi-modern central departments took care of the king's business, taxation, warfare, mining and trading. A new division of the provinces (S. *län*) was instituted in 1634. Local bureaucracy was reorganised. Courts of Appeal were established and the system of local courts made more effective. Crown offices became permanent, the civil officers becoming servants of the Crown. Compared with the previous century these were great changes.

How much say did the Crown's subjects have in this society that has been described as a 'power state'. Two opposing answers have recently been given to this question.[30] On the one hand it has been assumed that the state machinery of the seventeenth century was able to suppress peasant society so effectively that open violent protest was no longer possible. Local controls were intensified at all levels of society. Above all, the effective military machinery of the 'power state' monopolised violence as a political weapon of the state. The peasantry as a political estate was drowned in the mud at the bottom of society. The counterpart to all this was the abrupt rise of the nobility at all levels of Swedish society. This is essentially how the Finnish historian Heikki Ylikangas has explained the disappearance of peasant revolts from Swedish society after the Club War.[31]

The other view, presented especially by the Swedish scholar Eva Österberg, can be labelled with the concept of interaction. From this perspective, the state-building process and its outcome can also be viewed in the light of interactive processes in which the bureaucracy could not act without taking account of the opinions of the peasantry. The peasants were the greatest estate in terms of numbers. They produced the food for the realm, provided recruits for the army and were one of the political estates in the Diet. They could therefore not be pressed too far. The peasants, too, could thus make their voice heard in the 'power state'. The old violent culture was displaced by legal ways of handling conflict, especially at the local (judicial) level. According to Österberg this was also the main reason why no large-scale violent revolts took place on Swedish-Finnish territory after the Club War.[32] Whatever the case – suppression or interaction (or both?) – the changes in the political life and culture of Swedish society were fundamental.

The monarch had a central position in early modern Swedish political life. However, during most of the period he was by no means an absolute ruler. Absolutism in Sweden was only a rather short forty-year episode from 1680 to 1719. The Great Northern War, for most of which the king was absent from his kingdom, covers half of the absolutist era. The other centres of political power were the Council of the Realm and the Diet. The Council of the Realm consisted initially of twenty members of the highest aristocracy. From 1660 on, they numbered forty. The affirmation of Gustavus II Adolph in 1611 confirmed the right of the Diet to take part in enacting laws, in major decisions of foreign policy (declaring war, etc.), in deciding on the raising of new military recruits from the peasants and in imposing new taxes. Four estates sat in the Diet: the nobility, the clergy, the burghers and the peasants. From 1626 on, the nobility was divided in three: the first class consisted of the 'old nobility', the 'cream' of counts and barons; the second comprised the 'ordinary' nobility; and the third was the military officers, judges, wealthy burghers and so on who had recently been raised to the nobility.[33]

The division of power between the monarch, the Council of the Realm and the Diet was not at all clear in the first half of the century. Views underlining the importance of the Diet and supporting the sovereignty of the monarch compete in the learned scriptures of the era. The Swedish political system in which power was divided between the monarch and the Diet was called *monarchia mixta*. Natural law concepts of the rights of the subjects that they had transferred to the government or the king were already well known in Sweden at the beginning of the seventeenth century.

In Johannes Althusius' *Politica* (1603), a book of great importance at the time, the commons were seen as the prime source of authority. This authority was transferred to the monarch in a 'contract'. If the ruler did not fulfil his duties or ruled badly, it was possible to break the contract. The concept of 'double majesty' (S. *det dubbla majestät*) was in use. The commons held the 'real power' (L. *majestas realis*), while the monarch had his personal power (L. *majestas personalis*) that the commons had transferred to him. Other important Swedish authors of similar ideas were archbishop Laurentius Paulinus Gothus (in *Ethica Christiana* 1617–1639) and Johannes Canuti Lenæeus (in *De Jure Regio* 1633–1634).[34]

The power and rights of the Swedish monarch were tied to the law and especially to what were referred to as 'fundamental laws' (S. *fundamentallagarna*). These were the Law of the King in the Law of the Realm (from 1442) and the oaths and other statements that were given when the monarch assumed power. In *Synopsis juris publici svecani* (1673), Johannes Loccenius included in the fundamental laws the Lutheran confession of faith, the royal inheritance order, the royal oath, the Constitution of 1634 and the decisions of the Estates at the Diet.[35] From the 1650s onwards, absolutist ideas grew in importance, culminating in the establishment of absolutism in 1680.

Chapter VII

Fixing a hole in the Crown's purse: the struggle for reduction

Gustavus II Adolph died in battle at Lützen in 1632. The successor to the throne, the king's daughter Christina, was only five. The realm was left in the hands of a regency. There was a desperate need for money to fund the warfare in Central Europe. There were four main ways for the Regency to raise money quickly: 1) to simply borrow it in a straight loan, 2) to give taxation rights as a pawn against a loan, 3) tax farming, i.e. leasing the rights for collecting the taxes on the peasants from a certain area for a limited period, and 4) to sell the rights for collecting the taxes of defined peasant houses, villages or parishes.

The first alternative was not at all attractive, as there was no guarantee as to when the loans could be paid back. It was also not very easy to find a lender for such a large amount of money. The second alternative was actually used. The rights to taxing several areas were given against the loans. However, it soon became evident to the lenders that the profit gained in this way was rather small. In the early 1630s, the Regency attempted to lease almost all the taxation in the country. There were immediate protests everywhere. The peasants complained about various abuses by the tax farmers, who were often burghers, officers or lesser nobility. Soon the Regency had to abandon the leasing. Selling the rights for collecting the taxes now seemed a very alluring alternative.

However, there were a number of obstacles in the way. In the first place, reducing the Crown property to be inherited by the successor to the throne was forbidden in the Law of the King of the Law of the Realm and the Constitution of 1634. The latter specifically forbade the government or regency from cutting the number of peasant holdings that paid their taxes to the Crown during the absence of the monarch or his/her immaturity.[36] Secondly, two of the estates in the Diet, the peasantry and the clergy, were most fervently opposed to this plan. The peasantry feared that these areas would be understood as fiefs and the freeholders whose taxes were sold to the nobility would soon be turned into tenants. The freeholder and the tenant had a very different status in society. In a nutshell, the tenant lacked political rights, while the lord had the right to evict him from the holding if he so wished. But the tenant was never actually tied to the soil or understood as the property of the landlord like the serfs in the feudal manorial system.

Despite the protests of the peasant–clergy opposition, the Regency decided to begin selling the taxes. This was done twice, in 1638 and 1641. In both cases the value of the taxes sold was considerable, about 400 000 dalers (S. *Riksdalar*). Only the nobility were allowed to buy taxes from the Crown.[37] In practice, the buyer became the landlord of the holdings. He had permission to build a manor on the purchased territory, and, in proper legal order (if, for example, the taxes were left unpaid for three years), to redeem the rights to the freeholder's holding. In this case the freeholder peasant was turned into a tenant. The fear of the peasantry would seem to have been well justified.

Selling the taxes was not, however, the most significant cause of the increase in the number of fiefs in the early seventeenth century. Of course, the old nobility already held landed property as fiefs. As the officers and financiers of the long wars had to be rewarded, the granting of noble titles and fiefs was a suitable way in which to do this. Sometimes fiefs were even given in lieu of salaries for the officers. Under Swedish law, a fief only gave the landlord the right to collect the ordinary taxes from their peasants. No juridical or other power was transferred to the lords. However, the landlords, who were often officers from areas around the Baltic or from Scotland, in many cases interpreted their status vis-à-vis their peasants in a different way. Here we have the seed of contention for the seventeenth century.

The peasant estate was always opposed to all efforts to increase the number and proportion of the fiefs in the country. And so was the clergy. The peasantry was not a solid group, even in the Diet. Accordingly, we can distinguish different grounds on which the 'parties' among the peasantry opposed increases in the numbers of landed fiefs. The freeholders complained that their burden of taxes grew when the number of peasants under the fiefs was increased. An ever smaller number of freeholders had to pay the same taxes. The freeholders that were placed under the fiefs insisted that the landlord could not demand a higher rent than they had paid in taxes to the Crown. The lords had been given or purchased the right to their Crown taxes, not to the holdings. The tenants had no representation at the Diet, but their voices were nevertheless sometimes heard there under the aegis of the freeholder-peasant estate. The tenants demanded a reasonable burden of rent service and rents. They also wanted rights that could guarantee security of tenure on the holdings they were cultivating.

Officially, the clergy supported the doctrine of two governments: the clergy took care of religious matters, while politics was the purview of the secular estates (i.e. the nobility). In reality, the clergy was most political estate, especially during the first half of the seventeenth century.

The clergy had at least two reasons to resist the rise of the nobility and the increase in the number of fiefs. The first was ideological. The rise of the nobility was not reflected only in the increase in the number of noble houses. The Swedish nobility began to take their model from the Continent. They built pompous castles and manors, espoused snobbish manners and began to despise the other estates; they wanted nothing to do with the peasant estate and wanted the clergy kept out of politics, while they viewed the burgher estate as just an unimportant collection of shopkeepers from tiny provincial towns. This was all ill-suited to the ethics the clergy had adopted from the Lutheran faith, and the clergy bitterly criticized this new-look nobility with its wasteful way of life.

The other reason was political. The rise of the nobility, and especially the growth in its landed properties, reduced the power of the king and the other estates. At the Diet of 1650, archbishop Johannes Lenæus proclaimed:

> "When the nobility gets all the peasants for their tenants the peasant estate will no longer have a voice at the Diet. With the peasant estate neutralised, the clergy and the burghers will be easily suppressed. Then there will only be one estate in the entire realm: the nobility. And if the nobility owns all the lands and holdings in the realm, where then is the power of the king?"[38]

Viewed thus, it is easy to understand that the fiefs in particular were an issue around which the clergy and peasant estates (and sometimes the burghers) could find common cause at the Diet.

The peasantry and the clergy were already active in the Diet of 1612. They proposed that most fiefs should be reduced to the Crown. Some reductions had already been carried out during the fourteenth and fifteenth centuries. So this was in no way an impossible idea. In fact, the king accepted the proposal and actually decided on a reduction. However, it was never carried through. When the peasantry raised the issue again at the Coronation Diet of Gustavus II Adolph in 1617 it got no support from either the other estates or the king.[39]

The next time the issue of a reduction was raised was at the Diet of 1634, remembered better for confirming the Constitution. The atmosphere in the peasant estate was very turbulent. In the end, no proposal on a reduction was made, only an unsigned ultimatum to the Council of the Realm with the threat of an uprising if a reduction was not carried out.[40] The Diet of 1635 saw the peasantry and the clergy in open alliance for the first time. Their energy was now directed against the 'small toll', an extra tax collected in the marketplaces for maintaining the army. Although these efforts proved fruitless, they served to consolidate the alliance of the three common estates. The bishop of Västerås, Johannes Rudbeckius, spokesman of the clergy, turned in his speech at the closing of the Diet to the peasant and burgher estates and presented a wish that these three estates would from now on "with faithful hearts and souls keep together".[41]

The peasants from the provinces sent complaints protesting over the Regency's policies in selling the peasants' taxes to the nobles. The peasants of Western Gothia complained that their landlords were attempting to turn them from freeholders into tenants. The former were simply swept under the carpet, while the latter complaint was passed to the provincial governor. Increasing numbers of similar complaints were presented to the Diets of 1642 and 1643, but the Regency was still able to settle the conflict.[42]

The Diet of 1644 saw Queen Christina taking over the reins of government. The Regency had bypassed the passages in the King's Code and in the Constitution forbidding the alienation of Crown property by adding to the contracts of sale a provision which made it possible for a new monarch to annul the deal within a year of coming to power. Of course, the price was to be paid back to the buyer. This was a clever ruse, as no new ruler would have the necessary sums of money available for such a purpose within a year.[43]

The peasants nevertheless tried their luck. They sent a complaint to the queen proposing that the bargains the Regency had made over the Crown taxes should be annulled. They also proposed a change to the queen's sovereign pledge. The monarch should not be tied to any time limit in deciding on a reduction. The Regency decided attack was the best form of defence. A peasant delegation was ordered to come to the Council of the Realm. The aristocrats severely admonished the members of the delegation for the peasantry having advised the Estates and the queen. They were asked if they were "trying to bring down the whole realm". The frightened peasants withdrew their proposals. The queen awarded the nobility new fiefs and new privileges.[44]

As the 1640s gave way to the 1650s, the situation in the country was highly flammable. Crop failures had hit the countryside hard, while there had been a growth in political tension between the nobility and the other estates. The lower clergy criticized the nobility in their sermons, accusing them of leading a wasteful and pompous life while part of the commons were forced to beg in the countryside. In many parts of the realm the tenants left their rent service undone. There was a general demand for a reduction. The political tensions exploded at the Diet of 1650, when Queen Christina was crowned. Three estates – the peasantry, clergy and burghers – appointed a commission to prepare a common request for a reduction to be presented to the queen.[45]

The idea was not to complain over abuses by the landlords. The arguments in the request were based on the Crown finances. If most of the fiefs were reduced, Crown income from the ordinary taxes of the peasants would grow to such an extent that there would no longer be any need for extraordinary taxes. This complaint expressed succinctly the main dividing line in the competing ideas over how best to organise the Crown finances. The nobility claimed that the cultivation of the land would be more effective if it was organised in large units like fiefs around a manor. They proposed that the Crown should derive its income from customs duties and other similar payments. The peasantry, in contrast, believed the Crown finances should be based on the ordinary taxes from the peasants working the land.[46]

The queen initially seemed to favour this complaint from the three estates, but this was mere bluff. The complaint was only a device for her to pressurise the nobility into accepting a new form of inheritance for the Crown. The queen was unmarried and had decided to remain so. She demanded that her successor be her German-born cousin, Count Charles Gustavus. The nobility wanted her to marry and give birth to an heir. Frightened at the prospect of reduction, the nobility decided to accept the queen's will. After this, there was no longer any talk of reduction. On the contrary, during the following few years the queen awarded the nobility numerous titles for counts and barons, and greater fiefs than had ever been seen in the kingdom.[47]

Queen Christina abdicated in 1654 and, as she had wished, Charles X Gustavus rose to the Swedish throne. The Diet assembled in 1655 and the peasantry tried once again to organise a united front of three estates to push for the reduction. However, the clergy had been purged of the bishops who had been active in the 'rebellious' alliance with two other estates in 1650. The clergy also knew the plans of the new king, and they were therefore not interested in supporting the peasant's demands. Charles had plans for warfare in the east, but the Crown was in desperate need of cash. Reduction seemed the only possibility. Yet, the voice of the peasantry was not heard. The king negotiated directly with the nobility, who had to bow to his will. A motion for a limited reduction was brought before the Diet. The nobility demanded that the decision include a clause securing the rest of the fiefs to them in perpetuity. The three other estates rose in opposition and made it clear that no such clause would pass the Diet. The nobility were forced to yield in order to get the 'quarter reduction' through the Diet at all. However, in the event it hardly reduced the fiefs at all. The principle was soon accepted that the landlords could avoid reduction by paying annually a quarter of the tax income from their fiefs. So, this 'reduction' brought no relief for most of the peasants under the fiefs.[48]

When Charles X Gustavus died in 1660, his successor, his son Charles, was only four. A regency ruled the realm during the years 1660–1672, a period favourable to the interests of the nobility. Although the Estates attempted to return to the issue of reduction at the Diets of 1664 and 1668, the slow progress that had been made during the war years 1656–1658 was now totally bogged down in bureaucracy. The Manorial Law, giving the landlords some juridical power over their tenants, was accepted by the Regency in 1671. Charles XI took the reigns in 1672, at the age of seventeen. Soon this young man proved to be a strong minded-ruler. The 'quarter reduction' was carried through with speed. Large fiefs that had been given against the law in 'forbidden areas' (for example Ostrobothnia) were totally reduced in 1675. Despite the exasperated protests of the nobility, the Diet of 1672 did not confirm the Manorial Law. The Diet of 1675 was particularly strong in its refusal to apply this enactment.[49] However, this was only the beginning.

During the years 1676–1679 Sweden was at war with Denmark. The Crown's outgoings were much greater than its income, leading to a large deficit in government funds. Charles XI did not make any proposal to the Diet of 1680 on how to make up this shortfall. Instead, he asked the Estates to propose a solution. He undoubtedly knew what would happen. It took less than ten days for the peasant estate to produce a proposal for a general reduction of the fiefs and how to go about executing it. The clergy and the burghers were talked into supporting the proposal. Together, the three estates brought their proposal to the king. The proposed reduction applied only to fairly large fiefs with annual tax incomes greater than 600 dalers. Many third rank nobles, who often had quite small fiefs, endorsed the proposed reduction. For most members of the second and first ranks it represented catastrophe. The noble estate fell into havoc. In the estate session, the first and second ranks were in such disorder that they were unable to vote on the proposal. In this chaos, the chairman of the estate proclaimed the reduction accepted. The nobles prepared their own submission on how the reduction of the fiefs should proceed. The Diet accepted and confirmed this proposal.[50] The act is called Great Reduction.

This was a great political victory for the peasant estate. For seventy years they had been proposing a general reduction of the fiefs. Now it came true. The noble estate also managed to save face. The inevitable reduction proceeded along the lines it had formulated. The freeholder peasants under the fiefs would now become freeholders paying taxes to the Crown. The tenant of a landlord would be a Crown tenant. This was the principle, and this was also what actually happened in many cases. However, as we shall see later, there were some significant exceptions to the rule. The reduction did not cover all fiefs. Large numbers of small fiefs were left untouched. The fiefs of 'old nobility', meaning those given before the seventeenth century, were also left alone. And, as we shall see, in some cases the reduction was annulled.

All in all, we must now ask whether the actions of the peasant estate at the seventeenth century Diets reflect a weak and politically incapable peasantry that was totally suppressed in the Club War. The answer must be a resounding "no"! The peasantry was undoubtedly in difficulties during the seventeenth century, that much is true. Even so, it was capable not only of reacting to the pressures from the nobility, but also of acting when the time seemed right for the proposals about the reduction. An essential component of this action was allying with the other 'lower' estates, especially the clergy, who brought their ideological and legal knowledge to support the claims of the commons. We must now turn to the local level and see if we can find any signs of peasant protests and conflict there.

Varieties of local unrest

To get a full picture of the character of peasant resistance in seventeenth-century Finland, we must focus our attention on some representative examples from different sides of the territory. These examples are: the disputes over possession of the peasant holdings in Elimäki in eastern Uusimaa, the combat over the fixed tax at the manor of Jokioinen in Tavastia, the struggle over the tax tar and peasant autonomy in the fiefs of Ostrobothnia, and the resistance against extra taxes and tax farming in Karelia, in the province of Käkisalmi.

Elimäki: struggle over meadows and fields turns into defence of holdings and peasant freedom

In 1605, Charles IX landed on Livonian soil with an army. In a battle with Polish troops near the village of Kirkholm, the king's horse was shot. A Baltic officer among the Swedish troops, Henrik Wrede, gave his horse to the king, but in saving Charles's life he lost his own. This was such an heroic deed that it could not be left unrewarded, even though the hero himself was dead. A large fief consisting of a whole Elimäki parish and about 200 peasant holdings was given to Wrede's sons Carl and Casper. As the heirs were still infants – Carl having been born after his father's death – the widow Gertrud von Ungern, who, in 1610, married the governor of Riga, Jochim Berndes, took care of the new fief.[51]

The first steps by the new landlords already provoked peasant protests. Peippola, the wealthiest of the villages in the parish, was chosen as the site for the manor. Peasants from ten farms were evicted and the manor built on their land. Although new lands were given to the evicted peasants, they were still unhappy. However, their complaints and protests were in vain. The king had instructed that the patroness of the fief had permission to freely choose the site for the manor. During the 1610s and 1620s, three more manors were built in the villages of Hämeenkylä, Moisio and Anjala. Cattle and cultivation required meadows and fields around the new manors. These were bought from or exchanged with the peasants. It seems evident that in some cases the peasants were even coerced into contributing the common lands to the manors. During the 1630s and 1640s, numerous disputes between the peasants and the landlords over these meadows and fields were handled at the local court. In almost all cases, the peasants ended up on the losing side.

One dispute led to another. The Elimäki freeholder peasants began to complain to the authorities about their landlords. They claimed that the landlords had illegally coerced them into surrendering the proprietary rights to their holdings with the aim of turning the freeholders into tenants of the manor. If a peasant holding had tax arrears over several years, as very often happened, the landlord had a legal right to buy out proprietary rights to the holding. The peasants felt this to be unjust.

From the 1630s onwards we can discern two main levels of peasant resistance in Elimäki: on the local level there were strikes in paying taxes and performing statutory labour service; on the political level there were complaints to the Regency or the Diet. Research has usually paid most attention to the strikes, which were intended to support the complaints and press the bureaucracy to handle the case with dispatch. Matti Sihvo, a peasant from the village of Anjala, rose to the head of this peasant movement. It is evident that Sihvo had already taken part in the Diet of 1634. He delivered to the Regency a complaint about the meadows and fields and about fishing rights on the River Kymi.

The Regency ordered a court of investigation to be held in Elimäki. This special court sat in 1635. We have very little knowledge of the court session, but the demands of the Elimäki peasants for the restoration of their lost meadows and fields were abandoned.[52] The outcome did not satisfy the peasants. The following summer, 1636, Matti Sihvo and two fellows were once again in Stockholm. They complained to the Regency that the patroness Gertrud von Ungern had coerced the peasants into surrendering their legal proprietary rights to their holdings.[53] Thus, the dispute no longer concerned individual meadows, fields or fishing waters, but the peasant holdings themselves. The case was transferred to the provincial governor, but nothing is known of the outcome.

In 1637, the Elimäki peasants reached an agreement with their patroness over 52 days of statutory labour service per holding per year. In addition, they also had to perform a similar number of 'help days'. This agreement became one of the long-lasting causes of dispute between the peasants and their landlord. In 1642, Matti Sihvo was once again in Stockholm with a complaint. This time the Elimäki peasants claimed that Gertrud von Ungern had increased the amount of statutory labour and the burden of taxes so heavily that they could not bear it. As a result of this heavy labour and taxation the peasants would fall into arrears, and the landlord would then buy out their proprietary rights to their holdings. These issues were the focus of attention at the Diet held the same year. The Regency ordered the provincial governor to investigate the case.

The special court sat in Elimäki in 1643. Most of the complaints, but not all, were shown to be groundless. A couple of abuses were nevertheless proven, and some peasants got their holdings or fields back. The number of days of statutory labour was confirmed at 52. None of the alleged abuses in tax collection were substantioted.[54] The Regency confirmed this judgement at the end of the year. However, this case would seem to have been of general interest and importance nationwide. The peasant estate put up similar complaints to those of the Elimäki freeholders at the Diet in autumn 1643, soon after the trial in Elimäki but before the Regency's confirmation of the court's judgement was issued.

The Regency's answer to the Diet and the peasant estate set the policy in these matters for years ahead. Landlords were not to pressurise their freeholders with heavier taxes or statutory labour service than the peasant had paid or performed for the Crown. However, because the freeholders under the fiefs received some relief from extraordinary Crown taxes, they had to 'thank' their patrons for this in a manner agreeable to both parties. Most often this involved an increase in the number of days of statutory labour. If the peasant had been a Crown tenant before the fief was granted, or if he had lost his proprietary rights to the landlord, he only had the status of a tenant. The possessor of the fief had the right to order whatever rent and rent service from his tenant as he wished. If he was unsatisfied with the terms imposed upon him, the tenant's only right was to leave the holding provided he was up to date with all his rent payments.[55] We can scarcely wonder if the peasants were afraid becoming tenants.

The peasants in Elimäki were highly dissatisfied with the Regency's decision. They evidently protested furiously at the local level, because in February 1644 the Elimäki landlords, Carl and Casper Wrede complained to the Regency that their peasants were unwilling to bend to the will of the court and the Regency. The sons of Henrik Wrede had grown into men. Only Casper now lived permanently in Elimäki. Carl was a member of Svea Court of Appeal in Stockholm. He was also favoured at the royal court. So it was no untrained rural gentry the Elimäki peasants were opposing. Irritation can be seen in the Regency's orders to the provincial governor to investigate the case of the recalcitrant peasants. The same attitude can be seen in the results of the court session that took place in summer 1644. Three of these peasant "hecklers" and "instigators" were arrested and imprisoned in Viipuri Castle.[56]

Queen Christina had meanwhile ascended the throne. She took the Elimäki peasants under her royal protection "against all violence and injustice". The queen ordered an inspection to see if the peasants had been mistreated by the court and demanded the restoration of calm. The Turku

Court of Appeal sent a two-member commission to Elimäki in summer 1645 and finally issued its judgement in April 1646. Three peasants got their lands back. Some fines were imposed on Casper Wrede and Gertrud von Ungern for acting in an arbitrary manner. All the other claims of abuses were found to be malicious. The landlords had incontrovertible rights to their lands. The amount of statutory labour for the freeholders under the fief was confirmed, while the amount of tenant's rent service was purely a matter for the landlords. For Matti Sihvo, the main troublemaker, the Court ordered deportation for three years.[57]

Immediately after the Court's judgement had arrived in Elimäki, another four peasants sailed in a small boat to Stockholm. The complaint they delivered to the queen was the same as before. The landlords were attempting to coerce the freeholders into becoming their tenants. The peasants complained that Carl Wrede was acting like a tyrant. He had imprisoned eighteen peasants in the jail at the manor. Furthermore, the fines the Court of Appeal had imposed on the peasants had been collected in an unjust manner, while the hatred of the landlords towards Matti Sihvo had ruined this poor peasant and his family. These accusations were investigated by the local court and found to be groundless.[58]

These same questions were handled on a general level at the Diet of 1649. The peasant estate complained that the landlords were attempting to alienate the freeholders from their rights and make them their tenants. The queen explained to the Estates that the fief did not give any other rights to the landlords vis-à-vis their freeholders than the right to collect the tax the peasants had previously paid to the Crown. It was forbidden to exert pressure on the freeholders. However, the landlords had to be compensated in some way for the relief the freeholders got from extra Crown taxes under the fiefs.[59]

At the same time as the Diet was discussing the amount of statutory labour and the freeholder's proprietary rights under the fief, Matti Sihvo was again on trial at the local court in Elimäki. He had returned from deportation to the parish and begun immediately to rouse the peasantry to resistance. The Elimäki peasants once again prepared a complaint about the statutory labour and tax increases. This time it was delivered to Per Brahe, governor-general of Finland, and bolstered with a strike in statutory labour. The accusations and the strike were investigated at the local court. Harsh fines were imposed on Matti Sihvo for stirring up the commons and refusing to obey royal orders. His arrest was also ordered. But, in spring 1650 he was once again in Stockholm with two fellows presenting a new complaint to the queen.[60]

The peasants continued their strike on statutory labour. A small skirmish occurred at one of the disputed fields. While the folk of the manor were harvesting in the field, about forty villagers from Anjala gathered with sticks and clubs on the other side of the fence. The leaders of the peasants barged into the field. The bailiff and his hands were threatened and forced to flee. The peasants took the corn and transported it to their own stores. These events and complaints were handled at the local court in August 1650. The court performed the investigation, but the case had to be referred to the Turku Court of Appeal. During the investigations it had come clear that, because they had left their taxes unpaid and statutory labour unperformed, most of the peasants had lost their proprietary rights to the holdings they cultivated. They had become tenants at least in part because of their resistance.[61]

Queen Christina herself now took the reins into her own hands. She ordered governor-general Brahe to arrest the man who had stirred up the commons, Matti Sihvo, have him tried in the Court of Appeal and sentenced to death. However, Matti had absconded and was nowhere to be found. The strike in statutory labour continued. The situation in the Elimäki fief was highly charged. It took two years for the Court of Appeal to resolve the case. In its judgement of February 1653 all the peasants in Elimäki fief were strictly warned not to show anymore disobedience. Matti Sihvo was sentenced to death as the 'prime mover' of all the disorder. Three of his fellows who had been in Stockholm with him were deported for three years. Stiff fines were imposed on those who had taken part in the skirmish in the manor's field.[62] Sihvo was evidently captured later the same year and put to death immediately.

Matti Sihvo's fate became a byword for noble injustice for a large part of the Finnish peasantry. His name was widely known. For example, the peasants of four provinces wrote in their complaint in the mid-1650s:

> "Our lords and masters threaten us with the same punishment that the late Carl Wrede let his peasant Matti suffer, he who was innocent and against all justice was executed and killed, as all the Finnish commons highly bewail and testify before God and your Royal Highness."[63]

Thus, it is no wonder the resistance at Elimäki still continued through the 1650s. During the 1660s and 1670s sporadic resistance always arose whenever there was any opportunity for protest. Stockholm was the target of the complainants from the fief in 1654, when Charles X Gustavus ascended the throne. In the 1660s, the years of unrest were 1661, 1662 and 1664. The next decade saw protests in 1673 and 1674. The Great Reduction of 1680 was eagerly saluted by the Elimäki peasants. They immediately suspended performance of statutory labour for the manors. Minor attacks against the tax collectors were carried out in the dark of night.

However, the fief was now owned by Baron Fabian Wrede, a man in favour and with great influence at the royal court. The king decided in 1683 that only four villages from the Elimäki fief had been reduced. The official reason was that the fief having been given for such a great heroic deed, saving the king's life, it could not be taken away from the heirs of Henrik Wrede. The peasants under the fief were dumbfounded. The protests began again. Statutory labour was left undone, the tax collectors were threatened, complaints were taken to Stockholm, court sessions were held, the peasants were fined and warned. The wheel turned round and round until the Great Northern War. The first half of the eighteenth century was a period of calmness in Elimäki fief. However, knowing the long history of resistance and the result of the reduction in Elimäki, it is no wonder this parish was one of the hotspots of Finland during the unrest that took place across the realm in the early 1770s.

Jokioinen: struggle against fixed tax turns into fight for the holdings

The 'quarter' of Jokioinen in Tammela parish in southwest Tavastia was given to Jesper Mattsson Cruus in 1602. This fief consisting of 26 villages and 132 peasant holdings was confirmed as his "eternal hereditary property" in 1613. Around 1618, Cruus founded a manor on his fief. Building the manor did not cause any protests among the peasants. The lands for the buildings were bought from the peasants and new holdings presented to them in replacement. Jesper Cruus held major posts in the central bureaucracy in Stockholm and never visited his Finnish manor or fief, his bailiffs taking care of the fief for him.[64]

In 1622, the peasants agreed with their landlord about paying a fixed tax. However, they soon found that the fixed tax was not in their interests. They had thought that the extraordinary taxes payable to the Crown were also included in the contract. Now, when the Diet decreed a new tax for billeting the military, the peasants under the fief refused to pay it to the manor. They thought everything should be included in the fixed tax. Otherwise they wanted to annul the agreement. This dispute was taken to the local court in 1628. The court ordered the peasants to pay their tax arrears a quarter higher than the original sum. The statute in the Law of the Realm applied by the court sets out the responsibility of the tenant to pay his land rent on time. The local court thus treated the peasants of Jokioinen purely as tenants. The bailiff demanded a death sentence for the leaders for rebellion against the landlord and the authorities. "Crying on their knees", the peasants begged for mercy, and none were executed.[65]

The early 1650s was a period of unrest in Jokioinen. The landlord was now Carin Oxenstierna, widow of Johan Jespersson Cruus. The peasants questioned the fixed tax. Chancellor of the Realm Axel Oxenstierna, the true ruler of Sweden during the Regency, was Carin's father. Chancellor Oxenstierna wrote a bitter letter to the peasants. He insisted that they agree the taxes with their landlord. Otherwise the governor-general and the provincial governor were to chastise them severely. The governor, Lorentz Creutz negotiated an agreement with the peasants in which they promised to do 24 statutory labour days per year. The agreement also gave them some relief from extraordinary taxes.[66]

Despite the agreement, the tax protests did not come to an end completely. When Johan Oxenstierna, the brother of the patroness, visited Jokioinen in 1652, he still had to threaten the disobedient peasants with arrest and punishment. Encouraged by the words of the high lord, the bailiff of the manor acted. A peasant who did not arrive in court to answer the charges of the bailiff was arrested and put in the manor jail (actually a small hole in the ground with bars). A group of peasants gathered, went to the manor and freed their jailed comrade. These events were tried in the local court in August 1652. With "screams and shouts" the peasants announced that they wanted to pay taxes in the manner of Crown freeholders. They did not even want to hear about the old fixed tax.[67]

The peasants sent two men to Stockholm. Their task was to present a complaint to their patroness Carin Oxenstierna about the bailiff and the taxes. The atmosphere in Jokioinen was extremely tense. In October 1652 the Crown sheriff went to the villages to collect the tax arrears. About a hundred peasants gathered with ramrods in their hands to oppose the sheriff and his retinue. A small skirmish occurred on the bridge of the little river that separated the parties, but no-one was seriously hurt. The peasantry shouted that they would not pay a coin of the fixed tax before their delegates returned from Stockholm. The collectors of the tax arrears had to return with empty hands.[68]

Carin Oxenstierna ordered an investigation into the case, and this was duly arranged at the manor in February 1653. The peasants demanded to be able to pay their taxes to the patroness according to the Crown tax rolls, as stipulated in the decree from the Diet of 1650; failing this, they wanted relief on their fixed tax. The peasants made an offer of a new agreement. This was quite similar to the agreement from the 1620s, yet the amounts of goods collected as taxes were set at their lowest limits. The report of the investigation was sent to the patroness, who answered her peasants with a new tax roll on which the fixed tax was set at quite a similar level to before.[69]

The next skirmish occurred at the beginning of the 1660s. Two men from Jokioinen fief brought a complaint to the king about alleged abuses by Pehr Söfringsson and Johan Jacobsson, respectively bailiff and clerk to the manor. The special court investigating this case was held at the end of October 1661. The peasants claimed that the bailiff had used false standards in collecting grain and other goods for taxes. He had also demanded too many statutory labour days. The clerk had, according to the peasants, pounded the tax grain into the barrels with his hands so that the barrels would hold more than usual. One peasant claimed that the clerk had beaten him so badly that he had been in his sickbed for a week. All charges were shown to be false. The standards of the manor were adjudged correct, while the number of statutory labour days in the manor rolls were equal to the agreement the peasants had made with governor Creutz in 1651. The peasants could not prove the pounding of the barrels, but clerk Jacob confessed that he really had struck an obstinate peasant twice on the back with a stick. For this deed he was fined six marks because – says the minute – "a man must enjoy law, not slashing".[70]

The real reason for the discontent and complaints now became evident. The peasants said that their patroness Carin Oxenstierna had in her new tax roll raised the number of assessment units for tax. The tax per unit itself was no higher than before, but raising the number forced them to pay more. The peasants claimed this was contrary to their agreement over the fixed tax. For formal reasons, the court did not handle this matter. However, the provincial governor, Ernst Johan Creutz (brother of Lorentz) came to the conclusion that in the 1630s the number of assessment units had in fact been set at too low a level. The land rents for the manor and the extraordinary taxes for the Crown had been paid for about thirty years according to this under-assessment. In his decree, the governor obliged the peasants to compensate for this loss of tax income to the manor and the Crown.[71] The complaint of the peasants was thus turned against them.

The dispute over the taxes came into the open again in 1677. The peasants now claimed that the new bailiff of the manor had raised the taxes. They demanded that their taxes should be similar to the Crown freeholders or collected according to the old fixed tax from the 1620s. The landlord, Anna Maria Cruus – granddaughter of the late Jesper Cruus – asked the provincial governor to punish these "rebellious peasants" who had once again dug up their old "whims".[72]

A special court was held at the manor in February 1678. The peasants were divided into two parties: those who had no complaint, and the 51 peasants who demanded changes in the taxes. The peasants explained that because they now had a real king – Charles XI had been crowned in 1675 – they wanted to be taxed like the Crown freeholders. The demands of the peasants were found to be groundless. The agreement over statutory labour from 1651 and the new tax rolls of Carin Oxenstierna from 1653 were judged to be legal documents between the landlord and her peasants. This was an entirely private matter. Neither Crown, king nor Diet had anything to say about it.[73]

The first half of the 1680s was a turbulent time in the Jokioinen fief. There were continual strikes in statutory labour. And this time the peasants' contention was not in vain. On December 10, 1683 Charles XI decreed that the freeholders under the fiefs were freed from statutory labour. Their only obligation to the landlord was to pay the ordinary taxes. However, this decree did not change the status of the tenants in any way. The peasants under Jokioinen fief therefore began to acquire documents to prove their proprietary rights to their holdings as freeholders. After the decree was issued, the statutory labour was left unperformed in many fiefs, including Jokioinen. Charles XI then prepared a new order in which he warned the tenants not to be refractory in respect of their rent service. If this were to happen, the governors would be entitled to use military force to subdue the resistance.[74]

The peasants in Jokioinen were stunned. The bailiff wrote to the governor that it was not possible to repeat the words the peasants had used when the decree was proclaimed to them. The peasants claimed that they were freeholders, and therefore the decree did not apply to them. Moreover, the Great Reduction had raised the hopes of the peasants that their wish to come under the Crown would soon come true. The taxes of the peasant holdings were indeed assessed for Crown taxation. However, the reduction was nullified in Jokioinen. The king gave Anna Maria Cruus the right to substitute holdings in other areas for the reduced holdings on her fief at Jokioinen. It was more profitable for the landlord to save a large fief with a manor than to hold onto small holdings scattered around the realm. As the amount of taxes collected from these separate holdings was equal to that from the holdings of Jokioinen fief, the Crown lost nothing in this exchange.

The result was continual disputes in the local court over the nature of each peasant holding. Now it had become crucial for the peasants to prove that they were freeholders, free from rent service and the fixed tax. However, this was not always easy to prove. The documents about their proprietary rights – if there ever had been such – had often been lost or burned in fires. The processes in the courts became very complicated. In 1695 a special court investigated the nature of 70 peasant holdings in Jokioinen. 43 peasants were able to prove that they owned the proprietary rights to their holdings. Most of the others insisted that they were freeholders but were unable to prove it. Only five were proved to be tenant holdings. These two latter groups were ordered to pay their taxes according to the old fixed tax. The freeholders had the opportunity to choose if they wanted to pay taxes according to the Crown's calculations or according to the fixed tax.[75]

The Great Northern War began in 1700. The Russians conquered Tavastia in 1713. At the beginning of 1714 they left Jokioinen manor and took the grain and cattle with them. The peasants demolished the empty buildings of the manor. The timber was used partly for the peasants' own buildings and partly chopped for firewood. In 1722, when these events were handled in court, there was no stock left on the manor.[76] However, the story of Jokioinen manor and the struggle with its peasants was not yet over.

Ostrobothnia: disputes over the tax tar and local autonomy

The policy of Queen Christina to alienate whole parishes or even larger areas to the nobility resulted in a ribbon of earldoms and baronies along the Ostrobothnian coast. The owners of these fiefs – counts and barons – usually lived in the capital and only rarely visited their distant properties. These donations saw a series of conflicts differing in an interesting way from those presented above.[77]

The earldom of Korsholma was donated to the Chancellor of the Exchequer, Count Gabriel Bengtsson Oxenstierna in 1651. This earldom of more than two parishes was situated near the town of Vaasa. Strikes in statutory labour began as early as 1653 and led to the peasants being fined in court for recalcitrance. The count, or actually his peasants, had to furnish soldiers for the Crown. However, the bailiff of the earldom used these men for work on the manor; some were even transported to work on the count's Swedish manors. The peasants protested. The funds they had paid for furnishing these soldiers were meant for the defence of the province not for paying the wages of the count's hands.

In 1655, the peasants of Korsholma earldom sent a delegate to Stockholm. His task was to deliver a complaint to the king. They complained that eighteen days of statutory labour was an unbearable burden and claimed that their taxes were now ten times higher than before the establishment of the earldom. The peasants insisted on their right to pay their taxes according to the Crown's taxing rolls. The peasants proposed to the king that the whole earldom be reduced to the Crown.

The main reason for the conflict were the operation of two price systems for the goods used to define the peasants' taxes. The Crown had fixed 'tax prices' for these goods, which were in the long run much lower than the market prices of the day. If a peasant first sold his goods at market for the price of the day and then paid his tax in money according to the Crown's fixed price, the difference between the two sums was kept by the peasant. On the other hand, if the bailiff of a fief collected the taxes in goods according to the Crown's low fixed prices, he would accumulate a lot of goods. If he then sold the goods at market, the surplus would constitute profit for himself or his lord. This was what was essentially at stake in the disputes in the Ostrobothnian fiefs.

The conflict between the bailiff of the Korsholma earldom and the peasants continued for several years. In 1656 the bailiff wrote to Oxenstierna that the peasants were even hatching plans of mutiny. With war with Russia at the door (the 'rupture' of 1656–1658), the bailiff lamented to the count that he did not know from which party to expect the more hostile actions, from the Russian enemy or from the peasants of the count's fief. Indeed, a peasant had shouted in public: "It is now better to serve the Duke of Russia than Swedish counts, those limbs of the Devil."

The complaints were handled in the local court in October 1656. Almost all the demands of the peasants came to nought. The count was found to have the legal right to be paid according to the market prices of the tax goods. It was not the fault of the bailiff if the prices had risen. The number of statutory labour days was also adjudged correct. The unrest in the earldom continued to the end of the 1650s and, although the next decade was a period of apparent calm, the delegates of the earldom's peasants to the Diets of 1660, 1664, 1668 and 1672 nevertheless presented the same complaints as they had done in 1655. They always proposed that the earldom should be reduced immediately to the Crown. Their wish was fulfilled in 1675 in what was known as the 'quarter reduction'.

Next to the earldom of Korsholma was the earldom of Kaarlepori. This large fief had been given to Klaus Åkeson Tott, a member of the Council of the Realm, in 1652. It consisted of three parishes, the small town of Uusikaarlepyy and peasant houses from a fourth parish. The conflict between the bailiff and the peasants was to do with the price of the tax tar. The bailiff wanted the taxes paid in tar and according to the Crown's fixed price, the tar then being transported to Stockholm where the market price was even better than in the Finnish towns. The peasants wanted to sell their tar to the local burghers at the price of the day and then pay their taxes in cash.

There was a third party to this conflict, namely the local burghers. They had traded with the peasants for a long time. The new demands of the landlord and his bailiff would have wreaked havoc with the traditional trading bonds and economic systems of the area. Each peasant had his 'own' burgher in the town with whom he traded. The burgher furnished the peasant with salt, iron, drapery and other necessities, often also for credit. In return, the peasant brought his tar to him. One part of this 'agreement' was that the burgher even paid the peasant's taxes. The burgher himself had his own mercantile links, most often with Stockholm. He consigned the tar to his own burgher in the capital, from whom he had often borrowed money for trading. When the new party – the bailiff of the fief – came and tried to cut this chain, the result would have been the collapse of the local trading structures. It is no wonder that the resistance of all the parties was long and hard, and their commitment total.

The crop failure of 1657 worsened the situation. In 1658 the peasants had almost nothing else to use in paying their taxes than tar. A strange scene was then played out in the town. The peasants wanted to sell the tar to the burghers at the market price and then pay their taxes in cash, but the bailiff had decided against this. The peasants arrived along the river with their long tar boats at the mayor's pier. The bailiff's hands ran to the pier and 'crowned' the tar barrels with the mark of the count. However, the peasants refused to move the barrels to the count's storehouses. They marched to the house of the mayor and soon returned with the burghers' hands. The tar boats were taken to the stores of the mayor.

Over the next few days this scene was repeated several times. The bailiff attempted to force the peasants to bring their tar to his stores. Often he and his hands could only observe impotently from the shore as the peasants rowed past them in their boats. Some boats were nevertheless taken to the bailiff's pier. As the peasants refused to give their names, the barrels were marked with the letters of the alphabet. In the dark of night these barrels, too, were taken to the mayor's stores. The bailiff got nothing from the tar and complained to his lord about the peasants' behaviour. The advice of the count's proxy was to accept the taxes in cash. This was a complete victory for the peasants and burghers.

However, the conflict between the bailiff, burghers and peasants did not end here. The situation in the earldom was very inflamed. Complaints of abuses by the bailiff and his clerk were sent to the count and the king in the early 1660s in particular. On one occasion over 300 peasants placed their mark under the document. These complaints were handled in the local courts. Most of the claimed abuses were found to be groundless. Severe punishments were handed out to the leaders of the peasant movement. Finally, the count ordered a special investigation into his earldom. This took place in 1667. It was found that about 150 peasants had paid too much taxes, while about 100 peasant holdings had tax arrears. This clearly impartial investigation calmed the situation in the fief. The earldom was eventually reduced in the Great Reduction of 1680s.

Our last example of the conflicts in the Ostrobothnian fiefs comes from the barony of Ikalapori. This barony was donated to the governor of Stockholm, Schering Rosenhahne in 1652. His son Axel Rosenhahne, a member of Svea Court of Appeal, inherited the fief in 1663. The first conflicts were over the fishing rights in the river and alleged abuses by the tax farmer to whom the fief was leased from 1656 to 1670. After the period of tax farming, the fief was returned to the governance of the landlord. The rule of the new Swedish bailiff, Hans Burgmeister gave rise to conflict with local peasant society. Without hearing the views of the peasants or the parson he appointed a new sheriff and clerk of the parish. The latter was Swedish-born and unable to write in Finnish, while the former was for other reasons unacceptable to the commons. The peasants and the parson protested. They sent a complaint to the provincial governor and requested the appointment of their own candidates for the post.[78]

The next dispute was over the representatives to the Diet. The bailiff nominated two men and paid no attention to the opinion of the peasants. However, one of the representatives took the complaint of the peasants with him to the king. The peasants complained about the appointments of the local officials and violence against the peasants. In November 1672, the young Charles XI ordered the provincial governor to seek reconciliation of the quarrels, but also forbade the baron from encroaching upon the rights of the peasants. It was an absolute right of the peasantry to elect the clerk of the parish. The dispute was, however, not resolved until 1675, when the barony was reduced back to the Crown.

Karelia: protests against tax farming lead to armed food riots

Organising the administration of the remote province of Käkisalmi was a special problem for the Crown. After the Treaty of Stolbova in 1617 the ceded territory was leased to General Jacob de la Gardie. This period of tax farming lasted until the early 1630s. During this period the lessee took care of the administration of the province. From the 1630s to the early 1650s the area was under Crown administration. The bailiffs of the Crown collected the taxes, and new Lutheran parishes were founded in this traditionally Orthodox area. As a part of Queen Christina's policy of rewarding the nobility, the whole province was distributed in fiefs in the early 1650s. The landlords – counts and barons – almost never visited their remote possessions. The bailiffs and their hands took care of the fiefs and the manors built on them. Many fiefs were also leased to tax farmers, who were often military officers.[79]

These earldoms and baronies were reduced to the Crown in the Great Reduction of the early 1680s. However, this gave no relief to the peasants of Karelia. The manors and old fiefs in all the conquered Baltic provinces, as these ceded territories were called, were soon leased to tax farmers. This was not done in other parts of the realm. The tax farmers were often former bailiffs, officers or civil officials, who ruled their leases like fiefs and treated the peasants as tenants. This behaviour was based on the fact that in 1617 all the conquered territories had been proclaimed Crown lands. It therefore followed that there were no freeholders in the area and the peasants had the status of Crown tenants. This superiority of the Crown vis-à-vis its subjects was, according to the lessees, transferred in the leasing contracts from the Crown to the tax farmer.

A special Karelian peculiarity was the system of assessing peasants' taxable property and crops annually. The taxes were set according to an examination conducted on each peasant holding by the tax farmer or his bailiff and several elected peasants. These taxes came to the tax farmers, while, although collected by the lessee, the fixed extraordinary taxes were paid to the Crown. The tax farmer paid a fixed annual sum in cash and grain to the Crown, keeping for himself the surplus from the difference between the lease and the ordinary taxes paid. Disputes over the taxes were an almost daily occurrence. The peasants repeatedly claimed that the tax farmer had over-assessed their taxable property in crops. They therefore petitioned the governor and the king for a fixed tax based on cultivated land to be set for each holding. The tax farmer had the right to use peasants' labour service for building the manor for his residence and for slash-and-burn cultivation of the fields and forests under the lease.

Tax farming was a hated system that always provoked peasant protest. All kinds of accusations were made of abuses by the lessees: hard taxing, hard work at labour service, use of false standards in tax collecting, violence and arbitrariness. Karelia was no different in this respect. During the 'era of earldoms and baronies', the peasants brought numerous complaints to their landlords and the king about the abuses of the tax farmers. The bitterness of individual peasants sometimes also exploded in the murder of the bailiffs.

The parish of Tohmajärvi was given as an earldom to Lars Kagg. The fief was subsequently leased in the 1660s to its former bailiff, Simon Örtken. Peasant resistance was not long in coming. The rule of the tax farmer so annoyed the peasants, that the lessee was forced to call for military help in collecting the extraordinary taxes. However, about 80 armed peasants formed up to oppose the detachment and the soldiers were forced to take to their heels.[80] The peasants had continued to experience problems in paying their taxes and in 1675 had complained about the situation to their landlord.[81] There were severe crop failures in 1674–1676, which did not make the situation any easier.

Örtken left the fief in 1676 and a new bailiff by the name of Sven Stille took the reins. Tax farmer Örtken never stayed in the small manor that was built in Tohmajärvi. However, the new bailiff Sven Stille moved to the manor with his family. He began to demand from his peasants the payments in goods for the manor that were normal in other fiefs. He also demanded rent for the needs of the fief. All these payments and duties had previously been paid in money. This caused great irritation among the peasants, who became incalcitrant towards the bailiff and also failed to pay their taxes properly.[82]

In December 1679, the governor sent a small detachment of soldiers to help the bailiff collect the *statio* tax (collected for the upkeep of troops at the local citadel in Käkisalmi town) from the "lazy and obstinate" commons. In some villages the detachment succeeded in its task, but in the village of Värtsilä a group of peasants gathered with guns and spears to oppose the tax collectors. After a small skirmish, the soldiers and the bailiff captured two peasants they saw as the leaders of the resistance. One of them was Tuomas Paakkunainen, the man who had been in Stockholm in 1675. The prisoners were locked up in the bakery of the manor. The peasants sent word to the other villages in the area, and soon a group of fifty men had assembled. At dawn this armed group attacked the manor, threatened the bailiff and his men and freed the prisoners. The peasants then proceeded in triumph to the church to hear the Sunday service.[83]

The freed peasants were recaptured, but during their trial at the local court the commons freed them yet again. The bailiff Stille travelled to Stockholm, as did Tuomas Paakkunainen and two companions. Their delivered a humble complaint to the king where they asked to be freed from the tyranny of bailiff Stille. They wanted themselves to elect a Finnish man they could trust to be their bailiff.[84] However, the complainants were arrested; Paakkunainen was jailed and the others sent back home. Turku Court of Appeal gave its judgement in the case on October 1680. Paakkunainen and one of his fellows were sentenced to death and every tenth peasant drawn from the hat who had been involved with the mutiny was also to be executed.[85] The king confirmed the sentences of Paakkunainen and his fellow. However, the other mutineers were spared to death sentence. Instead of the execution they were to run the gauntlet.[86]

Paakkunainen rotted in jail in Sweden until the following summer, when he was transported to his home parish. His execution, which apparently took place in late autumn 1681, was made into an awesome and frightening spectacle for the other peasants. The governor himself was present with a detachment of soldiers and drummers as the executioner's axe fell and chopped the head and limbs off the troublemaker.[87] However, there is no knowledge that a mass running of gauntlet was ever organised. This particular event, known as the Värtsilä mutiny, was now over.

The introduction of tax farming to the province gave rise to peasant protest. The resistance was keenest in the northern parts of the province. Dozens of complaints against the tax farmers were sent to the governor-general of the ceded provinces and to the king. Complaints, tax strikes and other forms of peasant resistance inflamed the atmosphere, especially during the 1680s. The peasants of the parish of Pielisjärvi were heavily fined for their constant contention. Two of their leaders were arrested and deported to forced labour in the distant province of Pomerania. But there was more to come.[88]

Crop failures were common, especially during the 1680s and 1690s, but the total losses in 1696 and 1697 were unprecedented. These years have been termed the 'Great Famine' of Finnish history. Crowds of beggars wandered the countryside, disease following in their wake and taking its predictable toll. The dozens and even hundreds of dead were quickly buried in common graves. However, these hard times did not alter the contract between the tax farmer and the Crown. The Crown demanded its share from the tax farmer, who in turn demanded his from the peasants. The subsistence of even the wealthiest peasants was now in danger.

In summer 1696 a rumour spread to the province that the Court of Appeal in Turku was to send a high-powered delegation to assess the tax burden of the peasants in the province. According to the rumour, the taxes were to be lowered, a fixed tax imposed on holdings and tax farming ended. These hopes, that had spread to most parishes in the northern parts of the province, collapsed in late autumn. No-one came from Turku. Instead the bailiffs of the tax farmers visited the villages to collect the tax arrears. The hatred towards the tax farmers and their bailiffs burst into flames. An open riot ensued.

The peasants tried to murder the bailiffs of the tax farmers in the parishes of Pielisjärvi and Suistamo. The next step was to attack the manors. In Pielisjärvi, the smaller of the two manors was robbed three times in December 1696. The main manor was attacked twice. In the first attack, gunshots from the manor made the peasants retire. However, the second attack after Christmas 1696 succeeded. The bailiff had fled from the manor. About eighty peasants looted all the property, cattle and horses from the manor. The building itself was destroyed as far as possible. The peasants dared not set it on fire because it was too near the church.

While this was happening, about a hundred armed peasants gathered around the manor in the parish of Suistamo with the aim of attacking the manor. A small detachment of soldiers had arrived to help the tax farmer and the sight of their arms made the peasants retire. Meanwhile, news of the success of the Pielisjärvi peasants emboldened the peasants in the parish of Liperi, and in January 1697 about forty armed peasants attacked the manor there. The tax farmer himself was not present. One of the attackers was killed in a skirmish with a hand of the manor who tried to defend the building. When he was finally beaten, the manor was comprehensively looted. The windows and fireplaces were smashed, the building ruined and the boats belonging to the manor broken. Nothing was left untouched. At the parish of Kitee a tax collector and his entourage were held up and robbed.

News of these events was carried to Käkisalmi citadel and a detachment of about 50 soldiers sent to defeat the rebels. The first contact occurred in the parish of Kitee, where the peasants had begun to gather to continue looting the manors. One soldier was killed and another wounded in a small fight. The peasants fled into the forests. Discipline was strictly reimposed in the rebellious parishes. The rebels in the forests were captured. Some were tortured and some killed immediately. Many innocent peasants also suffered from the terror carried out by the soldiers. About fifty suspects were transported to the jail in Käkisalmi citadel. At a special trial in March 1697 about forty death sentences were handed out. Several of the accused already died in jail from mistreatment and disease.

Entering the Age of Liberty

The Swedish half of the realm, too, saw some smaller disturbances during the seventeenth century. The leasing of the extra tax known as 'small toll' to tax farmers caused disturbances in Stockholm during the 1620s. This payment was keenly resisted in several small Swedish market towns in the 1630s. An armed peasant group of as many as 300 men were on the march, but the uprising was eventually settled by negotiation. However, two peasant leaders were executed during the disturbances against the small toll in the town of Hova.[89]

'The uprising of the morning star' (*Morgonstjärneupproret*) occurred in the woods of central Sweden in 1653. During the sixteenth century there had been Finnish immigration into these areas. Five brothers of Finnish origin started the rebellion. Their aim was no less than to conquer the manors, kill the nobles and establish a commonwealth. The name for the uprising came from the peasant weapon: a thorn-headed club resembling a star figure. There were never any significant numbers of rebels involved, and the uprising was easily suppressed. Queen Christina ordered a delegation of judges from the Court of Appeal to investigate the case. In her letter to the delegation, the queen already gave detailed orders as to how the rebels should be punished. We must remember that at precisely this time she was proceeding in similar vein with Matti Sihvo of Anjala. All the leaders of the uprising were executed in an impressive manner in Stockholm and several towns around the area of the rebellion.[90]

The ill-starred war with Denmark stimulated peasant protests, especially in the areas that were near the battlefields. In Scania and Halland, the provinces ceded to Sweden from Denmark, there was a peasant movement that went by the name of 'fly-catcher' (*Snapphanarna*). The aim of the 'fly-catchers' was to get these provinces ceded back to Denmark. The first strikes by Swedish miners took place in the 1670s. In 1679, the same year as the Finnish peasants were rebelling in the parish of Tohmajärvi, the Swedish miners marched in a large group to Stockholm to present their demands. The fatal crop failures of 1696–1697 saw no significant peasant movements in the Swedish half of the realm. Some miners went on strike for better wages, and the tenants of some of the southern provinces protested over the harsh burden of rent service. But nothing serious happened.[91]

Times of war have a character all their own, a character that extends to the social conflicts within society. War demands a lot not only from the military and from those recruited to serve as soldiers. The civil population must also bear their share of the burden in extra taxes, transporting military materiel, billeting the troops and – especially – sending their own sons to the battlefields. Troop recruitment for the Great Northern War led to ill-tempered protests, especially in Dalecarlia. A war somewhere across the sea in the remote east meant little to the Swedish peasantry if the price was the life of a son or two. In the Finnish part of the realm, the war marks the peak of court cases dealing with the recalcitrance of the peasants in repairing the roads, building bridges, transporting military materiel and so on. However, the resistance of the commons against the increasing demands of the authorities during the war was merely passive in nature. The desertion of recruits from the ranks was in no way exceptional.[92]

Sometimes war can rekindle old local conflicts. So it was in the province of Käkisalmi in Karelia. In 1708 the peasants from Pielisjärvi parish near the border attacked the villages on the Russian side. The aim was not only to rob and loot; they were particularly keen to provoke the Russian peasants to attack the Swedish side and destroy the hated manor. When this attempt proved fruitless and the Russian troops had entered the town of Käkisalmi in 1710, the peasants of Tohmajärvi, Liperi and Pielisjärvi parishes in particular joined the enemy. Secret negotiations were held. The commander of the Russian troops, General Jacob Bruce prepared a proclamation ordering the peasants to arrest their superiors and deliver them to the Russians. This actually happened in Tohmajärvi. In Pielisjärvi the peasants attacked the manors, were able to take them, but could not capture the tax farmer.[93] This treason by the peasants shows clearly how deep the hatred of the manors and their tax farmers was among the common people.

Meanwhile, there was also a lot happening in Swedish politics. The turning point in the war was the defeat of the Swedes at Poltava in 1709. Charles XII escaped to Turkey, where he lived in exile for several years attempting to lead both the war and his kingdom. After his return to Sweden he launched an operation against Denmark-Norway, only to meet his death from a bullet on the mountains of Norway. A quick political about-turn was now just ahead. New constitutions were affirmed in 1719 and 1720. The era of absolutism was over. The Diet was to be the supreme political authority in the realm. Anyone attempting to restore absolute monarchy would be proclaimed a traitor and guilty of treason. Swedish politics took on a new complexion. The period 1718–1772 is known as the 'Age of Liberty' in Swedish historical writing. The new era and a new kind of politics ushered in new forms of protest for the peasants, too. However, before we begin to examine these phenomena, we must sum up the experiences of the seventeenth century.

The modern bureaucracy built during the reign of Gustavus Vasa and extending its influence at local level had to compete with the 'communal' principles of peasant society. The peasants carried in their minds the 'horizontal' medieval principles of fairly autonomous peasant societies with their own ways of organising common tasks. Common property had now become the property of the Crown and the goods collected for common purposes had become Crown taxes. This was not accepted at once, as we can see in the Lappee revolt of the mid-1550s. Violence played a very small, essentially symbolic role in these skirmishes. The political influence of the peasantry was channelled through complaints to the king. Gustavus Vasa consciously sustained this medieval link between the commons and the highest echelons of the realm. It was his way of controlling his newly constructed bureaucracy. The political culture of the sixteenth century carried at all levels of society strong echoes of the old medieval mentalities while simultaneously giving birth to the new ways of the early modern systems of governance.

The Club War was the last 'late medieval' peasant uprising in the Swedish realm. The long-lasting hatred towards the *borgläger,* the terror wreaked by the soldiers in the villages, the crop failures, and the weight of taxes and other burdens were the factors that provoked peasant resistance. However, the opportunity for the peasants to ally with Duke Charles, the pretender to the throne, was what led them to organise such a desperate action as armed revolt. This closely resembles the pattern of many late medieval revolts in Sweden and was the last time the pattern was repeated in Swedish history. In the Swedish political culture of the seventeenth century it was necessary to look elsewhere for allies.

The actions of the peasant estate at the seventeenth-century Diets clearly demonstrate that it had not lost its political potential in the emergence of the Swedish 'power state'. Not even in Finland was it totally suppressed by the Club War. At the beginning of the seventeenth century the peasant estate was already ready to attack the nobility with proposals for the reduction of the fiefs. Despite political setbacks, this policy was systematically pursued throughout the century until the Great Reduction of 1680s. This was made possible only with the help of powerful allies, who were now to be found in the clergy and burghers at the Diet. A substantial strand of this policy was to seek support from the monarch. The monarch only – and a new monarch especially – had the power to carry out the reduction. Here we have the principal reason for the support of strong monarchy in early modern peasant politics. A strong king was the only really effective ally for the peasantry against the nobility in the Diet. All the parts of this jigsaw were present in 1680 when the reduction was first carried through.

If we look at the local disturbances in Finnish territory (and Swedish too) during the seventeenth century, we see that their timing is quite close to the political fermentation at the Diet. Does this mean the local disturbances and conflicts were merely reflections of the political agitation by the clergy, as has sometimes been proposed? Definitely not. A closer look at the sources shows that the local conflicts between the landlords and their freeholders and tenants came first. The political fermentation at the Diets of the 1640s and 1650s directly reflected the conflicting relations at local level. The peasantry of the seventeenth century made politics.

Here we come to our another explanation for the cessation of large-scale violent revolt in Sweden at the beginning of the seventeenth century. The systems intermediating between local society and the authorities were actually created for the Swedish 'power state'. This process has usually been connected to the enhanced role of the local courts and the founding of the Courts of Appeal. This was certainly an important channel for solving conflicts between peasants and between nobles. However, when the conflict was between the peasants and their landlords this channel soon proved fruitless for the peasants. Only rarely and only in crystal clear cases did the judges of the local courts wish or dare to oppose the noble landlords. The remaining channel for the peasants to have a say in society was the political organisation of the Diet.

Surveying conflicts from different areas of Finnish territory has clearly shown us that there was no single reason for conflict between the landlords, their hands and tax farmers and the peasants, if the system of fiefs and manors as such is not considered a single reason. The conflicts touched on the proprietary rights of the peasantry to their holdings, the principles of taxation, the right to pay the taxes in cash and the autonomous rights of local peasant society. Tax farming was a hated system that caused a great deal of trouble for the peasants and, by extension, the authorities. Despite the diversity of conflicts, in all cases the peasants came to the conclusion that the fiefs had to be reduced. This was the guiding star in all their acts and in the policies they pursued at the Diet. The authorities described these policies as "unrest", "mutiny" and "rebellion". Much had changed in political culture and peasant protest by the time Sweden entered the Age of Liberty. However, as we shall see, a strong king was still one of the cornerstones in the political calculations of the peasantry.

NOTES

1. See Pirinen 1939 unless otherwise stated.
2. Gustavus Vasa to the complainants from the parish of Lappee 20 October 1551. In Arwidsson VIII, no 40.
3. The complaint of the Lappee peasants against Bertil Jörensson in 1551. VA 2511, 17–18v. Vanhempi tilikirjasarja. KA; The complaint of the Lappee peasants against Bertil Jönsson in 1551, VA 2511, 323. Vanhempi tilikirjasarja. KA; The complaint of the parish of Lappee in 1552. VA 2511, 27–28v. KA.
4. Answer of Bertil Jörensson to the complaints in 1552. VA 2511, 19–23v. Vanhempi tilikirjasarja. KA.
5. Complaint of Bertil Jörensson against the Lappee peasants in 1552. VA 2511, 24–2v. Vanhempi tilikirjasarja. KA.
6. Gustavus Vasa to the peasants of Lappee parish 12.12.1552. In Arwidsson III, no. 98.
7. Ibid.
8. Henrik Classon Horn and Gustavus Fincke to the king 1553. Arwidsson III, no. 106.
9. Henrik Classon Horn and Gustavus Fincke to the king 1553. Arwidsson III, no. 106; The sentencing of Maunu Nyrhi and Inki Multiainen 1553. Arwidsson III, no. 99.
10. Pirinen 1939, 46.
11. See for example Wohlfeil (hrsg) 1975.
12. For the 'Twelve Articles' translated into English see Blickle 1981b, s. 195–201.
13. See Zagorin 1982 I, 208–214; Beer 1982, 81–138.
14. Tawastjerna 1918–1920, 531–555; Pirinen 1965, 130–153; Kirkinen 1976, 169–198; Katajala and Tšernjakova 1998, 65–67; Kiuasmaa 1987, 246, 275–277.
15. Pohjolan-Pirhonen 1960, 388–393; Fagerlund 1991, 69–71; Ylikangas 1996, 94.
16. These abuses by the soldiers are described in several studies. See Tawastjerna 1918–1920, s. 213, 473, 638–640; Renvall 1945, 40–41; Renvall 1949, 169–171; Ylikangas 1977, 80–84; Fagerlund 1991, 74–76.
17. Renvall 1939, 40–41; Renvall 1949, 169–170; Kiuasmaa 1987, 284; Fagerlund 1991, 75–80; Ylikangas 1996, 94–98.
18. Koskinen 1929, 268–275; Luukko 1950, 527–533, 553; Ylikangas 1996, 118–119, 123.
19. Grönblad III, 1.
20. Koskinen 1929, 150–153; Ylikangas 1996, 100–101.
21. Ylikangas 1996, 100–101.
22. Koskinen 1929, 276–293; Luukko 1950, 540.
23. Koskinen 1929, 276–293; Ylikangas 1996, 128–129.
24. Markkanen 1980, 193–205; Ylikangas 1980, 178–191; Ylikangas 1996, 142–146.
25. Ylikangas 1996, 142.
26. Koskinen 1929, 292–293; Kiuasmaa 1987, 287; Ylikangas 1996, 164.
27. Ylikangas 1977, 42–50.
28. Maarbjerg 1992.
29. Luukko 1978, 287–288.
30. The dichotomy presented here has recently been given an explicit formulation in Ylikangas – Johansen – Johansson – Næss 2000, 97–98.
31. Ylikangas is not alone in adopting this approach, but he has perhaps been the strongest proponent of it in reference to the question of peasant unrest. See Ylikangas 1990, 82; Ylikangas 1996, 362; Ylikangas 2000, 150.
32. Eva Österberg presented her interpretation of the interactive processes in the early modern state as far back as the early 1970s. Since then, many Swedish scholars have used this view in their studies of the era. In reference to peasant unrest see especially Österberg 1987, 321–340; Österberg 1989, 73–95.
33. Rystad 1985, 65–66; Karonen 1999, 207–210.
34. Lindroth 1975, 349–366; Runeby 1962, 144–152, 217–219.

35 Lindroth 1975, 357–361; Rystad 1985, 68–70; Nilsson 1994, 151.
36 KrLL, Law of the King, chapter 4, § 5; The Constitution of 1634, § 60. Stiernman 1729, 919.
37 Wittrock 1948, 202–203.
38 Ahnlund 1933, 268–269; Jutikkala 1958, 162; Karonen 1999, 202.
39 Ahnlund 1933, 126, 241; Magnusson 1985, 5.
40 Odhner 1865, 26; Lövgren 1915, 8–10; Ahnlund 1933, 204; Wittrock 1948, 56–57.
41 Lövgren 1915, 14; Ahnlund 1933, 213; Runeby 1962, 140–144; Nilsson 1994, 149–151.
42 Lövgren 1915, 30–31; Wittrock 1948, 298–299, 440–457.
43 Ahnlund 1933, 246–247; Wittrock 1948, 462–465.
44 Odhner 1865, 128–129; Lövgren 1915, 37; Ahnlund 1933, 247–248; Wittrock 1948, 274–276.
45 Lövgren 1915, 84, 105, 133–145; Ahnlund 1933, 261, 265–266, 269; Jokipii 1956, 42–48; Jutikkala 1958, 162–163; Rystad 1985, 70; Nilsson 1994, 151.
46 Magnusson 1985, 5.
47 Lövgren 1915, 125; Ahnlund 1933, 269–274; Jokipii 1956, 42–48; Jutikkala 1958, 162–163; Rystad 1985, 70.
48 Ahnlund 1933, 282, 293–298; Jokipii 1956, 35–38; Jutikkala 1958, 163–165; Dahlgren 1964, 57–118; Magnusson 1985, 8; Englund 1989, 28, 33–35; Karonen 1999, 203.
49 Grauers 1932, 18–27; Ahnlund 1933, 361–362; Jokipii 1956, 37–38, 67; Jutikkala 1958, 165; Rystad 1985, 73.
50 Grauers 1932, 60–70; Jutikkala 1958, 185–187.
51 This presentation is based on the descriptions in Oksanen 1981, Oksanen 1985 and the most extensive presentation of the events in Katajala 2002. The primary sources are noted here only when really necessary.
52 Our knowledge of the results of the special court of 1635 is based on the minutes of Elimäki court 30.8.–4.9.1643. Justitierevisionen, oresolverade revisionsakter. RA.
53 Wittrock 1948, 141.
54 See the minute of the special court in Elimäki 30.8.–4.9.1643. Justitierevisionen, oresolverade revisionsakter. RA.
55 The Regency's decree in response to the complaint of the peasant estate 27.11.1643. Stiernman 1729, 1037–1040.
56 Turku Court of Appeal to governor Carl Mörner 7.9.1644. Justitierevision, oresolverade revisionsakter. RA.
57 Judgement of Turku Court of Appeal 25.4.1646. Justitierevision, oresolverade revisionsakter. RA.
58 Complaint of the peasants from two villages of Elimäki fief, undated (1646). Copy nos 2038–2039. Rahvaanvalitukset. KA.
59 Queen Christina's decree in response to the complaint of the peasant estate 19.3.1649. Stiernman 1729, 1117–1118.
60 Minute of the local court in Elimäki 24.11.1649. Justitierevision, oresolverade revisionsakter. RA; Minute of the local court in Elimäki 7.–8.8.1650. Justitierevision, oresolverade revisionsakter. RA.
61 Minute of the local court in Elimäki 7.–8.8.1650. Justitierevision, oresolverade revisionsakter. RA; Minute of the local court in Elimäki 26.–27.7.1651. Justitierevision, oresolverade revisionsakter. RA.
62 Judgement of Turku Court of Appeal 28.2.1653. Justitierevision, oresolverade revisionsakter. RA.
63 See Halila 1949, 431.
64 Anttila 1991, 20–26.
65 Minute of the local court in Somero and Tammela 23.9.1628. Jockis handlingar no 14. fol. 69–72. Jokioisten kartanon arkisto. HMA.
66 Chancellor Axel Oxenstierna to the peasants of Jokioinen 22.5.1651. Jockis handlingar no. 2. fol 72–73. Jokioisten kartanon arkisto. HMA; Governor Lorentz Creutz to Chancellor Axel Oxenstierna 9.6.1651. Jockis handlingar no. 13. fol 560–561. Jokioisten kartanon arkisto. HMA.
67 Minute of the local court in Tammela and Somero 26.–27.8.1652. Jockis handlingar

no 14. Jokioisten kartanon arkisto. HMA.
68 Crown bailiff Michell Eskilsson and Crown sheriff Hans Larsson's report, undated. Jockis handlingar no 2. fol 74v–75v. Jokioisten kartanon arkisto. HMA.
69 Report of the investigation 28.2.1653. Jockis handlingar no 14. fol 65–67. Jokioisten kartanon arkisto. HMA; Decree of governor Ernst Creutz 24.1.1662. Jockis handlingar no. 14. fol 84–85. Jokioisten kartanon arkisto. HMA.
70 Minute of the special court at Jokioinen manor 30.–31.10.1661. Jockis handlingar no. 14. fol 78–84. Jokioisten kartanon arkisto. HMA.
71 Decree of governor Ernst Creutz 24.1.1662. Jockis handlingar no. 14. fol 84–85. Jokioisten kartanon arkisto. HMA.
72 Decree of governor Axel Stålarm 30.11.1677. Jockis handlingar no. 14. fol 27–28. Jokioisten kartanon arkisto. HMA; Countess Anna Maria Cruus to governor Axel Rosenhahne 29.9.1677. Jockis handlingar no. 14. fol. 45–46. Jokioisten kartanon arkisto. HMA.
73 Minute of the special court at Jokioinen manor 10.2.1678. Jockis handlingar no. 14. fol 29–40. Jokioisten kartanon arkisto. HMA.
74 Governor Johan Gripenberg to the Crown bailiffs 9.10.1684. Jockis handlingar no. 15. fol 269–270. Jokioisten kartanon arkisto. HMA.
75 Minute of the local court in Tammela and Somero 9.5.1695. Jockis handlingar no. 2. fol 160–168. Jokioisten kartanon arkisto. HMA.
76 Minute of the investigation 4.8.1722. Jockis handlingar no. 4. fol 281–289. Jokioisten kartanon arkisto. HMA.
77 This presentation is based on the descriptions in Luukko 1945, 586–631; Jokipii 1956, 209–216.
78 Virrankoski 1956, 299–320; Jokipii 1956, 67, 314, Jokipii 1960, 175, 222–225.
79 See Katajala 1994.
80 Katajala 1994, 152.
81 See the minute of the local assizes in Tohmajärvi on 18.10.1679. Justitierevisionen, utslagshandlingar 7.9.1680. RA.
82 The minute of the local assizes in Tohmajärvi on 7.9.1679. Justitierevisionen, utslagshandlingar 7.9.1680. RA; the minute of the local assizes in Tohmajärvi on 6.–7.2.1680. Justitierevisionen, utslagshandlingar 7.9.1680. RA.
83 The minute of the local assizes in Kitee, Ilomantsi and Suojärvi on 20.–22.12.1679. gg 2. 994. KA.
84 Complaint of Tuomas Paakkunainen to the king, reached the king's council on 25.6.1680. Justitierevision, utslagshandlingar 7.9.1680. RA.
85 Judgement of Turku Court of Appeal on 7.4.1680. Justitierevision, utslagshandlingar 7.9.1680. RA.
86 The minute of the local assizes in Tohmajärvi on 2.–3.3.1681. gg 2. 524–524v. KA.
87 See Jokipii 1960, 234.
88 This and following description is based on Katajala 1994.
89 Wittrock 1948, 216 passim: Lundberg 1987, 7–10; Vuorela 2000, 87–107.
90 Melander 1939, 28–30; Silvén–Garnert & Söderlind 1980, 190–191; Lundberg 1987, 11–14.
91 Silvén–Garnert & Söderlind 1980, 193–203; Florén 1987a.
92 Villstrand 1992; Linde 2000, esp. 127–186; Kujala 2001, 87–155.
93 See Kokkonen 2002, 128–146.

CHAPTER VIII

Marching to Stockholm
Repertoires of peasant protest in eighteenth-century Sweden

Karin Sennefelt

"All for one and one for all," Sven Hofman concluded his letter to the burghers of Borås, sitting, as he said, "on the edge of a field at Fläskjum on the 14th day of May 1766."[1] He was, together with approximately 500 other men, on a march towards Stockholm, their aim to "honour God and restore the authority of the king."[2] However, the burghers of Borås were not persuaded by Hofman's letter, despite his claim that his objectives were honourable and perfectly suitable for a humble subject. Instead, the people of the town rose to defend their community against the expected attack from the peasants, as the town was en route to Stockholm. Every able-bodied man was ordered to arms, guards were posted around the town, reconnaissance troops were sent out into the surrounding countryside in search of stray rebels, and Borås' seven canons were placed strategically outside the town gates. News of the mobilisation reached the marchers, who began to desert. When they were met by troops from Borås the following day, they had been reduced to 190 men who had already arrested their own leaders and declared they had been inveigled into coming along. They were all brought to Borås, arrested and put on trial.[3]

Only twenty-three years had passed since the Swedish realm had last been subjected to what became known as an uprising, when the peasantry of Dalecarlia had marched to Stockholm in the early summer of 1743. Both then, and in 1766, the political situation in Sweden was extremely unstable, with intense party and social struggles during the meetings of the Diet. These were exceptional times in Swedish history, with the peasant estate in the Diet wielding greater influence than ever before. But uprisings occurred all the same, and of a magnitude not seen since the sixteenth century. Although these two uprisings were very different in extent and duration, they share certain crucial characteristics unique to peasant protest in the eighteenth century, intimately linked as they are with state centralisation, the political system of the Age of Liberty and the peasantry's new role in Swedish politics.

The Dalecarlia uprising

The grievances that emerged during the uprising that began in the province of Dalecarlia in 1743 can be traced back a few years to the beginning of the war between Sweden and Russia.[4] This had begun in 1741 and almost immediately brought great losses of land in Finland and heavy casualties, among them soldiers from Dalecarlia. Equipping new soldiers, which was a household obligation to the state, was an expensive business. Peasants in Dalecarlia considered this obligation unjust – why should the peasants and burghers bear the responsibility for defending the country by recruiting and equipping soldiers, while the nobility and clergy had no responsibilities at all?[5] The crop failures of 1741 and 1742 spread destitution and added to the discontent.

In preparation for the Diet of 1742–1743, the peasantry of Dalecarlia elected new representatives for the peasant estate, replacing those who had agreed to the war against Russia at the previous Diet. During the war, the queen had died, leaving her husband with no heirs. A successor to the throne had to be chosen. In the event, the succession became caught up in international politics, as both Russia and Denmark favoured different candidates and the choice of successor would inevitably affect Sweden's foreign relations. The first candidate to be chosen by the Diet became heir to the Russian throne instead, and the issue then escalated into a problem of domestic politics. Russia favoured a new candidate, Adolf Fredric of Holstein-Gottorp, and made his election a condition of peace. The peasantry, however, wanted a strong king and preferred the crown prince of Denmark, which unlike Sweden was still an autocracy. During the Diet, peasant delegations were sent from Dalecarlia over this issue, and the peasant estate, acting alone, opted for the Danish crown prince as heir to the Swedish throne. The issue did not end here, however, as the other estates preferred Adolf Fredric and a favourable peace.

There was also great discontent in Dalecarlia over the generals who had been in command during the war. It was felt that they ought to be held responsible for the unfortunate outcome of the war and brought to trial for having betrayed the soldiers and led them into unnecessary danger. As the Diet drew to a close, the peasants in Dalecarlia felt that the grievances they had aired at the beginning of the Diet had still not been resolved. They decided to march to Stockholm to ensure a hearing for their grievances over the generals and the succession. Messages were sent to all the parishes of Dalecarlia urging them to join the march. On 8 June 1743, the peasants assembled in the provincial capital of Falun, and a few days later they set off for Stockholm. The march took ten days, provisions being supplied by the towns along the route.

On 20 June, 4 500 peasants and soldiers arrived at the gates of Stockholm and after some commotion entered the city. Negotiations continued for two days, during which time, and independently of the demands of the peasants, peace was made with Russia and the successor to the throne was chosen. Troops gathered in Stockholm for defence against the peasants. The negotiations between the peasants and the government collapsed, leading to a battle in the centre of the city within sight of the royal palace. Over one hundred peasants were either killed or wounded, while a further three hundred died later in prison from injuries and disease. A total of three thousand peasants were arrested immediately, and, while the majority were led on a humiliating march back to Dalecarlia, six were executed for their participation in the uprising and another forty were sentenced to terms of imprisonment.

The Hofman uprising

The second uprising studied here has not left much impression in historical writing, although it evoked great attention in its day and was the first national news item reported in the official newspaper *Inrikes tidningar*.[6] As its name, the Hofman uprising, suggests, it was initiated and led by one central figure, Sven Hofman.

The uprising originated in Hofman's unsuccessful attempts to become a member of the peasant estate in the Diet. Hofman was elected by the hundred of Veden in the province of Älvsborg to be its representative at the Diet of 1765–1766. However, on his arrival in Stockholm he was denied entry to the peasant estate because of an incident ten years earlier when he had been found unworthy of pleading anyone's cause by a local court after having, as a delegate, instigated an illegitimate court case. The peasant estate urged the hundred of Veden to elect another representative to replace Hofman, but the hundred persisted and elected Hofman once again, regardless of the instructions from the estate and requests from the provincial governor. Although the government intervened on Hofman's behalf, he was not accepted by the estate, which considered him far too notorious to be admitted as a member. Hofman finally made inflammatory comments about the peasant estate and its speaker, and was expelled from the Diet.[7]

Hofman's letters home to friends and electors in Veden provide ample evidence of his discontent with how he had been treated, and he did not return home peacefully.[8] Rather, for the duration of the Diet, Hofman travelled back and forth between his home and Stockholm, meeting up with other discontented people in the capital to discuss altering the Constitution in favour of an autocratic regime. Hofman also accused a judge in his home hundred of having tampered with the elections of representatives for the peasant estate. The local court found these accusations false and at the end of April 1766 ordered Hofman's arrest. He managed to escape and began speaking openly of the peasantry coming together and rising in order to restore autocracy. He tried to persuade the peasantry that if they would only start marching towards Stockholm, Crown Prince Gustavus would come to their assistance.[9]

Hofman later stated in court that he had thought it would be easy to persuade the peasantry to join his venture because there was so much discontent in the country over the Constitution. In his home hundred, his friends began discussing when and what had to be done while Hofman was still a fugitive. When he returned to Veden in mid-May he held a meeting with approximately twenty men, who soon marched to the nearest inn to spread the word that they were on a march to Stockholm to restore the monarchy. At most, the marchers amounted to an estimated 500 men. Support for their cause was not as widespread as they had expected, and the marchers' enthusiasm began to wane. Only a few days after setting out, the march came to an end when troops arrested the marchers outside Borås.[10]

Besides the special Court of Appeal held in Borås, the Diet soon decided to appoint a commission in Stockholm to investigate Hofman's contacts in the capital. The court in Borås sentenced forty-two men to death, although the commission later commuted all but three of these sentences, sending the remaining thirty-nine men to prison. Three years later, after a proposal by the peasant estate, an amnesty was declared for those who had taken part in the Hofman uprising.[11]

Repertoires of protest and how they change

The question arises as to why peasants have used certain forms of protest at certain times and not at others. Why did peasants in Sweden during the Age of Liberty choose to march to Stockholm in order to protest? The range of action from which protesters choose can be referred to as their repertoire of protest. Peter Burke, Charles Tilly, James C. Scott, and Rod Aya have all used this type of thespian analogy in connection with collective action, everyday forms of protest, and rebellion.[12] The term describes the relation between protesters and what they do and is oriented towards the actions of the protesters rather than their beliefs.[13]

In essence, the expression 'repertoire' indicates that a protest is not merely an improvised show of contention in any form that seems practical at the moment. Rather, people have different options of action at all times, although these options are always limited – they have a certain repertoire of collective action. A protest repertoire implies "not only what people *do*" when they protest, it is also "what they *know how to do* and what others *expect* them to do". Forms of action are thus not chosen at random; they are learned and understood by the protesters and sometimes even planned and rehearsed. It is essential for the protesters to decide what form to use for their protest, under what circumstances it will be possible for them to carry it out, and when the form can be used legitimately.[14] This depends on both opportunity and capacity. Repertoires of protest are not entirely rigid, but there are innate limitations to their scope – the repertoire has limitations because it is conditioned by the power relationships in society. There is, however, room for innovation and creativity, and innovative aspects can gradually become commonplace.[15]

Just as the protesters must learn forms of protest, the object of the protest must themselves also learn to understand it. The form a protest takes is a message in itself, and the intent of the protesters is of course to get their message across. It is important to view forms of protest as means of communication, as methods to make discontent known rather than just as protest per se. In fact, the communicative aspect of protest can sometimes be the whole point of the protest. The form has considerable impact on how a protest is perceived.[16]

Repertoires of protest have the potential to change, and change dramatically, under certain conditions. Since a form of protest is a means of communication between two parties, a change in the relationship of power between the parties also alters the forms of protest. Charles Tilly's model of how repertoires of collective action change is essentially evolutionary: from the protest repertoires of the seventeenth through to the nineteenth century which were mainly parochial, reactive and relied greatly on the patronage of local powerholders, to those of the second half of the nineteenth century which were more national in scope, active and autonomously formed in relation to powerholders. A change developed in the repertoires of protest around the mid-nineteenth century: grain seizures and invasions of fields evolved into strikes and demonstrations. Successive changes in the structure of economic, social, and political life have, according to Tilly, affected the development of protest repertoires. More specifically, the changing power relationships that he has referred to as repertoire-altering are state building and the growth of capitalism.[17]

The development of protest repertoires in early modern Sweden is, however, not as linear as this bird's-eye view might suggest. In comparison with medieval uprisings in Scandinavia, the uprisings of the Age of Liberty show some noteworthy differences. The most striking difference between medieval peasant uprisings and those discussed here is that the medieval uprisings were strongly marked by the use of violence, whether on a small scale in meetings with the representatives of central power, or in large-scale military confrontations. Moreover, peasant uprisings seldom spread beyond regional borders.[18]

These characteristics also hold true of smaller uprisings in the seventeenth and early eighteenth centuries. Several riots occurred at markets in the late 1630s against a new toll introduced by the central government. The culmination came in the riots in Hova and Bro in 1638. Protesters there, as in other towns where the toll met opposition, attacked local officials, and the fence guarding the area where the toll was to be paid was torn down and burned along with several merchants' booths.[19] In 1653, in the 'uprising of the morning star' (*Morgonstjärneupproret*), the protesters' aims, at least according to a contemporary account, were to "go to the manors and exterminate the nobility, among other mad things".[20] Peasants refusing to enrol soldiers in Vadsbo hundred in the province of Skaraborg in 1710 did not direct their protests towards the political centre of the country. They merely beat a sheriff to death and left it at that.[21] These protests were aimed at local officials who were not necessarily directly responsible for what they were officiating over, and the parochial element of the protest repertoire is evident. Another striking feature in comparison with the Dalecarlia and Hofman uprisings is the violent nature of the protests, either towards officials or in the means of sabotage.

However, it is not my intention to portray the Dalecarlian and Hofman uprisings as early examples of a modern protest repertoire, as direct forerunners of the strikes, demonstrations, and social movements that are characteristic of nineteenth-century protest repertoires. Rather, it is quite evident that the protests that occurred in the Age of Liberty in Sweden were closely connected to current political and social conditions. Sweden in the middle of the eighteenth century exhibits a few crucial factors which affected repertoires of protest. The conditions of political life were quite different from the preceding royal autocracy. In addition to this, state building played a large part in shaping repertoires of protest, while capitalism had not yet made its mark. These factors in turn had consequences for the identities of political actors.

The political conditions of the Age of Liberty

Both the uprising in Dalecarlia and Sven Hofman's uprising occurred during a unique period in Swedish political history. The Age of Liberty, as it was dubbed by its contemporaries, began with the new Constitution adopted on the accession of Ulrika Eleonora in 1719 after the death of her brother Charles XII. The Constitution abolished royal autocracy in Sweden and placed sovereignty in the hands of the Diet, while the monarchy was more or less reduced to a symbolic justification for the reign of the Diet. From 1719 to 1772, when royal autocracy was restored, the Estates held governmental power and according to the Constitution were to meet at least once every three years for a session of three months. The estates (the nobility, the clergy, the burghers and the peasantry) had one vote each, and no decision could be taken without a majority. The Secret Committee (*sekreta utskottet*), from which the peasant estate was excluded, was the most important of the Diet's committees and was the true centre of power in the country, as it dealt with sensitive matters such as foreign affairs and finances.[22]

After the initial domination of political life by Arvid Horn, who simultaneously held several influential positions in government, the first signs of an emerging party system were visible by the end of the 1730s. Political opponents of Horn, emerging as the Hat party, mobilised against him and managed to overthrow the entire Council of the Realm at the meeting of the Diet in 1738–1739. The rise of the Hats, with their strong organisation and party propaganda, soon led to the mobilisation of their political opponents, the Caps, by the next meeting of the Diet in 1740–1741.[23]

The emergence of a party system in Sweden during the Age of Liberty can be attributed to the fact that sovereign power lay in the hands of the Diet and its electorate; some sort of structure was needed to avoid public life becoming bogged down in conflicting private interests.[24] The party system brought an increase in propaganda and political activity. Important political debates were no longer conducted solely in the noble estate. All four estates became important to the parties in their endeavours to muster support. There was a process of political socialisation that also included the delegates of the peasant estate.[25] Thus, by the beginning of the 1740s, the peasant estate had become an important political actor despite being constitutionally the least influential estate in the Diet. Taxes still had to be approved by all the estates, and it was important for more powerful political figures to cultivate informal political contacts with influential representatives of the peasantry.[26]

The state-building process thus far

The changes in the Constitution in 1719–1720 and 1723 were mainly changes of political form. They did not bring about a structural shift in the division of power. Central state power had expanded greatly during the seventeenth century – the Swedish state was one of the strongest in Europe – and did not diminish in the following century.[27] State administration was centralised, bureaucracy extensively developed, and the state finances were based on taxation. With the end of autocracy in 1719, there was a decline in the previous importance to the state of the military and war, although this did not disappear altogether. The political élite remained virtually unchanged, although new groups gained political influence through the new constitutional reign of the Diet. Neither was there any dramatic alteration in the relationship between the central state authorities and local communities. Local and regional administration was already well developed and intimately linked to the state. The parish assembly gained in influence in the eighteenth century, becoming a useful administrative tool, both for the local community and for the state.[28] However, the state did have difficulties implementing central decisions at local level. Local politics were largely under the control of the local community.[29]

The eighteenth-century Swedish state was not, however, based solely on the extensive state-building process of the previous century. Indeed, the process continued in new forms. Instead of basing state building on the demands of war or territorial integration, the development of society as a whole was adopted as a deliberate strategy. In accordance with this, the creation of a strong and well-ordered economy became a government priority during the Age of Liberty. The government legislated in many different areas that had never been addressed before, including industry and agriculture, infrastructure and social welfare.[30]

The extent of state and political centralisation during the Age of Liberty is illustrated in the frequent suggestions and the final attempt to move the meeting of the Diet to a town other than Stockholm. Norrköping was considered suitable because it was conveniently located for the Finnish delegates to the Diet. Here, it was assumed, the Diet would be free of foreign ambassadors and the central bureaucracy meddling in its business, while at the same time the delegates to the Diet would be unable to meddle in the business of the bureaucracy. The Diet began its sitting in Norrköping in 1769, but soon ran into problems: it could not function without the assistance of its committees, which were not permitted to leave

Stockholm. After a few weeks, it was forced to relocate to Stockholm, where its work was eventually completed.[31]

One consequence of state building is integration: territorial and political. Integration has many aspects; it can, for instance, refer to the integration of peripheral areas in competition with other power holders, or to integration directed towards the existing state in order to replace older units and build a new administrative system.[32] As far as political integration through formal channels is concerned, the well-developed interaction between local community and central power meant that every subject could be reached by the authorities, and, in turn, every subject could, at least in theory, reach the central authorities. Peasants were represented in institutions from the village assembly to the Diet. And in addition to the imposed local political institutions, peasants often sought out the central authorities and those in positions of power in order to voice their complaints. Sending a delegation of trustworthy representatives from the local community to supplicate the king, the Council, committees, or representatives in the Diet was a common, and accepted, practice in early modern Sweden.[33] For example, shortly before the Club War of 1596–1597 in Finland, large numbers of peasants were sent with supplications to powerful figures in the kingdom. The political centre of the realm was unclear after the death of John III, and a power struggle was raging between king, Council, and Duke Charles – the supplicators decided to seek the help of Charles[34] (see chapter VII).

Smiths from Jäder ironworks sought meetings with the Council, the College of Mining, and the queen in the 1640s and 1650s. Queen Christina was in Uppsala at the time, and the smiths had plans to see her there in order to bring their complaints before her. After the accession of Charles X Gustavus, they sought out the king at the palace in Strömsholm to deliver a list of grievances.[35] In 1683, peasants from Mark in Western Gothia sent a man to Stockholm to speak with the province's representative in the Diet and to supplicate the king in order to contest the conscription of soldiers.[36] In 1720, miners in Falun protested to the mine inspector over the shortage of grain and their general poverty. Despite efforts to calm the situation, the miners sent representatives to Stockholm to deliver a written complaint to the queen, who in turn referred the matter to the College of Mining.[37]

By the Age of Liberty, the king's influence was greatly reduced, and, while supplications were still frequently employed,[38] it was not as important as before to reach the king himself. Stockholm, site of the Diet and the seat of the Council, was the political centre in the Age of Liberty. It was in Stockholm that the political parties were based, intimately connected as they were with the politics of the Diet. Local manifestations of party politics can only be found to a small degree in a few towns besides Stockholm, and then mainly concerning political mobilisation before meetings of the Diet.[39]

The peasantry also became integrated into informal politics during this period. The meetings of the Diet and the development of a party system created an array of informal political activity in the capital in the form of clubs and coffee houses. For instance, the peasant estate had its own political club where the representatives gathered to discuss politics, the speaker of the estate complaining that some representatives spent more time in the clubs than at plenary sessions.[40] Sven Hofman tried several times to visit the peasant estate's club, but was not admitted since he had been rejected by the estate. Instead, he visited another club, where he conferred with others discontented with the Constitution. Among these was a second lieutenant who said that "they" were now in power and that soon "father's [the king's] hands will be freed and he will reign." The Constitution seemed to be on everyone's mind, according to Hofman. In order to gauge the political climate in the capital, Hofman had walked about town at night, following people around in the dark, eavesdropping on political conversations.[41]

The measures Hofman used were of course extreme, although they do indicate something of the intensity of political activity surrounding the meetings of the Diet. Dinners and other shows of patronage towards the peasantry were not at all uncommon. For instance, a prominent leader of the Hats regularly had morning tea with members of the peasant estate.[42] A representative at the Diet from Dalecarlia, Skinnar Per Andersson, who later became one of the leaders of the uprising, together with a delegation of peasants from Dalecarlia sought out the Danish ambassador to Stockholm hoping that he would advise them on the succession to the throne and the candidature of the Danish crown prince. Peasants in Dalecarlia also wrote a letter to the ambassador asking whether or not they should recruit soldiers for the war, and what the crown prince himself felt about this. Several peasants from Dalecarlia were also treated to dinner by a burgher of Stockholm who supported their views on the succession.[43]

When it came to protest, the peasantry was, like the other estates, well aware of where it made most sense to turn. It was no longer as important to reach the king as it had been previously – and was to become again after the renewal of royal autocracy in 1772.[44] The king's power was greatly restricted and, although peasants often expressed monarchist views, they knew that he had no real power. Protests were instead aimed at the centre of political power. Because that power was centralised in Stockholm and was largely in the hands of the Diet, that was where peasants directed their protests.

Peasant political identity in the Age of Liberty

It is clear that during the Age of Liberty there was a remarkable change in the political identity of the peasantry and the peasant estate in particular. Its role in the new Constitution was initially quite ambiguous – not least for the estate itself. It initially held on to the belief that it was best served by an autocratic monarch and was forced to fight hard battles against the other estates to ensure and defend its rights and liberties.[45] In the long run, however, the peasant estate found that its interests were best served by cooperation with the burghers and the clergy, rather than by an autocratic monarch, and when autocracy was finally restored, the peasantry was the only estate to voice regret.[46]

By the end of the Age of Liberty, it is clear that the peasant estate and the peasantry as a whole had developed greater 'political confidence' and had become more aware of the political potential of the Diet, which became the most important political arena for the peasantry.[47] The social base of political influence had broadened thanks to the constitutional changes which had taken place, and this had led to a strengthened political position for the peasantry in comparison with the seventeenth century.[48] During this period, the peasantry as a whole became increasingly socially differentiated, with the emergence of a socioeconomic peasant élite. This development coincided with the peasant estate's rise to political influence and importance. With the Diet of 1742–1743, there was an overall increase in peasant political activity at both national and local level. Social unrest, such as the threat of an uprising in Dalecarlia, led the other estates in the Diet to show extraordinary goodwill towards the peasantry, and many peasant grievances were resolved in their favour.[49] In 1742, the peasant estate made clear what it thought of its role in public affairs when its speaker appealed to the other estates for the peasantry to be represented on the all-powerful Secret Committee. He told the other estates that the peasantry would be very disappointed if this reasonable request were denied:

> "[Now] when the realm was in need of the presence and assistance of the peasant estate, which carried the greatest burdens and whose toil with the axe and the plough did not hinder it from having a good and natural understanding of that which could serve the common good."[50]

For the first and only time, the peasant estate was admitted to the Secret Committee at the Diet of 1742–1743.[51]

Later during the same Diet, the peasant estate to a great extent acted alone in the issue of finding an heir to the throne. A delegation of peasants from Dalecarlia visited the peasant estate, urging it to vote in favour of the crown prince of Denmark. These peasants were not alone. There was a great degree of agreement in the estate over this issue – the view being that the estate (and the rest of the Diet) must choose an heir itself before Russia forced one upon it. The discussion ended with the estate resolving to elect the crown prince of Denmark as heir to the Swedish throne while the other estates opted to delay their choice and link it to the peace treaty with Russia.[52]

Political activity among the peasantry had increased dramatically by 1742 and did not diminish after the elections of delegates to the Diet. On the contrary, propaganda and the burning issues of the war with Russia and the election of an heir to the throne kept political interest running high not only in Stockholm, but throughout the country. The peasantry also made the most of its participation in the Diet. During the twenty years following the Diet of 1742–1743, there was an enormous increase in the sending of written grievances to the Diet.[53]

The Diet of 1765–1766 was equally turbulent to that of 1742–1743, the temper of political debate running high thanks to the rise to power of the Caps. This shift also meant that the nobility, which had dominated the Hats, lost influence in the Diet to the three other estates. The 1765–1766 Diet shows an overall increase in political confidence on the part of the common estates, and the peasantry in particular. At this Diet, the three common estates decided to appoint a commission in Stockholm to investigate Sven Hofman's contacts in the capital, and this without waiting for the nobility to vote on the issue. They also carried through the taxation of the nobility against the will of the noble estate, in direct violation of the Constitution. From 1766 until the end of the Age of Liberty the peasant estate cooperated on many issues with the burghers and the clergy, especially over the redistribution of privileges from the nobility to the other estates.[54]

The actions of the peasant estate by the end of the Age of Liberty certainly show a rather different picture of the estate's identity from the early years, its demeanour no longer humble and subservient. Peasant political identity having evolved due to the changing relations of power in state and society, this not surprisingly also affected the repertoires of peasant protest.

Political identity is a factor which should be included in this equation. When people share a sense of unity, this facilitates mobilisation. Group identity is not only based on a view of oneself as part of a group, but on a conception of the nature of society, and this in turn affects the forms of protest adopted.[55] Altered relationships of power not only lead to changes in repertoires of protest; they also affect political identities. Identities and interests are constituted in relationship to other groups and change in conjunction with these relationships.[56] Political identities are always relational and collective and subject to change as political networks, opportunities and strategies change. Therefore, political identity rests not only on a sense of solidarity with others, but also on a shared relation to an enemy (as it were) or rather to an individual or organisation controlling concentrated means of coercion. Situations such as elections assert, display, or confirm political identities. But political identities also need to be validated. This is done through interaction with other groups, which either accept or reject the group and its claims.[57]

It is important to note that the recognition of the right to make a claim helps stabilise and secure political identity. In essence, recognition of a group's right to make claims grants it legitimacy as a group. This gains in effect if the claim is successful.[58] This is evident during the Age of Liberty, when the peasant estate's claims in issues concerning agriculture and forestry were quite successful. Peasants were acknowledged in political life to a greater extent than before, although they were by no means seen as equals.[59]

The march as a form of protest

It had been clear from the outset that the Dalecarlian peasants' aim was for a massive march on Stockholm, as this had been discussed for over a year before the uprising actually took place.[60] Marching to Stockholm was initially spoken of in terms that resemble a protest march, and during the year preceding the uprising several delegations from Dalecarlia had visited the capital. For example, the peasant estate received delegations of peasants from Dalecarlia on the issue of the succession. A delegation from Dalecarlia also called on the commission investigating the alleged crimes committed by the generals in the ongoing war, urging that they be punished immediately.[61] These visits to the capital in smaller groups did not have the desired effect – the crown prince of Denmark was not accepted by any other estate, and the peace negotiations with Russia and the investigation and trial of the generals dragged on. By marching to Stockholm the peasants in Dalecarlia would be able to 'have their right', as they put it, and they wanted the generals to be sentenced to death and the crown prince of Denmark chosen as heir to the Swedish throne. They also had more traditional grievances over new taxes and sought relief for their hardship.[62] On the last day of May 1743, messages were sent all over Dalecarlia from a meeting held in Mora with orders for all men, both peasants and soldiers, who were capable of marching the distance to Stockholm to assemble in the provincial capital of Falun one week later.[63]

Smaller marches towards the provincial capital began in parishes around Dalecarlia. During a few days at the beginning of June, Falun was occupied by the thousands of peasants and soldiers who assembled there before beginning their march. In Falun a leader was chosen, a bookkeeper at a local copper works and former soldier, Gustav Schedin. Major Wilhelm Gustav Wrangel was chosen as the military leader of the march. Essentially, these persons were only leaders of the march, not the uprising, and Wrangel seems to have taken on the responsibility quite reluctantly. The peasants were still essentially in charge, and Schedin's orders were often overridden by leading peasant representatives. The peasants brought along on the march representatives of the authorities, local clergy, and even the provincial governor himself. Messages were sent to parishes in the rest of the province and to the provinces the march would pass through on its way to Stockholm, urging other peasants to join the march on the capital.

It took the peasants ten days to reach Stockholm. During this time, the marchers totalled about 4 500 men. Peasants from the parishes passed through en route soon followed. Specific rules were made for the marchers to adhere to, stating the order in which the march was to be conducted. The rules were written down and signed by representatives of the peasants, and copies spread among the participants. The participating parishes alternated in taking the lead and flew their parish flags, drummers and pipers accompanying the marchers into towns on the way. Religious services were held every day.[64] The towns of Västerås and Uppsala were called on to provide provisions for the marchers, and they complied in fear of being overrun by violent rebels, although they never were. Despite what these fears suggest, the march was actually exceptionally peaceful. No serious cases of maltreatment were reported, and although about half of the peasants were armed with firearms and another third with other types of weapons they did not engage in any violence until the final battle in Stockholm.

The central authorities, of course, wanted to avoid having rebellious peasants roaming the capital. In an attempt to prevent this, a delegation was sent from the king and the Estates to meet the marchers before they reached Stockholm. The delegation met the marchers in the town of Sala and tried to persuade them to stop there. Since the delegation lacked any military support, the peasants could easily ignore the message from the government and continue their march. They were also met by a smaller delegation with a message from the king two days' march from Stockholm. If the peasants stayed where they were, they were to receive provisions for all those on the march and could send representatives to Stockholm to speak to the king and Council. The peasants did send their grievances to the government, but continued their march all the same.

In a final attempt to spare Stockholm from the rebellious peasants, King Fredric led a minor force out to meet the march outside the gates of the city. But not even the king's attempts at persuasion could prevent the peasantry from finishing their march. The peasants successfully avoided the troops, some canons were seized, and Stockholm found itself hosting thousands of peasants, while marches had now begun from other parts of the country.

When the peasants finally arrived in Stockholm on June 20, it seems as though the main part of their goal had already been achieved. Many of the issues that had been important for the mobilisation of the march had now been resolved: the generals who were on trial had both been sentenced to death and peace made with Russia while the peasants were on their way to Stockholm. Even the question of the succession was resolved, since the choice of Adolf Fredric was a condition of the peace treaty. The arrival in Stockholm therefore became something of an anticlimax. Negotiations were held between the peasants from Dalecarlia and representatives of the Estates, and the peasants were finally presented with an ultimatum. They could either retreat to outside the city gates, or face the consequences. Who actually began the subsequent battle in the city centre is a matter of debate – the authorities claimed that the peasants had commenced by firing a canon at the troops, while peasants described the battle as a massacre.[65]

In the Hofman uprising in 1766 the march began gradually. The first twenty men walked to an inn and announced what they had in mind: to march to Stockholm and not come back until they had an autocratic monarch, whether it be the king or the crown prince. As the men passed through the parishes of their home hundred, they sent messages ahead urging others to join them. The march divided after a while in order to spread the uprising to as large an area as possible. Mobilisation went well to begin with. Two days after the march had begun the marchers totalled an estimated 500 men, and an observer commented that only women and children were left in the villages. The marchers' weaponry consisted of rifles and knives. They seemed quite confident of being successful in their aims, saying they would return in triumph from Stockholm. Nor would they have to continue their march alone. It was rumoured that the crown prince would meet them halfway to Stockholm to be their leader. According to some rumours, the crown prince was in fact already among them, in disguise. At Fläskjum, Hofman requested lunch and schnaps from the local clergy, and this was duly delivered to the marchers.[66] During his trial, he related that he had been inspired by the Dalecarlian march and intended to write to the provincial governors for provisions for the marchers. But this apart, he was rather vague on how the march was to get to Stockholm.[67]

As the march continued from Fläskjum, fewer and fewer new arrivals came to join it. The peasantry in the parishes they passed through fled from the marchers rather than joining them, and some even buried their money and silver in order to save it from the rebellious peasants. This discouraging fact led the marchers to turn around and return to Fläskjum. Hofman, hoping for support, sent a letter to the town of Borås in the hope of evoking some solidarity on the part of the burghers there. He explained that it was not their intent to pillage Borås, and neither had they any intention of being disrespectful to the king – quite the contrary.[68]

Besides the letter to Borås, other messages urging people to join the march were sent to the parishes lying ahead. The marchers spent another night at Fläskjum. The following morning they awoke to the fact that their group had been reduced during the night to half its size and the messengers who had been sent ahead had been arrested. The march disintegrated. Hofman fled into the woods, but was soon caught by troops sent out from Borås. The remaining 190 marchers declared they had been inveigled into coming along.[69]

In Borås, Hofman's letter did not have the desired persuasive effect; the rumour of the peasant march had preceded the letter and preparations had already been made to avoid being overrun by rebellious peasants. Not only did the town of Borås decide to defend itself, but the surrounding hundreds and provinces were also prepared for the arrival of the marchers – troops from several regiments took part in apprehending them. While some troops were sent to intercept the marchers, others scouted the countryside in order to prevent other areas joining the march, and yet others cut off the two possible routes to Stockholm.[70]

In comparison with the Dalecarlia uprising twenty-three years earlier, the local authorities acted with remarkable zeal to prevent this uprising approaching Stockholm. Orders sent by the government in Stockholm became superfluous after the swift measures taken locally. A plenary session of the noble estate noted that: "We tremble before an unbridled commonalty [...] so it was in 1743, and so it is today."[71] And before news of Hofman's arrest had arrived in Stockholm, the government made sure that its burghers were patrolling the capital and that they were properly armed.[72]

While Hofman and his accomplices awaited trial in Borås, a letter was found outside the town gates with details of plans to help them escape from prison. The letter also reminded its intended recipient that Hofman and the other peasants had risen "for the sake of our sins" and that what had been accomplished had happened thanks to the zeal of two men. More worrying for the authorities was that the writer of the letter again urged all peasants to come to Stockholm. This time they would not bring any weapons, and according to the writer their accounts of their distress would be heard when they brought them before the king, who was merciful and gracious.[73]

The goal of the march

There were several advantages in using a march to the capital as a means of protest. Firstly, it immediately put the protesters in contact with the central authorities, transcending local authorities and local political institutions. Secondly, the march itself, while being a relatively peaceful form of protest, posed the threat for the central authorities that the social unrest underlying the protest could easily escalate from the form the protesters were using. And finally, the march was an effective means of communication – not only did the authorities get the message of widespread discontent and exceptional organisation, but so did sympathisers, who could see how widespread and openly expressed the opinions were. Indeed, the march incorporated an invitation to others to join.

However, a march to the capital is not a form of protest that can be used by anyone, anywhere. Not surprisingly, the marches to Stockholm were undertaken by peasants who held a certain position in society and were politically informed, acting in a political context which was quite unusual.

Centralisation, integration, and bureaucratisation distinguished the Swedish state in the Age of Liberty. The Constitution provided the Diet with legislative, executive, and sometimes even judicial power. Social differentiation created a peasant élite, which was broadly represented in the Diet. The peasant estate gained in political influence and experience, and this influenced peasant political activity on all levels. In the Diet, the peasant estate was increasingly successful in obtaining its goals. National issues were discussed on the local level. In essence, the relationship between the peasantry (or rather, those peasants who were represented in the Diet) and the state was different from that of the seventeenth century. This altered relationship also affected peasant political identity, which now became much more self-assertive, as several researchers have pointed out, and the peasant estate gained greater 'political confidence'. The development of a party system and the consequent bartering for votes allied to the particularly turbulent Diets of 1742–1743 and 1765–1766 legitimised and developed peasant political identity, giving peasants an important role in the politics of the day.

These changes facilitated a shift in peasant political culture that incorporated an altered repertoire of protest. This was manifested when peasants protested in the eighteenth century: the march to Stockholm was simultaneously a consequence of state centralisation and a development of protest repertoires in conjunction with the development of a strong political identity among the peasantry represented in the Diet.

The march to Stockholm was not primarily just a useful way to get there; it was important in itself. This form of protest had in fact been learned and even rehearsed on numerous delegations to Stockholm on a variety of issues, even if actual uprisings were rare. This is also evident in the strong connections with military marches, especially in the Dalecarlia uprising. What is important here is the use of a common practice in a new context. I believe that the sending of delegations and the final march are related and constitute part of the same repertoire. The aim of delegations and these two uprisings were virtually the same: to come into contact with those the peasantry believed could and would intervene on their behalf. In a centralised and highly bureaucratised state, where could they turn but to the capital? The communicative aspects of the protests were vital – for delegations, meetings with those in power were essential, but the marches were also a communicative medium in themselves. In some cases the march could be compared to a modern day demonstration in communicating that the protesters were discontented, with the actual stay in Stockholm perhaps not so important.

The aspects of responsibility and active participation in politics are evident in the marches. The protesters were not heavily armed and there was hardly any violence during the uprisings until, in the case of the Dalecarlia uprising, the protesters were actually confronted by armed troops. Neither was there any pillaging or destruction of property. The peasants even received provisions for their marches just as a military march would be entitled to. These uprisings were true *peasant* uprisings; they were in fact initiated by peasants and led by peasants, albeit not the most politically disadvantaged of peasants. The peasants from Dalecarlia admittedly had help from a major to organise the march, but the uprising itself originated in the peasantry's will and interest to be involved in issues of national importance. This is also true for Sven Hofman's uprising, where the aim of restoring royal autocracy implies that the Constitution had been discussed within the local community. Although much effort was expended on finding instigators from social groups other than the peasantry, no connections vital to the form or contents of the protests were found. Thus, the marches were a highly politicised form of protest and illustrate a remarkable assertion of political identity.

The peasants in the uprising in Dalecarlia and in Sven Hofman's uprising had got their point across merely by marching towards Stockholm. Their grievances were instantly transformed from a local to a national issue and were heard without their having to use institutional political channels. The march incorporated the threat of social unrest with a peaceful method, while the severity of the peasants' grievances was made perfectly clear. They were protests with a national scope, a non-violent means of protest rooted in peasant political identity.

Chapter VIII

NOTES

1. Inrikes tidningar, no. 41, 29.5.1766.
2. The Estates' commission on Hofman, minute 20.8.1766. RA.
3. Inrikes tidningar, no. 41, 29.5.1766; Malmström 1900, 364–366.
4. The following account of the uprising in Dalecarlia is based on Beckman 1930 unless otherwise stated.
5. Letter from the peasantry in Dalecarlia to His Majesty the King, supplement to provincial governor Wennerstedt to His Majesty the King, 14.4.1743, letters from the provincial governor of Kopparberg to the king 1741–44. RA.
6. Burius 1984, 212.
7. The minute of the peasant estate at the Diet 16, 28 (w. extraktprotokoll), 29.1.1765, 14.3.1765, 27.1.1766, 1.2.1766, 8.2.1766, 3.5.1766. RA; Malmström 1900, 364.
8. See letters from Sven Hofman collected in connection with the trial against him in Borås. Estates' commission on Hofman, records. RA.
9. Ibid.
10. Letter from the provincial governor's office to the commission appointed by the Diet, 21.5.1766. Estates' commission on Hofman, records. RA; Malmström 1900, 365–366, 372.
11. Inrikes tidningar, no. 62, 11.8.1766; Malmström 1900, 372; Alexandersson 1975, 174.
12. Burke 1983b, 7; Tilly 1984, 307; Tilly 1986; Scott 1990; Aya 1990, 54. For a recent example of Charles Tilly's influence on the study of collective action and the use of the term 'repertoire', see Hanagan et al 1998.
13. Hanagan, Moch & te Brake 1998, xvii.
14. Tilly 1984, 307–308, quoting Tarrow 1994, 31.
15. Tarrow 1994, 114–115. For examples of the flexibility of protest repertoires see Maier 1970a and 't Hart 1998.
16. Ibid.
17. Tilly 1984, 308; Tilly 1986, 5–8, 391–398; Hunt 1984, 247.
18. Würtz Sørensen 1988, 33–35, 40–42; Harrison 1997a, 14–16, 94.
19. Wittrock 1948, 212–216.
20. Lundberg 1987, 11.
21. Bolmskog 1995; Lennersand 1999, 146.
22. For an overview in English of the constitutional situation during the Age of Liberty, see Roberts 1973, Metcalf 1977 and Gustafsson 1994a, 47–51.
23. Nilzén 1971, 222–224.
24. Metcalf 1977, 287.
25. Metcalf 1977, 267, 285–286; Gustafsson 1994a, 132–133.
26. Alexandersson 1975, 183–191.
27. Frohnert 1993, 12, 24.
28. Florén 1987b; Melkersson 1997, 42–43, 47–48, 50–52, 60.
29. Frohnert 1993, 13, 21.
30. Melkersson 1999, 6–8.
31. Lagerroth 1934, 13–16.
32. Gustafsson 1991, 200.
33. Frohnert 1985, 251.
34. Ylikangas 1999, 142.
35. Florén 1987a, 142–144, 147.
36. Jameson 1986, 15.
37. Ericsson 1970, 17–18.
38. Frohnert 1985, 252.
39. Metcalf 1977, 284.
40. Alexandersson 1975, 181–182.

41 Estates' commission on Hofman, minute 19.8.1766. RA.
42 Carlsson 1981, 98.
43 Svea Court of Appeal, minutes on Dalecarlian uprising 21.7.1743, 12.8.1743, 19.8.1743. RA.
44 Smedberg 1972, 97–101.
45 Olsson 1926, 88, 100; Lennersand 1999, 224–230.
46 Alexandersson 1975, 205–207, 211.
47 Alexandersson 1975, 211; Ericsson & Petersson 1979, 26; Aronsson 1992, 336; Frohnert 1993, 18; Gustafsson 1994b, 223.
48 Olsson 1926, 88–89, 101–106; Bäck 1984, 293–294; Gustafsson 1994a, 132; Melkersson 1997, 48.
49 Bäck 1984, 137–138.
50 The minutes of peasant estate at the Diet 31.8.1742. RA.
51 Frohnert 1985, 196.
52 The minutes of the peasant estate at the Diet, 8.–9.3.1743, 14.3.1743, 18.3.1743; Malmström 1897, 145.
53 Bäck 1984, 137–138, 294.
54 Malmström 1900, 368–369; Roberts 1986, 155–158, 194–198.
55 Reddy 1977, 66, 82.
56 Hanagan, Moch, & te Brake 1998, xxix.
57 Tilly 1998, 7–8, 14.
58 Hanagan, Moch, & te Brake 1998, xviii.
59 Bäck 1984, 294, 302.
60 The following account of the uprising in Dalecarlia is based on Beckman 1930 unless otherwise stated.
61 The minutes of the peasant estate at the Diet, 8.3.1743, 14.3.1743. RA; The Estates' commission on the war, minutes 11.3.1743. RA.
62 Svea Court of Appeal, minutes on Dalecarlian uprising, 21.– 23.7.1743, 26.7.1743. RA; Handlingar rörande Skandinaviens historia I, 289–298, III, 243–245.
63 Svea Court of Appeal, records on Dalecarlian uprising, Orders to march 30.5.1743. RA.
64 Svea Court of Appeal, records on Dalecarlian uprising, Rules for the march, 17.5.1743. RA; Svea Court of Appeal, minutes on Dalecarlian uprising, 19.7.1743, 217.1743, 26.7.1743. RA; Aarsberetninger, 362; Anders Koskull's memoirs, 61.
65 Kopparberg provincial chancellery, incoming letters from the king, letter from Nils Jansson and Erik Andersson to the peasantry of Dalecarlia, undated. ULA.
66 The Estates' commission on Hofman, records, letters from rider Sandström, 13.5.1766, J. F. Strömbom, 14.–15.5.1766, the provincial governor's office, 21.5.1766, and report from the court in Borås 6.5.1766, to the commission appointed by the Diet. RA.
67 The Estates' Commission on Hofman, minute 20.8.1766. RA.
68 Inrikes tidningar, no. 41, 29.5.1766; the Estates' commission on Hofman, records, letter from A. W. Sparre, 19.5.1766, report from the court in Borås, 9 July 1766, to the commission appointed by the Diet. RA.
69 The Estates' commission on Hofman, records, letter from the provincial governor's office to the commission appointed by the Diet, 21.5.1766. RA.
70 Inrikes tidningar, no. 39–41, 22.5.1766, 26.5.1766, 29.5.1766.
71 Roberts 1986, 192–193.
72 Malmström 1900, 366.
73 The Estates' commission on Hofman, records, Letter from Per Andersson to his father, 20.6.1766, RA; Skaraborg provincial chancellery, incoming letters fron Göta Court of Appeal, 4.7.1766, 9.7.1766. No attempts were made to free the prisoners. GLA.

CHAPTER IX

For the king, farms and justice
Swedish peasant politics and tenant movements in the eighteenth century

Kimmo Katajala

The Swedish peasantry in the Age of Liberty did more than march. Non-violent forms of protest such as tax strikes and complaints to the king and Diet were still in use, as they had been for centuries. The Diet had been a channel of influence for the freeholder peasantry for a century. However, the tenants of the landlords and the poor commons were still excluded from the political estates. So it is natural that the freeholder peasants pursued their aims mostly through the Diet, while the tenants of the landlords had to use other channels in attempting to achieve their goals and express their demands.

Peasants at the Diet and in the law courts

The Swedish constitutions of 1719 and 1720 that put an end to the period of absolutism in Sweden had their origins more in natural law than in the Enlightenment. Nevertheless, the slogans of liberty, brotherhood and equality were soon being repeated in the speeches and pamphlets of the era – the Age of Liberty as the period 1718–1772 is called in Swedish history.[1] The Constitution saw 'the people' as the primary source of political authority. This authority was exercised in the Diet by the Estates. The king was relegated to the margins of politics. However, the official political doctrine of the era did not see the Estates in the Diet as representing 'the people'. They were 'the people' when they exercised their primary political authority. The imperative mandate was discussed, but from the 1740s onwards was a forbidden topic.[2]

New 'parties', the Caps and Hats, emerged in Swedish politics. The difference between these two parties is usually described through their posture on foreign policy. The Hats supported aggressive policies towards Russia, while the Caps sought to settle the eastern conflict. It is said that they even went as far as cringing before the Russians. The division can also be discerned to some extent in internal policies. The Hats were close to the policies of the noble aristocracy, while the Caps derived much of their support from the burghers, clergy and Finnish peasantry. However, it must be stressed that the line between the parties was not simply drawn between the estates. Both parties were supported by members from all estates.[3]

From the 1740s onwards new groupings can be traced inside the estates and the parties. Those who, for different reasons, disfavoured the unfettered power of the Estates, set to work to the strengthen the power of the king. We can even speak of a 'court party'. This group was opposed by those who supported the Constitution and the supremacy of the Estates. However, this was not a division between 'royalists' and 'democrats'. The nobles, who wielded a great deal of influence in the Diet, were notable supporters of the power of the Estates. The 'court party' was supported mainly by the Caps and the peasants. A strong king was seen in this political structure as a counterweight to the nobles in the Diet and the aristocratic high bureaucracy.[4] The 'royalism' of the peasant estate took its sharpest form in the Dalecarlia uprising of 1743 and the Hoffman uprising of 1766 (see chapter VIII).

The Diet was very quarrelsome during the Age of Liberty. There were even periods when decision-making was totally paralysed. In normal political situations the Diet was now the main channel for the peasants represented there to wield political influence. However – as the Swedish historian Kalle Bäck has shown – when this channel was jammed by political disputes the peasantry made use of local, non-violent but illegal forms of resistance. According to Bäck, they were the same forms of resistance the serfs and tenants in Central Europe had been using, namely tax strikes, strikes in rent service, failing to comply with the orders of the establishment, and so on.[5]

There were several reasons for the conflicts between the Swedish eighteenth century peasantry and the Crown. The most common of these were new taxes, the recruiting of soldiers, legislation restricting slash-and-burn cultivation and the prohibition on the distilling of spirits from grain. However, this combat was more like normal political struggle than what we understand by the concept of 'peasant unrest.'.

The seeds of the quarrel between the noble and peasant estates were still the rights of the manors. The Great Reduction of 1680 did not set all the peasants free from their responsibilities to the manors. The fiefs of 'old nobility' were left untouched. In some cases, presented later, the reduction was cancelled and the tenancy continued unchanged. Most of the manors were given as residences to military officers and civil servants. Often the surrounding peasant holdings – whether their occupants were freeholders or tenants – were given as 'auxiliary holdings' to the local manor. These auxiliary holdings were known as 'augments'. A freeholder or tenant living on an augment was obliged to pay his taxes and perform rent service to the manor. If a manor was purchased by its occupier, the tenants' augments became the full property of the landlord. However, the status of a freeholder cultivating an augment remained unchanged.

The augment tenant who cultivated the landlord's holding was in a very weak position. If he was dissatisfied with his rent or other terms in his contract, the only legal way to protest was to give notice and leave the holding. However, all the rents had to be paid, rent service had to be performed and the buildings on the holding had to be left in good condition. If not, the tenant was obliged to make up the loss to the landlord.

The status of a freeholder cultivating an augment was also not very secure. If the taxes of the augment were left unpaid for three years, the proprietary rights to the farm were put up for sale. The freeholder himself and his nearest relatives had right of precedence to save the holding by paying the back taxes. However, if they were unable to do this, the landlord was second in line to redeem the holding. In this case the holding would become his full property and the peasant cultivating it his tenant. This was one of the areas of contention between the peasant and noble estates in the Diet during the Age of Liberty.

First the nobles tried to persuade the Diet to set the price of the peasant holdings on public sale so high that the peasants themselves or their relatives would probably be unable to afford them. This would have made it easy for the landlord to redeem the holding. But this effort did not meet with success at the Diet. However, in 1756 the nobles succeeded in pushing through a royal decision that gave them precedence in redeeming the proprietary rights of augments that came up for public sale within ten kilometres of a manor. The peasant protest was not slow in coming, especially from Finland. The peasant estate persuaded the clergy and the burghers to take their side at the Diet of 1760–1761 and succeeded in having the decision annulled. However, those bargains that had already been concluded during the intervening five years under the royal decision were left in force.[6]

Jokioinen

The competition between the landlords and the peasants cultivating the augments had its counterpart at local level too. In many places, especially in Finland, the freeholders and tenants of the augments attempted to resist the efforts of the landlord to redeem their holdings. Their protests were usually in vain. However, simultaneously with the combat over the augments at the Diet in the 1750s, the peasants of Jokioinen manor in Finland began again to agitate over their rights to their holdings. The seventeenth century saw continuous quarrels between the peasants and their masters, first over the taxes and rent service, and after the Great Reduction of the 1680s over the proprietary rights to the holdings (see chapter VII). In 1754, seven peasants claimed they were freeholders and insisted on their right to pay their taxes according to the taxing levies of the Crown. The landlord Reinhold Jägerhorn saw them as tenants and demanded payment of the rents according to the private taxing roll dating back to 1692 plus the performance of rent service according to the old agreement from 1651.[7]

The local court, where the case was first taken, agreed with the landlord and ordered the peasants to pay their taxes and to do their rent service according to the private agreements. The peasants, who had fetched old documents from the Treasury in Stockholm to prove their freeholder status, appealed to the Court of *Lagman*[8]. From the decision of the *lag-*

man court they appealed to the Court of Appeal in Turku. The result was in both cases the same as in the local court. Still believing in their rights, the peasants appealed to the king, but also to the Chamber of Treasures. The king took the same view of the case as the local court, *lagman* court and the Court of Appeal. The Chamber, however, announced that the case must be examined again and resolved by the local court.

Along with its decision, the Chamber sent the peasants an excerpt from the land book of Jokioinen parish from 1685. In this document, half the holdings in the parish were marked as freeholder holdings. This evoked new hope among the peasants, and in 1759 forty-four of them appealed again to the local court for their freeholder rights. The court session saw a heated debate between the advocates hired by the landlord and the peasants. Old documents were cited against other old documents. Both parties tried their best to prove their ownership of the proprietary rights to the holdings. However, the judge sitting in the court viewed the documents the landlord had presented as more reliable than those of the peasants. They were all tenants, decided the court.

The peasants did not surrender. Once again they appealed to the Court of *Lagman* and the *lagman* saw these new documents as proving that the peasant holdings of Jokioinen possessed freeholder status. This was a victory for the peasants. But their joy was to prove short-lived. The landlord appealed to the Court of Appeal, which decided that only those five holdings that had initiated the whole process had freeholder status and the freeholder status of the others would have to be established separately. Until such time, they were tenant farms. In 1767, the king confirmed the decision of the Court of Appeal in respect of these five freeholder holdings. As for the other holdings, however, the king took the view their case should be examined again by the local court. The king set the wheel of bureaucracy rolling yet again.

The case reached its final conclusion in 1782, twenty eight years from its first being raised. The local court had again decided that all forty-nine holdings involved in the case were tenant holdings. The landlord, who was now Gustav Reuterholm, had hired the best lawyer available, Matthias Calonius, professor of jurisprudence at the Academy of Turku. Calonius was an expert on the history of landowning. It was his invention to develop a kind of mediating nature for the holdings under the Jokioinen manor. According to him these peasants had the right to sit on their holdings as long they paid their taxes and behaved properly. The landlord had no right to evict them without a legally valid reason. However, the holdings were still to be counted as tenant farms. In 1782, Gustavus III decided that, with the exception of the five holdings which had been proved to be freeholder farms, all other holdings under Jokioinen manor should be treated according to the principles outlined by Professor Calonius.

As we can see, these eighteenth-century events at Jokioinen were nothing like the peasant revolts or unrest of preceding centuries. Although the local atmosphere between the peasants and the landlord was occasionally extremely heated, there was absolutely no open violence. The peasants chose to use legal procedures in pursuit of their goals. The contents of the quarrel took on a jurisprudential nature. The fight took place in the courts between the advocates of the parties. Old documents showing the nature of the peasant holdings took the place of arms. The long combat was successful for some of the peasants. Nevertheless, the establishment labelled these peasant acts as 'unrest', 'mutiny' or even 'rebellion'.

Joensuu

At Joensuu manor, near the town of Turku in Finland, vigorous and even violent acts by Hinric Buch, the new manager, or 'director', of the landed estate upset the peasants under the manor. They complained about their new estate manager to their landlord, Count Uldrich Barck, who was living in Stockholm. The count had no ear for the laments of his peasants. On the contrary, in 1771 Buch ordered the eviction of fifty-two peasants who had joined the protest. According to him the peasants were tenants. If they were not satisfied with his command, they had to leave their holdings.[9]

The peasants appealed first to the governor and, after it became clear that no help could be expected from that quarter, to the Court of Appeal. The Court of Appeal ruled that the case should be examined by the local court. The peasants had hired an advocate to help them in court, which sat in 1772. The bone of contention turned out to be labour service. The peasants claimed that they had done too many days of service, while 'director' Buch took the opposite view. No compromise was reached, and the eviction remained legal.

The day the peasants – now fifty-six in number – had been ordered to leave their holdings was in spring 1773. Instead of obeying the command of the estate manager, they appealed again to the local court. Their aim was to win time by complaining about the taxes and labour service. The court did not even take up the complaints of the peasants. The judge confirmed the eviction of fifty-one peasants. The other five, who had not legally been given notice to quit, were permitted to stay on their holdings. Those under threat of eviction appealed to the Court of *Lagman*.

The court sat in June 1773. The new advocate hired by the peasants tried to turn the conflict in a new direction. He claimed that the farms under Joensuu manor were not tenant holdings but freehold farms. This meant neither the landlord nor the estate manager had the right to evict the peasants, although he was entitled to their taxes and labour service. The court did not scrutinize this matter at all. It simply ordered the peasants to leave the holdings.

Most peasants gave up. They prepared a letter in which they apologized to 'director' Buch for their obstinacy. The peasants were made to sign an agreement about the duties of a tenant. In this document they confirmed that their farms were tenant holdings. They also accepted even harder terms for taxes and rent service than before. Only seven peasants were actually evicted from the farms. 'Director' Buch, who had prepared the document, writes in one of its paragraphs:

> "...however, a peasant under a manor, as little as cottagers or servants, owns not a single piece of turf in the Realm, which must be stated clearly here, because the tenants have had a contrary opinion on this matter."

These two examples from Jokioinen and Joensuu show that there was disagreement between the landlords and their tenants at local level about the proprietary rights to the peasant holdings. In some very few cases the combat over the rights to the holdings resulted in success for the peasants. If a farm was found to be held as a freeholding, this restricted the rights of the landlord to taxes and labour service. He had no authority to increase the taxes or demand more labour service than the freeholder had done to the Crown. In other cases, the tenant holding and its rents were under the total control and power of the landlord. However, these skirmishes presented above were only an overture to the peasant movements which arose in several areas of the Swedish realm after Gustavus III took power.

The restoration of absolutism in 1772

The politics of the Age of Liberty had at least two faces. Slogans like freedom of speech, the natural rights of man and even equality were in diligent use in political speeches and pamphlets. The other face was the censorship of the press, heated quarrels in the Diet and the great influence of foreign powers – especially Russia and Denmark – in the politics of the realm. Decision-making in the Diet was occasionally totally paralysed because of the incompetence of the political parties to make compromises. Although this political system had plenty of supporters, the number of critics was also growing, especially from the 1760s onwards.

Gustavus III was crowned king in June 1772. Nearest to the young monarch there were some skilful men who were fed up with the endless quarrels in the Diet, and prominent among their numbers was the Finnish-born general Jacob Magnus Sprengtporten. A plan was made to restore the absolute monarchy. According to the Swedish Constitution and the General Law from 1734 this was unadulterated treason. Sprengtporten was sent to Finland, officially to inspect the possibility of political unrest because of a pamphlet published earlier that year. The real reason was to prepare a coup d'état. According to the plan, the coup was to begin simultaneously in Finland and in the province of Scania in the middle of August 1772. When the messages about the revolutionaries reached the Diet that had assembled in Stockholm, the king with his guards took power from the frightened Estates. The Diet was forced to accept the new Constitution. Sweden was now once again an absolute monarchy. The coup d'état had succeeded.

The new absolute ruler held a speech from the throne on 21 August 1772 in which he presented lofty arguments for his coup using the political vocabulary of the Enlightenment. Pointing to the period of estate power he declared:

"This way freedom, the most noble of the human rights, has been turned in the hands of the ruling party into aristocratic despotism... Those most virtuous, valuable and first citizens (*medborgare*) have been sacrificed... yes, and the folk itself has been pressed, its complaints have been labelled rebellion and freedom is turned in this way into an aristocratic yoke, intolerable for every Swedish man... A part of the people have borne this yoke, moaning and groaning, but keeping calm without knowing where to find salvation or how to achieve it... However, God has blessed my work and I have seen the same love for the fatherland living in the soul of my people that in olden times burned in the hearts of Engelbrekt and Gustavus Eriksson... I have promised to rule a free nation."[10]

If Gustavus really was afraid of tumults because of the writings of an unknown scribbler, he was certainly wrong in estimating his own capacity to ensure the tenants that the time for their freedom had now come. His speech was read aloud in all the churches of the realm. It was also translated into Finnish. The response was immediate. Men bringing requests from the tenants to be freed from their landlords and to receive their holdings as their own property were sent to the king from almost all over the realm. The aftermath of the coup saw the last large-scale Swedish peasant movement of the *ancien regime*.

Tenant movements of the 1770s

Elimäki

Elimäki fief was the hotbed of Finland during the seventeenth century. The partial annulment of the Great Reduction in the fief was a real disappointment for the peasants sitting on the holdings left under the manors. Although the first half of the eighteenth century turned out to be quite calm in Elimäki, the coup d'état of 1772 became the starting shot for the last large-scale peasant protest in the area.[11]

After the king's speech was read aloud in the church, the peasants on Elimäki fief stopped performing their rent service. Two men were chosen to take a complaint to the king about the rents being too high and the heavy level of rent service. In Stockholm these couriers hired an advocate to present a written complaint to the king's chancellery. The advocate gave promises of freedom from rent service and lower taxes on the holdings. The two delegates already returned home with their encouraging messages in autumn 1772.

The result was a full strike in rent service in Elimäki fief. Eighty-two peasants renounced their fidelity to their landlord, Ullrika af Forselles, the widow of a rich trader who had bought most of the Elimäki fief from the Wrede family. The possessor of the other half of the fief was Count Rabbe Gottlieb Wrede, a scion of Henrik Wrede (see chapter VII). His tenants also stopped performing rent service. About 200 peasants joined the movement.

Nothing was heard of the advocate during the winter. The governor informed the king about the situation in Elimäki, and as a result, instead of positive news, there arrived from Stockholm a royal declaration to all the tenants in Finland. The king ordered the tenants to be loyal to their landlords. Those continuing in their recalcitrance would be severely punished. This declaration was read and translated into Finnish in the church. Gustavus III had not had the tenants in his mind in August 1772 when he spoke about the folk pressed under the yoke of aristocracy.

Thus, in spring 1773 it became clear to the peasants that a new delegation to the capital was required. In Stockholm it became evident that their advocate had vanished with the money they had given him for costs and payment. The peasants had to hire a new advocate. His task was to find documents proving the freeholder nature of the peasant holdings and to prepare a complaint to the king. A vast sum of about 1 000 dalers in copper was collected from the peasants of Elimäki and sent to Stockholm to pay the advocate. The complaint was delivered to the king's chancellery on 5 May, and the king issued his decree on the matter on 18 May. This stated it was not the king's task to scrutinize a handful of peasant holdings; the examination should be carried out at the local court. In the meantime, however, a lot had happened in Elimäki.

At the end of April, governor Anders Henrik Ramsay held an examination at Elimäki parish. The governor commanded the tenants to obey the king's declaration given in February and be loyal to their lords. They were to pay their taxes and perform their rent service. The recalcitrant would be severely punished. As a warning to the peasants he even read aloud the death sentence the Court of Appeal had given to Matti Sihvo in 1653 (see chapter VII).

The peasants did not heed the governor's admonishment. They had heard and understood the king's declaration, but they claimed it had been invented by the governor himself. They were the king's humble subjects and soon the king would free them from the manors. So there was no reason to pay their rents or perform rent service. The upshot was that the governor arrested the fourteen most outspoken members of the crowd. They were taken as prisoners to the citadel of Svartholma on a tiny island outside the town of Loviisa.

The recalcitrance of the Elimäki peasants was examined in the local court. This gave its judgement on 17 May, just one day before the king issued his decision on the peasants' complaint. The court took the view that it had no power of sentence in a such serious case as the recalcitrance of the Elimäki peasants. The case was submitted to the Court of Appeal. However, the judge decided that others who had joined the recalcitrants should also be arrested. About one hundred peasants were taken as prisoners to the citadel of Svartholma, where they had to sit and await the decision of the Court of Appeal.

The summer of 1773 was a very restless time in Elimäki. Most of the peasants were sitting under arrest in the citadel. The rest of the commons refused to cooperate with the landlords and the establishment. The manors lacked labour because of the strike in rent service. The hay needed gathering in for the cattle for the winter, and it was almost harvest time. Governor Ramsay sent a small unit of soldiers to the parish to force the peasants to perform rent service. However, in the villages the soldiers saw only angry and hostile women and children who met them with stones and sickles in their hands. Even some small violent affrays occurred, and the governor sent more soldiers to the area. All this only served to increase the hatred of the commons towards the governor and the landlords.

A special court was set up in Elimäki to scrutinize the case at the end of September. The aim of the court was to inspect the crimes of the peasants, not their complaints and their claimed proprietary rights to the farms. Moreover, those arrested were taken the long way from Svartholma to the court, although half of them were in fever and suffering from bloody flux (dysentery). Some prisoners had died of the disease and the bad conditions in the damp vaults of the citadel. The peasants were evidently not ready to cooperate. They wanted to appeal to the king for justice and their farms. The court was preparing to pass harsh sentences on the peasants.

At the beginning of October, the court session was moved from Elimäki to the town of Loviisa. General Jacob Sprengporten was once again in Finland, and the king, who had followed the process at Elimäki with growing irritation, ordered him to resolve this Gordian knot. Sprengporten had discussions with the arrested peasants. Promising the king's mercy and the right to appeal to the king he extracted a promise from the peasants to return to performing rent service. Soon most of the arrested were set free, and the peasants began once more to perform rent service and pay their taxes to the manor. Two peasants were sent to Stockholm to appeal to the king for the freedom of their holdings. The Court of Appeal gave its judgement in December, and this was submitted to the king.

The king gave his decision in the case on 11 April 1774. All the recalcitrant peasants of the movement were pardoned apart from the leaders. However, they were all severely warned from further opposition against the establishment or the landlords. The Court of Appeal had proposed that three leaders of the movement be sentenced to death and broken on the wheel. However, the king moderated this punishment to lashes. Two peasants were punished with thirty cut-pairs of lashes and one with twenty cut-pairs, three cuts of a lash in a pair. According to the king, the peasants were under an absolute obligation to perform their duties to the manor. So, the peasants achieved none of their goals and the outcome of the resistance was a total defeat. Be that as it may, the fief of Elimäki remained rather calm for the rest of the century.

Nastola

Nearby the Elimäki fief, in Nastola parish, the peasants living in tenant augments began in spring 1773 to seek freedom for their holdings. The idea was taken from the Elimäki peasants. Three men were sent to Stockholm. The goal was to get the holdings returned to the Crown. The line of events resembles those in Elimäki. The men who were sent to Stockholm hired an advocate, who wrote a complaint for them and delivered it to the Chamber of Treasures. The Chamber gave a note to the peasants acknowledging receipt of their complaint, and with this paper the men of Nastola returned home.

The effect was immediate. The tenants went to the lords of the manors and gave them a copy of the note from the Chamber. In one voice they renounced all fidelity to their landlords. According to the peasants the document gave them the right to break off their rent service to the manors. This happened although the paper was translated to the peasants several times and it was clearly shown to them that it was only a note acknowledging receipt of the complaint. Later, when accused over the strike, the peasants claimed that they had not understood what kind of paper the note was. This was a white lie. In the mind of the peasants, they were under no obligation to fulfil the disputed responsibilities while the case was still pending – and the fact that it was pending was clearly attested in their note. After the king's decision it would be a different matter.

The establishment thought otherwise. The tenants were summoned to the local court for failure to perform their duties. Some of them were soon evicted from their holdings. However, although several attempts were made, it proved impossible to get the tenants to attend the court. Most of them hid in the forests. Only two of those who had been in Stockholm were caught. However, the other tenants violently freed one of the prisoners while he was being transported from the jail to the court. Without extra manpower it was hopeless trying to catch the hiding tenants.

The governor ordered a military detachment into the parish. Their task was to unearth the tenants and bring them to the court. One by one, the hiding tenants were caught and brought to the jail. The king had given his decision on the tenant's complaint in May 1774. Gustavus III explained that it was not his task to examine the nature of a handful of tenant holdings or the lawfulness of the decisions of the Chamber of Treasures from the 1750s, when most of these holdings were placed under the manor. This was the task of the local court. However, according to Gustavus the complaint itself was written in so bilious a manner that the advocate was charged fifty dalers in silver.

The court was set up to handle the case in June 1774. The tenants were heard, but no judgement was reached because not all the persons involved in the case were present. The tenants were returned to the jail in the castle of Hämeenlinna. There they had to sit almost the whole of the following winter. The next examination was held in spring 1775. Judgement was referred to the Court of Appeal, which gave its judgement in the autumn, and the king confirmed it in November 1775.

Three "most criminal" tenants were sentenced to twenty days' imprisonment on bread and water. All other tenants who had joined the movement got a sentence of eight days on bread and water. These sentences do not at first sight look too harsh. However, the conditions in the prisons of those days were appalling. Three weeks, or even one, in such a place without any real sustenance was surely an experience a prisoner would remember for the rest of his life. In addition to this, the tenants were sentenced in joint and several liability to indemnification of over one thousand dalers, and many of them were evicted from their holdings. The advocate that the tenants had hired in Stockholm was sentenced to imprisonment of twenty-eight days on bread and water. Meanwhile, there was one more area in Finland where unrest arose after the coup of 1772.

Pälkjärvi

Those donations of land given as a pledge against a sum of money in the seventeenth century were not returned to the Crown in the Great Reduction of the 1680s. They were to be bought back by the Crown at a later date. However, in some cases this never happened and these donations remained in the hands of the landlords. Over a period of decades the donations or parts thereof were sold on to other persons. With this buying and selling the nature of the pledge was forgotten and during the eighteenth century they began to be ruled as the full property of the landlords – which had not been the intention of the original donation in the seventeenth century.

One such donation was in Northern Karelia – one of the hotbeds of the seventeenth century – in the parishes of Pälkjärvi and Ilomantsi.[12] At the turn of the 1770s, the possessor of this donation was the director of the post office and royal secretary Niclas Gustaf Duncan, who died in 1771. His young widow, Catherine Birgitta Duncan and two minor children were to hold the landed estate with help of the bailiff Otto Wilhelm Polack. Many peasants on the donation openly opposed this harsh bailiff, even resorting to violence. The peasants on the donation viewed their conditions as worse than those of other parishes of the county that were taxed by the Crown. Thus, there was already discontent when the news of the king's coup of 1772 reached Northern Karelia.

The immediate result of the king's famous speech and the news that echoed from the Elimäki fief was a tax strike and refusal to perform rent service. More than one hundred peasants presented a complaint about the taxes to governor Ramsay on his visit to the county in spring 1773. However, the governor did not react in any way to the appeals of the peasantry. Soon three men from northern Karelia were sent to Stockholm to bring a letter of complaint to the king. The petition contained complaints over taxation and accusations about the harshness of the bailiff. However, the petition ended in an appeal for the peasant holdings to be brought under Crown rule.

The governor, who had heard about the tax strike and the complaint sent to Stockholm, warned the peasants against continuing their obstinacy. The taxes were to be paid and rent service performed for the landlord. Otherwise the governor would have no other resort than to send troops to the area. We must remember that just at that time there were soldiers occupying Elimäki parish at the behest of the governor. The petition was delivered to the king in November 1773. He passed it on to General Jacob Magnus Sprengtporten, who was engaged in sorting out the mess in Elimäki. Sprengtporten, who desperately wanted to return to Stockholm, sent the complaint to the local Crown bailiff in Karelia, Gabriel Wallenius with advice to organise negotiations between the landlord and the peasants.

It is not known if the meeting actually took place that winter. Be that as it may, the situation seems to have calmed down for two years. We know of no complaints from the peasants or the landlord until 1775, when the tension between them again emerges into the light of day. The peasants sent a letter of complaint about their taxes to the king. The complaint argued that because the donation had initially been given as a pledge, it had involved only the right to collect the taxes, not the holdings. The holdings should now be returned to the Crown and taxed as Crown holdings. The peasants had hired an advocate in Stockholm to help them with writing the document and digging judicial arguments from the archives.

The king sent the document to the governor with an admonition to settle this discontent. Several meetings were held between the peasants and the landlord over the next few years, but without success. Neither of the parties had any will to compromise. The recalcitrance over payment of taxes and rent service continued. The possessor of the donation, Catherine Birgitta Duncan had married the local judge of Karelia, Eric Philip Didron. This was why the peasants did not appeal to the local court, as they should have done according to the law. After a final meeting between the peasants and the governor (the landlord Didron and his wife were absent) in March 1778, the peasants gathered at the manor. They called judge Didron out and renounced all their fidelity to him as their landlord. The result was a brawl between the judge and his bailiffs on the one side, and the peasant leaders on the other.

The peasants appealed to the king to order the newly established Court of Appeal in Vaasa to organise an impartial investigation into the case. The king accepted the motion of the peasantry. An examination that took several weeks was organized at the manor of Pälkjärvi. However, no decision was taken on site. The peasants had to wait the judgement of the Court of Appeal. This did not so much as glance at the peasants' petitions and complaints. All its effort went into solving the problem of how to punish the recalcitrant peasants? The judgement was eventually submitted to the king.

The king accepted the proposal of the Court of Appeal almost in its entirety. A peasant called Henrik Kuronen, who had been twice in Stockholm carrying petitions to the king, was sentenced as the prime mover of the movement to forty pairs of lashes, three cuts in a pair. He was also sentenced to forced labour for two years in a citadel. Another peasant was also sentenced to forty pairs of lashes, and several others received a punishment of smaller numbers of lashes. However, there were still more than 200 peasants to be punished. They were sentenced to draw lots, with every tenth one of those who had joined the movement but not taken an active part to suffer corporal punishment with twenty pairs of lashes.

Now there remained only the task of executing sentence. Punishing those leaders of the movement who were already jailed was not a problem. However, the others had fled to the woods, where it was impossible to reach them. The king ordered a military detachment under Colonel Robert Montgomery to enforce punishment on these men. A plot was hatched. The colonel announced publicly that he had arrested judge Didron and that the peasants were now free to return to their homes. Lured out of the forests, the peasants were immediately arrested and the punishments duly executed. This mass corporal punishment of November 1779 ended the peasant movements of the 1770s in Finland. However, we must still take a glimpse at those tenant movements that took place in the most southerly parts of Sweden, in areas that had previously been Danish and were ceded to Sweden during the seventeenth century.

Scania and Halland

The relations between landlords and their tenants in the southernmost Swedish provinces of Scania and Halland differed from the rest of the country. These relations had their origins in the earlier Danish times. In the other parts of Sweden the peasants were mostly freeholders. In these southern provinces, where a great number of manors were situated, tenancy was a much more common phenomenon. The tenants of the area had a lifelong right to occupy their holdings. However, the landlord had the right to demand an unlimited amount of rent service. If a peasant did not fulfil his duties the landlord had the right to evict him from the holding.

In November 1772, soon after the famous speech of Gustavus III, the governor of these provinces, Olof von Nackerej reported skirmishes in some manors of the area.[13] The tenants had stopped performing rent service. Several complaints of the tenants about the taxes and rent service were brought to the king. These individual signs of unrest were still unrelated to each other. The king answered the tenants in November 1772 with a warning. He forbade them to show any obstinacy towards their landlords. They were to be loyal to their masters and perform rent service without any recalcitrance. The king's declaration was very similar to the warning he gave the Finnish tenants the following February.

In autumn 1772 there were troubles only on one or two individual manors. But during spring 1773 the tenant resistance developed into a real movement. There was organised cooperation between the tenants of several manors. Violence played no role in the movement. The violent encounters that did occur were rare, sporadic events and unrelated to each other. The tenants sent numerous complaints to the governor. However, they did not give him any time to act. As early as April 1773 three tenants travelled to Stockholm and conveyed the common complaint of the tenants to the king. The immediate result at local level was a large-scale strike on rent service. The aim of the tenant movement was to gain a specified limit to rent service, and by extension more certain conditions for their rights of occupancy to the holdings.

The king passed the case on for examination in the law courts. The landlords were accordingly summoned to court in autumn 1773, where the tenants urged examination of the their real rights to the holdings. The tenants and their complaints were drawn through the whole Swedish judicial bureaucracy: from the local court to the Court of *Lagman*, from there to the Court of Appeal and finally to the royal Supreme Court. At all judicial levels the judgements went against the tenants. The royal

Supreme Court gave the final judgement in 1776. Before this, during the course of 1775, many tenants who had joined the movement were given notice to quit and evicted from their holdings with the help of military detachments.

The peasant unrest tamed

The main combat over the proprietary rights to the augment holdings took place in the Diet. The case was in the interests of the peasant estate, which represented freeholders and Crown tenants. Tenants of private landlords had no right to take part in the Diet. Lacking political rights, the tenants had to send their complaints to the governor and the king. However, the bureaucracy and the law forced them to bring their demands to be examined in the courts. We can identify certain high points of peasant and tenant unrest in eighteenth-century Sweden. Unrest always peaked when the highest power in the realm was ambivalent – when a new king was elected, as in 1743, and after the coup by Gustavus the III in 1772. At times like these there was always a rise in peasant protests and tenant demands.

The course of events in the eighteenth-century tenant protests follows the same pattern every time. The tenants hear about the coup of 1772 and Gustavus III's speech is read aloud to them in church. Their interpretation of the speech is that the political situation is favourable for them to present their demands and complaints. First they turn to the governor, but in every case the governor ignores their complaints or does not have time to act before the tenants take their next step. Men are sent to Stockholm, where they hire a learned man, an advocate to write their complaint in a style presentable at court. The complaint is delivered to the king, who passes it on to the local law court. The peasants then have to face the long journey through the various levels of the judicial system. This rocky and expensive road is always run to the end, but with essentially negative results. The tenants are usually severely punished with lashes, imprisonment and fines because of their attempts to renounce their fidelity to their landlords. Many recalcitrant peasants are also evicted from their holdings.

Although it is hard to understand the sense in this bull-headed and clearly disadvantageous process of litigation over the proprietary rights of the tenant holdings, it is clear it was the tenants' only hope. All other ways of influencing their conditions were blocked off. The argumentation of the tenants and the advocates they hired shows clearly that the proprietary rights to the tenant holdings were not at all an unacceptable argument in the jurisprudential discourse of the era. However, the ideas of the Enlightenment favoured in the rhetoric of the political speeches of the era played no role in these practical judicial proceedings over the proprietary rights to the tenant holdings.

1789, the year of the French Revolution saw a kind of coup in Sweden too. The king and the freeholder peasants were allied again. With help of the peasant estate, a detachment of soldiers and peasant troops gathered from Dalecarlia, Gustavus III persuaded the other estates in the reluctant Diet to accept the Act of Union and Security. On the one hand this document, referred to as the Constitution of the realm, strengthened the king's power. However, the other side of the Act was that it secured the ownership of the peasant holdings for the freeholder peasants. This was a direct blow against the aims of the nobility to expand their influence in the politics of the state and at local level. The freeholders had once again made a very successful move with the help of a strong king. From now on the freeholders were safe from the demands of the local manors. However, this all weakened the position of the tenants and the poor commons at local level. They were pushed to the margins of political life for a long time ahead.

The conditions of the tenants were widely discussed during the latter half of the nineteenth century. In Finland, annexed to the Russian Empire as an autonomous Grand Duchy in 1809, the main focus of attention was on the conditions of the tenants under the donations in the area known as Old Finland. These donations were given to Russian nobles from 1721 onwards after the easternmost parts of Finland had been ceded to Russia after the Great Northern War. The question was resolved in 1867, when the Finnish Diet decided to redeem the donated holdings from the landlords for the tenants. However, the tenants and cottagers in the other parts of the country had to wait until 1918 when the Parliament of the newly independent Finland gave them the right to redeem their own holdings at a reasonable, low price.

The absence of violence by the tenants is a significant feature of the unrest of the eighteenth century. When violent skirmishes occurred they were small in scale and extremely localised, usually outbursts of individual hatred having no relation to the organised tenant movements. As we have already seen with the case of the marching peasants it was the authorities who used organised violence in suppressing the movement. The military was used for several purposes. First of all, the soldiers were used to force the striking peasants to return to the performance of rent service. They were to aid the landlords in getting their labour to the work at the manors. The second task was to hunt down the tenants hiding in the woods and bring them to court. Thirdly, the military was used in executing the corporal punishments inflicted on recalcitrants. And finally, the soldiers were ordered to attack the marching peasants on the streets of Stockholm in 1743. In Weberian terms, the state had monopolised the use of organised violence.

This brings us to our last major question, to examine how the establishment attempted to handle peasant unrest. There have been two major conflicting views of the relationship between peasant unrest and the process of the centralising state. The main view has been that centralisation, creating the bureaucracy and transferring power from local communities and into the hands of state officials and central government formed the main fundamental grounds for the unrest. On the other hand, good reasons have also been presented in favour of the view that the centralisation process was in large measure due to the peasant unrest. It has been proposed that society and its ruling strata had to create structures that could cope with the rioting masses. Legislation plays a fundamental role in organising society. Our last main chapter therefore turns to the task of investigating developments in legislation. We must pose the question as to whether or not peasant unrest had any influence in generating provisions to secure the internal peace of society.

NOTES

1. Lindroth 1978, 43, 498–502, 530–532.
2. Thanner 1953, 37–38; Roberts 1973, 11–12.
3. See for example Olsson 1963; Carlsson 1981.
4. Ylikangas 1964, 177–181.
5. Bäck 1984, 283–284.
6. Paloposki 1961, 344–352; Alexandersson 1975, 171–172; Lindroth 1978, 533; Bäck 1984, 280, 291.
7. The presentation is based on Katajala 2002, 415–423.
8. The Court of *Lagman*, a court in civil cases between the local assizes and the Court of Appeal. *Lagman* (literally 'law man'), a title given to a judge having dominance over the local courts and the judges of some provinces.
9. For the events at Joensuu, see Jutikkala 1932, 386–400; Ylikangas 2000, 313–314; Katajala 2002, 413–415.
10. Speech of Gustavus III from the throne to the Estates of the Realm 21.8.1772. Modeé X 1781, 3–5.
11. The presentation of the events at Elimäki is based on Katajala 2002, where substantial primary sources are presented.
12. The presentation is based on Katajala 2002, where the substantial primary sources are presented.
13. These events are presented in Smedberg 1972. The presentation here is based on that study.

CHAPTER X

Swedish medieval and early modern treason legislation
A consequence of peasant uprisings?

Mia Korpiola

Revolt and the law

In this chapter, I consider the legal aspects of peasant revolt from the angle of treason. This is not without its difficulties, as treason is both a broad subject and an elusive one. I have therefore chosen one major aspect, the interaction between treason legislation and peasant revolt, to provide an approach to the whole complex mass of treason doctrine. My aim here is to answer the question of whether or not Swedish treason legislation really was a consequence of peasant uprisings.[1] This has required me to dwell on the earliest origins of Swedish treason legislation in order to establish when and for what reason treason law first emerged in medieval Sweden. I have also had to consider the legal means employed and developed by the early modern state on the one hand to limit and on the other hand to channel peasant protest. In addition to this, I have devoted space to the impact of state formation on treason law in the sixteenth and seventeenth centuries. As the time span of this chapter covers about six centuries and so little research has been done on treason, I have also had to sketch in the framework of treason legislation to some extent.

The work of several researchers active in the field of peasant protest would seem to imply a possible link between the peasant revolts and the criminalisation of treason, making treason legislation a post-revolt reaction of kings and nobility. Admittedly these researchers do not claim a quasi-causal link between the peasant revolts and treason legislation in the broad sense, and their intention has been to explain the occurrence of peasant revolts in the framework of the slowly emerging territorial state. However, as they do use as evidence cases where treason has been criminalised, it is surely not inappropriate to take them as a starting point, especially as so little research has been done on treason as such.

Professor Peter Blickle has discussed the subject in his much-cited article 'The Criminalization of Peasant Resistance in the Holy Roman Empire: Toward a History of the Emergence of High Treason in Germany'. His main thesis is that peasant assemblies and riots as such were criminalised after the Grat German Peasant War of 1525. According to Blickle, it was mainly peasant resistance, even in a passive form, that brought about this criminalisation, despite its former acceptance. As he himself puts it: "The emperors and the imperial princes had created the concept and criteria for high treason (*Hochverrat*) in response to the peasant unrest."[2] Yet the "epidemic spread of resistance" was not the only contributing factor, as the imperial sensitivity to the need for peace also played a role in developments. The peace of 1495, forbidding feuds and war, did not settle the issue.[3] The wave of peasant revolts in the closing years of the fifteenth century and the early sixteenth century provoked legislation against sedition and passive resistance first on the territorial level and, after the Peasant War of 1525, on the imperial level.[4]

In Finland, professor Heikki Ylikangas, who has done much to set the Finnish peasant war of 1595–1597, the Club War, in its international context,[5] has taken up Blickle's theory in his attempt to explain the historical connections of European peasant uprisings. His reading of Blickle is that "the concept of high treason was deliberately developed as a weapon in the fight against rebellion" within the Holy Roman Empire, and that the effectiveness of the instrument is demonstrated by the long period of peace after the Peasant War of 1525.[6] He considers the question of whether the centralised modern state was the cause or consequence of peasant revolt, correctly linking the strengthening concern to uphold public order and the growing severity of the criminal law to the emerging early modern state.[7]

Ylikangas has interpreted the background to the 1442 Swedish Law of the Realm by King Christopher of Bavaria from this point of view. He sees it as "direct evidence" of the view that the peasant revolts contributed to the birth of the centralized state.[8] According to Ylikangas, the law of 1442 was mainly a consequence of the Swedish Engelbrekt uprising of 1434–1438 and its aftermath. He has further suggested that Engelbrekt uprising directly inspired the Swedish nobility and king to retaliate by introducing certain new categories of crime: "the law [of 1442] created two new kinds of criminal, namely the robber and the pirate."[9] To cite Ylikangas further, "[t]his law criminalised a number of actions which had clear connections with revolt and also increased punishments for crimes related to it."[10]

Kimmo Katajala has accepted Ylikangas's claim that the criminalisation of robbers and pirates in the Law of the Realm of 1442 was a novelty.[11] Yet in a later article –"Swedish Treason Legislation and Peasant Unrest from the High Middle Ages to the Era of Enlightenment (1300–1800)" – he has adopted a somewhat more critical stance regarding the link between the paragraph in question and Engelbrekt uprising.[12] In fact, in this article Katajala has developed Blickle's and Ylikangas's thoughts further in seeking "to discover if there is a connection between the legislative change which occurred and social unrest."[13] After his analysis he concludes that "[b]y and large the evidence seems to support the impression that peasant uprising and political turbulence did indeed result in fundamental alterations and amendments to the law". This process, as far as peasant uprisings were concerned, began with the law of 1442. However, he modifies his view by suggesting a three-fold legislative policy as far as treason was concerned: firstly, there was the medieval "traditional pattern", secondly "*ad hoc* solutions" and thirdly the reinterpretation of *ad hoc* statutes. Katajala distinguishes two major long-term Swedish trends: a progressive stiffening of punishments for "political offences" until the very end of the eighteenth century, and the progressive extension of the area of treason legislation culminating in the law of 1734.[14]

The questions I set out to answer in this chapter revolve largely around these issues. If one were to generalize and talk in terms of a theory that peasant revolts generated treason legislation, would such a theory be plausible in the case of Swedish legal history? When did the bulk of treason legislation appear in Sweden and why? Did the law of 1442 contain new crimes of treason? Against whom was the Swedish treason legislation aimed? Did the punishments for treason grow more severe with time? What was the relationship between the emerging early modern state and treason law? But before moving on to address these questions, some general comments are called for on the crime of treason itself.

The crime of treason

Treason is a vague and indistinct crime which has strong links to control policy, state trials and military discipline. Reasons of state have played an important part in the administration of justice in treason trials. In addition, the content of the crime has fluctuated along with the temporal changes in the concept of treason. As the crime our present legislation calls treason covers only a small part of the mass of treason legislation in medieval and early modern Europe, it would not do to approach the subject with the present-day concept in mind. This would be misleading and produce unhistorical or anachronistic results.[15]

However, I shall make no attempt here to draw a clear-cut distinction between the words 'treason', 'sedition', 'high treason' or even 'lese-majesty'. There are several reasons for this. Firstly, only a fraction of the cases where treason is criminalised in our medieval laws are expressly framed as such. Secondly, in the case of the last two it would seem somewhat unhistorical, as contemporaries made no clear distinctions between the various crimes. The king was closely assimilated with the realm and the Crown. As the Swedish lawyer David Nehrman (1695–1769) explained: "I talk here and elsewhere of the King and Realm together as inseparable because the goods, rights and interests of the king and realm should never be distinguished... and the king uses his power in order to ensure the public good of the realm... so that all offences against the king touch and harm the realm and all machinations and crimes against the realm result in damage and harm to the king."[16]

The English legal historians Pollock and Maitland have called treason "a crime which has a vague circumference and more than one centre".[17] Scholars have traditionally distinguished two such centres: on the one hand, there is the Germanic tradition emphasizing the meaning of the mutual duties in contractual or quasi-contractual relationships. A traitor was a betrayer who broke his oath and fealty.[18] The Roman tradition, strongly influenced by the oriental notions of divine kingship, gave much weight to the notion of majesty, and its influence can be seen even in twelfth and thirteenth-century England.[19] A sovereign, whose word was law, could demand absolute obedience from his subjects.[20]

In any case, at least three centres, in the Pollockian-Maitlandian sense of the word, can be distinguished in medieval and early modern treason legislation. The first of these, the oldest and probably the most original, deals with crimes committed against the community as such. This group includes military crimes, such as cowardice in battle, desertion, espionage, delivering secrets to the enemy and more generally aiding the enemy or invader. The second group consists of crimes against one's lord. These crimes were strongly influenced earlier by Germanic, later by feudal notions of bilateral contractual relations, mutual duties and oaths of fidelity. A breach of such duties, treachery or murdering one's lord were the extreme examples of this infidelity. The third centre, strongly influenced by Roman law, contained crimes and offences against the king or sovereign. Such crimes were usually called lese-majesty (from the Roman *crimen laesae maiestatis*) and could comprise anything from regicide or rebellion to counterfeiting money or embezzling royal revenues. In fact, all acts that could be construed to lessen royal authority, majesty or prerogatives were offences against the royal person and consequently treasonous.[21]

The crimes falling under the concept of treason might seem rather an odd, sporadic assortment of criminal acts. However, there is a clear logic behind this *mélange* based on the three-fold centres of treasonous crimes, even if these centres tended to get blurred with time. The group of lese-majesty crimes, in particular, was very broad and expanding at the expense of the others.

Peace legislation comes very close to this area of crime. As Floyd Seward Lear has observed, while the breaches of such 'peaces' cannot be unequivocally labelled as treason, "yet they occupy a peculiar intermediate position between purely private offences against individuals and treasonable attacks against public authority or a body politic."[22] After all, breaking a special peace law guaranteed by the king was certainly not very far removed from lese-majesty. Yet, for reasons of space, I have largely omitted peace legislation insofar as it was not used in practice for punishing peasant revolt. Peace legislation appears in the Swedish laws in the late thirteenth century, at the same time as the first steps to criminalise treason, and the aim was to limit the use of violence and promote peace. This also succeeded in extending the king's judicial powers in a significant way. I have for the most part omitted general references to the history of crime, although we may note in passing that the medieval Scandinavian laws referred to some serious crimes, including some types of treason, as 'nidingsverk' (*niþingsvärk*), infamous and unatonable crimes.[23]

However, these did not aim as strongly as the criminalisation of treason at the protection of the community and the state, but rather labelled certain crimes as cowardly and despicable. We must attempt to draw a distinction between treason and ordinary crime. Although any crime could be understood to be an insult to the laws or the king, in whom justice was personified, treason was understood more narrowly. It broke special bonds of fidelity, jeopardized the security of society and defied the prerogatives or authority of the ruler. Peasant uprisings fall by their nature in the first and last of these categories but, depending on their scale, they could naturally threaten the peace and stability of society as well.

In order to approach the problem of the relationship, if any, between peasant uprisings and treason legislation, we must first discover when notions of treason first began to emerge in Swedish laws and documents. These roots can be found in the Middle Ages, and more precisely in the provincial laws, which are the oldest Swedish medieval laws, and royal statutes from the late thirteenth century.

The emergence of treason legislation in Sweden: when, what and why?

The oldest and most resilient conception of treason in Sweden is the betrayal of the community to the enemy.[24] This is evident in the only paragraph on treason in the provincial law of Eastern Gothia. It was considered treacherous to help and assist the enemy to plunder, burn and kill in one's own country:

> "If there be a man who brings foreign troops against his country, bears a shield over the shore and through the wood, lays waste and burns in his own country, ties up and abducts people, if this can be proven by witnesses, then he has forfeited his lands and his life and also all that he owns within the country and province."[25]

The older provincial law of Western Gothia, preserved in a manuscript from the 1280s, also contains the same criminalisation, but in less detail.[26] In fact, later it was clearly considered treasonous to aid, assist, comfort or abet the enemies of the king or country in any way. As medieval documents show, even trade with such enemies was regarded as treasonous.[27] This was still the prevailing view in the eighteenth century. "When a war has begun," wrote David Nehrman, "all dealings, trade and correspondence with the enemy become forbidden as they can easily endanger the realm."[28]

However, the crimes linked to betrayal of king and lord emerged in the thirteenth century through feudal and Romano-canonical influences. In medieval Sweden we can talk with certainty of growing royal powers in the latter half of the thirteenth century at the latest. In the neighbouring kingdoms of Denmark and Norway, the notions of theocratic kingship, filtering in especially through canon law, can be observed earlier in the century in the *arenga*s of royal letters and literature such as the Norwegian King's Mirror (*Kongespeilet ca.* 1250~1257).[29] It is scarcely far-fetched to suppose that the doctrine of theocratic monarchy, perhaps tinged with notions of the king's majesty influenced by Roman law, was circulating in Sweden in the late thirteenth century.

This development, paralleled with growing royal powers in the fields of legislation and the judiciary, largely contributed to the appearance of a wider concept of treason. By the thirteenth century at the very latest Scandinavian monarchical rhetoric included mention of the king's majesty and offences against it. By this time Swedish royal letters concerning disputed property adjudicated by the king were starting to threaten with reprisals and royal displeasure anyone who disregarded the royal judgement. Occasionally such an offence was referred to as a matter touching the king's majesty.[30] Some scholars have interpreted the punishments for offending the king's majesty as a consequence of the royal peace legislation, based on the "ancient privilege of the king to punish with outlawry".[31] Others stress the increasing royal powers and their legal legitimation.[32] The increase in the rhetoric of theocratic monarchy and practice should be seen against the background of judicial development from the thirteenth century onwards.

The thirteenth-century rivalry between parties fighting for the Swedish throne was resolved in 1250, when the family of the influential Earl Birger (Birger *jarl*, d. 1266) captured the crown. As the policy of the defeated *Folkunga* party rested on elective monarchy, giving the people the right of resistance, and a national Church with bishops chosen by the people and installed by the elected king, we should not be surprised that the Church helped to suppress the later revolts of the *Folkunga* party.[33] Furthermore, the pope expressly exhorted the high clerics to remain loyal to the king and help him against rebels. An example of this is a letter of 1252 from Pope Innocent IV (r. 1243–1254) to the archbishop of Uppsala and the suffragan bishops enjoining them to help King Valdemar Birgersson (r. 1250–1275) and Earl Birger maintain justice and fight evildoers and rebellious forces.[34]

But the turbulence in the realm by no means came to an end after the execution of Holmger Knutsson of the *Folkunga* party by Earl Birger in 1248. The revolt of Holmger's brother Filip Knutsson and father-in-law Filip Petersson against Earl Birger ended in their execution in 1251. Filip Knutsson's sons Johan and Birger also rose against Magnus Birgersson Ladulås (r. 1270–1290) in 1280. The Roman law of majesty began to exert an influence around this time. In a document of 1282, revolt against the Swedish king was expressly stated to fall under the *Lex Julia Majestatis*. According to this document, the attempt of Holmger and Filip on the life of the king had caused the Crown to confiscate their and their spouses' property.[35] This seems to be the first time that Roman law was explicitly applied to a Swedish case, and it is made all the more interesting by the existence of domestic treason law as well. It should therefore be interpreted as a sign of knowledge of Roman law and of an ability to adopt and introduce foreign doctrines when this served the purposes of the rulers. At this stage the law of treason was used mainly against noble conspirators rather than peasants.

The kings were probably somewhat over-enthusiastic in their adaptation of this concept of treason influenced by Roman law: the confiscation of the culprits' property, in particular, was excessive.[36] It would seem that the Swedish nobility were later able to insist that only Swedish legislation could be applied to such crimes. The demands of the knightly class in 1308 concerning protection of the life and property of the aristocracy – that forfeiture of goods and life was possible only after due judgment – and the stress laid on Swedish law may have been a reaction against the Roman law provisions that had been used against the most important noble families in the late thirteenth century.[37] In addition, the Statute of Skenninge in 1284 forbade all secret conspiracies, especially those of noblemen, which again strengthens the case for arguing that the nobility rather than the peasantry were perceived as a threat to the Crown at this stage.[38]

Harald Hjärne supposes that a now lost statute concerning crimes of lese-majesty was issued around 1280, and that it was this statute that has influenced the treason paragraphs of the northern Swedish provincial laws (the *Svea* laws).[39] This seems quite plausible, especially as mid-thirteenth-century Denmark saw Roman law treason vocabulary used in the Latin lese-majesty statutes of Christopher I (1252~1259) and Erik Glipping (1276). In Norway, Roman law also influenced some criminalisations of treason.[40] There is no reason to suppose the Swedish king was unaware of the statutes issued in neighbouring Denmark or uninfluenced by these ideas. The provincial laws used the expression "bära avog skiöld" (to carry a turned shield) to signify revolt, aiding the king's enemies and making an attempt on the king's life:[41]

> "Everyone who turns his shield against the all-powerful king or against his realm, where he himself was born, shall forfeit his life if he is caught, and in addition will his lands and chattels come under the Crown no matter if he is caught or no."[42]

The laws applying throughout Sweden defined the same crime in greater detail but still rather loosely, leaving much room for extensive interpretation.

> "He who raises troops against the king or the lord of the realm, or makes an ambush in order to take him prisoner or kill him, or commits any violent acts or injustice by letter, counsel, acts or aid will lose his lands, chattels and life..."[43]

Any verbal insult against the king's majesty or the king's councillors was also criminalised in King Magnus Ericsson's mid-fourteenth century town law.

> "If anyone should slander the king or the king's Council, insulting their honour and reputation, and six men have witnessed this, he shall be put into the gaol of the town and lose his head."[44]

The paragraph was repeated in the 1437 Statute of Strängnäs, King Christopher's (r. 1441–1448) Law of the Realm in 1442[45] and later laws. Although the paragraph mentioned only slandering the King's majesty, any disrespectful or offensive act could also be interpreted as lese-majesty.

In a case from 1566 it was specifically stated that although no written law criminalised such an act, the matter was interpreted as slandering the king by analogy with the Court Articles and the law of 1442.[46] The only addition in the law of 1734 was the slandering of the queen or the heir to the throne: it could be libellous (in writing) slanderous (in speech) or take place with other outward acts.[47] But even this would have fitted into the mid-thirteenth century Danish law on lese-majesty, which also protected the *membra regis*, including the bishops, dukes, the queen, royal children and relatives.[48] But then, the Swedish concept of lese-majesty, at least that of written law, was probably narrower at this stage than the Danish.

That one could commit a treasonous crime against one's lord was a construction based on feudal law, and the doctrine considered killing or attacking one's lord, whom one was particularly bound to obey, an offence punishable by death. The intentional killing of the master or mistress, to whom particular obedience was due, had found its way into most of the Swedish provincial laws by the late thirteenth century, to be later repeated in the royal laws.[49]

> "If someone kills or betrays his master, whether rich or poor, and he is taken in the act, he will be condemned to the wheel and all his lands and goods will be divided into three parts... It may happen that a male or female servant, male or female slave kills or betrays the master or bailiff, their wives or children; then the man will be broken on the wheel and the woman stoned..."[50]

It is doubtful that this criminalisation was taken into the Swedish laws as an extension of the *ledung* or defence system, so that all free peasants who could possibly perform military service were protected from their servants and tenants as Hjärne has suggested.[51] It is more likely to be of Germanic origin, probably of the same tradition as the *hirð* ordinances, and later strengthened and developed further by Continental feudal influences.[52] The oldest Swedish mention of the paragraph is the laconic sentence in the older law of Western Gothia, which shows influence from Norwegian and Danish law: "If someone kills his master, it is an unatonable crime." This means that the paragraph existed at least in the 1280s.[53] In the late fifteenth century the killing of one's master was explicitly called treason (*forrädilsse*).[54]

What about treason under the law of arms and martial law, both of which had their roots in medieval customary law? The law of arms, and martial law in particular, offered the King a simplified procedure for dealing with traitors in cases of open rebellion: if the royal army was in the field with the royal banner unfurled, a state of war existed. Any resistance could be dealt with by martial law, or summarily by the law of arms. Acts like surrendering a castle, garrison or other strategic place to the enemy without proper resistance or for financial gain were undoubtedly treason.[55] Later in medieval and early modern Europe martial law and the law of arms became for kings a channel to extend their judicial powers.[56]

The Scandinavian kings began to issue statutes, or manorial law (*lex castrensis*; *gårdsrätt*), guaranteeing the peace and discipline in the royal household and among the troops stationed in the various royal castles.

These disciplinary statutes included severe punishments like execution for neglecting guard duties, considered to be a breach of the guard's duty "against the oath and loyal service he had promised and sworn to the king's majesty".[57] The emphasis on oaths and duties has a clear feudal ring which also appears in coronation oaths, officials' oaths and military oaths. These statutes had older Scandinavian roots in the norms regulating the king's entourage. The earliest known manorial laws, the Danish *vederlov* and Norwegian *hirð* ordinances, contain stipulations against traitors to the king. Especially the Latin versions of Danish manorial law display a good knowledge of the treason terminology in Roman law: *proditio, mortem machinari* and *crimine maiestatis*.[58] The first Swedish manorial law is thought to have been issued by King Magnus Ladulås before 1284.[59]

The Statute of Telge concerning knightly service, issued by Magnus Ericsson in 1345, dealt with the wartime duties of the royal troops: when it was time to confront the enemy, desertion from under the royal banner, the service of the king, his officials or his emissaries was punishable by death if the king was unwilling to show mercy. If the deserter managed to escape uncaught, he was outlawed, while a jury of twelve men was to decide the matter.[60] Carl Knutsson (r. 1448–1457, 1464–1465, 1467–1470) reissued this provision in 1448.[61] The punishment for desertion, especially in the heat of battle, did not change from the Middle Ages to the eighteenth century: it was always death. The paragraphs on mutiny in the Swedish fifteenth century manorial laws of Queen Margaret (r. 1389–1412) and Carl Knutsson were less severe than the Danish and Norwegian laws, which order that the culprit lose both life and property.[62]

However, a clear German influence is visible in the terminology of Swedish manorial law. Many words relating to administration and war were of German origin, as was the word for mutiny, *rothaskap* or *rotoskap*. This word also appeared in the German-influenced town law of Visby.[63] When Gustavus Vasa (r. 1523–1560) began to reshape the Swedish army in the 1520s, he relied increasingly on Swedish and foreign mercenaries, which brought further German influences into Swedish military law. His Articles of War were based on the oath of fidelity of the mercenary or soldier, and they contained stipulations on mutiny and breaking the duty to obey. However, as to mutiny or revolt, there was not much difference between medieval law and Gustavus Vasa's Naval Articles (1535) and Articles of War (1545), except that the crime was now unequivocally punishable by death.[64]

Then to the question of whether the Swedish peasant uprisings had an effect on the emergence of treason legislation. Although there were admittedly some smaller local uprisings or revolts in medieval Sweden, the major event was the revolt of 1434–1438 led by the minor nobleman Engelbrekt Engelbrektsson. Although it has been claimed that this uprising generated new legislation aimed against peasant revolts, the flaw in this theory is the fact that the supposedly new paragraph concerning the punishment of pirates and robbers did not appear for the first time in the law of 1442.[65] The criminalisation can actually be found in several much earlier laws, including royal statutes, Magnus Ericsson's Law of the Realm and most Swedish provincial laws.[66] The example below is from the provincial law of Uppland, confirmed in 1296:

> "Now a man is lurking in a forest or on a boat or elsewhere and gives himself to murdering and robbing; if he murders or robs and is caught in the act he will be taken to the assizes... If he who is accused of murder or robbery is found guilty, the murderer will be sentenced to [be broken on] the wheel, and the robber [will be put] under the sword."[67]

In other words, these acts were criminalised at least 150 years earlier, the earliest known criminalisation being that of pirates in the manuscript of the older law of Western Gothia from the 1280s.[68] Although the paragraph in the 1442 law gives the most thorough treatment of the crime, it was certainly no novelty. Not all researchers even consider the 1442 law a real, independent law, but rather a new edition of Magnus Ericsson's Law of the Realm, and the 'political' crimes therein had not changed their character since the law of 1348.[69] Furthermore, piracy was a constant, pestering nuisance which did much harm to maritime traffic and commerce in the Baltic Sea region, inspiring a number of international agreements as early as the fourteenth century.[70]

Although Engelbrekt uprising had some legal consequences and the political power of the nobility *vis-à-vis* the newly elected king, Christopher of Bavaria, was emphasised in the 1442 Law of the Realm,[71] there was no new treason legislation after the revolts of 1434–1438 because the surviving and imprisoned rebels could be dealt with under the existing laws. An example of this is the Finnish revolt of 1438, David's uprising, named after its leader. In the document containing the oaths of fidelity and obedience by the representatives of the rebellious regions, their uprising was labelled treason against their king, lords and the realm. The signatories acknowledged that they had forfeited their right to their lives, property and lands by their treason according to the Law of the Realm, and that if they revolted again the punishment would follow the law without mercy.[72]

Were the prohibitions on wearing certain weapons, which could be invoked to reduce the risk of violent revolt or riot, provoked by the peasant revolts? Especially the 1437 ban on the bearing of certain arms by the peasantry has been considered a consequence of peasant revolt, namely Engelbrekt uprising. Peasants were forbidden to wear certain kinds of weapons, swords, armour or crossbows in church, at assizes, markets or towns and such places where people assembled.[73] This statute represented a conscious effort on the part of the leading noblemen to pacify the country and reduce the political power of the peasantry after they had achieved their political aims as a consequence of Engelbrekt's revolt.[74] But once again a quasi-causal relationship between the uprising and subsequent legislation cannot be shown, as the statute had several predecessors unlinked to peasant revolt. Feuds, blood vengeance and private war had been discouraged and restricted for centuries, not only in Scandinavia but also elsewhere in Europe. Bans on bearing certain arms were a means to secure peace and control peasants as well as nobles.[75]

The newer provincial law of Western Gothia forbade all peasants to carry swords on penalty of a fine, soldiers or those in danger excepted, while the 1335 statute forbade people from riding around the country fully armed unless they had committed yet uncompensated homicides which they wished to atone with a fine.[76] In 1347, Magnus Ericsson forbade the common people of the copper-mining area from carrying weapons other than knives for eating. The mining masters were allowed weapons such as swords and shields, but they were allowed to be fully armed only under certain conditions and only in the event of an uprising. A breach of the statute was punishable with a fine of three or forty marks.[77] In some versions of the 1414 Statute of Skara all except noblemen and their servants were forbidden from carrying crossbows into the towns.[78] These statutes were largely aimed at the peasantry, but some provincial laws were not as discriminating. They included bans on wearing certain weapons at assizes or when the king was touring the province unless royal permission had been granted.[79] In some laws, manslaughter by "murderous weapons" was considered a more serious crime, and the subsequent fine was therefore higher.[80]

In 1441, all people, and especially peasants, tenants and their servants, were forbidden to carry swords or weapons in church, town or in the king's presence, the only exception being members of the king's Council and royal officials. Offenders were to pay a fine of forty marks.[81] In 1442, a peace ordinance covering the whole of Scandinavia took the matter still further. Nobody was allowed to ride around with certain weapons for fear of someone getting hurt. The nobility were totally prohibited from bearing arms, with the exception of a dagger, in church, town, or where the king was residing. Peasants were forbidden to wear weapons at weddings or assizes, at guild meetings or in church. Offenders were to be punished with excommunication, but if this was to no avail the secular arm was to act in the matter[82] As we can see, the statute of 1437 can be rightly interpreted as a reaction by the nobility to Engelbrekt uprising, but it can with equally good reason be seen as an instance in a longer-term development of control and state monopoly on violence.

Thus, the conclusion to be drawn from the development presented above is that the Crown did not have any problems in dealing with violent forms of treason, as these were well covered by the medieval core of treason law. The dilemma facing the authorities, therefore was not how to handle overt and armed opposition to the ruler, whether from noble or peasant; the existing treason legislation provided the Crown with adequate tools to deal with open rebellion, homicide and pillaging. It was the less demonstrative and more peaceful protests that needed effective remedies. However, as the existing law provided none, what were the methods employed in suppressing such threats to the establishment?

How to deal with non-violent protest?

As noted above, the Swedish medieval peasant uprisings had no direct impact on treason legislation: the criminalisation of treason against the king and realm had occurred well before Sweden experienced its first 'peasant' uprising. In the sixteenth century there was still some understanding towards peasant uprisings and a tendency to clemency, provided that peasant protest did not result in homicide or was not interpreted as explicitly defying the king's authority and majesty.

In 1574, in the village of Marttila in southwest Finland, 260 peasants attacked the house of the local sheriff (S. *länsman*), robbing and battering some cavalrymen who had unlawfully collected hay from them, and butchering their horses. Although the court ordered that the the hay be returned to the peasants, every tenth peasant had to pay a fine of 26 marks and 8 öres. A similar incident where no lives were lost took place in Somero and Kiikala, the punishment also being much the same as in Marttila. However, in Uusikirkko in 1579 a similar but considerably smaller-scale event resulted in eight peasants having to pay a fine of 40 marks – presumably for assaulting and attacking cavalrymen. This time the verdict emphasized that the guilty peasants should really have been beheaded. In 1586–1587, the 126 recalcitrant peasants of Paimio were to pay the substantial collective fine of 300 dalers as punishment for their refusal to assist in the upkeep of cavalrymen. In 1590, at assizes held in Kyrö by the governor Axel Leijonhufvud, three peasants were sentenced to lose their lives for revolt, but the king later pardoned them. Finally, in a revolt in Kyrö and Lapua in 1594, again concerning the upkeep of the cavalry, the leaders were fined and one of them imprisoned in the castle of Oulu for a time.[83] Nevertheless, where homicides were committed, as seems to have been the case in Tavastia in 1592–1593, executions of the leaders of the uprising followed.[84]

The decapitations of the peasant Maunu Nyrhi and the juror (S. *nämndeman*) Ingi Multiainen for treason in 1553 were based on somewhat different grounds. By the time the king's representatives arrived at Lappee, disagreement concerning taxation had been going on for two years and the royal assizes were convened to investigate and settle the issue. Nyrhi, who had threatened people not to pay up, was seen as the main instigator of the tax strike and denounced to the court as a rebellious traitor (*wproriske forrædare*). When Multiainen defied the king's decision in the matter of the taxes in open court, he, too, was tried for treason – probably for blatant treason, possibly even verging on lese-majesty. Both Nyrhi and Multiainen were executed, and overt opposition ceased after these two warning examples had been made (see chapter VII).[85]

No new treason legislation concerning revolt was enacted immediately after either the Swedish peasant war of 1542–1543, named after its leader Nils Dacke, or the Finnish Club War 1596–1597. This discovery should not surprise us as both were so violent and extreme that they could easily be dealt with under the existing treason laws. The executions and punishments of the leaders and participants in the Club War were based either upon treason or peace legislation.[86] The same applies to the punishments of those north Karelian 'food rioters' of 1696–1697 who were guilty of house-breaking and subsequent robbery. The court had no difficulty in sentencing them to death under the peace legislation.[87]

The Swedish Crown, whether in the Middle Ages or in the early eighteenth century, crushed violent revolts and uprisings with the help of peace legislation and criminalisations of serious crime. Non-violent forms of treason, however, were another matter – especially when there was a change in the political culture making popular protests less bloody affairs.[88] It has been pointed out that there were hardly any proper peasant uprisings at all in the seventeenth century.[89] The explanations for this vary, but it posed a much more serious dilemma to the authorities: the lack of a legal arsenal against non-violent protest became a nuisance when peasant resistance increasingly took on more peaceful forms. As Katajala has also pointed out in his article, it was a greater challenge to suppress and punish non-violent resistance like day-labourers' strikes, tax strikes or blatant recalcitrance.[90]

The unobtrusive addition of the town law paragraph concerning revolts against the royal bailiff, mayor or aldermen into some versions of the law of 1442 was a way of partly solving the problem.[91] By the fourteenth century, learned jurisprudence considered that lese-majesty could be committed against any sovereign, independent community or king, although in classical Roman law the crime could only be against the emperor or the Roman people (*respublica Romana*).[92] According to post-glossators, lese-majesty, inciting people to disorder, changing the form of government by armed force or forging money, could be committed against the people of a sovereign city-state without a ruler. Traces of this thought of internal attacks against a town can be seen in Italian, German and Swedish town law.[93]

Popular gatherings or assemblies were places for venting one's grievances, but they could quickly develop into something more serious – a riot or a revolt. This threat was perceived by the authorities, and the first step in their suppression in medieval Sweden was the statute of King Eric Magnusson in 1357, given for the town of Stockholm together with the king's Council. It stipulated that, if anyone revolted (literally, gathered together and assembled) against the royal bailiff, mayor or aldermen, the punishment was death, accompanied by royal confiscation of the culprit's chattels. The penalty, contrary to peace legislation, was expressly said to be death even if there was no killing, violence or breaking and entering. All participants were to be punished, and those who sheltered them would incur "the wrath and vengeance of the king".[94]

The forerunner of the town law, the Biärköa law, did not contain any stipulations concerning treason, while the later, German-inspired town law of Visby considered even unarmed revolt (*myterij* or *rotenskap*) against the town council a crime punishable with death. Such traitors, like murderers, were to be executed.[95] There is no suggestion that this paragraph was a consequence of popular revolt, nor is there any reason for supposing so. Yet, as there are some town law versions, such as the law book of Söderköping of 1387, in which the paragraph from 1357 is not found, the stipulation cannot have been part of the original town law.[96] When new copies of law books were made, this paragraph was incorporated into the Town Law of King Magnus Ericsson.[97] The text can be found in some surviving manuscripts of King Christopher's Law of the Realm, with some adaptations making it more suited for circumstances in the countryside. Namely, while the original text spoke of the mayor and aldermen in addition to the bailiff, in the 1442 law it was altered to the bailiff, the judge (*häradzhöffdinge*) and the twelve jurors (*the XII men – i nempdenne*). Still this paragraph is not part and parcel of the original version of the 1442 law.[98]

By the late seventeenth century the pressure to modernize the medieval laws had become stronger. A law commission had been active since 1686, but quick relief was not available as its work took almost fifty years to complete – the new General Law was finally completed in 1734. Judges had to show skill and subtlety in order to find a suitable paragraph to condemn and punish protesters. As the Crown could hardly release persons regarded as inciters to revolt or resistance but the existing legislation did not give the judges much help, the recourse to analogy was necessary.

In at least a few cases, broad interpretations of treason norms were used in order to secure a conviction. The 1694 process against Johann Reinhold Patkul and several other leading members of the Livonian noble opposition to royal autocracy was clearly political, part of an ongoing campaign to crush the relatively autonomous status of the Livonian nobility. Despite the fact that a conviction was clearly called for in order to make an example, allegedly treasonous acts presented a problem from the point of view of both procedural law, mainly the existing requirements of proof, and treason law. The majority of the members of the temporary commission established in order to investigate and judge the affair were of the opinion that an inciter or abettor to sedition was equally guilty of lese-majesty even if the desired result, namely sedition against Sweden, had not taken place. A minority of the commission took a more restricted view on treason. The majority considered chapter 9 of the Law of the King (*Kungabalken*), on slandering the king or his councillors, chapter 8 of the Law of the Heinous Crime (*Högmålsbalken*) in the Law of the Realm of 1442, and chapter 7 of the Law of the Heinous Crime (*Högmålsbalken*) in the Town Law, levying troops etc. against the king, to be applicable.[99]

Another case where the judge resorted to creative interpretation was in connection with the north Karelian 'food riots' of 1697. Once again the problem was how to punish the non-violent protesters who had organized and delivered the peasants' complaints to the king and were therefore seen as the instigators of the trouble, but who were not guilty of breach of the peace of the home or robbery. Here the paragraph of the Statute of Örebro of 1617 concerning those spreading rumours within the country was invoked to justify the death penalty regardless of the fact that the statute had originally been issued against the Polish king, Sigismund, who had lost the Swedish throne, and his mostly noble allies.[100] The decision of the Diet of Stockholm in 1604 that a bailiff who unlawfully collected taxes from the people would be punished as a traitor was also extended in the 1697 'food riots' to those representatives of the peasantry who had collected money for their travel expenses to Stockholm.[101]

Here we can once more see signs of the adaptability of treason legislation, though it was atypical of Swedish lower courts to show such initiative in interpreting the law, as this was normally the role of the higher courts. Writing of the English sixteenth-century development in treason law, John Bellamy has said: "[i]t is obvious that, when there was some doubt about the scope of the law, the professional judges were pressured to interpret in the manner most beneficial to the prince, and usually their conferences ended with their doing just that."[102] A strong case could be made of a similar approach in late seventeenth-century Sweden.

The law code of 1734 described treasonous acts more thoroughly than the 1442 law, but, even though it did take into consideration the statutory developments in the sixteenth and seventeenth centuries, mostly concerning the non-violent forms of treason, it still built largely on the medieval tradition of treason. The treasonous acts were included in three chapters: treason (*förräderi*), slander and libel of the king, the queen, the heir to the throne or the king's councillors, and mutiny or revolt.[103] In 1756, when David Nehrman defined uprising and mutiny, which he thought of as one and the same, he talked of "common men's conspiring to disobedience towards the king, or those who rule and give orders on the king's behalf". If this conspiring took place with intent to act against the king, the royal house, the safety of the realm or the freedom of its inhabitants, the crime was treason. If not, it was an uprising or mutiny. People who had either legally or illegally called an assembly were guilty of the crime if they in their "wickedness" (*af arghet*, i.e. intentionally) conspired to oppose the orders of the king or his representatives by word, writing or deeds. In addition, the offence included acting in a manner likely to cause a breach of the peace, endangering the security of life or property and causing harm to the realm. However, Nehrman expressly excluded from the crime of uprising a conspiracy with intent to commit a violent deed, crimes or robbery.[104] The instigators of mutiny were to be punished by death, as was every tenth man of the remainder, to be selected by the drawing of lots, while the rest were to be flogged with forty pairs of lashes or imprisoned for a month on bread and water.[105]

Although the treason paragraphs of the 1734 law were a compact compilation of earlier statutory developments which was surely meant to cover all non-military treason, they did not prove to be sufficient to cope with peasant assemblies. Thus new statutes were issued in lieu of expanding the interpretation of the existing paragraphs. In 1743 a dramatic statute forbidding the calling of a peasant assembly was issued after the Dalecarlia uprising, during which peasant protesters from Dalecarlia marched on Stockholm. Once again the government had no problems in sentencing the leaders for treason, but it seems to have wanted a deterrent so as to quash trouble before it arose. Anyone trying to call a peasant meeting, whether orally, by the traditional 'message stick' (*budkavel*) – which had also been used several times during the revolt in Dalecarlia – or by letter, was to suffer the draconian punishment meted out for treason: his right hand was to be cut off, he was to be broken on the wheel and decapitated. If a royal servant called an assembly for unlawful business, he was to be similarly punished.[106]

The message stick was a very old custom in Scandinavia, mention of which can be found in sources as early as the twelfth century. It was a means of communication: for calling a peasant assembly to discuss important business, for defending the country, and even for protest or uprising. However, procedural law spoke of it as a means for assembling persons on the business of the law, and in the village ordinance (*byordning*) of 1742 it was the prescribed way for calling a village assembly.[107] The statute of 1743 against use of the message stick would have made it impossible to call a village assembly, as the inhabitants of some villages pointed out. According to the new statute, people attending an unlawful assembly were to be punished as rebels. A person who merely helped to pass on a message stick or command to assemble was to be punished by 40 'pairs' of lashes, three strokes to the 'pair'. People were obliged to report immediately to the authorities in the event of an attempt at unlawful assembly, and for this they could be rewarded with 100 dalers.[108] Nevertheless, this ordinance seems not to have been applied in all its severity in Halland in 1775, while in Scania the punishments in the first instance were much less lenient.[109]

It should be noted that in medieval Denmark this question had been handled by interpreting as treason such cases in which the message stick had been passed or burning torches (*vidje og brand*) sent out in order to start an uprising. Documents talk expressly of "passing the message stick or sending flaming torches against the king" or "carrying the message stick against a royal official in defiance of the king".[110] Thus, carrying the stick was considered a treasonous act in itself. In the aftermath of an unsuccessful revolt the Danish peasants had been made to promise the king they would never again organize an assembly without his knowledge.[111] Furthermore, there is a Swedish case from 1486 where several men had resisted the government's tax policy for three years, instigated others to withhold their taxes "against the will of the Council", sent out message sticks (*skooret budkaffle medh brandh och snara*) to assemble the people, conspired against the Council and refused to obey its letters. The leaders of the tax revolt were condemned to death under paragraph seven of the Law of Heinous Crime (*högmæles balken*), which points to the fact that the rebels were condemned according to the mid-fourteenth-century Magnus Ericsson's Law of the Realm. The usual forfeiture of property followed in due course.[112]

The largest peasant protest, the Dalecarlia uprising in 1743, was dealt with harshly. Although the masses were pardoned by the king, six of the leaders were executed while over forty others were punished with various combinations of imprisonment on bread and water, flogging and hard labour in royal fortresses.[113] Still, in judging whether the reaction of the state was or was not disproportionate, we should bear in mind the fact that this uprising was much larger in scale and not only threatened the peace but also the political system in a different way than mere local manorial trouble. The march of thousands of peasants into the heart of the capital, Stockholm, despite several attempts to keep them outside and make them disperse, was a traumatic experience for the rulers. It explains the fright when Sven Hofman, accompanied by five hundred men, tried to repeat the march to Stockholm two decades later. The sentences were almost as harsh as in the Dalecarlia uprising: the Council, the highest instance to judge the case, confirmed three death sentences, while thirty-nine were commuted to terms of imprisonment.[114] The uprising of the Skaraborg region in 1710 had resulted in similar punishments: fines and lashes for the rioters, except for the instigators and participants in homicides, who were sentenced to the wheel.[115]

In comparison with the Middle Ages, the Crown's tolerance of uprising and riot had grown very strained. After the pacification of peasant revolt, the repressive policy of the authorities and the harsh punishments imposed on peaceful protesters seem rather like hysterical overreaction. Could it perhaps be that the early modern state was the cause of this change? This might be a suitable moment to take a closer look at Swedish early modern treason legislation.

Treason legislation and the state-building process in early modern Sweden

Although early modern kings issued many statutes and ordinances on treason, most of these did not deal in any way with peasant uprisings. What they did was largely to supplement existing statutes and make them more precise. Olaus Magnus (1490–1557), the pre-Reformation archbishop of Uppsala, supplied his readers with a very conventional definition of treason in his book *Historia de gentibus septentrionalibus* ('History of the northern people'), published in 1555. According to his description, all were traitors who deliberately sought to kill their lords or take over their castles at night. The concept of traitor also applied to anyone who tried to inveigle a neighbouring people into attacking his own country or who led foreign princes into the country. Also traitors were those who entreated help from their king's enemies, while constantly slandering and accusing him of all possible crimes, and also those who tried to make themselves king.[116] Olaus Magnus' traitors were noblemen, royal officials or officers, and other evidence points to the threat perceived as coming from the same direction. In the 1560s, the re-established counts and barons had to pledge themselves not to call an assembly of the peasants on their own estates or in their counties or baronies.[117]

The influence of Roman law, whose impact on Swedish treason legislation came via Germany, was growing again from the mid-sixteenth century on. This development, mainly in respect of the concept of lese-majesty, was much to the advantage of the Vasa dynasty, which was busily expanding the royal powers.[118] In 1567, Eric XIV (r. 1560–1568) had a man accused of sending falsified letters in the king's name "by which the king's majesty's title is usurped and a great falsehood taken place", a typical lese-majesty crime.[119] The decision of the Diet of Stockholm in 1604 that a bailiff who unlawfully collected taxes from the people would be punished as a traitor was a lese-majesty construction.[120] Moreover, the influence of Roman law and learned jurisprudence in, for example, the seventeenth century helped to assimilate coining offences with lese-majesty.[121]

The early seventeenth-century Swedish notion of lese-majesty seems to have been even wider, judging by its definition in the 1621 Articles of War. Not only did lese-majesty include attempts on the king's life or attacks on his honour, or similar offences against the life or honour of his heir or certain of his officials, but also conspiracy, correspondence or communications with the enemy, planning to cede a fortress, military camp, troops or vessels into enemy hands or levying war against the king or the realm (*förer afwogan Sköld*).[122] Furthermore, in 1689 the Estates (section 1) had decided that infidelity towards the king or mere ill will towards the realm constituted lese-majesty.[123] Thus, in Sweden, as on the Continent, the categories of lese-majesty crime were in fact clearly on the increase.

Broadening the concept of treason and ruthless executions of traitorous foes were a means to an end for these kings. It has been suggested that powerful sixteenth-century kings like Christian II of Denmark (r. 1520–1523), Gustavus Vasa, Eric XIV and Charles IX (r. 1599–1611) were not loath to permanently rid themselves of their political opponents.[124] Indeed they were not, and there is quite an impressive number of cases to suggest that treason trials were used for such purposes. Examples include Gustavus Vasa's ruthless suppression of the revolt in Western Gothia in 1529, the Swedish 'Gunpowder Plot' of 1536, the Dacke War of 1542–1543 and the Lappee peasant troubles of 1551–1553. Gustavus accused his former favourites Olaus Petri and Laurentius Andreae of treason by concealing knowledge of the conspiracy of 1536.[125]

Eric XIV's lese-majesty trials were notorious and eventually contributed to his downfall. Between 1562 and 1567 his High Council handed down 50 death sentences for treason or war-related crimes, and in 1563 he had the Estates declare that his brother, the future John III (r. 1568–1592), had committed high treason.[126] After his coup d'état and accession, John had to deal with attempts to release his captive brother Erik and restore him to the throne, and these, too, resulted in treason trials and executions.[127]

Charles IX was merciless in dealing with the pro-Sigismund opposition to his accession to the throne. His nephew, the deposed King Sigismund (r. 1592–1599), having brought foreign troops into the country, was considered to have forfeited the crown through his treason. These foreign troops were Polish, as Sigismund was King of Poland through his mother, Catharina Jagellonica, and thus the noble opposition had conspired to have foreign troops enter their native land. The noblemen lost their heads and property, while the traitors of lower status were fined a third of their lands or property and forfeited their offices or enfeoffments.[128]

Besides all this, the early modern kings were very fussy about their powers and easily interpreted independent action, even if sanctioned by tradition, as an offence against these powers. Local border peace agreements are a good example of this. It had been customary in the Middle Ages for the representatives of the inhabitants of border regions to negotiate peace with each other across the frontier in order to minimize the ravages of war and ensure trading opportunities. This happened in Sweden on the southern border with Denmark and the eastern border with Russia as late as the seventeenth century, while in England it was customary on the northern border with Scotland. However, by the sixteenth century the practice was beginning to be considered treasonous in both countries: in 1564, Eric XIV of Sweden fumed against "a treasonous peasants' peace", while Henry VIII of England (r. 1509–1546) prosecuted for treason many of his officials and ambassadors who had negotiated a local peace treaty with the enemy without royal permission or were suspected of treasonous contacts with the enemy.[129]

When treason legislation was found to be insufficient, existing legislation could be reinterpreted to suit new needs, or new statutes could be issued. The latter solution was usually chosen, because royal law was the most important source of justice in Sweden and the role of jurisprudence was much smaller than in most Continental countries.[130] Neither did precedents have the status they held in England. Despite the hegemony of written law, the severe punishments for crime prescribed in the law were often disregarded until the late sixteenth and early seventeenth centuries. Local courts used discretion in the punishments they meted out within the community. As a more stratified society emerged, especially in sixteenth-century and seventeenth-century Sweden, and as successive kings brought the justice system under royal control, this discretion came to an end. Punishments became more severe as the local courts followed the law to the letter, the power of discretion being transferred to the Courts of Appeal, the first of which was established in Stockholm in 1614.[131]

Thus the strengthening position of Swedish kings gave a prominent role to royal legislation. The Courts of Appeal were under instructions to refer to the monarch all matters for which there was no written law or there was doubt over the meaning of the law.[132] Furthermore, the tightening grip of the state on the Swedish justice system, especially in the seventeenth century, encouraged the development of a professional judiciary. There were few university-educated lawyers in the royal service before the seventeenth century, and the legal profession as such began to emerge only at this time.[133] The good king was the personification of justice, and royal justice, especially in criminal cases, was a privilege for all of his subjects. If an official or nobleman tried to prevent a criminal case from appearing in court, Charles IX stipulated that he should be punished as a traitor.[134]

To some extent, however, the need for more control, especially of tumultuous or riotous behaviour, was met through statutes and ordinances such as were issued all around early modern Europe. Starting in the late fifteenth and early sixteenth centuries, public order and control became more and more important issues. This trend is also discernible in Sweden, where the numbers of police ordinances increased, especially after the middle of the seventeenth-century.[135] For example, the Swedish Penal Ordinance of 1563 mentions the king's desire with the help of God to further his loyal subjects' wellbeing and best interests. In addition, he wanted to uphold good policy (*politie*) and government to the glory of God and the wellbeing of the common man throughout the realm.[136]

This was language typical of police ordinances (*ius politiae; Polizeygesetzgebung*), which dealt with an extremely wide range of matters from promotion of commerce to regulation of the common good. Even so, public order and discipline were definitely not neglected, as witnessed by the inclusion in the ordinances of measures to criminalise treason. The same can be seen in English sixteenth-century statutes.[137] The penal ordinance of 1611 by Charles XI made slandering the authorities punishable by branding on the forehead and the cutting off of both ears, while a decision of the Diet of Stockholm in 1612 forbade on pain of the highest penalty the spreading of any rumours that could harm the country.[138] Nevertheless, it should be noted that in judicial practice the spreading of treasonous rumours was already being punished fifty years earlier, in 1563.[139]

In 1617, the Statute of Örebro made treasonous all communication, correspondence and relations with the vanquished Sigismund, his family or his allies. Similarly punishable were Polish spies and those who aided them plus those who conspired orally or in writing against the king or the realm. Spreading idle gossip and rumour around the country (section 7) was also punishable by death.[140] It was probably the precarious state of the succession to the throne after the death of Gustavus II Adolf (r. 1611–1632) that provoked the Diet, assembled in Stockholm in 1633 and 1634, to once again address the Polish question.[141]

The categories of treason criminalised in the disciplinary Court Articles of the sixteenth and seventeenth centuries were more numerous than in their precursors, the medieval manorial laws. The new articles concerned mainly lese-majesty and military treason: offending the honour of the king, his Council or his closest servants, taking part by word, deed or counsel in secret conspiracies or illicit assemblies against the king, knowledge of such machinations, contacts with the king's enemies or divulging of the king's secrets.[142] The Court Articles of 1655 (sections 5–8) merely extended the criminalisation of overt or secret conspiracies to cover all action against the queen and the king's heir.[143] The Court Articles of 1687 mainly repeated the earlier criminalisations and referred in a rather general way to treason under regular Swedish law.[144] As we can see, these 'new' paragraphs in manorial law were mostly included in the concept of treason expressed in ordinary legislation and scarcely merit being described as very innovative or extensive.

Compared to their medieval and sixteenth century predecessors, the royal Articles of War of 1621 (sections 127, 133) and 1683 (sections 71–84) and the royal Naval Articles of 1685 (sections 227–234) seem to originate in quite another, more efficient and professional era of warfare. These statutes were much influenced by continental, mainly German and Dutch, military law.[145] The Articles of War and Naval Articles gave a more thorough treatment of treason than their precursors. They labelled many different kinds of activity as treasonous: communicating or conspiring with the enemy in various ways, giving the enemy secret information, ceding a ship or fortress to the enemy, mutiny, illicit assembly, and slanderous talk about the admiral or field marshal.[146]

The Naval Articles and Articles of War of 1755 primarily repeated the treason criminalisations of these earlier military codes, with only minor additions.[147] Looking only at the norms, a revolution would seem to have taken place in the treason paragraphs in military law. In actual fact, the change was more superficial than it may at first glance appear. Mutiny or illicit assembly had been criminalised in medieval and sixteenth-century versions of the law. Slandering the king or his councillors had been criminalised in the Town Law of 1350, and the commander-in-chief of the army could be compared to a royal councillor. As to communicating or conspiring with the enemy, adhering to the enemy, leaking confidential information, or even surrendering a castle, fortress or vessel to the enemy except under extreme necessity, these were all included in the medieval concept of treason. Not only did they constitute lese-majesty, but they were also treacherous actions in medieval customary military and feudal law. They were probably followed as customary law in medieval (and early modern) Sweden.[148] They fitted into the ample treason paragraph (the Law of Heinous Crime, section 8) of the 1442 law, and they were written down in the Swedish Naval Articles and Articles of War after the arrival of continental military law in the seventeenth century. Although new paragraphs in the text of the law, they were not, as such, novelties.

The strict punishments for the killing of one's master were upheld. In 1699, King Charles XII (r. 1697–1718) wrote a letter to all Swedish Courts of Appeal in which he gave instructions on how to deal with murder or attempted murder, assault and battery or slander committed by a servant or tenant towards his master, mistress or their representative. The punishment for murder, based on medieval legislation, was always death. Even less serious misdeeds like threatening one's master or mistress were to be punished by imprisonment, while slander could only be atoned for with fines four times higher than were normally given for the offence – though the fines were only three times higher if it was just the master's representative who had been slandered.[149] A proclamation of 1776 punished more severely, with flogging and over a year of hard labour at a royal fortress, any attempt by a tenant or servant to kill, assault or physically harm his master. Moreover, while serving his sentence in the fortress the culprit was to be flogged on each anniversary of the attack on his master.[150] Anners has assumed that this sort of punishment, aiming at an extended deterrent effect, was adopted from Denmark.[151]

In 1774, the question of freedom of the press provoked a new criminalisation concerning treasonous printed matter. The king tightened the law regulating freedom of the press so that anyone writing or printing anything critical of the fundamental laws, constitution, acts of succession, sovereign pledge, or the majesty, highness and justice of the king or realm would be considered the enemy of the king and the realm, and consequently guilty of treason. Naturally, nearly all kinds of written or printed criticism of the royal person or policy would then fall under treason law. Even so, this was mostly only a more precise version of section

V:1–2 of the 1734 law, and in practice the punishments for dissenting pamphleteers were not that severe.[152]

The mostly non-violent and local peasant troubles in Scania, Halland and Finland in the 1770s fell under the treason legislation: even if none of the peasants were executed, the repression cannot be described as entirely lenient.[153] The concern for public order explains the punishments of the leaders of the peasant movements in Halland and Scania in 1772–1776. The sanctions were usually at their most lenient at the level of the Court of Appeal, as both the local assizes and the royal Supreme Court (*Justitierevision*) commonly gave stricter sentences. It has been assumed that the local assizes were more susceptible to pressure from the local notables or authorities than the Courts of Appeal, which were freer from political pressure. Among the reasons given by the Court of Appeal in justification of its more lenient treatment was that a particular assembly "had not been aimed in any way against the king's high person or the public safety of the realm." In contrast, the royal Supreme Court viewed the disturbance as indeed touching on public safety and therefore meriting severe punishment. For example, the Court of Appeal sentenced Bengt Persson, one of the peasant leaders of the Halland disturbances, to 30 'pairs' of lashes, at three strokes a 'pair', while the Supreme Court added two years hard labour at the fortress of Marstrand.[154]

In 1778, the King's Council took a more conservative view than the law commission on the abolition of capital punishment for certain types of treason. It placed a higher value on public safety and wanted to preserve the death penalty, except in cases of the spreading of rumours affecting the security of the realm. According to the Council, the definition of this paragraph was too broad and gave the judge too much leeway in a crime punishable by death.[155]

All the same, in the late eighteenth century the sentences in the peasant revolts followed the general policy of the time, namely the trend of fewer enforced capital punishments. After the accession of Gustavus III (r. 1771–1792) no death sentences were given for peasant or popular disturbances in the 1770s.[156] Treason and public order were taken seriously and punishments duly meted out, but in ordinary circumstances there were relatively few death sentences. According to statistics presented by Olivecrona, only five persons lost their lives for treason between 1749 and 1801, apart from the executions of the noble rebels of 1756, Colonel Hästesko and the regicide Ankarström. While the noble Lieutenant-Colonel Tigerstedt, executed in 1790, was one of the five, another had murdered his master, while a third had joined the enemy.[157] The same phenomenon can be observed in Denmark-Norway in the 1760s: none of the four leaders were executed for their part in the rising against extraordinary taxation in Bergen, although in 1768 the Supreme Court sentenced all of them to death. The king commuted the sentence to life-long hard labour in a royal fortress.[158]

To sum up, we can justifiably say there was relatively little expansion of the medieval concept of treason in the early modern period. The sixteenth and seventeenth century ordinances mainly repeated and extended medieval provisions, such as section 8 in the Law of Heinous Crime of the 1442 law, and did little to expand the existing concept of treason. However, they did provide the Crown with improved legal sanctions against acts such as spreading dangerous rumours, holding illicit assemblies or maintaining contacts with the enemy that could develop into something more dangerous and jeopardize the stability of the realm.

Their other function was of a declaratory nature: they emphasized that a certain policy or certain acts were punishable, and, as they were read aloud from the pulpit to the church-going populace, the message was effectively transmitted around the country. Besides, by issuing laws, the king was doing what was expected of him: exercising his legislative powers. The law of 1734 for the most part merely restated, clarified and crystallized previous legislation on treason. This has also been noted by Katajala,[159] but I would be inclined to lay more stress than he has done on the medieval concept.

It has also been shown that a lack of major peasant uprisings, especially in the seventeenth century, did not prevent the Crown from issuing treason laws. But the threat of peasant uprisings nevertheless persisted. As Peter Englund has noted, the fear of revolt lived on, although the aristocracy tended to blame priests or burghers for inciting the common man – a theme which often recurred in seventeenth-century and eighteenth-century peasant troubles.[160] The fact that the seventeenth-century peasant disturbances were mostly only minor and local should not be taken to mean that the Crown did nothing in this area, as the steady flow of regulations, statutes and police ordinances provides evidence to the contrary. The level of behaviour tolerated in the developing early modern state was simply becoming stricter all the time, and the authorities now wanted to nip all peasant discontent in the bud before it could develop into something more threatening to the establishment.

Nipping discontent in the bud

According to Eva Österberg, after the 1540s the peasants in the central areas of Sweden tended largely to use legal channels and peaceful methods in their conflicts with the state, while the central government avoided being too heavy-handed in demonstrating its power. She sees in this a change in the political culture related to the frightening experiences on both sides of the bloody sixteenth-century uprisings, a mutual though unequal interdependency of the Estates based on a traditional patriarchal sense of solidarity and an institutionalisation of the local channels of influence and local government in which peasants took part.[161]

This would be the equivalent of what Blickle and Ylikangas, referring to Winfried Schulze, call the "juridification of social conflicts".[162] Schulze's notion means that the state developed judicial means not only to suppress revolt but also to provide an alternative to violent action. These legal alternatives ranged from ways within the justice system to complain about the landowners to special commissions to investigate popular grievances.

Where such legal and peaceful methods were available, they often helped to channel conflict and determine peasant resistance strategies. Where such means were not at hand, the peasants had to react in other ways.[163]

But, unlike Blickle, who sees high treason as "a condition and prerequisite" to the development, Österberg sees the impact of peasant revolts as more direct. It was the bloody aftermath of the peasant revolts rather than the subsequent treason legislation that caused the change in political culture. Ylikangas agrees with Österberg as far as the "pacification" of the peasant uprisings goes. He admits that the peasants, having both a political and a legal channel to express their complaints since the seventeenth century, were more inclined to engage in more peaceful conflicts with the state and nobility. However, he lays more stress on the fact that there were certain means available to control and punish those responsible for the complaints. Besides, in the seventeenth century the peasants were too poor and powerless to be able to protest in any very effective way, and local government was less and less in the hands of the people themselves. The political significance of the peasantry was reduced as the peasants were increasingly seen as passive subjects of the king.[164] Peter Reinholdsson has also observed the change in the political culture and its expressions, feuding and self-help. The emergence of the early modern state in the mid-sixteenth century challenged and finally denied the legitimacy of uprisings and interpreted them as always being against the state.[165]

After the change in the political culture in the later sixteenth century, violent uprisings were no longer the norm, although smaller-scale local disturbances or attempted revolts did occur.[166] One might suppose that the government would find it easier to tolerate less threatening action once violent uprisings and revolts were no longer as likely as before. This was, however, not the case. The necessity to maintain public order was important to the expansionist Swedish military state, and the seventeenth-century monarchs were in a better position than ever before to enforce it. The tightening grip of the state was visible in all fields of life: in religious issues, in economic considerations, in administrative matters and in the justice system. The courts were taken under royal supervision, local government was made more effective and local officials, including the clergy, were transformed into royal spokesmen.

After the Lutheran Reformation, which had been introduced with the support of King Gustavus Vasa, the new religion, combined with the Lutheran absolute duty to obey the secular rulers and superiors, became a useful weapon. The Church Ordinance of 1686 told priests who learned of lese-majesty or treason to exhort the sinner to report it to the local officials. If this was not successful, the priests were obliged to warn the authorities so that they were able to prevent any damage taking place. However, it was not necessary to name any persons involved.[167]

"And, now in particular [i.e. after the Reformation] it is known," wrote Nehrman, "that the clergy following the word of God has taught that infidelity, revolt, disobedience and contempt towards the authorities and the realm are serious and horrible sins..."[168] The clergy, having been robbed of its independent status and separate jurisdiction, increasingly became royal servants whose duty was to preach obedience and submission to their flocks both in the pulpit and at local administrative meetings. They were also to inform the civil authorities of any unusual goings-on in their parish. In connection with a number of peasant protests, they did just that.[169] A failure to restrain their parishioners or suspicion of provoking and assisting them could result in serious reprimands from the secular authorities or their ecclesiastical superiors.[170]

At times, the Janus-faced role of the local administration and clergy must have resembled balancing on a tightrope. On the one hand they had to maintain an equilibrium with their parishioners and inferiors, whose complaints and needs had to be given sufficient attention, while on the other hand they had to maintain order and discipline. This double role was particularly strained in times of peasant unrest.[171]

In the course of the seventeenth and early eighteenth centuries the Crown, though listening to peasant complaints and petitions and setting up commissions to deal with them, was also directly and indirectly trying to hinder this flow. There are several examples of such a policy. The local royal officials played an important role in trying to smooth down trouble before it began to ferment. The Constitution of 1634 made it the task of the local governor to report to the central government on the popular mood, whether there were signs of war, revolt or such in their province, and this was indeed what the governors actually did in practice.[172] They were to watch diligently and alertly for possible enemy spies or malicious persons, so that these could not infiltrate the country and poison people's minds against the authorities, realm and government. The governors were to investigate those who were behind treasonous conspiracies and see to it that no one offended against the king's or the realm's justice and majesty.[173]

The situation of the governors, too, was somewhat equivocal, as they were not only meant to control the inhabitants, but also to protect and promote their interests if, for example, the crops failed.[174] If a local governor dealt with peasant troubles too leniently or showed too much understanding, he could be replaced by a firmer supporter of order and harsh punishments, as happened in 1775 when Olof von Nackreij, governor of Halland, was replaced by Colonel H. H. von Saltza.[175]

The royal and noble ideology also emphasised good kingship and lordship, and the relationship between superiors and inferiors was seen as a personal, mutual bond. The position of the powerful was compared to that of a strict but loving father, while the subordinated were likened to obedient children. While the superiors were to be mild, protecting and forgiving, they were equally entitled to discipline and punish the disobedient.[176] These patriarchal tendencies contributed to the establishment of commissions to investigate popular supplications in order to pacify the peasants and look into their grievances. Furthermore, the peasant estate could voice its dissatisfaction in the Diet and thereby place issues on the agenda for discussion.[177] Nevertheless, although complaints of maladministration and the excesses of landlords or local authorities were common, the grievances usually remained unremedied, as they could only rarely be proven. This was the result of many factors, but particularly of differences in how the cases were investigated and the strict rules of evidence under the statutory theory of proof.[178]

The opportunity to participate in the meetings of the Estates and send local representatives to Stockholm certainly played a role in this pacifying process. The peasant estate never exercised any great influence in the Diet, as it was not even represented on the Secret Committee. This has been described as the real power centre of the Age of Liberty (1718–1772), and it dealt with the most important issues relating to defence, state finances, interior and foreign affairs. Despite this, it has been assumed that during the Age of Liberty the position and influence of the peasant estate were improving and that it actively furthered a policy advantageous to its own interests.[179]

The tours of inspection by the attorney-general, an institution founded in 1719, had a twofold aim: on the one hand the attorney-general was to listen to the grievances and complaints of the people as a visible demonstration of the king's paternal care for his subjects, on the other to report whether there were false rumours circulating and remind the people of their duty to obey the king and his officials. As one attorney-general put it, he had exhorted the people to obey or suffer ("*lyda eller lida*"). The main aim of the tours was to demonstrate the king's concern for the wellbeing of the common people, not to provide them with an effective channel to issue concrete complaints against the administration.[180]

The landowners and royal officials could refuse to give passports to dissatisfied peasants, thereby hindering them from travelling to the capital with their complaints.[181] It was also possible to fine a person for abuse of the justice system if he had taken his case to all instances and lost in all of them. The punishment for a frivolous complaint to the king without clear cause was an astronomical fine of 500 dalers for the appellant and gaol for his representative.[182] Such fines and spells in gaol were in fact meted out to the peasants and their representatives after the Halland and Nastola troubles in the 1770s.[183] If anyone spoke against the King's judgement, this was construed as an insult to the king and his justice. Nehrman, writing in the eighteenth century, attributed the leniency of the punishment – a fine of a mere 500 dalers instead of death – to the feelings of understanding and pity on the part of the authorities towards those who were blinded by their self-love and false thoughts.[184]

Another means to nip protest in the bud was the 'ordinance of supplicants' (*sollicitantsförordningen*), which was intended to prevent direct complaints to the king unless the matter had either been taken to court or the local governor had been petitioned. The fact that such ordinances had to be repeated several times – in at least 1680, 1682, 1687, 1689 and 1723 – indicates that they were largely disregarded, because it was customary to take matters straight to the king. The last of these ordinances forbade any direct complaints or petitions to the king on pain of a fine of ten dalers, fifteen for repeated offences.[185] However, the punishments in the ordinance seem not to have been in use in the 1770s, although many such cases were turned away from the royal Supreme Court (*Justitierevision*) and the bureau of internal affairs (*inrikes-civil-expedition*). Furthermore, when the king travelled around the country, people approached him in the customary fashion with petitions and complaints of various sorts.[186]

It was also a punishable offence to complain to the King over a matter that had already been resolved if there were no special reasons for doing so. The punishment was a fine of 300 dalers, or alternatively a spell in prison.[187] On 29 June 1773 a still more severe ordinance was issued which made it possible to punish even the writer of a letter of complaint, even if he was not the actual complainant but merely wrote the letter for a fee or on request. He was seen to be inciting simple folk to initiate unfounded court cases and make unreasonable supplications. The ordinance further insisted that the name of the writer should be stated in the letter.[188]

The timing of this ordinance suggests a link with the peasant troubles in Scania, Halland and Finland, which seems quite plausible. The governors could issue local proclamations related to the ordinances on supplicants, forbidding assemblies and threatening peasants with punishment if they should attempt to assemble in order to make a complaint or to organise such an assembly. This happened in Käkisalmi in 1684, but the proclamation was completely disregarded and the number of assemblies and complaints only gathered pace with the discontents of the following years.[189] Ylikangas's point about the Crown's efforts to restrict the peasants' channels of complaint seems quite valid in this light.

As we have seen, the insistence on obedience was still strong in the eighteenth century. As late as the 1810s the landowning peasants of Kuhmo in north-eastern Finland were to learn the hard way what resistance to the authorities could lead to in the early modern state. The peasants of Kuhmo showed most obstinate recalcitrance and disobedience by not building their new church at the place ordered by the authorities. Despite several express decisions first by the governor, then by his Imperial Majesty Czar Alexander I, construction work was begun at the site of the old church. As a result, in 1814, the peasants faced charges of treason, and two of the leaders of what was called the 'church rebellion' were sentenced to death, while the lesser players faced fines and imprisonment.[190] Although the issue was local and scarcely a threat either to peace or to the Crown, such lengthy and headstrong shows of local independence were no longer acceptable in a new world that insisted on discipline and obedience.

Continuity and interpretation

Treason legislation appeared in Sweden in the second half of the thirteenth century, and by the mid-fourteenth century the fundamental criminal categories of treason can be found in provincial and common laws of the realm and in several royal statutes. This period can therefore be seen as the crucial period for Swedish treason legislation. The development coincided with the growing powers of the king and his role as the fountain of justice and protector of the peace. According to Åqvist, it was during the period from around 1280 to the 1360s that the king's legislative powers became established, although it took some time before the laws of Magnus Ericsson, the Town Law and the Law of the Realm, were in use all over the kingdom.[191]

At this stage the criminal categories of treason or lese-majesty were used primarily as a weapon against pretenders from rival families, aristocratic attempts at a coup d'état, and all those in breach of the royal prerogative. There is no evidence that this earliest layer of norms was a result of peasant revolt; it has even been claimed rather recently that there were no 'true' peasant revolts in medieval Sweden.[192] Nor has any substantial support been found for the view that the Swedish uprisings of the 1430s inspired new treason legislation, especially considering the law of 1442 contained no new categories of treason.

The lack of explicit and detailed paragraphs on many different treacherous acts in medieval law is not evidence of their non-existence in practice. Many treasonous crimes, such as delivering a castle into the hands of the enemy, do not figure in the Swedish medieval laws. Still, this was without doubt considered treason under customary military law, the law of arms, before the general codification of 1734 expressly classified it as treason for the whole realm. The possible discrepancy between law texts and unwritten practice explains why a 'novel' paragraph or criminalisation filling what seems to be a gap in the law need not really be so novel after all.[193] The question may have been regulated by customary law such as the international law of arms. Or the presumed void may have been filled by an extensive interpretation of law in legal practice, as occurred in the case of some lese-majesty crimes. Alternatively, a gap in a specific law could signify that the treason criminalisations in the general law were applied in cases other than those specifically mentioned in the text of the law. Special laws like the Articles of War and the Naval Articles or the Court Ordinances supplemented the general law of 1442 and regulated more precisely the special circumstances of a royal castle, military camp or man-of-war.

As the powers of the king began to grow, especially in the early modern period, this was accompanied by the development of broader treason legislation. As we have seen, the Vasa kings such as Charles IX skilfully used the law of treason to label their political opponents as aiders and abettors of the enemies of the realm or as offenders against the king's majesty. During the sixteenth and early seventeenth centuries, lese-majesty and non-violent forms of treason, including spreading rumours, illicit assemblies and various ways of aiding the enemy, were given more legislative attention than in earlier years. It has been observed of France that "the law of treason was made more precise on points of detail, but departed little from medieval precedents" from the late fifteenth to the mid-seventeenth century.[194]

Admittedly the medieval French precedents were both more extensive and more numerous than the Swedish, but the observation nevertheless rings true. New statutes were undoubtedly issued in early modern Sweden, but generally speaking they were not particularly remarkable, since they mostly repeated and slightly extended older criminal legislation. The scope to build on these ideas by use of analogies and extensive interpretation was not greatly used, and so authoritative and declaratory but hardly very innovative statutes appeared quite regularly. Action which had been more or less tolerated in earlier times was increasingly regarded as a threat to authority from the sixteenth century onwards, and mere peasant assemblies began to be seen in this light. The Crown provided the peasantry with means to take part in politics at the Diet and make known their grievances, but it also restricted the opportunity for complaining directly to the king. Almost any large scale disobedience to the authority of the king, government or estate owner could be interpreted as treason, and, on the whole, the process of state formation undoubtedly meant stricter control in various sectors of society.

In Sweden, the Law of the Realm of 1734 scarcely affected the existing treason laws, as its general conservativeness is visible even in its treason doctrine, the basis of which was still strongly medieval. There were no really new ingredients to the concept of treason in the 1734 law, since it mostly codified and incorporated older, seventeenth-century statutory criminalisations. Despite its intended scope, it cannot be seen as the culmination of previous developments, since new acts were also criminalised as treason later in the century, even as late as the 1770s, some of which can be said to be a direct response to peasant revolts. The criminalisation of summoning peasants to assemble in 1743 after the Dalecarlia uprising, the ordinance of 1773 enabling the Crown to punish persons serving as clerks to complainants, and the proclamation of 1776 punishing severely any attempt of a tenant or servant to kill, assault or physically harm his master could all be mentioned as a reaction of the authorities to recent peasant unrest.

The punishments for treason were usually extremely severe: execution was the norm, especially for ringleaders and those considered a special threat. There were no great changes in this principle from the Middle Ages to the eighteenth century. Moreover, in the case of violent revolt, the death penalty was usually enforced. However, the crime of treason followed in some respects the general trend of control policy. The growing, though at first very relative leniency of the punishments for crime in general from the later eighteenth century onwards has been attributed to the changes in the policy of the enlightened despots, who relied increasingly on the support of the lower estates. The political force of the lower estates was emphasized and the social differences between the estates grew smaller.[195]

In spite of this, such a change in the punishments for treason is not immediately noticeable after the accession of Gustavus III. Although the punishments for crime were in general less severe than a century earlier, and the use of capital punishment had generally declined in legal practice, the king and the ruling classes were keen to maintain peace and discipline. Draconian statutes were meant as deterrents even if considerably fewer criminals than before actually lost their lives in practice.[196] In actual fact, apart from the punishments of the leaders of the 1743 Dalecarlia uprising, proportionately more nobles than peasants lost their lives for treason in the eighteenth century.

As S. H. Cuttler has observed in the case of late medieval France, the scope of treason "was a wide one by design". Several factors contributed to this. First of all, the possibility to punish opposition and treachery at all levels of society was a useful weapon to control dissenters. In addition, the deterrent aspect of the punishments helped to improve public order. And last, although certainly not least, was the material advantage gained by confiscation of the traitors' property. "[T]he broadest possible interpretation was in the best interests of the king personally and of the crown."[197] This applies perfectly, no doubt, to the Swedish situation.

Still, Swedish medieval and early modern treason legislation was neither paranoid nor growing indiscriminately. In comparison with England or especially France, Swedish treason legislation was clearly more conservative, concentrating on more basic treasonable acts.[198] The Swedes were unwilling or unable to extend the scope of treason to the extent that Roman law would have allowed, although the sixteenth-century and seventeenth-century expansion especially of lese-majesty, due to a reception of foreign, Roman and German law, was of considerable benefit to successive Swedish kings.

Some aspects of the long-term development in Sweden sketched here are probably also applicable to the kingdoms of Denmark and Norway. The Scandinavian medieval laws surely influenced each other: earlier the borders of the kingdoms were not rigidly defined, later the same king could be the ruler of several monarchies. Magnus Ericsson was king of both Sweden and Norway, and during the Kalmar Union the Danish kings and queens ruled the whole of Scandinavia. Nevertheless, we should make some allowances for differences stemming from such factors as earlier state formation, wider reception of Roman law, and variations in the status of the peasantry and the type of monarchy (elective *versus* hereditary). If anything, one might tentatively suspect that in Denmark and Norway the concept of treason was wider than in Sweden. This might have even implied more severe punishments.[199]

As far as Sweden is concerned, any notion of the concept of high treason being the result of peasant revolts in medieval or early modern Sweden can be finally put to rest. Apart from some specific exceptions, peasant revolts did not generate treason legislation on a large scale. Treason legislation was not meant as a special weapon against the power of the peasantry: peasants fell victim to the law of treason like all other groups which threatened the inner stability and peace of the realm. Despite further statutes, particularly on non-violent treason, later medieval and early modern legislation brought no fundamental changes into the main principles of the Swedish law on treason.

NOTES

1. I do not wish this to be understood as a contribution to the controversy over the proper definition of 'feuds' or 'uprisings' raised by Reinholdsson 1998. I simply choose here to use the conventional term.
2. Blickle 1986c. The citation is on S93.
3. Blickle 1986c, S88–89.
4. Blickle 1986c, S90–94.
5. Ylikangas 1990, 62–82; Ylikangas 1991; Ylikangas 1996, 354–362.
6. Ylikangas 1991, 98.
7. Ylikangas 1991, 97–99.
8. Ylikangas 1991, 99.
9. Ylikangas 1990, 76, 122–128. The citation is on page 122.
10. Ylikangas 1991, 99.
11. Katajala 1994, 378–379; Katajala 1999, 18–19.
12. Katajala 1999, 17–23, 53.
13. Katajala 1999, 8.
14. Katajala 1999, 55–56.
15. See also Bauman 1970, vii–viii.
16. Nehrman 1756, 142–143. Cf. ibid., 147. Kantorowicz 1981; Post 1964, 442.
17. Pollock & Maitland 1898, II, 503.
18. Pollock & Maitland 1898, I, 52; Lear 1965, 38–40, 74, 87–90, 142–144, 185–186, 192–193; Cuttler 1981, 4–7; Bar 1968, 101–102, 163–164; Bellamy 1970, 1–6.
19. Lear 1965, 66–72, 141–142; Bauman 1981; Bellamy 1970, 6–14.
20. In general, see Kantorowicz 1981, e.g. 95–97, 104–105, 148–150; Ullmann 1980, II, 214–215; Ullmann 1966, 9–19; Lear 1965, 16–25.
21. Bauman 1970, passim.
22. Lear 1965, 205; for Sweden, see also Korpiola 2001.
23. For example the older law of Western Gothia (hereafter VgL I), Urb (balken om urbotamål, Law on Unatonable Crimes) in SLL V; LKMH, IV.3–4, 92–99.
24. Tacitus, 38–41; Lear 1965, 6–7, 15, 27, 42, 44, 87–93, 147–150, 184–185, 190–194; Brecht 1938, 27–75; Bar 1968, 101.
25. Östgötalagen (hereafter ÖgL), E (edsörebalken, Law of the King's Peace) 30 in SLL I. The earliest surviving and complete version of the law is from the mid-fourteenth century, although it is thought to have been compiled in the 1290s. Inledande anmärkningar, 3, in SLL I.
26. Inledning, in SLL V, xvii–xix; VgL I, Urb §4, in SLL V.
27. VgL I, Urb §4; newer law of Western Gothia (hereafter VgL II), Urb 1 §8, in SLL V. Law of Uppland (hereafter UL), M (manhelgsbalken, Law of Homicide) 15 in SLL I; Law of Södermanland (hereafter SdmL), M 36 in SLL III; Law of Hälsinge (hereafter HL), M 24 in SLL III. MELL H (högmålsbalken, Law of Felony) §8; MESL, H 7; Söderköpings lagbok 1387, H 7; KrLL, H §9. DS II, doc. 1125, 184; DS VI, doc. 4462, F122; FMU IV, docs. 3617 and 3620, 422–423.
28. Nehrman 1756, 153–154. See also Rosén 1955, 125.
29. For example Bagge 1987, esp. 203–204, 209, 218–223; Damsholt 1970, esp. 98–101; Christensen 1978, 32–34; Fenger 1977, 62–63; Åqvist 1989, 20–22, 53–60, 95, 129, 164–175.
30. DS I, doc. 116, 141, doc. 439, 383; doc. 675, 549; doc. 843, 697; Ödberg 1875, I, 48–49; Bååth 1905, 91–92.
31. Bååth 1905, 91–92.
32. Åqvist 1989, 53–54, 95.
33. Lönnroth 1944, 8–9, 18–26.
34. DS I, doc. 396, 356–357; Lönnroth 1944, 12–14, 19–20; see also DS I, doc. 692, 566; DS II, doc. 980, 63–64.
35. DS I, doc. 753, 615. See also DS I, doc. 744, 605–606; Bååth 1905, 95–97.
36. Hjärne 1951, 47–49.

37 Rosén 1939, 342–343; Bååth 1905, 97–99; Bjarne Larsson 1994, 182, 193–197, 206–208; Fritz 1987, 102–103.
38 DS I, doc. 813, 669.
39 Hjärne 1951, 43–44, 78–81, 88, 158, 176; Fritz 1987, 102–103.
40 DRL, 58–61; LKMH, IV.4 2, 96–97.
41 SdmL, M 36; HL, M 24.
42 UL, M 15.
43 MELL, H §7; MESL, H §6; KrLL, H §8.
44 Söderköpings lagbok 1387, KB 8.
45 MESL, Kg (kungabalken, Law of the King) 8; UUB B 9, 132v; KrLL, Kg 9.
46 Rosén 1955, 93–94. See also ibid., 110; Schmedeman 1706, 36.
47 For example SRL 1734, MB (missgärningsbalken, Law of Crime) V:1–2; Nehrman 1756, 162–165, 167–168.
48 DRL, 59; Fenger 1977, 80.
49 VgL II, Urb 1; VgL II, Add. 7 §31. See also VgL Exc. Lyd. 72. UL, M 15 §1; Law of Västmannaland (hereafter VmL), M 13 in SLL II; HL, M 24. MELL, H 9; MESL, H 8; KrLL, H 10. Cf. Katajala 1999, 24. However, some versions of the town law included versions whereby this paragraph also applied to cases where the wife murdered her husband. This was a crime which in English law, due to feudal influences, was classified as petty (or lesser) treason. Statute of Treason 1352, SECH, 183–184; Bellamy 1970, 225–231.
50 SdmL, M 36 §1.
51 Hjärne 1951, 82.
52 Bååth 1905, 97. See also Ullmann 1966, 63–67; Brunner 1984, 215–220, 283–285, 288–290; Reynolds 1994, 18–21, 29–31, 36–38, 86–89, 128–130, 282–284; Leges Henrici Primi c. 13, 12, pp. 118–119; c. 43, 3–7, pp. 152–153; c. 55, 1–3b, pp. 172–174.
53 VgL I, Urb §7; see also Inledning in SLL V, xv–xviii, xxi.
54 SST 1483–1492, 135.
55 Keen 1996, esp. 135, 139–143, 149–166; Keen 1965, passim; Capua 1977, esp. 152–161; Skyum-Nielsen 1964, 148; Cuttler 1981, 34–37.
56 Capua 1977, 161–173; Anners 1961, 96; Leges Henrici Primi c. 13, 7–8; 13, 12, pp. 118–119; c. 80, 1, pp. 248–249.
57 Två finländska gårdsrättsredaktioner, esp. 28–35, 39–43; Uppländska konungsdomar, 12.5.1540, 91–92, 110–111, 115.
58 Hirðskrá, 5, 14–15, 19–22, 50, 53–54, 56–57; the law of King Magnus Hakonarson, LKMH, III.10.4, 72–73, III.13.1, 78–79; different versions of the Vederlov mainly from the 1180s in DRL, 2, 22–24, 33–34, 37.
59 Hjärne 1979–1981, II, 154–156; Fenger 1983, 63, 80–82; Åqvist 1989, 6–7.
60 DS V, doc. 3972, 478; Skyum-Nielsen 1964, 148–149.
61 Konung Carls 8vi Stadgar eller Artiklar, 1, Hadorph 1687, 50.
62 Drottningh Margretas Gårdz Rätt 20, Hadorph 1687, 34.
63 Maurer 1877, 49, 75–79; Två finländska gårdsrättsredaktioner, 35, 42; Drottningh Margretas Gårdz Rätt 20, Hadorph 1687, 34; Gothlandz Gambla Stadz Lag I:3, 39–40, Hadorph 1688, 3, 20.
64 GVB, 64–65, 71–74; Schmedeman 1706, 24–25; Anners 1961, 89–93, 96; Ylikangas 1996, 320.
65 KrLL, E 42.
66 Treaty between the Danish king Valdemar and the Swedish king Magnus Eriksson in 1343, documents 3743 and 3744 in DS V, 216 and 220–221; VgL II, Urb 1 §10; VmL, M 25; SdmL, M 13; HL, M 16. MESL, E 24; Söderköpings lagbok 1387, E 24; MELL, EB 45. See also the Danish and Norwegian thirteenth-century criminalisations in LKMH, III.16.1, 84–85 and JL 3.67, 160–161.
67 UL, M 31.
68 VgL I, Urb §10.
69 Åqvist 1989, 125–127; Larsson 1984, 237–243; Bjarne Larsson 1994, 123.

70 For example DS V, docs 3743–3744, 216, 220–222; doc. 3242, 515; doc. 3788, 265.
71 Letto-Vanamo 1995, 147–148: Bjarne Larsson 1994, ch. 4, esp. 98–100, 116, 118, 128–129, 210–212.
72 REA, doc. 476, 368–369; Voionmaa 1916, 377.
73 UUB 9, 132v; Strängnäs Stadgan 1437, Hadorph 1687, 45; Bøgh 1988, 154; Bjarne Larsson 1994, 76, 78.
74 Larsson 1984, 222, 230.
75 For example Brunner 1984, 14–16, 29–35, 57–59; Kaeuper 1988, 244–246.
76 VgL II, FB (förnämesbalken, The Law of Homicide) 50; DS IV, doc. 3175, 464–465. See also the Statute of Uppsala of 1344, DS V, doc. 3864, 374–375.
77 King Magnus' privilegiebrev för Kopparberget, DS V, doc. 4142, 638.
78 SD II, doc. 1975, 830; Bjarne Larsson 1994, 70; Konung Erickz aff Pomern Stadga 1416, 13, Hadorph 1687, 43.
79 For example HL, R XIV §3, 398.
80 For example SdmL, M XXVI §3, 176.
81 Kon: Christophers Placat til Linkiöpigz Stifft 1441, 3–4, Hadorph 1687, 47. For Malmö see also Lamberg 2001, 235–236.
82 Bøgh 1988, 156–157; Bjarne Larsson 1994, 82. Cf. the 1462 statute of King Christiern, 5, Hadorph 1687, 55, and the 1537 Recess of Nyköping, Schmedeman 1706, 6.
83 Ylikangas 1996, 94–99, 101.
84 Ylikangas 1996, 99–100.
85 Arwidsson 1849, docs. 98–99, 175–181; Pirinen 1939, esp. 48–50. See also Hallenberg 2001, 230.
86 Ylikangas 1996, 211–212, 230–231.
87 Katajala 1994, 378–383, 386–388; KrLL 1442, E §1, 19, 21, 28, 35, 40, 42.
88 This change in the political culture is discussed in more detail below.
89 Ylikangas 1990, 80–82.
90 Katajala 1999, esp. 39, 45.
91 Schlyter XII, KrLL, addit. B, 6, 401–402.
92 Bauman 1970, 1–28, 87–90, 124–125, 132, 222, 228–233, 270–274.
93 Canning 1987, 121–123; Knapp 1896, 292–295; Conrad 1954, 445; DS VII, document 5823, 253–254.
94 DS VII, document 5823, 253–254; MESL, E 27.
95 Biärköa Rättär, Hadorph 1687, 1–15; Gothlandz Gambla Stadz Lag I:3, 39–40, Hadorph 1688, 3, 20.
96 Söderköpings lagbok 1387, XII, 96.
97 Schlyter XI, MESL, E 27, 318–319. Cf. Lamberg 2001, 41, 235 for punishments in Denmark.
98 Schlyter XII, KrLL, addit. B, 6, 401–402; cf. KrLL, E, 120–131.
99 Isberg 1953, 224–225, 244–246, 256, 261–272, 278–279, 282–284.
100 Katajala 1994, 382–387.
101 Decision of the Diet of Stockholm 1604, Stiernman 1728–1733, 556; Katajala 1994, 317–319, 325–328; Katajala 1999, 43.
102 Bellamy 1979, 81–82.
103 SRL, Law of Crime, chapters 4–6, 128–131. See also Erich 1934, 749–757; Katajala 1999, 30–47.
104 Nehrman 1754, 176–180.
105 Nehrman 1754, 180.
106 Modée III, 2053–2055.
107 Würtz Sørensen 1988, 35–37, 42–43, Rasmussen 1988, 125, 128; Letto-Vanamo 1995, 43; By-Ordning I.), Modée III, 1848. See also e.g. the Norwegian thirteenth-century law of King Magnus Hakonarson, LKMH, III.3.1–3 (*skera upp herorfar*), 58–61, III.4.1, 60–61, III.9.1 (*boð upp skera*), 70–71, III.16.2–4 (*oruar skurð; or skera*), 72–73.
108 Smedberg 1972, 182; Modée III, 2054.

109 Smedberg 1972, 86–87, 160–163.
110 Rasmussen 1988, 125, 128.
111 Rasmussen 1988, 131.
112 Styffe IV, docs. 74–75, 110–113. Unlike document 75, document 74 refers to the wrong section (§ 6). Sections 6 and 7 in the Law of Heinous Crime of the 1442 law talk about homicide by witchcraft and murder of a stepchild for its inheritance, so they cannot have been applied in this case.
113 Modée III, 2047–2048, 2051–2053, 2055–2070, 2123; Beckman 1930, 387, 412–413, 417–429.
114 See the chapter written by Karin Sennefelt in this book.
115 115. Lennersand 1999, 146–147.
116 Olaus Magnus, 8, ch. 34, 101–103.
117 Reinholdsson 1998, 107.
118 Modéer 1997, 72–73; Rosén 1955, 13–14, 45, 48–63, 73–74, 95–97, 109–111, 115, 119, 140–142, 149–157, 159.
119 Rosén 1955, 62; Cf. Lamberg 2001,238: in Denmark this was the practice since the early fifteenth century, at latest.
120 Decision of the Diet of Stockholm 1604, Stiernman 1728–1733, 556; see also Lennersand 1999, 93–98, 175, 178, 190–193, 202–203, 252, 274 and Hallenberg 2001, 98–101, 113, 122–123.
121 Thyrén 1895, 66–67; Munktell 1934, esp. 772–782, 784–786, 804; Nehrman 1756, 148, 168–169.
122 Schmedeman 1706, 213.
123 Isberg 1953, 262.
124 Harrison 1997b, 270–273.
125 GVB, 119–122, 130, 169; Stiernman 1728–1733, 97–98, 171–172; Pirinen 1939; Ylikangas 1988, 29–39; Rosén 1955, 55, 58. See also Hallenberg 2001, 163–165.
126 Stiernman 1728–1733, 257–260; Rosén 1955, 37, 43; Modéer 1997, 74–75.
127 Elander 1958, 268–282.
128 Decision of the Diet of Stockholm in 1599, Stiernman 1728–1733, 483, also 491–493, Decision of the Diet of Linköping in 1600, Stiernman 1728–1733, 506–508; Katajala 1999, 25–29.
129 For Sweden see GVB, 75–78; Venge 1980, esp. 41, 48, 57, and chapter VI in this book and for England see Korpiola 1996, 59–61 and the literature mentioned there.
130 Björne 1995, 22–51, 375–380.
131 Kekkonen–Ylikangas 1982, 50–64; Thunander 1993, 7–15.
132 Schmedeman 1706, 1208–1209; Thunander 1993, 8, 186–187.
133 Letto-Vanamo 1989, esp. 10–27; Blomstedt 1958, esp. 222–226, 261–266.
134 Schmedeman 1706, 119; Decision of the Diet of Stockholm 1604, Stiernman 1728–1733, 556.
135 Scribner 1987; Pihlajamäki 1999, 513, 515–516. Cf. GVB, 116–118, 152–153.
136 Patent om Högmåhls Saker 1563, Schmedeman 1706, 47.
137 Scribner 1987, 103–105, 108–112; Tudor Proclamations II–III, passim; Bellamy 1979, 15–82.
138 Schmedeman 1706, 131; Stiernman 1728–1733, 670–671.
139 Rosén 1955, 13, 51.
140 Schmedeman 1706, 167–170; Stiernman 1728–1733, 709–711; repeated in the decision of the Diet of Stockholm in 1624, Stiernman 1728–1733, 763–764. See also the criminalisation in 1727, Modée I, 662–663.
141 Stiernman 1728–1733, 851, 875.
142 Schmedeman 1706, (King Gustav's Manorial Law 1544 §6–7), 17–18, (King Erik XIV's Court Ordinance 1560 § 6–7, 9–13, 16, 19–20, 25), 36–39; (King Johan III's Manorial Law 1569–73 § 1–2, 4–8, 11–12, 18), 44–46.
143 Schmedeman 1706, (§ 5–8, 10–11, 14) 302–303.
144 Schmedeman 1706, (§ 6–9, 24, 30–32), 1153–1155, 1159–1162.
145 Anners 1961, 95–96.

146 Schmedeman 1706, (1545, § 3–4) 24 , 212–213. See also ibid., 1477–1478.
147 Modée V, esp. 3754–3757, 3804–3808.
148 See, for ex. DS V, doc. 3743, 215 ("*vtputa lese maiestatis, castrorum aut terrarum prodicionem vel. eorum consimilia..*"); SD I, doc. 1193, 212. See also Strickland 1996, 214–216, 224–229, 230–257; Keen 1996, 149, 158; Cuttler 1981, 35–36, 151–152, 221–222; Elton 1972, 287.
149 Schmedeman 1706, 1565–1566; Cf. KrLL, H 10; SRL 1734, MB 6:1–3.
150 Modée X, 621–622.
151 Anners 1965, 259.
152 Modée X, 289–290; Almén 1940, 269–270, 305–307. Cf. Modée II, 1271; III, 2386, 2448–2449; SRL 1734, MB V:1–2.
153 For example Smedberg 1971, passim; Kerkkonen 1931, 177–179, 183; Jutikkala 1931, 279; Jutikkala 1932 I, 363–371. See also Modée X, 103, 120–122.
154 Smedberg 1972, 80, 160–162, 182–183.
155 Anners 1965, 236, 241.
156 Katajala 1999, 48–50; Jutikkala 1932, I, 369–371, 378–379, 385; Olivecrona 1891, 110–149.
157 Anners 1965, 188–189; Olivecrona 1891, 110–149. The statistics should be taken with a pinch of salt, however, as it would seem that these figures do not include the executions after Hofman's uprising in 1766.
158 See e.g. Sætra 1998, 306–307.
159 Katajala 1999, 30–45.
160 Englund 1989, esp. 98–99, 198–199. For example Melander 1939, 31, 33; Katajala 1994, 279–282; Jutikkala 1932 I, 353, 359–361, 365, 396.
161 Österberg 1989, 87–91.
162 Blickle 1986c, S97; Ylikangas 1991, 98, 102.
163 Schulze 1982, 35–37, 41. See also Theibault 1992.
164 Ylikangas 1990, 67, 80–82, 108–111, 115–118; Ylikangas 1991, 103–104; Ylikangas 1996, 360–362; Lennersand 1999, 56–57. See also Jutikkala 1932 II, 138–139, 143.
165 Reinholdsson 1998, esp. ch. 6:1, 103–107.
166 For example Melander 1939.
167 Church Ordinance of 1686, ch. 7, § III.
168 Nehrman 1756, 144, 164; Church Ordinance of 1686, ch. 2, § II.
169 Kalm 1948, 184–185, 196–205; Englund 1989, 31–32, 110–111; Heikkinen 1988, 228, 231–233.
170 Katajala 1994, 206–211, 281–291, 314.
171 Frohnert 1985, 222–225; Frohnert 1993, 159–161, 168, 222–231, 240–241; Katajala 1994, 279–291.
172 The Constitution of 1634, Stiernman 1728–1733, 904–905; Melander 1939, 28–31.
173 Instruction för Landshöfdingarne 1734, Modée II, 1071–1072, 1080.
174 Frohnert 1985, 215–216; Frohnert 1993, 191, 202–203.
175 Smedberg 1972, 18, 114–115, 165–174, cf. ibid. 174–175. For a contrary example of Governor A. H. Ramsay during the simultaneous Finnish disturbances, see Jutikkala 1932 I, 367–368.
176 Englund 1989, 91–102, 120–121, 202–204; Peterson 1985, esp. 318–321.
177 Frohnert 1985, 250–255, 258–259; Peterson 1985, esp. 308–309, 312, 333–335; Frohnert 1993, 136–138, 219–220, 243–277; Katajala 1994, 217–223; Lennersand 1999, 56–57, 62–63, 128–129, 162–163, 275; Holm 2003.
178 Peterson 1985 esp. 310–311; Katajala 1994, 98–99 and passim; Frohnert 1993, 249–252, 254–257, 262–269.
179 Beckman 1930, 4–5; Peterson 1985; Frohnert 1985, 196–197; Frohnert 1993, 238–239.
180 Modée I, 109; Peterson 1985, 320–322; Frohnert 1993, 246–247, 271.

181 Kerkkonen 1931, 163, 170; Jutikkala 1932 I, 380; Katajala 1994, 195–196; Smedberg 1972, 100–101.
182 SRL 1734, R (rättegångsbalken, Law of Procedure) 29:2, 30:16.
183 Smedberg 1972, 107, 161–162; Jutikkala 1932 I, 374, 376, 379.
184 SRL 1734, R 28:1–2; Nehrman 1756, 167.
185 Schmedeman 1706, 715–717, 754–756, 1136, 1229–1230, cf. 797–798, 1104–1105; Modée I, 393–395. Pirinen 1939, 41–42, 50–51; Katajala 1994, 175–182; Frohnert 1985, 250–255.
186 Smedberg 1972, 83, 157–158; Jutikkala 1931, 278–279; Jutikkala 1932 I, 379, 401, 407–408; Frohnert 1993, 257–258.
187 For example Modée I, 731–732.
188 Modée X, 166–167.
189 Katajala 1994, 236.
190 Heikkinen 1988, 216–289.
191 Åqvist 1989, 129.
192 Reinholdsson 1998.
193 Cf. Elton 1972, 267, 273, 287.
194 Cuttler 1981, 242–244.
195 Kekkonen–Ylikangas 1982, esp. 58–67.
196 Anners 1965, 125–128; Olivecrona 1891.
197 Cuttler 1981, 54.
198 Cuttler 1981, 1–2, 6–9, 28; Bellamy 1970, 102–137; Bellamy 1979, 15–82; Elton 1972, 263–292.
199 See also Sjöholm 1988, 159–160, 191, 244–245; Lamberg 2001, 235–236, 238.

CHAPTER XI

Conclusions
Peasant unrest and political culture

Kimmo Katajala

Most research on peasant unrest has concentrated on analysing individual revolts or tumults. This has made it possible to encroach deep into the events and the societies surrounding the protests. However, this approach has also had an impact on the interpretations and explanations reached on the basis of the available material. Be the inspected unrest a nationwide peasant war or a modest local tumult, geographical comparisons and analyses over long periods of unrest have been rare.[1] The persistent characteristics of popular unrest from the Middle Ages to the birth of the modern era become visible only in a long-term analysis (*la longue durée*). However, there were also essential changes in the nature of peasant unrest over the centuries. Analysing the unrest and its changing forms as a part of the political culture of each era reveals the main turning points in the development processes of the societies in question.

The aim of this final chapter is to bring together the experiences of the preceding chapters and attempt to meet the need for a long-term comparison for northern Europe. The period under inspection covers over five hundred years, and the comparisons made are between territories of five present-day nation states. The main aim is to identify any similarities and differences in peasant unrest inside the 'family' of Nordic medieval and early modern realms, but also to compare peasant unrest in the north with that in the rest of Europe. Only in this way can we identify the political cultures behind the patterns of peasant unrest. Thus, the main aim is to see if there was a specific 'Nordic model' of peasant unrest.

Economics

The fourteenth century has been called the century of popular revolutions *par excellence*.[2] And during this century, western Europe certainly saw a lot of peasant contention. Of these numerous and large-scale violent protest movements we can mention the examples of the uprising in Flanders in 1323–1328, the *Jaquerie* of the French peasantry in 1358 and the English rising in 1381, or the revolt of Wat Tyler, as it is also called. These were all armed and violent movements involving thousands of peasants.

The rebels numbered in the tens of thousands, and the movements were often well organised.

In the English rising, a body of about 100 000 peasants marched to London and demanded the abolition of serfdom and introduction of unified land rents. However, the immediate stimulus for the revolt was the newly established poll tax. In Flanders, the peasantry attacked the manors and castles because the landlords had imposed new taxes. The revolt was well organised, and support from the burghers of Bruges enabled it to last for several years. The French *Jaquerie* was merely an attack on the manors and castles by separate groups of armed peasant troops. However, the total numbers involved in these separate actions has been estimated as up to 10 000 peasants.

Research primarily links these fourteenth-century movements with rising taxes. They were also serious attacks against the landlords and the manors. The causes of these medieval revolts have traditionally been sought in economic changes: rising taxes and land rents, falling wages, changes in the price of grain, and so on. Economic ups and downs have been seen as the prime movers of the peasant risings. This view has also long dominated Scandinavian research into the medieval risings. The Engelbrekt uprising in Sweden, Halvard Gråtopp's uprising in Norway and the David's uprising in Finland are all said to have originated in economic changes.

Besides rising taxes, land rents and grain prices, another salient feature is crop failure. The Club War occurred during one of the many crop failures of the early modern era. The years 1595–1597 were a climatic catastrophe across almost all of Europe, and there were peasant uprisings in many areas. There was a large-scale peasant uprising (*Croquant*) in France in 1593–1595, food riots in several English counties in 1596, especially in Essex, and an all-out peasant war raging in Upper Austria (*Oberösterreich*) in 1596–1598, to mention just a few examples. The middle of the seventeenth century also saw many bad harvests at the same time as much of Europe was in political chaos. The English Civil War (1642–1651) led to great political changes, and France was trembling in the pains of the *Fronde* (1648–1653).[3] As we have seen, political life in Sweden, which suffered bad harvests in the 1640s, was also extremely inflamed at this time. And, finally, we have in the eastern corner of the Swedish realm the Karelian uprising during the years of the Great Famine in 1696–1697.

We must therefore ask if crop failure was the prime mover behind the early modern political disturbances and peasant uprisings? The answer must be an absolute no! There were numerous bad harvests and even almost total losses of yield that did not give rise to any open protests at all. The victims of crop failure usually sought other ways to influence the establishment than the path of open revolt. Revolt had to have a social and political basis on which to grow, and this would often lie in the relations between the peasantry and their landlords or the Crown. Crop failures increased the price of grain and sharpened social contradictions by causing tax arrears. In already inflamed social and political situations a bad harvest would give the protesters tools with which to voice their discontent, but it is important to stress that the crop failures themselves were not the reason for the unrest.

Religion

Many medieval peasant social movements were at the same time also religious movements. In the English rising, for example, the preachers among the commons played a role in giving the rebels an ideological context for their rebellion by spreading a message of the basic equality of man based on the writings of scripture. The slogan of the rebels, "When Adam delft and Eve span, who was then a gentleman", asked that if all men were the children of Adam and Eve, what was the justification for the inequality in society.[4]

This religious proclamation of equality can also be traced in many protest movements of the fifteenth and sixteenth centuries. A good example is the Hussite War of 1419–1433 in Bohemia. In this long-lasting conflict the demands for reforms in the Church and religion, social inequalities and the tensions between the Germans and Czechs become entangled with each other. The reformative ideas of Jan Hus (1373–1415) and his followers elicited a response from the Czech peasantry, the other side being taken by the German-speaking landlords and priests supporting the papal church.[5]

The medieval and late medieval periods (meaning in Nordic historical writing the fourteenth and fifteenth centuries) saw many violent uprisings in the Nordic realms too. The 1430s, in particular, were times of tumult in every corner of Scandinavia. The Engelbrekt and Puke uprisings in Sweden and the revolts of Amund Sigurdsson Bolt and Halvard Gråtopp in Norway are the most memorable events from this particular decade. There were also uprisings in Denmark and on Finnish soil at this time. The risings in Sweden, Norway and Denmark were closely interwoven with the politics of the day, while the Finnish revolts were local events only very loosely related to the political tumults of the period. There are, however, no signs that religion played any role in these disturbances.

The religious ethos was a substantial component in the peasant revolts of the late fifteenth and sixteenth centuries in Germany, and also in France and the British Isles. For example, in England, the Pilgrimage of Grace in 1536, the Prayer Book Rebellion of 1548 and also the more secular Kett's rebellion of 1549 were closely connected with religious disputes.[6] In the German *Bundschuch* revolts at the end of the fifteenth century the peasantry attacking the manors and castles of the landlords and bishops swore by the name of the 'common father': Adam.[7]

The Reformation played a fundamental role in the Great German Peasant War of 1525. The war itself was essentially a series of attacks by separate peasant armies, although there was a strong effort to organise joint leadership and governance. The ideological clue to this mass movement can be found in the writings of the reformer Martin Luther. This can be clearly seen in the 'Twelve Articles of Memmingen', the document that became a genuine programme for the German rebels. The main secular demands in these articles are the abolition of serfdom and rights to the use of natural resources such as forests. However, all these demands were grounded in the biblical message of the equality of man. On the other hand, demands that at first sight appear to be purely religious, like the demand to give parishioners the right to elect their own (Lutheran) priest and the right to pay his salary, were in fact serious attacks against the landlords, who had traditionally possessed these rights (*jus patronus*).[8]

Nothing like this can be found in the peasant uprisings in the Nordic countries. With the possible exception of Denmark, there was no reformist movement among the common people. The Reformation was brought to Scandinavia by order of the Crown. Besides religious motivations, the Reformation, at least in Sweden, was carried through by the Crown for fiscal reasons. Confiscation of Church land and movable property was one way of acquiring the funds needed for state-building: establishing the first embryo of the permanent central administration and military warfare needed to secure the territory and economic power of the newly emerging quasi-modern state. At the same time, it also crushed the main pillars of the strong secular power the Church had enjoyed in late medieval society.

However, all the Nordic countries – Iceland excluded – had their last great uprisings during the sixteenth century. The last large-scale uprisings occurred in Norway in the 1520s, in Denmark in the 1530s, in Sweden in the 1540s and on Finnish soil in the 1590s. In these uprisings of the Reformation period religion played almost no role, and where it had any impact it was against the Reformation, not on behalf of it. In the Norwegian Telemark revolts of the 1520s the peasants rose against the labour service imposed because of the newly opened mine and the upkeep of the mine-workers brought into the area. The fact that these newcomers were German and Protestants must have increased the suspicions and hatred among the local Norwegian peasantry, who were still Roman Catholic. All in all, it seems that the reluctant attitude of the Norwegians to the Reformation was due to the fact the 'purified religion' was introduced to Norway by order from Denmark.

Sweden saw some genuine uprisings against King Gustavus Vasa and his reformation policies. These movements were led by some Catholic bishops, and they are not considered in the historical literature as peasant uprisings.[9] However, the rebels of the Dacke War in the 1540s also criticized confiscation of the parish properties and the 'theft' of Church valuables by the Crown. The peasants felt that they themselves were the victims of these acts. In addition to this, the rebels also complained that the new reformed liturgy was so simple that any herdsman was able to whistle it through.

In the tax unrest in Lappee, in Finland, in the 1550s, the fact that the Crown judge had in the name of confiscation removed the valuables from the local church only to keep them in his own manor caused a great deal of irritation among the rebelling peasantry. Nevertheless, neither of these revolts could be claimed to have had their origins in the Counter-Reformation. During the political disputes surrounding the events of the

Club War in 1596–1597, the Finnish peasants chose the side of Duke Charles. Although Charles attempted to present himself as a guarantor of the Lutheran faith against the Catholic King Sigismund, religion played no role in the events of the war.

It has been clearly shown that one essential difference between the late medieval and sixteenth-century peasant revolts in western and northern Europe lay in the role of religion. In central and western Europe the religious disputes were closely intertwined with the social and political ones. In the north, religion played a much smaller role in politics and it had almost no part at all in peasant unrest. This is a feature common to all the Nordic countries. But, if religion cannot provide the answer, where can we find the prime mover behind the peasant revolts?

Instigation

The thought of the peasantry being capable of political action was almost impossible for the nobility in early modern society. The peasant was viewed as a simple, clumsy and somewhat amusing creature, capable only of ploughing the fields and working in the forests and mines.[10] The nobles and the learned men wrote all the documents that have survived from these times, and they have mediated to us this view of political incompetence on the part of the commons. The rising of such simple men to resistance or protest was a mystery to the establishment. The only possible solution they could conceive of was that someone from the learned estates had incited the peasantry to protest. This instigator was keenly sought through the centuries, but almost never found.

The example of Finnish peasant unrest in the 1640s and 1650s shows how the politics of the realm and the local disputes were intertwined with each other. The enlarging of the manorial estates at the expense of the peasants was the main local cause of dispute. Bad harvests sharpened these disputes, and peasant complaints were sent to the Diet. At the Diet, these complaints (similar ones being sent from the other parts of the realm) were used as a tool by the three common estates in their struggle against the aims of the nobility to enlarge the number of manorial estates and fiefs. The clergy took the ideological lead in this three-estate alliance. Now Lutheran ethics were turned against the nobles: the construction of their manors and castles and the pompous lifestyle of the nobility were bitterly criticised, especially during the times the commons were suffering in poverty due to bad harvests.

There is an evident contemporaneousness in the British, French and Swedish political turbulence of the 1640s and 1650s. The clergy were certainly aware of the Protestant struggle for Commonwealth in the British Isles. Moreover, the ideas for strengthening the power of the Diet which were presented in France during the *Fronde* were apparently known in Sweden. So we must ask if the peasant estate was simply a tool of the clergy in this struggle? Absolutely not! The peasant protests with their origins in local disputes came first and were genuine peasant grievances, not inflamed by the local priests. At the Diet these became entangled with the greater figures on the political stage.

The ability of the peasant estate to pursue independent politics at the Diet can be seen in their continuous demands for the reduction of the fiefs and manorial estates. The reduction of the fiefs was the main goal of the peasant estate throughout the seventeenth century, and one that was taken up at every Diet where they perceived any chance of achieving their goal. This demand was eventually realized in the Great Reduction of 1680s. However, we must not overestimate the political capacity of the peasant estate. The precondition for successful peasant politics at the Diet was cooperation between the three non-noble estates, and this was based on mutual interests in opposing the nobility. In many cases where these common interests did not pertain, such an alliance was impossible and the peasant estate did not wield much influence at the Diet.

The pacification of society

If the peasants did not have much say at the Swedish Diet, then we must ask why their representation there was necessary at all. They were not present at the Diets in other European countries! There are two main ways to explain this. The first possibility is that when the peasants were represented at the Diet, decisions about new taxes and other payments were more readily accepted in the provinces. The other possibility is that the aim was to create a genuine channel of interaction between the peasants – who supplied the country with food, other goods and recruits for the army – and the central government. Whatever the truth, both explanations point to the exceptionally strong position of the peasantry in early modern Sweden. The fear of peasant discontent and even uprising was still present and the basic needs of the peasantry could not be overlooked.

The peasantry in Sweden, Finland (with the exception of riots in the easternmost corner of Karelia in the 1670s, 1680s and 1690s), Norway and Denmark never again rose in violent revolt after the turn of the seventeenth century. Seventeenth-century Europe, in contrast, experienced numerous violent peasant revolts and riots: the English peasantry protested especially against the enclosure movement, the French peasants had their own uprisings (for example the *Croquant* of 1636 and the *Nu-Pied* of 1639) and the peasants in German areas also organised several violent protests.[11] It is important to remember that during the first half of the seventeenth century the Thirty Years War was raging around Europe until the Treaty of Westphalia in 1648. In the latter half of the century the peasant protests in Germany especially were no longer crushed with military force. In many cases the protesters were tried by commissions or at the Supreme Court. This process has been called *Verrechtlichung*, or the juridification of conflicts. And this is also what we can see in the Nordic countries.

There were no real large-scale peasant uprisings in the Nordic countries during the seventeenth century. Instead, we can see peasant protests in the form of petitions, complaints, strikes on rent service and taxes, and so on.

The main scene of conflict was in the local courts (*ting*). Thorn-headed clubs were replaced as weapons by documents, and instead of rebellious peasant troops against cavalry it was the advocates of the contending parties who took the measure of each other in legal combat. Although these disputes between the peasants and their landlords were almost totally non-violent, they were long-lasting quarrels that the establishment labelled as "peasant rebellions".

The pacification of peasant protest happened rather quickly in the seventeenth-century Nordic kingdoms. This development must be seen in connection with the general pacification of these societies. The level of violent crime in general (per 100 000 persons per year) declined throughout almost the whole of Europe. In the Nordic countries this decline in the level of violence in society as a whole is very clear.[12] Behind this pacification there were several processes at work. Firstly, military and police organisations extended territorial control over their societies. The emergence of the 'power state' (*Machtstaat*) made it almost impossible to organise any large-scale violent attacks against the establishment. Secondly, new channels of peasant influence were developed, or the old ones strengthened. Developing the judicial system and consolidating the work of the Diet in Sweden served as alternative ways of trying to have a say in society. Bringing complaints to the king and the central authorities in general was another essential means of protest in all the Nordic countries. And thirdly, a factor of importance for organised violent peasant movements, the traditional horizontal organisation of peasant society was pulled apart and replaced with local administration under Crown control. This process of demolishing the traditional principles of peasant organisation had already begun by the beginning of the sixteenth century.

Peasant communalism

Nordic historians have used the concept of communalism – taken from Peter Blickle's vocabulary – in describing the horizontal elements in late medieval Scandinavian society. We have shown above that local peasant society had a fairly autonomous position in the late medieval Scandinavian kingdoms. One aspect of this autonomy was the military power of the armed peasantry. It was possible to organise this power at least at provincial level. The organisation of the province to rise in revolt took place at special provincial assemblies (*landting*), as we have seen in the context of the Engelbrekt uprising. However, we have only quite scanty knowledge about how this organisation actually happened in practice. This military power of the peasantry was one essential piece of the puzzle when crown pretenders competed with each other and the peasantry tried as best they could to benefit from the struggle. In this, we have one of the basic structures underlying the peasant uprisings of the fifteenth century, especially in Sweden.

In Norway, the late medieval alliances between peasants and local aristocracies cannot be traced as clearly as in Sweden, but the logic of the events would nevertheless seem to be somewhat similar. The rebelling peasants almost always had a noble at their head. The situation in Finland was totally different. In the David's uprising at the end of the 1430s we can see only rioting peasants who were attacking and looting the local manors. The main organisational unit seems to have been the parish, as far as we can tell from the sources available. The final reconciliation was made between the peasant delegates of six parishes on one side and the governor of Turku Castle on the other. However, the settlement was confirmed on the side of the peasantry with the seal of the province of Satakunta.

The Norwegian example examined in this book shows the complexity of the processes involved in rising in open revolt. In the areas with little social and economic differentiation and strong institutions of self-government, and relatively free from the power of the establishment, conflicts were handled in legal institutions (or institutions understood as such) and did not develop into open revolts. On the contrary, government repression and strong social and economic differentiation increased the danger of revolt and, if open protest was impossible, passive resistance was resorted to instead. A balance of rights and duties was reached in an 'agreement' between local peasant society and the Crown and their respective representatives. As long as the mutual commitments were met, peace was maintained in society. These communal structures of peasant society were broken in the changes the Nordic realms endured during the sixteenth and seventeenth centuries.

In Sweden, many of the old communal practices of peasant society were replaced with new systems dominated by the central government during the reign of Gustavus Vasa. The medieval conception was that taxes represented a collective compensation on the part of peasant society for the shelter guaranteed the subjects by the power of the prince. The reorganisation of the tax system in the first half of the sixteenth century replaced these old collectively paid taxes with personal duties from every holding. This was one of the disputes underlying the Dacke War in 1542, but it can also be discerned in the background to the unrest in Lappee in 1551–1553.

Comparing the Norwegian experience with the Swedish uprisings of the fifteenth century and the Club War in Finland at the end of the sixteenth century highlights the importance to the risings of local horizontal organisational structures. The late medieval decision-making structures in the provinces were crucial for organising the peasant troops of the province. These provincial assemblies (*landting*) were also a party to be negotiated with over the terms of support. The Engelbrekt uprising rested on a foundation of the local corporative organisations involved in iron production.

These local governmental structures were dominated by the wealthiest peasants. This can be seen in the Finnish Club War, especially in the important role played by the local peasant sheriffs and peasant tax collectors in organising the peasant troops. In summing up, we can say that the peasant revolts in the Nordic countries were not uprisings of the poor; they were risings by the well-to-do peasants led by the wealthiest ones. The difficulties or even collapse of the economy of the well-to-do peasantry was the one prime mover behind many revolts. However, other groups of commons joined these protests at a later stage.

The consolidation of the Swedish Diet was an essential part of this process of rescinding the local communal principles of peasant society. Previously, the Crown had had to agree – at least in theory – with the provinces over new taxes and the taking of new recruits for the army. Now these decisions were centralised in the Diet and there was no longer any need to communicate directly with the provinces. In 1660, a royal statute even prohibited the provincial meetings. The local structures essential for organising the armed peasant troops were now finally dissolved.

The idea here is somewhat opposite to Peter Blickle's original ideas about peasant communalism. Blickle explained the rise of peasant revolts in the fourteenth and fifteenth centuries by a process whereby feudal principles were replaced by new local structures of communal organisation.[13] In the Scandinavian context, we have explained the peasantry's ability to organise armed forces by appeal to local medieval communal organisational structures. The vanishing of the large-scale violent uprisings after the sixteenth century is here connected with the rescinding of peasant communalism. However, although the day of violent uprisings was now over, the peasant movements did not vanish. The peasantry's ability to organise resistance and protest was not swept under the carpet, but in the changed circumstances it took on new forms. Finally, we must consider these changing circumstances through the concept of political culture.

Political culture

At the beginning of this book the concept of political culture was defined as "the patterns of the game" in politics. These patterns include established political practices (praxis), the norms and values guiding these practices, and the symbols used in 'doing' politics.[14] These practices, norms, values and symbols form a system characteristic to each epoch. Each system of political culture can bear traits from preceding political cultures. For example, in the case of peasant revolts, the idea of an 'agreement' on the reciprocal duties and responsibilities between lord and subject (or communal local peasant society) as the basis of the hierarchical relations of loyalty and protection can be traced every bit as much from the fifteenth-century David's uprising as from the tenant movements of the late eighteenth century. The tenants in eighteenth-century Finland did renounce their loyalty to their landlords, and, to the establishment, this marked the movement as rebellion.

However, there were both differences and similarities between the political cultures of the Nordic realms. For example, the peasant unrest in Norway and Finland had much in common. The medieval unrest in both territories was directed primarily against the growing demands of the clergy. In Sweden, where the elective monarchy made the political 'parties' compete, an alliance between the pretender to the throne and the peasantry can be found as early as the Uppland uprising in 1247. This arrangement paved the way for the Swedish peasant uprisings of the fifteenth century. In late medieval Norway and in Finland the peasant revolts were usually – with only a few exceptions – rather small-scale disturbances with their origins in local disputes. The connection to state politics was weak, although not entirely absent. Most of these disturbances occurred during periods of political confusion. However, they did not arise because of the inflamed situation, but parallel to these political struggles. The Swedish revolts of the era had an altogether different character. In these events, the Swedish peasantry took part in state politics. The aim was usually to influence who should be crowned king. Swedish revolts were also usually large-scale events, and in two cases – the Engelbrekt uprising of 1434–1436 and the Dacke War of 1542–1543 – an alternative governmental organisation was even constructed.

The change of political culture in all the Nordic kingdoms during the sixteenth century was drastic. The medieval societies composed of fairly autonomous territories led by local gentry were replaced by state-like societies with central bureaucracies and a stronger position for the king. In Sweden, the competition between pretenders to the throne in alliance with peasant armies from the provinces came to an end. In Iceland, there was an end to the conflicts between the local chiefs, and the peasants gradually began to get shelter from the Crown, its representatives and its law. The state began to dominate and local structures to vanish or adapt to the new system.

Two of the last great Nordic peasant wars, the revolt of Skipper Clemens in 1534 in Denmark and the Finnish Club War in 1596–1597, serve to illuminate the change from late medieval to early modern revolts. The revolt of Clemens occurred during the War of the Counts (1533–1536) in a situation where the exiled Christian II and Christian III, the successor to Frederic I on the Danish throne, were vying for power. At the end of the sixteenth century in Finland the scene was somewhat similar, with a struggle for power between King Sigismund and Duke Charles, who had begun to seek the Crown. In this situation the Finnish peasantry tried to ally with the duke to fight against their hated oppressors, the soldiers, and their commanders, the Finnish nobility faithful to the king. However, although these revolts had connections with state politics as they occurred while possession of the throne was still unresolved, in both cases the unrest had its local roots in social and economic contradictions or breakdowns in peasant society.

One aspect of the great change of the sixteenth and seventeenth centuries was that the newly constructed administrative structures begun to function as a legitimate channel of political communication. This is certainly true, but – it must be stressed – only partly true. There were many aspects of social life where the Crown listened to the complaints of the peasantry. For example, their consent was still needed in the sixteenth century – at least in theory – for setting new taxes. However, when the interests of the establishment were opposed to those of the peasantry, the peasants had little say in the matter. This can be seen clearly in the politics of the Swedish regencies of the seventeenth century and in local trials involving disputes between the peasants and their landlords.

In Iceland, there were no peasant revolts during the period examined here. However, the Icelandic example shows clearly how an examination of peasant protest can be a fruitful tool in research into the social relationships of all medieval and early modern societies. We have seen how conflicts arose between the Icelanders and Norwegian and later Danish rule, which represented the establishment and the central power. On the other hand, the conflicts between the Icelandic landowning elite and their tenant farmers were related to the taxes, rent service and cow rents. The political culture of Iceland began to change when the Danish establishment intervened on the side of the tenants from the 1550s onwards. The medieval mutual patron-vassal relationships based on the need for shelter were slowly replaced with early modern landlord-tenant relationships based on the law and agreements over the taxes and rent service. Without conflict-oriented research these kinds of processes within societies can easily be missed.

Denmark is an exception from the 'Nordic rule'. It is difficult to find almost any traces of organised large-scale peasant protest movements in Danish history after the revolt of Skipper Clemens in 1534. It is evident that the construction of a tight network of manors and the granting of judicial and economic powers to the landlords made it almost impossible for Danish peasant society to organise any protest movements. We have only scattered knowledge about local peasant protest in any form from the countryside of early modern Denmark. This supports the impression that the strong control over peasant society prevented the rise of open unrest. This definitely does not mean there were no conflicts in society, but they were hidden beneath the suppression and the protests took hidden forms.

The latter half of the eighteenth century saw a new rise of peasant protest and even marching columns of armed peasants in Norway, Sweden and Finland, but no longer in Denmark. And, we must add, this new wave of open protest in the eighteenth century had almost nothing in common with the late medieval and early modern uprisings apart from the scale of protest. The movements once again touched hundreds and thousands of peasants. In Norway, the peasants gathered and protested about the taxes, the Swedish peasants tried to have a say in the succession to the throne, and Finnish tenants struggled for proprietary rights to the farms they cultivated. It is important also to note that simultaneously with this there was a severe and large-scale peasant uprising in Russia (Pugachev's revolt).[15] Thus there would appear to have been a final outburst of peasant movements in northern Europe in the 1770s. However, they all appear to have had very different backgrounds and the only common feature seems to be the timing. In every case the main violence was that exercised by the Crown's troops.

Violence was one of the tools in the establishment repertoire for subduing peasant protest. Another tool was the law. The means at the disposal of the establishment for responding to and suppressing peasant unrest were part of the political culture. The law had at least two roles in this work: being a part of the system of norms and values in society it inhibited the rise of protest, and, if unrest nevertheless arose, the law was the code and legitimation for the punishments handed out to the rebels. It would seem that the establishment already had in the medieval Scandinavian statutes an adequate arsenal for handling peasant uprisings. This was usually via treason legislation. In inflamed situations, and after the uprisings had abated, new statutes were given or the old ones updated. However, there would appear to have been no need to make fundamental changes to the law as a result of peasant unrest.

NOTES

1. Exceptions to this general rule include Mousnier 1970; Tilly 1986; Ylikangas 1991; Tilly 1993; Katajala 2002.
2. Mollat–Wolff 1973, 11.
3. Kamen 1971, 309–317, 357–360; Aylmer 1975; Sharp 1980, 83–155, 223–225; Schulze 1980, 51; Kamen 1982, 138–155; Zagorin 1982 I, 217; Tilly 1986, 91–100, 140–145.
4. See for example Hilton 1975, 39–46; Hilton 1977; Fourquin 1978, 101–102; Dobson 1983, 374; Hilton 1984.
5. Seibt 1975; Fourquin 1978, 102–107; Mullett 1987, 110–122.
6. Beer 1982; Zagorin 1982 II, 22–31; Gunn 1989; Bush 1991.
7. Franz 1984, 56–70; Blickle 1988, 22–27.
8. Diwald 1975, 339–340; Vogler 1975, 209–210; Blickle 1981b, 19–20, 58–67, 195–201; Blickle 1988, 26–29.
9. See for example Rosén 1962, 384–391.
10. See Englund 1989, 90–102, 194–204.
11. Mousnier 1970, 77–86; Kamen 1971, 314–317, 347–348; Le Roy Ladurie 1974, 296–300; Bonney 1978, 214–237; Sharp 1980, 83–155; Schulze 1980, 54–55; Lindley 1982; Kamen 1982, 143–153; Zagorin 1982 I, 220–223; Zagorin 1982 II, 10–12; Tilly 1986, 91–100, 140–145; Blickle 1988, 38–40; Bercé 1990, 109–165.
12. See Ylikangas 1998.
13. See Blickle 1986a.
14. For recent discussion on the concept see Sennefelt 2001, 17–21.
15. See for example Alexander 1969.

Sources and references

Primary sources

National Archives of Sweden (Riksarkivet, Stockholm, Sweden RA)
    Justitierevisionen (Supreme Court)
Oresolverade revisionsakter (Unresolved cases)
    Kammararkivet (Chamber Archives)
Småländska handlingar 1543
Kungl. Maj:ts arkiv (King's Archive)
Landshövdingarnas skrivelser till Kungl. Maj:t, Kopparbergs län 1743–1744
Svea hovrätt, Huvudarkivet (Svea Court of Appeal, the Main Archive)
Protokoll i särskilda mål, Dalupproret 1743–1744 (abbr. Svea hovrätt, protokoll Dalupproret)
Handlingar rörande Dalupproret, vol. a–d (abbr. Svea hovrätt, handlingar Dalupproret)
Riksdagens arkiv (Diet's Archive)
Ständernas kommissioner (Estate's Commissions)
Kommission angående orsakerna till krigets olyckliga förlopp i Finland 1741–1742, Protokoll (abbr. Ständernas kommission över kriget, protokoll)
Kommission över Sven Hoffman och upproret i Vedens härad i Västergötland, Handlingar och protokoll (abbr. Ständernas kommission över Hofman, handlingar/ protokoll)

National Archives of Finland (Kansallisarkisto, Helsinki, Finland, KA)
    Vanhempi tilikirjasarja (Old register of accounts)
    Rahvaanvalitukset (Complaints of the commons)

National Archives of Iceland (Þjóðskjalasafn Íslands, Reykjavik, Iceland)
    Lénsreikningar 1597–1660
    Manntalið 1762, Norðuramt

Provincial Archive of Hämeenlinna, (Hämeenlinnan maakunta-arkisto, Finland, HMA)
    Jokioisten kartanon arkisto (Archive of Jokioinen manor)

Provincial Archive in Göteborg (Landsarkivet, Göteborg, Sweden, GLA)
Skaraborgs läns landskansli, inkommande skrivelser från Göta hovrätt, 1761–1766

Provincial Archive of Uppsala (Landsarkivet, Uppsala, Sweden, ULA)
Kopparbergs läns landskansli, inkommande skrivelser från Kungl. Maj:t, 1743–1746

National Library of Iceland, (Landsbókafsan Íslands)
    Handritadeild (Manuscript Divison)
        JÞ XIII

Uppsala University Library, Sweden (Uppsala universitetsbibliotek, UUB)
    UUB B 9

Published sources

Aarsberetninger: *Aarsberetninger fra det Konglige Geheimearchiv indeholdende Bidrag til Dansk Historie, vol. 5.* Published by C. F. Wegener. Copenhagen 1874–1875.

Alþingisbækur 1570–1650. Reykjavik 1912–1982.

Anders Koskull's memoirs: Anders Koskulls memoarer, Den av Quennerstedt opublicerade delen. In *Karolinska förbundets årsbok* 1977.

Árbækur Espólíns. Köpenhamn 1829.

Arwidsson III: *Handlingar till upplysning af Finlands häfder, III.* Ed. Adolf Iwar Arwidsson. P. A. Norstedt & söner. Stockholm 1849.

Bondeståndets riksdagsprotokoll 1742–1743 & 1765–1766, vol. 5 & 10. Published by Sten Landahl. Stockholm 1954 & 1973.

Church Ordinance of 1686: *Kircko-Laki ja Ordningi 1686.* Suomalaisen Kirjallisuuden Seuran Toimituksia 444, SKS. Juva 1986.

Diplomatarium Islandicum. Reykjavik 1857–1972.

DRL: *Den danske rigslovgivning indtil 1400.* Ed. Erik Kroman, Det danske Sprog- og Litteraturselskab. Denmark 1971.

DS: *Diplomatarium Suecanum.* Different editors. Kungl. vitterhets historie och antikvitetsakademien och Riksarkivet. Stockholm 1829–1987.

FMU: *Finlands medeltidsurkunder, I–VIII.* Ed. Reinhold Hausen. Finlands statsarkiv. Helsingfors 1910–1935.

Grönblad III: *Handlingar rörande Klubbekriget. Tredje häftet.* Utg. av. Edward Grönblad. Helsingfors 1846.

GVB: *Gustav Vasas brev.* Ed. Alf Åberg. Levande litteratur, Natur och kultur. Stockholm 1960.

Hadorph 1687: *Biärköa Rätten / Then äldsta Stadz Lag i Sweriges Rike.* Ed. Johan Hadorph. Hendrick Keyser. Stockholm 1687.

Hadorph 1688: *Wisby Stadz Lag på Gotland / Såsom then i Forna Tijder giord/.* Ed. Johan Hadorph. Hendrick Keyser. Stockholm 1688.

Handlingar rörande Skandinaviens historia I & III: *Handlingar rörande Skandinaviens historia, vol. I & III.* Stockholm 1816 & 1817.

HArk IV 1874: *Historiallinen Arkisto IV.* Ed. Historiallinen Osakunta. Suomalaisen Kirjallisuuden Seuran toimituksia. Osa 41. Helsinki 1874.

Hirðskrá: *Das norwegische Gefolgschaftsrecht* (Hirðskrá). Ed. Rudolf Meißner, Germanenrechte, Texte und Übersetzungen, Band 5. Schriften des Deutschrechtlichen Instituts, Abteilung Nordgermanisches Recht. Verlag Hermann Böhlaus Nachf. Weimar 1938.

Inrikes tidningar, no. 39–41, 62, 1766.

Íslenskir annálar 1400–1800. Reykjavik 1922.

JL: *Den Jyske lov.* Text med oversættelse, kommentar og ordbok. Ed. Peter Skautrup. Jysk selskab for historie, sprog og litteratur. Denmark 1941.

Kanc. brevb: *Kancelliets brevbøger vedrørende Danmarks indre forhold / i udrag udgivne ved L. Laursen.* 1885.

KrLL: *Kuningas Kristoferin maanlaki 1442.* Transl. Martti Ulkuniemi. Suomalaisen Kirjallisuuden Seuran toimituksia, SKS. Vaasa 1978.

Leges Henrici Primi: *Leges Henrici Primi.* Ed. (with Translation and Commentary) L. J. Downer. Oxford University Press. Great Britain 1972.

LKMH: *Landrecht des Königs Magnus Hakonarson.* Ed. Rudolf Meißner, Germanenrechte, Neue Folge. Schriften des Deutschrechtlichen Instituts, Abteilung Nordgermanisches Recht. Verlag Hermann Böhlaus Nachf. Weimar 1941.

Lovsamling for Island. Köpenhamn 1853–1855.

MELL: *Magnus Erikssons landslag i nusvensk tolkning.* Eds. Åke Holmbäck and Elias Wessén. Rättshistoriskt bibliotek, 6. Institutet för rättshistorisk forskning grundat av Gustav och Karin Olin. Lund 1962.

MESL: *Maunu Eerikinpojan kaupunginlaki.* Transl. by Abraham Kollanius, ed. Martti Rapola. Suomen kielen muistomerkkejä III, 2. Suomalaisen Kirjallisuuden Seuran toimituksia 82. SKS. Helsinki 1926.

Modée: *Utdrag Utur alle ifrån den 7. Decemb. 1718. utkomne Publique Handlingar, Placater, Förordningar, Resolutioner Och Publicationer, Riksens Styrsel samt inwårtes Hushållning och Författningar i gemen, jemwäl ock Stockholms Stad i synnerhet angå, I–XV.* Ed. R. G. Modée. Lorenz Ludwig Grefing. Stockholm 1742–1829.

Nehrman 1756: Nehrman, David: *Inledning til Then Swenska Jurisprudentiam Criminalem efter Sweriges Rikes Lag och Stadgar.* Gottfried Kiesewetter. Lund 1756.

Olaus Magnus: Olaus Magnus: *Historia om de nordiska folken, II.* Utg. genom Michaelisgillet. Uppsala 1912.

Piispa Henrikin surmavirsi 1999: *Piispa Henrikin surmavirsi.* SKS. Vaasa 1999.

REA: *Registratum Ecclesiae Aboensis eller Åbo Domkyrkans Svartbok.* Jyväskylä 1996.

Schlyter: *Corpus iuris Sueo-gothorum antiqui, X–XII.* Ed. C. J. Schlyter. Berlingska Boktryckeriet. Lund 1862–1869.

Schmedeman 1706: *Kongl. Stadgar, Förordningar, Bref och Resolutioner Ifrån Åhr 1528 in til 1701.* Ed. J. Schmedeman. Upsala 1706.

SD: *Svenskt diplomatarium, I–III.* Ed. Carl Silfverstolpe. Riks-Archivet. Stockholm 1879–1887.

SECH: *Sources of English Constitutional History.* Eds. Michael Evans & R. Ian Jack. Butterworths. Australia 1984.

Silvén-Garnert and Söderlind 1980: Silvén-Garnert, Eva and Söderlind, Ingrid: *Ett annat Sverige. Dokument om folkets kamp 1200–1720.* LTs förlag – Falköping 1980.

Skjöl um hylling Íslendinga 1649 við Friðrik konung Þriðja. Reykjavik 1914.

SLL: *Svenska landskapslagar, I–V.* Eds. and trans. Åke Holmbäck and Elias Wessén. Hugo Gebers förlag. Uppsala 1933–1946.

SRL 1734: *Sveriges Rikes Lag, Gillad och Antagen på Riksdagen Åhr 1734.* Rättshistoriskt bibliotek, Vol. 37. Skrifter utgivna av Institutet för rättshistorisk forskning grundat av Gustav och Karin Olin. Lund 1984.

SST: *Stockholms stads tänkeböcker, 1483–1492.* Ed. Gottfrid Carlsson. Utgifna af Kungl. Samfundet för utgifvande af handskrifter rörande Skandinaviens historia med understöd av samfundet Sankt Erik. Stockholm 1921.

Stiernman 1728–1733: *Alla Riksdagars och Mötens Besluth, Samt Arfföreningar, Regements-Former, Försäkringar och Bewillningar som på allmenna Riksadagar och Möter ifrån år 1633 intil år 1680 giörde, stadgade och beviljade äro; med the för hwart och ett stånd utfärdade allmenna resolutioner.* Ed. Anders Anton von Stiernman. Joh. H. Werner. Stockholm 1728–1733.

Sturlunga saga. Reykjavik 1988.

Styffe IV: *Bidrag till Skandinaviens historia, IV.* Ed. Carl Gustaf Styffe. P.A. Norstedt & Söner. Stockholm 1875.

Suomen historian dokumentteja 1 1968: *Suomen historian dokumentteja 1.* Otava. Helsinki 1968.

Söderköpings lagbok 1387: *Söderköpings lagbok 1387.* Ed. Elias Wessén. Rättshistoriskt bibliotek, Vol. 15. Skrifter utgivna av Institutet för rättshistorisk forskning grundat av Gustav och Karin Olin. Lund 1971.

Tacitus: Tacitus: *Germania.* Gaudeamus. Jyväskylä 1976.

Tudor Proclamations II–III: *Tudor Proclamations, II–III.* Eds. Paul L. Hughes & James F. Larkin. Yale University Press. USA 1969.

Två finländska gårdsrättsredaktioner: *Två finländska gårdsrättsredaktioner.* Ed. Nat. Beckman. Göteborgs högskolas årsskrift XXV. Göteborg 1919.

Uppländska konungsdomar: *Uppländska konungsdomar från Vasatiden intill Svea hovrätts inrättande.* Utg. genom Nils Edling. Uppländska domböcker utgivna av Kungliga humanistiska vetenskapssamfundet i Uppsala, III. Uppsala 1933.

Catalogues and others

Íslenskur söguatlas 1. bindi. Reykjavik 1989.
Íslenskur söguatlas 2. bindi. Reykjavik 1992.
Mårtensson 1952: Mårtensson, Ludvig: *Sakregister till Allmogens besvär till år 1720.* Stockholm 1952.

References

't Hart 1998: 't Hart, Marjolein: Rules and Repertoires: The Revolt of a Farmers' Republic in the Early-Modern Netherlands. In M. P. Hanagan, L. P. Moch, and W. te Brake (eds.), *Challenging Authority: The Historical Study of Contentious Politics.* University of Minnesota Press. Minneapolis 1998.
Aalto et al 2000: Aalto, Seppo, Johansson, Kenneth and Sandmo, Erling: Conflicts and Court Encounters in a State of Ambivalence. In Eva Österberg and Sølvi Sogner (Eds.), *People Meet the Law. Control and conflict-handling in the courts. The Nordic countries in the post-Reformation and pre-industrial period.* Universtetsförlaget. Otta 2000.
Aðils 1919: Aðils, Jón J.: *Einokunarverslun Dana á Íslandi 1602–1787.* Reykjavik 1919.
Ahnlund 1933: Ahnlund, Nils: Ståndriksdagens utdaning 1592–1672. Sveriges Riksdag. Förra avdelningen. *Riksdagens historia intill 1865.* Tredje bandet. Stockholm 1933.
Ahnlund 1948: Ahnlund, Nils: *Jämtlands och Härjedalens historia.* Förste delen inntil 1537. Stockholm 1948.
Alexander 1969: Alexander, John T.: *Autocratic Politics in a National Crisis. The Imperial Russian Government and Pugachev's Revolt 1773–1775.* Indiana University Press 1969.
Alexandersson 1975: Alexandersson, Erland: *Bondeståndet i riksdagen 1766–1772.* Bibliotheca Historica Lundensis XXXVI. Lund 1975.
Almén 1940: Almén, Folke: *Gustav III och hans rådgivare 1772–89. Arbetssätt och meningsbrytningar i rådkammare och konseljer.* Uppsala 1940.
Anderson 1980: Anderson, Perry: *Den absoluta statens utveckling.* Stockholm 1980.
Anderson 1984: Anderson, Perry: *Övergångar från antiken till feodalismen.* Lund 1984.
Andresen 1997: Andresen, Espen: *Landskap og maktstat. Jemtland 1613–1645.* Unpublished master thesis, Trondheim 1997.
Anners 1961: Anners, Erik: Vasatidens och stormaktstidens svenska militärstraffrätt. Några problemställningar. In *Tidskrift utgiven av Juridiska Föreningen i Finland,* 87–1961.
Anners 1965: Anners, Erik: *Humanitet och rationalism. Studier i upplysningstidens straflagsreformer–särskilt med hänsyn till Gustav III:s reformlagstiftning.* Rättshistoriskt bibliotek, Vol. 10. Skrifter utgivna av Institutet för rättshistorisk forskning grundat av Gustav och Karin Olin. Lund 1965.
Anttila 1991: Anttila, Olavi: *Kartanosta kunnaksi. Jokioisten historia.* Forssa 1991.
Appel 1999: Appel, Hans Henrik: *Tinget, magten och æren. Studier i sociale processer og magtrelationer i et jysk bondesamfund i 1600-tallet.* Odense 1999.
Arendt 1988: Arendt, Hannah: *Människans villkor.* Vita activa. Eslöv 1988.
Aronsson 1992: Aronsson, Peter: *Bönder gör politik. Det lokala självstyret som social arena i tre smålandssocknar 1680-1850,* Lund University Press. Lund 1992.
Axelsson and Cederholm 1997: Axelsson, Anders, Cederholm, Matthias: *Kungen på tinget – en implicit utopi i de senmedeltida bondeprotesterna.* Unpublished dissertation. Lund 1997.
Aya 1990: Aya, Rod: *Rethinking Revolutions and Collective Violence: Studies on Concept, Theory, and Method.* Het Spinhuis. Amsterdam 1990.

Aylmer 1975: *The Levellers in the English Revolution.* Ed. G. E. Aylmer. Thames and Hudson. London 1975.

Bagge 1987: Bagge, Sverre: *The Political Thought in The King's Mirror.* Odense University Press. Viborg 1987.

Bar 1968: Bar, Carl Ludwig von et al.: *A History of Continental Criminal Law.* The Continental Legal History Series VI. Rothman Reprints, Inc. & Augustus M. Kelley Publishers. USA 1968.

Bauman 1970: Bauman, Richard A.: *The Crimen Maiestatis in the Roman Republic and Augustan Principate.* Witwatersrand University Press. Pietermaritzburg 1970.

Beckman 1930: Beckman, Bjarne: *Dalupproret 1743 och andra samtida rörelser inom allmogen och bondeståndet.* Wettergren & Kerbers förlag. Göteborg 1930.

Beer 1982: Beer, Barret L.: *Rebellion and Riot. Popular disorder in England during the Reign of Edward VI.* The Kent University Press 1982.

Bellamy 1970: Bellamy, John: *The Law of Treason in England in the Later Middle Ages. Cambridge Studies of Legal History.* Cambridge University Press. Aberdeen 1970.

Bellamy 1979: Bellamy, John: *The Tudor Law of Treason.* Studies in Social History. Routledge & Kegan Paul Ltd. Great Britain 1979.

Bercé 1987: Bercé, Yves-Marie: *Revolt and revolution in early modern Europe. An essay on the history of political violence.* Manchester 1987.

Bercé 1990: Bercé, Yves-Marie: *History of Peasant Revolts. The Social Origins of Rebellion in Early Modern France.* Cornell University Press 1990.

Bjarne Larsson 1994: Bjarne Larsson, Gabriela: *Stadgelagstiftning i senmedeltidens Sverige.* Rättshistoriskt bibliotek, Vol. 51. Skrifter utgivna av Institutet för rättshistorisk forskning grundat av Gustav och Karin Olin. Lund 1994.

Bjørkvik and Holmsen 1952–1954: Bjørkvik, Halvard and Holmsen, Andreas: Kven åtte jorda i den gamle leilendingstida? In *Heimen. Lokalhistorisk tidskrift,* vol. IX, 1952–1954.

Bjørkvik 1996: Bjørkvik, Halvard, *Norges historie vol. 4: Folketap og sammenbrudd 1350–1520.* Oslo 1996.

Bjørn 1981: Bjørn, Claus: *Bonde, herremand, konge. Bonden i 1700-tallets Danmark.* København 1981.

Björne 1995: Björne, Lars: *Patrioter och institutionalister. Den nordiska rättsvetenskapens historia, I. Tiden före år 1815.* Rättshistoriskt bibliotek, Vol. 52. Skrifter utgivna av Institutet för rättshistorisk forskning grundat av Gustav och Karin Olin. Lund 1995.

Björnsson 2000: Björnsson, Lýður: "Íslendingar og danski herinn á 17. og 18. öld." *Lesbók Morgunblaðsins 29. apríl 2000.*

Blickle 1981a: Blickle, Peter: *Deutsche Untertanen. Ein Widerspruch.* München 1981.

Blickle 1981b: Blickle, Peter: *The Revolution of 1525. The German Peasants' War from a New Perspective.* The John Hopkins University Press. Baltimore 1981 (1st edition 1977).

Blickle 1986a: Blickle, Peter: Kommunalismus, Parlamentarismus, Republikanismus. In *Historische Zeitschrift,* 1986.

Blickle 1986b: Blickle, Peter: Das göttliche Recht der Bauern und die göttliche Gerechtigkeit der reformatoren. In E. Bodhof (Ed.), *Archiv für Kulturgeschichte.* Köln 1986.

Blickle 1986c: Blickle, Peter: The Criminalization of Peasant Resistance in the Holy Roman Empire: Toward a History of the Emergence of High Treason in Germany. In *The Journal of Modern History*, Vol. 58, Supplement (1986).

Blickle 1988: Blickle, Peter: *Unruhen in der Ständischen Gesellschaft 1300–1800.* R. Oldenbourg Verlag. München 1988.

Blickle 1997: Peter Blickle (Ed.), *Resistance, Representation and Community.* Clarendon Press. Oxford 1997.

Blomstedt 1937: Blomstedt, Kaarlo: Davidin kapina v. 1438. In *Historiallinen Aikakauskirja*, 1–1937.

Blomstedt 1952: Blomstedt, Kaarlo: Anian David. In *Suomalaisia talonpoikia Lallista Kyösti Kallioon.* WSOY. Porvoo 1952.

Blomstedt 1958: Blomstedt, Yrjö: *Laamannin- ja kihlakunnantuomarinvirkojen läänittäminen ja hoito Suomessa 1500- ja 1600-luvuilla (1523–1680).* Historiallisia Tutkimuksia LI. SHS. Forssa 1958.

Bøgh 1988: Bøgh, Anders: "Med Guds og Sankt Eriks hjælp". Sociale oprør i Sverige-Finland 1432–38". In *Til kamp for friheden. Sociale Oprør i Nordisk Middelalder*, eds. Anders Bøgh, Jørgen Würtz Sørensen and Lars Tvede-Jensen. Bogsmejden. Denmark 1988.

Bolmskog 1995: Bolmskog, Henrik: *Vi vill inte gå till Skåne! Överhet och undersåtar på kollisionskurs i Västergötland år 1710.* Unpublished paper at the Department of History at Stockholm University. Stockholm 1995.

Bonney 1978: Bonney, Richard: *Political Change under Richelieu and Mazarin 1624–1661.* Oxford University Press. London 1978.

Brecht 1938: Brecht, Christoph Heinrich: *Perduellio. Eine Studie zu ihrer begrifflichen Abgrenzung im römischen Strafrecht bis zum Ausgang der Republik.* Münchener Beiträge zur Papyrusforschung und antiken Rechtsgeschichte, 29. C. H. Beck'sche Verlagsbuchhandlung. München 1938.

Bregnsbo 1997: Bregnsbo, Michael: *Folk skriver til kongen: supplikene og deres funktion i den dansk-norske enevælde 1700-tallet. En kildestudie i Danske Kancellis supplikprotokoller.* København 1997.

Brunner 1962: Brunner, Otto: *Neue Wege der Verfassungs- und Sozialgeschichte.* Göttingen 1962.

Brunner 1984: Brunner, Otto: *Land and Lordship. Structures of Governance in Medieval Austria.* University of Pennsylvania Press. USA 1984.

Bugge 1925: Bugge, Alexander: *Den norske trælasthandels historie 1. Fra de ældste tider indtil freden i Speier 1544.* Skien 1925.

Burius 1984: Burius, Anders: *Ömhet om friheten. Studier i frihetstidens censurpolitik.* Diss. Uppsala University. Uppsala 1984.

Burke 1983a: Burke, Peter: *Folklig kultur i Europa 1500–1800.* Stockholm 1983.

Burke 1983b: Burke, Peter: The Virgin of the Carmine and the Revolt of Masaniello. In *Past & Present,* no. 99–1983.

Bush 1991: Bush, Michael: *Tax Reform and Rebellion in Early Tudor England.* History 1991. No 248.

Bååth 1905: Bååth, L. M.: *Bidrag till den kanoniska rättens historia i Sverige.* Stockholm 1905.

Bäck 1984: Bäck, Kalle: *Bondeopposition och bondeinflytande under frihetstiden. Centralmakten och östgötaböndernas reaktioner i näringspolitiska frågor.* LTs förlag. Stockholm 1984.

Canning 1987: Canning, Joseph: *The Political Thought of Baldus de Ubaldis.* Cambridge studies in medieval life and thought, 6. Cambridge University Press. Great Britain 1987.

Capua 1977: Capua, J. V.: The Early History of Martial Law in England from the Fourteenth Century to the Petition of Right. In *Cambridge Law Journal,* 36–1977.

Carlsson 1962: Carlsson, Gottfrid: *Nils Dacke och Europa.* In Engelbrekt, Sturarna och Gustav Vasa. Gleerups. Lund 1962.

Carlsson 1981: Carlsson, Ingemar: *Parti – partiväsen – partipolitiker 1731–43. Kring uppkomsten av våra första politiska partier.* Acta Universitatis Stockholmiensis 29. Almqvist & Wiksell International. Motala 1981.

Carlsson 1948: Carlsson, Sten: De småländska gränslanden under medeltiden. In *Historisk Tidskrift* (Sweden), 1948.

Carlsson 1951: Carlsson, Sten: Mellan Bolmen och Holaveden. In *Meddelanden från norra Smålands fornminnesförening.* Jönköping 1951.

Christensen 1978: Christensen, Aksel E.: *Ret og magt i dansk middelalder*. Gyldendalske Boghandel. Denmark, 1978.

Conrad 1962: Conrad, Hermann: *Deutsche Rechtsgeschichte 1, Frühzeit und Mittelalter.* Verlag C. F. Müller. Karlsruhe 1962.

Cuttler 1981: Cuttler, S. H.: *The Law of Treason and Treason Trials in Later Medieval France.* Cambridge University Press. Bristol 1981.

Dahlgren 1964: Dahlgren, Stellan: *Karl X Gustav och reduktionen.* Studia Historica Upsaliensia XIV. Svenska Bokförlaget. Uppsala 1964.

Damsholt 1970: Damsholt, Nanna: Kingship in the Arengas of Royal Danish Diplomas 1140–1223. In *Mediaeval Scandinavia 3*. Odense University Press. Odense 1971.

Danielsen et. Al 1995: Danielsen, Rolf et. Al.: *Norway. A History from the Vikings Our Own Times.* Oslo 1995.

Diwald 1975: Diwald, H.: *Propyläen Geschichte Europas. Band 1. Anspruch auf Mündigkeit 1400–1555.* Propyläen Verlag. Germany 1975.

Dobson 1983: Dobson, R. B.: *The Peasants' Revolt of 1381.* The Macmillan Press Ltd. London 1983 (first publ. 1970).

Døssland 1998: Døssland, Atle: *Strilesoga 3. Frå 1650 til 1800*. Bergen 1998.

Elander 1958: Elander, Rudolf: Upprorsförsök mot Johan III 1569 och prästens i Böne anklagelse mot honom i 1576. In *Historisk Tidskrift* (Sweden), 3–1958.

Elton 1972: Elton, G. R.: *Policy and Police. The Enforcement of the Reformation in the Age of Thomas Cromwell.* Cambridge University Press. Cambridge 1972.

Englund 1989: Englund, Peter: *Det hotade huset. Adliga föreställningar om samhället under stormaktstiden.* Bokförlaget Atlantis. Stockholm 1989.

Erich 1934: Erich, Rafael: 1734 års lags bestämmelser om brott av politisk karaktär. In *Minneskrift ägnad 1734 års lag, II.* Stockholm 1934.

Ericsson 1970: Ericsson, Brigitta: *Bergsstaden Falun 1720–1769.* Diss. Stockholm University. Uppsala 1970.

Ericsson & Petersson 1979: Ericsson, Brigitta & Petersson, Ann-Marie: Centralmakt och lokalsamhälle på 1700-talet. Presentation av ett internordiskt forskningsprojekt. In *Historisk Tidskrift* (Sweden), 1–1979.

Fagerlund 1991: Fagerlund, Rainer: *Sotilasrasitus Varsinais-Suomessa 1523–1617. Varsinais-Suomen historia V,7.* Laitila 1991.

Feldbæk 1993: Feldbæk, Ole: *Danmarks økonomiske historie 1500–1840.* Herning 1993.

Fenger 1977: Fenger, Ole: *Romerret i Norden.* Berlingske forlag. Denmark 1977.

Fenger 1983: Fenger, Ole: *Gammeldansk ret.* Centrum. Denmark 1983.

Florén 1987a: Florén, Anders: *Disciplinering och konflikt. Den sociala organisering av arbetet: Jäders bruk 1640–1750.* Acta Universitatis Upsaliensis. Studia Historica Upsaliensia 147. Uppsala 1987.

Florén 1987b: Florén, Anders: Nya roller, nya krav. Några drag i den svenska nationalstatens formering. In *Historisk Tidskrift* (Sweden), 4–1987.

Franz 1984: Franz, Günther: *Der Deutsche Bauernkrieg.* Wissenschaftliche Buchgesellschaft. Darmstadt 1984 (first publ 1933).

Fritz 1987: Fritz, Birgitta: Spår av en förlorad stadga från 1200-talet. In *Arkivetenskapliga studier* 6–1987.

Fourquin 1978: Fourquin, Guy: *The anatomy of popular rebellion in the Middle Ages. Europe in the Middle Ages.* Selcted studies vol 9. North-Holland publishing company 1978.

Frohnert 1985: Frohnert, Pär: Administration i Sverige under frihetstiden. In *Administrasjon i Norden på 1700-talet.* Universitetsforlaget. Oslo 1985.

Frohnert 1993: Frohnert, Pär: *Kronans skatter och bondens bröd. Den lokala förvaltningen och bönderna i Sverige 1719–1775.* Rättshistoriskt bibliotek, Vol. 48. Skrifter utgivna av Institutet för rättshistorisk forskning grundat av Gustav och Karin Olin. Lund 1993.

Gläuser 1983: Gläuser, Jürg: *Isländische Märchensagas.* Studien zur Prosalitteratur im spätmittelalterlichen Island. Basel und Frankfurt am Main 1983.

Grauers 1932: Grauers, Sven: Den Svenska Riksdagen under den karolinska tiden. Sveriges Riksdag. Förra avdelningen, *Riksdagens historia intill 1865.* Fjärde bandet. Stockholm 1932.
Grell (ed.) 1995: Grell, O. P. (ed.): *The Scandinavian Reformation. From Evangelical Movement to Institutionalisation of Reform.* Cambridge 1995.
Gunn 1989: Gunn, S. J.: Peers, Commons and Gentry in the Linconshire Revolt of 1536. In *Past and Present* no 123–1989.
Gunnarsson 1983: Gunnarsson, Gisli: *Monopoly Trade and Economic Stagnation. Studies in the Foreign Trade of Iceland 1602–1787.* Lund 1983.
Gurevic 1985: Gurevic, Aron: *Categories of Medieval Culture.* Routledge & Kegan Paul. London 1985.
Gustafsson 1985: Gustafsson, Harald: *Mellan kung och Allmoge. Ämbetsmän, beslutsprocess och inflytande på 1700-talets Island.* Stockholm 1985.
Gustafsson 1991: Gustafsson, Harald: Statsbildning och territoriell integration. Linjer i nyare forskning, en nordisk ansats samt ett bidrag till 1500-talets svenska politiska geografi. In *Scandia. Tidskrift för historisk forskning,* 2–1991.
Gustafsson 1994a: Gustafsson, Harald: *Political Interaction in the Old Regime. Central Power and Local Society in the Eighteenth-Century Nordic States.* Studentlitteratur. Lund 1994
Gustafsson 1994b: Gustafsson, Harald: Vad var staten? Den tidigmoderna svenska staten: sex synpunkter och en modell. In *Historisk Tidskrift* (Sweden), 2–1994.
Gustafsson 1997: Gustafsson, Harald: *Nordens historia. En europeisk region under 1200 år.* Lund 1997.
Gustafsson 1998a: Gustafsson, Harald: The Conglomerate State. A Perspective on State Formation in Early Modern Europe. In *Scandinavian Journal of History,* 1998.
Gustafsson 1998b: Gustafsson, Harald: Dansk historia i nordiskt perspektiv – eller tyskt? In *Historisk Tidskrift (Denmark),* 1998.
Habermas 1988: Habermas, Jürgen: *Borgerlig offentlighet. Kategorierna "privat" och "offentligt" i det moderna samhället.* Lund 1988.
Halila 1949: Halila, Aimo: Suurvalta-aika. In *Suomen historian käsikirja. Part I.* Ed. Arvi Korhonen. Porvoo 1949.
Hallenberg 2001: Hallenberg, Mats: *Kungen, fogdarna och riket. Lokalförvaltning och statsbyggande under tidig Vasatid.* Brutus Östlings Bokförlag Symposion – Stockholm/Stehag 2001.
Hanagan, Moch & te Brake 1998: Hanagan, Michael P., Moch, Leslie Page & te Brake, Wayne: Introduction. In Michael P. Hanagan, Leslie P. Moch, and Wayne te Brake (eds.), *Challenging Authority: The Historical Study of Contentious Politics.* University of Minnesota Press. Minneapolis 1998.
Hanagan et al 1998: Hanagan, Michael P., Moch, Leslie Page & te Brake, Wayne (eds.), *Challenging Authority: The Historical Study of Contentious Politics.* University of Minnesota Press. Minneapolis 1998.
Harnesk 1998: Harnesk, Björn: Kommunalism, makt och motmakt i det tidigmoderna Europa. In *Historisk Tidskrift* (Sweden), 4–1998.
Harrison 1997a: Harrison, Dick: *Uppror och allienser. Politiskt våld i 1400-talets bondesamhälle.* Lagerbringbiblioteket, Historiska Media. Lund 1997.
Harrison 1997b: Harrison, Dick: Murder and Execution within the Political Sphere in Fifteenth-century Scandinavia. In *Scandia. Tidskrift för historisk forskning,* 63: 2–1997.
Haug 1997: Haug, Eldbjørg: *Provincia Nidrosiensis i dronning Margretes unions- og maktpolitikk.* Trondheim 1997.
Heikkinen 1988: Heikkinen, Antero: *Kirveskansan elämää. Ihmiskohtaloita Kuhmon erämaissa 1800-luvun alussa.* WSOY. Juva 1988.
Helle 1995: Helle, Knut: *Aschehougs Norges Historie. Bind 3. Under kirke og kongemakt 1130–1350.* Oslo 1995.
Hilton 1975: Hilton, Rodney: Soziale Programme im englischen Aufstand von 1381. In Revolte ond Revolution in Europa. Hearusgegeben von Peter Blickle. *Historische*

Zeitschift. Beiheft 4 (neue folge). R. Oldenburg Verlag. München 1975.
Hilton 1977: Hilton, Rodney: *Bond Men Made Free. Medieval Peasant Movements and the English Rising 1318.* Methuen & Co Ltd. London 1977 (first publ. 1973).
Hilton 1984: Hilton, Rodney, H: Introduction. In *The English Rising of 1381.* Eds. R. H. Hilton and T. H. Ashton. Cambridge University Press. Cambridge 1984.
Hjärne 1951: Hjärne, Erland: *Fornsvenska lagstadganden I–III.* Almqvist & Wiksells Boktryckeri AB. Uppsala 1951.
Hjärne 1979–1981: Hjärne, Erland: *Land och ledung, I–II.* Rättshistoriskt bibliotek, Vols. 31–32. Skrifter utgivna av Institutet för rättshistorisk forskning grundat av Gustav och Karin Olin. Lund 1979–1981.
Holm 1988: Holm, Poul: De skånsk-hallandske bondeoprør. In *Til Kamp for Friheden. Sociale Oprør i Nordisk Middelalder.* Eds. Anders Bøgh, Jørgen Würtz Sørensen, Lars Tvede-Jensen. Boksmejden. Ålbog 1988.
Holm 2003: Holm, Johan: Att välja sin fiende – Allmogens konflikter och allianser i riksdagen 1595–1635. In *Historisk Tidskrift* (Sweden) 1–2003.
Hunt 1984: Hunt, Lynn: Charles Tilly's Collective Action. In T. Skocpol (ed.), *Vision and Method in Historical Sociology.* Cambridge University Press. Cambridge 1984.
Härenstam 1947: Härenstam, Kurt: *Det medeltida folklandet. Boken om Njudung.* Meddelanden från Norra Smålands fornminnesförening. Jönköping 1947.
Imsen 1982: Imsen, Steinar: Norske ad hoc-kommisjoner i forvaltning og politikk under Christian IV. In Imsen, Steinar and Sanvik, Gudmund (eds.): *Hamarspor. Eit festskrift til Lars Hamre.* Oslo/Bergen/Tromsø 1982.
Imsen 1990a: Imsen, Steinar: Bondemotstand og statsutvikling i Norge ca. 1300 til ca. 1700. In *Heimen. Lokalhistorisk Tidskrift,* 2–1990.
Imsen 1990b: Imsen, Steinar: *Norsk bondekommunalisme fra Magnus Lagaböte til Kristian Kvart. Del 1. Middelalderen.* Tapir forlag 1990.
Imsen 1994: Imsen, Steinar: *Norsk bondekommunalisme fra Magnus Lagaböte til Kristian Kvart. Del 2. Lydriketiden.* Trondheim 1994.
Imsen 1997: Imsen, Steinar: Oslofjordbygdene som politisk og sosialt stormsentrum under Erik av Pommern. In *Vestfoldminne* 1997. Tønsberg 1997.
Imsen and Vogler 1997: Imsen, Steinar and Vogler, Günther: Communal autonomy and peasant resistance in northern and central Europe. In Blickle, Peter (ed.): *Resistance, representation and community.* Oxford 1997.
Isberg 1953: Isberg, Alvin: *Karl XI och den livländska adeln 1684–1695. Studier rörande det karolinska enväldets införande i Livland.* Lindsteds Universitetsbokhandel. Lund 1953.
Jaakkola 1944: Jaakkola, Jalmari: Suomen sydänkeskiaika. Itämaan synty ja vakiintuminen. In *Suomen historia IV.* Werner Söderström Oy. Porvoo 1944.
Jaakkola 1950: Jaakkola, Jalmari: Suomen myöhäiskeskiaika I. Unionin alkukausi. In *Suomen historia V.* Werner Söderström Oy. Porvoo 1950.
Jameson 1986: Jameson, Ola: *Den gnista som förbårgat i askan ligger. Om bönder, utskrivningar och alternativa protester i Småland, Västergötland och Blekinge 1683 och 1710.* Unpublished paper at the Department of History at Uppsala University. Uppsala 1986.
Jespersen 1987: Jespersen, Knud, J. V.: Absolute Monarchy in Denmark. Change and Continuity. In *Scandinavian Journal of History*, 1987.
Jóhannesson 1956: Jóhannesson, Jón: *Íslendinga saga I.* Reykjavik 1956.
Jóhannesson 1968: Jóhannesson, Kristinn: "*Þættir úr landvarnasögu Íslands.*" Saga 1968.
Johansson 1997: Johansson, Kenneth: Rättens ansikten: ett svenskt härad under stormaktstiden. In S. Å. Nilsson and M. Ramsay (Eds.) *1600-talets ansikte.* Krapperup 1997.
Johnsen 1919: Johnsen, Oscar Albert: *Norges bønder. Utsyn over den norske bondestands historie.* Kristiania 1919.
Jokipii 1956: Jokipii, Mauno: *Suomen kreivi- ja vapaaherrakunnat I.* Historiallisia tutkimuksia 68:1. SHS. Forssa 1956.

Jokipii 1960: Jokipii, Mauno: *Suomen kreivi- ja vapaaherrakunnat II.* Historiallisia tutkimuksia 68:2. SHS. Forssa 1960.

Júlíússon 1997a: Júlíusson, Árni Daníel: "Þurrabúðir, býli og höfuðból. Félagslegt umhverfi 1100–1550. Heimildir og Þróunarlínur." *Íslenska söguÞingið 28.–31. maí 1997*, Ráðstefnurit I.

Júlíusson 1997b: Júlíusson, Árni Daníel: *Bønder i pestens tid. Landbrug, godsdrift og social konflikt i senmiddelalderens islandske bondesamfund.* Unpublished PhD thesis, University of Copenhagen 1997.

Jutikkala 1931: Jutikkala, Eino: Nastolan talonpoikaisrettelöt vv. 1773–75. In *Historiallinen Aikakauskirja* 1931.

Jutikkala 1932: Jutikkala, Eino: *Läntisen Suomen kartanolaitos Ruotsin vallan viimeisenä aikana, I–II.* Historiallisia tutkielmia 15:2. SHS. Helsinki 1932.

Jutikkala 1958: Jutikkala, Eino: *Suomen talonpojan historia.* Suomalaisen Kirjallisuuden Seuran toimituksia 257. SKS. Turku 1958 (2nd edition).

Kaeuper 1988: Kaeuper, Richard W.: *War, Justice and Public Order: England and France in the Later Middle Ages.* Clarendon Press. Great Britain 1988.

Kalm 1948: Kalm, Ingvar: *Studier in svenska predikan under 1600-talets förra hälft.* Svenska Kyrkans diakonistyrelses Bokförlag. Uppsala 1948.

Kamen 1971: Kamen, Henry: *The Iron Century. Social change in Europe 1550–1660.* Weidenfeld and Nicholson. London 1971.

Kamen 1982: Kamen, Henry: Die europäischen Volkaufstände 1550–1660 und die struktur der Revolten. In *Europäische Bauernrevolten der frühen Neuzeit.* Herausgegeben von Winfried Schulze. Suhrkamp. Frankfurt am Main 1982.

Kantorowicz 1981: Kantorowicz, Ernst H.: *The King's Two Bodies. A Study in Mediaeval Political Theology.* Princeton University Press. Princeton 1981.

Karonen 1999: Karonen, Petri: *Pohjoinen suurvalta. Ruotsi ja Suomi 1521–1809.* WSOY. Juva 1999.

Katajala 1994: Katajala, Kimmo: *Nälkäkapina. Veronvuokraus ja talonpoikainen vastarinta Karjalassa 1683–1697.* Historiallisia Tutkimuksia 185. SHS. Jyväskylä 1994.

Katajala 1999: Katajala Kimmo: Swedish Treason Legislation and Peasant Unrest from the High Middle Ages to the Era of Enlightenment (1300-1800). In *Crime and Control in Europe from the Past to the Present*, eds. Mirkka Lappalainen and Pekka Hirvonen. Publications of the History of Criminality Research Project. Helsinki 1999.

Katajala 2002: Katajala, Kimmo: *Suomalainen kapina. Talonpoikaislevottomuudet ja poliittisen kulttuurin muutos Ruotsin ajalla (n. 1150–1800).* Historiallisia Tutkimuksia 212. SHS – SKS. Vammala 2002.

Katajala–Tšernjakova 1998: Katajala, Kimmo & Tšernjakova, Irina: Karjalainen ihminen uuden ajan alussa. In *Karjala. Historia, kansa, kulttuuri.* Editors Pekka Nevalainen ja Hannes Sihvo. SKS. Pieksämäki 1998.

Kaukiainen 1978: Kaukiainen, Yrjö: Nuijasodan sfäärit ja projektiot. In *Historiallinen Aikakauskirja* 1978.

Keen 1965: Keen, M. H.: *The Laws of War in the Late Middle Ages.* Routledge & Kegan Paul. Great Britain 1965.

Keen 1996: Keen, Maurice: *Nobles, Knights and Men-at-Arms in the Middle Ages.* The Hambledon Press. Great Britain, 1996.

Kekkonen–Ylikangas 1982: Kekkonen, Jukka & Ylikangas, Heikki 1982: *Vapausrangaistuksen valtakausi. Nykyisen seuraamusjärjestelmän historiallinen tausta.* Oikeuden yleistieteiden laitoksen julkaisuja 1/1982. Helsingin Yliopisto. Helsinki 1982.

Kerkkonen 1931: Kerkkonen, Martti: Elimäen talonpoikaislevottomuudet v. 1773. In *Historiallinen Aikakauskirja* 1931.

Kertzer 1988: Kertzer, David I.: *Ritual, Politics, and Power.* Yale University Press. New Haven 1988.

Kirkeby 1995: Kirkeby, Birger: *Hallvard Gråtopp frå Lindheim skipreide.* Sauherrad 1995.

Kirkinen 1976: Kirkinen, Heikki: *Karjala taistelukenttänä. Karjala idän ja lännen välissä II.* Joensuu 1976.

Kiuasmaa 1987: Kiuasmaa, Kyösti: Valtaistuinriitojen ja uskonpuhdistuksen aika. In *Suomen Historia 2.* Weilin & Göös. Espoo 1987.

Knapp 1896: Knapp, Hermann: *Das alte Nürnberger Kriminalrecht nach Rats-Urkunden erlautert.* J. Guttentag Verlagsbuchhandlung. Potsdam 1896.

Koht 1926: Koht, Halvard: *Norsk bondereising. Fyrebuing til bondepolitikken.* H. Aschehoug & Co. Oslo 1926.

Kokkonen 2002: Kokkonen, Jukka: *Rajaseutu liikkeessä. Kainuun ja Pielisen Karjalan asukkaiden kontaktit Venäjän Karjalaan kreivin ajasta sarkasotaan (1650–1712).* Bibliotheca Historica 79. SHS–SKS. Helsinki 2002.

Korpiola 1996: Korpiola, Mia: *Pettureita ja pelinappuloita: maanpetos ja maanpetosprosessit Englannissa 1509–1547.* Unpublished candidate thesis in legal history. Faculty of Law, University of Helsinki, 1996.

Korpiola 2001: Korpiola, Mia: "The People of Sweden Shall Have Peace". Peace Legislation and Royal Power in Later Medieval Sweden. In *Expectations of the Law in the Middle Ages.* Ed. A. Musson. The Boydell Press. Bury St Edmunds 2001.

Larsson 1984: Larsson, Lars-Olof: *Engelbrekt Engelbrektsson och 1430-talets svenska uppror.* P. A. Norstedt & Söners förlag. Värnamo 1984.

Koskinen 1929: Koskinen, Yrjö: *Nuijasota, sen syyt ja tapaukset.* Historiallinen kirjasto I. Historian Ystäväin Liiton julkaisuja. Otava. Helsinki 1929 (3rd edition).

Kristinsson 1998: Kristinsson, Axel: "Embættismenn konungs fyrir 1400." *Saga* XXXVI 1998.

Kujala 2001: Kujala, Antti: *Miekka ei laske leikkiä. Suomi suuressa pohjan sodassa 1700–1714.* Historiallisia Tutkimuksia 211. SHS–SKS. Hämeenlinna 2001.

Kumlien 1933: Kumlien, Kjell: *Karl Knutssons politiska verksamhet 1434–1448.* P. A. Norstedt & Söner. Stockholm 1933.

Ladewig Petersen (ed.) 1984: Ladewig Petersen, Erling (ed.): *Magtstaten i Norden i 1600-tallet og de sociale konsekvenser.* Odense 1984.

Lagerroth 1934: Lagerroth, Fredrik: *Sveriges Riksdag: Frihetstidens maktägande ständer, I:6 vol. 2.* Published by the Swedish Parliament. Stockholm 1934.

Lamberg 2001: Lamberg, Marko: *Dannemännen i stadens råd. Rådmanskretsen i nordiska öpstäder under senmedeltiden.* Monografier utgivna av Stockholms stad, 155. Stockholmia förlag. Borås 2001.

Larsson 1984: Larsson, Lars-Olof: *Engelbreckt Engelbrecktsson och 1430-talets svenska uppror.* P. A. Norstedt & Söners förlag. Värnamo 1984.

Larsson 1979: Larsson, Lars-Olof: *Dackeland.* Växjö 1979.

Larsson 1964: Larsson, Lars-Olof: *Det medeltida Värend. Studier i det småländska gränslandets historia fram till 1500-talets mitt.* Växjö 1964.

Larsson 1975: Larsson, Lars-Olof: Förrädare eller frihetshjältar? Dackefejden i eftervärldens dom. In *Historia om Småland.* Växjö 1975.

Larsson 2002: Larsson, Lars–Olof: *Gustav Vasa, landsfader eller tyrann?* Bokförlaget Prisma. Stockholm 2002.

Lárusson 1967: Lárusson, Björn: *The Old Icelandic Land Registers.* Lund 1967.

Laxness 1987: Laxness, Einar: *Íslandssaga A–K.* Reykjavik 1987.

Le Roy Ladurie 1974: Le Roy Ladurie, Emmanuel: Über die Bauernaufstände in Frankreich 1548–1648. In *Wirtschaftliche und soziale Strukturen im saekularen Wandel. Festschrift für Wilhelm Abel zum 70 Geburtstag. Band I.* Schriftenreiche für Ländliche Sozialfragen. Western Germany 1974.

Lear 1965: Lear, Floyd Seward: *Treason in Roman and Germanic Law.* Collected Papers. University of Texas Press. Austin 1965.

Lennersand 1999: Lennersand, Marie: *Rättvisans och allmogens beskyddare. Den absoluta staten, kommissionerna och tjänstemännen, ca. 1680–1730.* Studia Historica Upsaliensia 189. Uppsala 1999.

Letto-Vanamo 1989: Letto-Vanamo, Pia: *Suomalaisen asianajajalaitoksen synty ja varhaiskehitys.* Suomalaisen Lakimiesyhdistyksen julkaisuja, A-sarja, 181. Suomalainen Lakimiesyhdistys. Vammala 1989.

Letto-Vanamo 1995: Letto-Vanamo, Pia: *Käräjäyhteisön oikeus. Oikeudenkäyttö Ruotsi-Suomessa ennen valtiollisen riidanratkaisun vakiintumista.* Oikeushistorian julkaisuja 2, Helsingin yliopisto, Rikos- ja prosessioikeuden sekä oikeuden yleistieteiden laitos. Helsinki 1995.

Linde 2000: Linde, Martin: *Statsmakt och bondemotstånd. Allmoge och överhet under stora nordiska kriget.* Acta Universitatis Upsaliensis 194. Stockholm 2000.

Lindley 1982: Lindley, Keith: *Fenland Riots and the English Revolution.* Heinemann Educational Books. London 1982.

Lindqvist 1988: Lindqvist, Thomas: *Plundring, skatter och den feodala statens framväxt. Organisatoriska tendenser i Sverige under övergången från vikingtid till tidlig medeltid.* Opuscula Historica Upsaliensia 1. Uppsala 1988.

Lindroth 1975: Lindroth, Sten: *Svensk lärdomshistoria. Stormaktstiden.* P. A. Nordstedt & söners förlag. Stockholm 1975.

Lindroth 1978: Lindroth, Sten: *Svensk lärdomshistoria. Frihetstiden.* P. A. Nordstedt & söners förlag. Stockholm 1978.

Lode 1978: Lode, Asgeir: *Tilhøvet mellom styresmakt og almuge i Jæren og Dalane sorenskrivari under den store nordiske krigen.* Unpublished master thesis. Bergen 1978.

Løgstrup 1987: Løgstrup, Birgit: *Bundet til jorden. Stavnsbåndet i praksis 1733–1788.* Odense 1987.

Lundberg 1987: Lundberg, Ulf: Morgonstjärnans uppgång och fall. Ett perspektiv på upproret 1653. In *Folkets historia*, 1–1987.

Luukko 1945: Luukko, Armas: *Etelä-Pohjanmaan historia III. Nuijasodasta isoonvihaan.* Etelä-Pohjanmaan historiatoimikunta – Oy. Ilkan kirjapaino 1945.

Luukko 1950: Luukko, Armas: *Etelä-Pohjanmaan historia II. Keskiaika ja 1500-luku.* Etelä-Pohjanmaan historiatoimikunta – Maalaiskuntien Liiton kirjapaino 1950.

Luukko 1978: Luukko, Armas: Mikä oli nuijasota? In *Historiallinen Aikakauskirja* 1978.

Lysaker 1987: Lysaker, Trygve: *Nidaros erkebispestol og bispesete 1153–1953. Vol. 2: Reformasjon og enevelde 1537–1804.* Trondheim 1987.

Lönnroth 1934: Lönnroth, Erik: *Sverige och Kalmarunionen 1397–1457.* Elander boktryckeri aktiebolag. Göteborg 1934.

Lönnroth 1944: Lönnroth, Erik: De äkta Folkungarnas program. In *Kungl. humanistiska vetenskaps-samfundet i Uppsala Årsbok 1944.*

Lövgren 1915: Lövgren, Birger: *Ståndstridens uppkomst. Ett bidrag till Sveriges inre politiska historia under drottning Kristina.* Uppsala 1915.

Maarbjerg 1992: Maarbjerg, John P.: The Economic Background to "The War of Clubs". In *Scandinavian Journal of History* 1992.

Magnusson 1985: Magnusson, Lars: *Reduktionen under 1600-talet. Debatt och forskning.* Liber Förlag. Malmö 1985.

Maier 1970a: Maier, Pauline: The Charleston Mob and the Evolution of Popular Politics in Revolutionary South Carolina, 1765–1784. In *Perspectives in American History*, vol. 4–1970.

Maier 1970b: Maier, Pauline: Popular Uprisings and Civil Authority in Eighteenth-Century America. In *The William and Mary Quarterly*, vol. 27–1970.

Malmström 1897 & 1900: Malmström, Carl Gustaf: *Sveriges politiska historia. Från Konung Karl XII:s död till statshvälfningen 1772, vol. 3 & 5.* P.A. Norstedt & söners förlag. Stockholm 1897 & 1900.

Markkanen 1980: Markkanen, Erkki: Nuijakapinan alku Rautalammilla – aika, paikka ja kapinoitsijat. In *Scripta Historica IV*. Tornio 1980.

Mathisen 1998: Mathisen, Runar: *Bøndene og militæret. Reaksjoner og problemer rundt militærutskrivingene i Stavanger len 1640–1660. En analyse med hovedvekt på krigene i perioden 1657–1660.* Unpublished master thesis. Oslo 1998.

Maurer 1877: Maurer, Konrad: *Das älteste Hofrecht des Nordens.* Christian Kaiser. München 1877.

Melander 1939: Melander, K. R.: Eräs suomalaisten v. 1653 alkuun panema kapinayritys Ruotsissa. In *Historiallinen Arkisto 46*. SHS. Helsinki 1939.

Melkersson 1997: Melkersson, Martin: *Staten, ordningen och friheten. En studie av den styrande elitens syn på statens roll mellan stormaktstiden och 1800-talet.* Studia Historica Upsaliensia 184. Uppsala 1997.

Melkersson 1999: Melkersson, Martin: *Att styra ett rike. Några funderingar kring statsbyggande och den politiska elitens syn på statens uppgifter under frihetstiden.* Conference paper presented at Svenska historikermötet 23.–25. April 1999.

Metcalf (ed.) 1987: Metcalf, Michael F. (ed.): *The Riksdag. A History of the Swedish Parliament.* New York 1987.

Metcalf 1977: Metcalf, Michael F.: The First 'Modern' Party System? Political parties, Sweden's Age of Liberty and the historians. In *Scandinavian Journal of History* 1977.

Modéer 1997: Modéer, Kjell Å.: *Historiska rättskällor. En introduktion i rättshistoria.* Nerenius & Santérus Förlag. Stockholm 1997.

Mollat–Wolff 1973: Mollat, Michel & Wolff, Philippe: *The Popular Revolutions of the Late Middle Ages.* The Great Revolution Series No. 6. George Allen & Unwin Ltd. London 1973.

Moseng et. al. 1999: Moseng, Ole Georg, Opshal, Erik, Pettersen, Gunnar I. and Sandmo, Erling: *Norsk historie 750–1537.* Oslo 1999.

Mousnier 1970: Mousnier, Roland: *Peasant Uprisings in seventten-century France, Russia and China.* Harper & Row Publishers 1970.

Mullett 1987: Mullett, Michael: *Popular Culture and Popular Protest in Late Medieval and Early Modern Europe.* Kent 1987.

Munktell 1934: Munktell, Henrik: Till förfalskningsbrottens historia. In *Minneskrift ägnad 1734 års lag, II.* Stockholm 1934.

Nilsson 1994: Nilsson, Sven A:.Politisk mobilisering i 1600-talets Sverige. In *Struktur og funktion. Festskrift til Erling Ladewig Petersen.* Odense University Studies in History and Social Sciences vol 174. Odense Universitetsforlag. Viborg 1994.

Nilzén 1971: Nilzén, Göran: *Studier i 1730-talets partiväsen.* Diss. Stockholm University. Stockholm 1971.

Nissen 1996: Nissen, Harald A.: *Bondemotstand og statsmodernisering. Bjelkekommisjonen i Trondheim len 1632.* Unpublished master thesis. Trondheim 1996.

Njåstad 1996: Njåstad, Magne: "...bønder som fører bønder." Bondemotstand i Trøndelag ca. 1550–1600. In *Heimen. Lokahistorisk tidskrift*, 3–1996.

Njåstad 1994: Njåstad, Magne: *Bondemotstand i Trøndelag ca. 1550–1600.* Unpublished master thesis. Trondheim 1994.

Nyström 1974: Nyström, Per: Feodaltidens lagar. In *Historieskrivningens dilemma och andra studier.* Stockholm 1974.

Odhner 1865: Odhner, C. T.: *Sveriges inre historia under drottning Christinas förmyndare.* P. A. Norstedt & Söner. Stockholm 1865.

Oksanen 1981: Oksanen, Eeva-Liisa: *Anjalan historia.* Myllykoski 1981.

Oksanen 1985: Oksanen, Eeva-Liisa: *Elimäen historia.* Anson Oy 1985.

Olesen 1980: Olesen, Jens E.: *Rigsråd, Kongemagt, Union. Studier over det danske rigsråd og den nordiske kongemagts politik 1434–1449.* Skrifter udgivet af Jyske selskab for historia, nr. 36. Universitetsforlaget i Aarhus 1980.

Olesen 1988: Olesen, Jens E.: Oprør og Politisering i Sverige 1463–1471. In *Til Kamp for Friheden. Sociale Oprør i Nordisk Middelalder.* Eds. Anders Bøgh, Jørgen Würtz Sørensen, Lars Tvede-Jensen. Boksmejden. Ålbog 1988.

Olivecrona 1891: Olivecrona, K.: *Om dödstraffet.* W. Schultz. Upsala 1891.

Olsson 1926: Olsson, Ragnar: *Bondeståndet under den tidigare frihetstiden. Val, organisation och arbetssätt.* Diss. Lund University. Lund 1926.

Olsson 1963: Olsson, Gunnar: *Hattar och mössor. Studier över partiväsendet i Sverige 1751–1762.* Studia Historica Gothoburgensia I. Akademiförlaget. Göteborg 1963.

Palola 1997: Palola, Ari-Pekka: *Maunu Tavast ja Olavi Maununpoika – Turun piispat 1412–1460.* Suomen Kirkkohistoriallisen Seuran Toimituksia 178. Saarijärvi 1997.

Paloposki 1961: Paloposki, Toivo J.: *Suomen talonpoikaissäädyn valtiopäiväedustus vapaudenajalla.* Historiallisia Tutkimuksia LVII. SHS. Forssa 1961.

Peterson, Claes 1985: "En god ämbetsman är bättre än en god lag..." Frågan om justitiekanslern som en allmogens besvärinstans i klagomål över kronobetjänternas ämbetsutövning (1747–1752). In *Administrasjon i Norden på 1700-talet.* Universitetsforlaget. Sweden 1985.

Pihlajamäki 1999: Pihlajamäki Heikki: Ius politiae – havaintoja politiaoikeuden pirstaloitumista ja rikosoikeuden kehityksestä 1800-luvulla. In *Lakimies*, 4–1999.

Pirinen 1939: Pirinen, Kauko: Lappeen talonpoikaiskapina vv. 1551–1553. In *Historiallinen Aikakauskirja* 1939.

Pirinen 1940: Pirinen, Kauko: Albrekt Mecklenburgilaisen ajoilta. Erään kuninkaankirjeen analysointia. In *Historiallinen Aikakauskirja* 1940.

Pirinen 1962: Pirinen, Kauko: *Kymmenysverotus Suomessa ennen kirkkoreduktiota.* Historiallisia Tutkimuksia LV. SHS. Forssa 1962.

Pirinen 1965: Pirinen, Kauko: Taistelut Savon ja Pohjois-Karjalan välisellä rajalla ennen Stolbovan rauhaa. In *Karjala IV.* Ed. Heikki Koukkunen. Joensuu 1965.

Pohjolan-Pirhonen 1960: Pohjolan-Pirhonen, Helge: Suomen historia 1523–1617. In *Suomen historia VII.* WSOY. Porvoo 1960.

Pollock & Maitland 1898: Pollock, Frederick & Maitland, Frederic William: *The History of English Law Before the Time of Edward I, I–II.* Cambridge University Press. Cambridge 1898.

Post 1964: Post, Gaines: *Studies in Medieval Legal Thought. Public Law and the State, 1100–1322.* Princeton University Press. USA 1964.

Rasmussen 1988: Rasmussen, Kristen J.: Jydernes gamle stivsind. Bondeoprør og adelsreaktion imod Erik Menved i 1313. In *Til Kamp for Friheden. Sociale Oprør i Nordisk Middelalder.* Eds. Anders Bøgh, Jørgen Würtz Sørensen, Lars Tvede-Jensen. Boksmejden. Ålbog 1988.

Reddy 1977: Reddy, William M.: The Textile Trade and the Language of the Crowd at Rouen 1752–1871. In *Past & Present*, 74–1977.

Reinholdsson 1998: Reinholdsson, Peter: *Uppror eller resningar? Samhällsorganisation och konflikt i senmedeltidens Sverige.* Studia Historica Upsalensia 186. Stockholm 1998.

Renvall 1939: Renvall, Pentti: *Klaus Fleming und der finnische Adel in den Anfangsphasen der Krise der neunziger jahre des 16. Jahrhuderts.* Annales Universitatis Turkuensis. Ser. B, Tom. XXIV. Turku 1939.

Renvall 1945: Renvall, Pentti: Eräitä huomioita 1500-luvun loppuvuosikymmenien talonpoikaislevottomuuksista. In *Historiallinen Aikakauskirja* 1945.

Renvall 1949: Renvall, Pentti: *Kuninkaanmiehiä ja kapinoitsijoita Vaasa-kauden Suomessa.* Tammi. Turku 1949.

Renvall 1962: Renvall, Pentti: *Suomen kansanedustuslaitoksen historia I. 1. Ruotsin vallan aika.* Helsinki 1962.

Reynolds 1994: Reynolds, Susan: *Fiefs and Vassals: The Medieval Evidence Reinterpreted.* Oxford University Press. Great Britain 1994.

Rian 1990: Rian, Øystein: Giftermål og familie som elitedannende faktor i 1600-tallets Brattsberg. In *Historisk Tidsskrift* (Norway), 4–1990.

Rian 1992: Rian, Øystein: Den frie og stolte norske bonde. Myter og realiteter. In Winge, Harald (ed.): *Lokalsamfunn og øvrighet i Norden ca. 1550–1750.* Oslo 1992.

Rian 1995: Rian, Øystein: *Aschehougs Norges Historie. Bind 5. Den nye begynnelsen 1520–1660.* Oslo 1995.

Rian 1997: Rian, Øystein: *Bratsberg på 1600-tallet. Stat og samfunn i symbiose og konflikt.* Oslo 1997.

Ringstad 1994: Ringstad, Jan Erik: *Oslobispens jordegods fram til 1407 med særlig hovedvekt på biskop Øysteins embedstid.* Unpublished master thesis. Oslo 1994.

Roberts 1973: Roberts, Michael: *Swedish and English Parliamentarism in the Eighteenth Century.* The Queen's University. Belfast 1973.

Roberts 1986: Roberts Michael: *The Age of Liberty. Sweden 1719–1772.* Cambridge

University Press. Cambridge 1986.

Rosén 1939: Rosén, Jerker: *Striden mellan Birger Magnusson och hans bröder. Studier i nordisk politisk historia 1302–1319.* A.-b. Gleerupska Univ.-bokhandeln. Lund 1939.

Rosén 1955: Rosén, Jerker: *Studier kring Erik XIV:s höga nämnd.* Skrifter utgivna av Kungl. humanistiska vetenskapssamfundet i Lund, 51. C. W. K. Gleerup. Lund 1955.

Rosén 1962: Rosén, Jerker: *Svensk historia I. Tiden före 1718.* Svenska bokförlaget/ Bonniers. Stockholm 1962.

Runeby 1962: Runeby, Nils: *Monarchia mixta. Maktfördelningsdebatt i Sverige under den tidigare stormaktstiden.* Studia Historica Upsaliensia VI. Svenska bokförlaget. Stockholm 1962.

Rystad 1985: Rystad, Göran: Stormaktstidens riksdag (1611–1718). In *Riksdagen genom tiderna.* Ed. Nils Stjernquist. Sveriges Riksdag 1985.

Salminen 1995: Salminen, Tapio: Davidin kapina ja Pirkanmaan kapinaherkkyys. In *Tampere. Tutkimuksia ja kuvauksia X.* Eds. Mervi Kaarninen ja Marjo-Riitta Saloniemi. Tampereen Historiallisen Seuran julkaisuja XV. Tampere 1995.

Salvesen 1979: Salvesen, Helge: *Jord i Jemtland.* Östersund 1979.

Sandmo 1992: Sandmo, Erling: *Tingets tenkemåter. Kriminalitet og rettssaker i Rendalen, 1763–97.* Oslo 1992.

Sandnes 1990: Sandnes, Jørn: *Kniven, ølet og æren. Kriminalitet og samfunn i Norge på 1500- og 1600-tallet.* Oslo 1990.

Sandvik 1992: Sandvik, Hilde: Rettsvesenets utbygging i Norge. Lokale konsekvenser og reaksjoner 1550–1750. In Winge, Harald (ed.): *Lokalsamfunn og øvrighet i Norden ca. 1550–1750.* Oslo 1992.

Sawyer & Sawyer 1993: Sawyer, B. & Sawyer, P.: *Medieval Scandinavia. From Conversion to Reformation circa 800–1500.* Minneapolis 1993.

Seibt 1975: Seibt, Ferdinand: Die hussitische Revolution und der Deutsche Bauernkrieg. In Revolte und Revolution in Europa. Herausgegeben von Peter Blickle. *Historische Zeitschrift. Boiheft 4 (neue folge).* R. Oldenburg Verlag. München 1975.

Sennefelt 2001: Sennefelt, Karin: *Den politiska sjukan. Dalupproret 1743 och frihetstida politisk kultur.* Gidlunds förlag. Hedemora 2001.

Sætra 1998: Sætra, Gustav: Norske bondeopprør på 1700-tallet, en trussel mot den dansknorske helstaten? In *Historisk Tidsskrift* (Norway), 3–1998.

Schulze 1980; Schulze, Winfried: *Bäuerlicher Widerstand und feudale Herrschaft in der frühen Neuzeit.* Stuttgart 1980.

Schulze 1982: Schulze, Winfried: Europäische und deutsche Bauernrevolten der frühen Neuzeit – Probleme der vergleichenden Betrachtung. In *Europäische Bauernrevolten der frühen Neuzeit*, ed. Winfried Schulze. Frankfurt am Main 1982.

Schulze 1983: Schulze, Winfried: Gegen Aufruhr und Aufstand Anlass zu neuen heilsamen Gesetzen". Beobachtunden über die Wirkungen bäuerlichen Widerstands in der Frühen Neuzeit, in Schulze, Winfried (ed.): *Aufstände, Revolten, Prozesse. Beiträge zur bäuerlichen Widerstandsbewegungen.* Stuttgart 1983.

Scocozza 1976: Scocozza, Benito: *Klassekampen i Danmarks historie. Vol 1: Feudalismen.* Carit Andersens Förlag. Copenhagen 1976.

Scott 1985: Scott, James C.: *Weapons of the Weak. Everyday Forms of Peasant Resistance.* Massachusetts 1985.

Scott 1990: Scott, James C.: *Domination and the Arts of Resistance: Hidden Transcripts.* Yale University Press. New Haven 1990.

Scribner 1987: Scribner, R. W.: Police and the Territorial State in Sixteenth-century Württemberg. In *Politics and Society in Reformation Europe.* Eds. E. I. Kouri and Tom Scott. Macmillan Press. Hong Kong 1987.

Seip 1942: Seip, Jens Arup: *Sættargjerden i Tunsberg og kirkens jurisdiksjon.* Oslo 1942.

Sharp 1980: Sharp, Buchanan: *In Contempt of All Authority. Rural Artisans and Riot in the West of England 1586–1660.* University of California Press 1980.

Sjöholm 1988: Sjöholm, Elsa: *Sveriges medeltidslagar. Europeisk rättstradition i politisk omvandling.* Skrifter utgivna av Institutet för rättshistorisk forskning. Serien 1. Rättshistoriskt bibliotek 1988.

Skrubbeltrang 1978: Skrubbeltrang, Fridlev: *Det danske landbosamfund 1500–1800.* København 1978.

Skyum-Nielsen 1964: Skyum-Nielsen, Niels: *Blodbadet i Stockholm og dets juridiske maskering.* Munksgaard. Denmark 1964.

Smedberg 1972: Smedberg, Staffan: *Frälsebonderörelser i Halland och Skåne 1772–76.* Studia Historica Upsalensia XXXIX. Uppsala 1972.

Spierenburg 1991: Spierenburg, Pieter: *The broken spell. A cultural and anthropological history of preindustrial Europe.* Macmillan – Basingstoke 1991.

Storm 1888: Storm, Gustav (ed.): *Islandske annaler indtil 1578.* Christiania 1888.

Strickland 1996: Strickland, Matthew: *War and Chivalry. The Conduct and Perception of War in England and Normandy, 1066–1217.* Cambridge University Press. Cambridge 1996.

Supphellen 1978: Supphellen, Steinar: Supplikken som institusjon i norsk historie. Framvokster og bruk særleg først på 1700-talet. In *Historisk Tidsskrift* (Norway), 2–1978.

Suvanto 1973: Suvanto, Seppo: *Satakunnan historia III. Keskiaika.* Satakunnan kirjateollisuus 1973.

Suvanto 1987: Suvanto, Seppo: Keskiaika. In *Suomen Historia 2.* Weilin & Göös. Espoo 1987.

Såghus 2000: Såghus, Svein Vik: Allianser under Lofthusreisinga 1780–1787. In *Heimen. Lokalhistorisk tidskrift*, 1–2000.

Tarrow 1994: Tarrow, Sidney: *Power in Movement: Social Movements, Collective Action and Politics.* Cambridge University Press. Cambridge 1994.

Tawastjerna 1918–1920: Tawastjerna, Werner: *Pohjoismainen viisikolmattavuotinen sota. Vuosien 1570 ja 1590 välinen aika.* Historiallisia Tutkimuksia 1. SHS. Helsinki 1918–1920.

Telnes 1991: Telnes, Bergit: *Bergverksdrift og bondeopprør. Vest-Telemark 1538–1549.* Unpublished master thesis Oslo 1991.

Thanner 1953: Thanner, Lennart: *Revolutionen i Sverige efter Karl XII:s död. Den inrepolitiska maktkampen under tidigare delen av Ulrika Eleonora d.y:s regering.* Almqvist & Wiksell. Uppsala 1953.

Theibault 1992: Theibault, John: Community and Herrschaft in the Seventeenth-Century German Village. In *Journal of Modern History*, 64–1992.

Thoroddsen 1919–1922: Thoroddsen, Þorvaldur: *Landbúnaður á Íslandi. Sögulegt yfirlit. 2. bindi.* Köpenhamn 1919–1922.

Thunander 1993: Thunander, Rudolf: *Hovrätt i funktion.* Rättshistoriskt bibliotek, Vol. 49. Skrifter utgivna av Institutet för rättshistorisk forskning grundat av Gustav och Karin Olin. Lund 1993.

Thyrén 1895: Thyrén, J. C. W.: *Förfalskningsbrotten med särskildt afseende på det objektive reqvisitet vid förfalskning.* Gleerupska Universitets-Bokhandeln. Lund 1895.

Tilly 1984: Tilly, Charles: Social Movements and National Poltics. In C. Bright & S. Harding (eds.), *Statemaking and Social Movements. Essays in History and Theory.* University of Michigan Press. Ann Arbor 1984.

Tilly 1986: Tilly, Charles: *The Contentious French: Four Centuries of Popular Struggle.* Harvard University Press. Cambridge Mass. 1986.

Tilly 1993: Tilly, Charles: *European Revolutions 1492–1992.* Ofxord University Press. Blackwell 1993.

Tilly 1998: Tilly, Charles: Political Identities. In M. P. Hanagan, L. P. Moch, and W. te Brake (eds.), *Challenging Authority: The Historical Study of Contentious Politics.* University of Minnesota Press. Minneapolis 1998.

Tretvik 2000: Tretvik, Aud Mikkelsen: *Tretter, ting og tillitsemnn. En undersøkelse av konflikthåndtering i det norske bygdesamfunnet på 1700-tallet.* Trondheim 2000.

Tvede-Jensen 1983: Tvede-Jensen, Lars: Clementsfejden. Det sidste bondeopprør i Dan-

mark. In *Til Kamp for Friheden. Sociale Oprør i Nordisk Middelalder.* Eds. Anders Bøgh, Jørgen Würtz Sørensen, Lars Tvede-Jensen. Boksmejden. Ålbog 1988.
Ullmann 1966: Ullmann, Walter: *The Individual and the Society in the Middle Ages.* The Johns Hopkins Press. USA 1966.
Ullmann 1980: Ullmann, Walter: *Jurisprudence in the Middle Ages.* Collected Studies. Variorum Reprints. Great Yarmouth 1980.
Vejde 1931: Vejde, Albert: Nils Dacke. In *Svenskt Biografiskt Lexikon.* Stockholm 1931.
Vejde 1943: Vejde, Albert: Nils Dacke och hans fejd. In *Hylten-Cavalliusföreningens årsskrift 1943.*
Venge 1980: Venge, Mikael: Bondefred og grænsefred. In *Historisk Tidskrift* (Denmark), 80–1980.
Villstrand 1992: Villstrand, Nils Erik: *Anpassning eller protest. Lokalsamhället eller protest. Lokalsamhället inför utskrivningarna av fotfolk till den svenska krigsmakten 1620–1679.* Åbo Akademis Förlag. Ekenäs 1992.
Virrankoski 1956: Virrankoski, Pentti: Uskonpuhdistuksesta isoonvihaan. In *Suur-Kalajoen historia I. Esihistoriallisesta ajasta isoonvihaan.* Keskipohjanmaan historiasarja I. Suur-Kalajoen historiatoimikunta. Kokkola 1956.
Vogler 1975: Vogler, Günter: Der Revolutionäre Gehalt und die Räumliche Werbereitung der Oberschwäbischen Zwölf Artikel. In Revolte und Revolution in Europa. Herausgegeben von Peter Blickle. *Historische Zeitschrift. Beiheft 4. (neue folge)* R. Oldenburg Verlag. München 1975.
Voionmaa 1916: Voionmaa, Väinö: Keskiajan kansankapinat Suomessa. In *Historiallinen Aikakauskirja* 1916.
Vuorela 2000: Vuorela, Piia: Pikkutullin voimaansaattamisen aiheuttamat konfliktit Tukholmassa 1620-luvulla. In *Rikos historiassa.* Jyväskylän historiallinen arkisto 5. Ed. Olli Matikainen. Jyväskylä 2000.
Wallentin 1978: Wallentin, Hans: *Svenska folkets historia, Verdandi-debatt 83.* Stockholm 1978.
Wangby 1975: *"Jämtlands reformator". Landsprosten Erik Andersson i Oviken och hans samtid.* Östersund 1975.
Westman 1908: Westman, K. G.: Konung och landskapliga myndigeter i den äldsta svenska rättegången. In *Historiska studier tillägnade Harald Hjärne på hans sextioårsdag den 2 maj 1908, af lärjungar.* Stockholm 1908.
Wittrock 1948: Wittrock, Georg: *Regering och allmoge under Kristinas förmyndare.* Skrifter utgivna av Kungl. Humanistiska Vetenskapssamfundet i Uppsala. Band 38. Uppsala 1948.
Wohlfeil (hrsg) 1975: *Der Bauernkrieg 1524–26. Bauernkrieg und Reformation.* Ed. Rainer Wohlfeil. Nymphenburger Verlagshandlung GmbH. München 1975.
Würtz Sørensen 1988: Jørgen Würtz Sørensen: Budstikken går. Bøndernes oprørspraksis i nordisk middelalder. In *Til kamp for friheden. Sociale Oprør i Nordisk Middelalder.* Eds. Anders Bøgh, Jørgen Würtz Sørensen and Lars Tvede-Jensen. Bogsmejden. Denmark 1988.
Würtz-Sørensen 1983: Würtz-Sørensen, Jørgen: *Bondeoprør i Danmark 1438–1441. En analyse af rejsingernes økonomiske, sociale og politiske baggrund.* Landbohistorisk Selskab. Odense 1983.
Wåhlin 1988: Wåhlin, Birgitte: Oprøret mod Knud den Hellige i 1086. Brydninger under stats- og klassedannelsen i Danmark. In *Til Kamp for Friheden. Sociale Oprør i Nordisk Middelalder.* Eds. Anders Bøgh, Jørgen Würtz Sørensen, Lars Tvede-Jensen. Boksmejden. Ålbog 1988.
Ylikangas 1964: Ylikangas, Heikki: Suomalaisten osuus levottomuuksiin vuoden 1755–1756 valtiopäivillä. *Historiallinen Arkisto 59.* SHS. Turku 1964.
Ylikangas 1980: Ylikangas, Heikki: Rautalammin kapina. In *Scripta Historica VI.* Tornio 1980.
Ylikangas 1988: Ylikangas, Heikki: *Valta ja väkivalta keski- ja uudenajan taitteen Suomessa.* WSOY. Juva 1988.

Ylikangas 1990: Ylikangas, Heikki: *Mennyt meissä. Suomalaisen kansanvallan historiallinen analyysi.* WSOY. Porvoo 1990.
Ylikangas 1991: Ylikangas, Heikki: The Historical Connections of European Peasant Revolts. In *Scandinavian Journal of History*, 16–1991.
Ylikangas 1996: Ylikangas, Heikki: *Nuijasota*. Keuruu 1996 (1st edition 1977).
Ylikangas 1998: Ylikangas, Heikki: What happened to violence? In *Five Centuries of Violence in Finland and the Baltic Area*. Publications of The History of Criminality Research Project. Helsinki 1998.
Ylikangas 1999: Ylikangas, Heikki: *Klubbekriget. Det blodiga inbördeskriget i Finland 1596–97.* Atlantis. Stockholm 1999.
Ylikangas 2000: Ylikangas, Heikki: *Aikansa rikos – historiallisen kehityksen valaisijana.* WSOY. Juva 2000.
Ylikangas–Johanssen–Johansson–Næss 2000: Ylikangas, Heikki, Johanssen, Jens Christian V., Johansson Kenneth & Næss. Hans Eyvind: Family, State, and Patterns of Criminality: Major Tendencies in the Work of the Courts, 1550–1850. In *People meet the Law. Control and conflict-handling in the courts*. Universitetsförlaget 2000.
Zagorin 1982 I: Zagorin, Perez: *Rebels and Rulers, 1500–1660. Volume I. Society, States and Early Modern Revolution. Agrarian and Urban Rebellions.* Cambridge University Press 1982.
Zagorin 1982 II: Zagorin, Perez: *Rebels and Rulers, 1500–1660. Volume II. Provincial Rebellion, Revolutionary Civil Wars, 1560–1660.* Cambridge University Press 1982.
Þorsteinsson 1980: _orsteinsson, Björn: *Íslensk mi_aldasaga*. Reykjavik 1980.
Åberg 1960: Åberg, Alf: *Nils Dacke och landsfadern*. Stockholm 1960.
Åqvist 1989: Åqvist, Gösta: *Kungen och rätten. Studien till uppkomsten och den tidigare utvecklingen av kungens lagstiftningsmakt och domrätt under medeltiden.* Rättshistoriskt bibliotek, Vol. 43. Skrifter utgivna av Institutet för rättshistorisk forskning grundat av Gustav och Karin Olin. Lund 1989.
Ödberg 1875: Ödberg, Fridolf: *Om Den Svenske konungens Domsrätt före Svea Hofrätts inrättande år 1614, I–II.* K. L. Beckman. Stockholm 1875.
Österberg 1987: Österberg, Eva: Svenska lokalsamhällen i förändring ca 1550–1850. Participation, representation och politisk kultur i den svenska självsyrelsen. Ett angeläget forskningsområde. In *Historisk Tidskrift* (Sweden), 1987.
Österberg 1989: Österberg, Eva: Bönder och centralmakt i det tidigmoderna Sverige. Konflikt – kompromiss – politisk kultur. In *Scandia. Tidskrift för historisk forskning*, 1–1989.
Österberg 1992: Österberg, Eva: Folklig mentalitet och statlig makt. Perspektiv på 1500- och 1600-talens Sverige. In *Scandia. Tidskrift för historisk forskning*, 1–1992.
Österberg 1995: Österberg, Eva: *Folk förr. Historiska essäer*. Stockholm 1995.

Authors

Gustafsson, Harald (b. 1953), PhD, professor, University of Lund, Department of History. (Sweden)

Johansson, Kenneth (b. 1952), MA, University of Lund, Department of History. (Sweden)

Juliusson, Árni Daniel (b. 1959), PhD, University of Copenhagen/ Reykjavik. (Iceland)

Katajala, Kimmo (b. 1958), PhD, Academy Research Fellow, University of Joensuu, Karelian Institute, Department of Human Sciences. (Finland)

Korpiola, Mia (b. 1971), jur.lic., University of Helsinki, Faculty of Law, Department of Criminal Law, Judicial Procedure and General Jurisprudential Studies. Legal History. (Finland)

Njåstad, Magne (b. 1962), PhD, The Norwegian University of Science and Technology (NTNU), Department of History. (Norway)

Sennefelt, Karin (b. 1972), PhD, Assistant Professor, Department of History, Uppsala University. (Sweden)

Index of persons

The names of researchers and authors whose works are referred to in the text are presented in italics.

A

Absalon, bishop 35–36
Adam 260
Adolf of Holstein, duke 48
Adolf Fredric (of Holstein-Gottorp), king of Sweden 189, 200
Afbragd, Jón 127
Albert of Mecklenburg, duke 69–70
Albert of Mecklenburg, king of Sweden 36–37, 69
Alexander III, pope 32
Alexander I, czar of Russia 248
Althusius, Johannes 161
Alvsson, Knut 93
Anckarström, Jacob Johan 243
Anderson, Perry 82
Andersson, Erik, priest 105
Andresen, Espen 106
Andrésson, Smidur 127
Anna, Swedish princess 80
Anners, Erik 242
Arason, Jón, bishop 130–131, 135
Ásbirningar family 121
Aslaksson, Øystein, bishop 97
Aya, Rod 191

B

Bagge, Nils 62
Barck, Uldrich, count 210
Bassason, Krok-Álfur 125
Bellamy, John 236
Bengt, bishop 33–34
Bengtsson, Sten 57
Bengtsson, Jöns (Oxenstierna), bishop 50
Berndes, Jochim, governor 167
Bielke, Axel Eriksson 61
Birger, earl of Sweden 227
Bjelke, Jens, chancellor 111
Bjelke, Henrik 139
Björn 118
Black Jens, bailiff 47
Blickle, Peter 13, 43, 222–223, 244–245, 264, 266
Blomstedt, Kaarlo 46
Bolt, Amund Sigurdsson 47, 91–92, 102, 260

Brahe, Per (older) 68
Brahe, Per (younger), governor-general 170–171
Bruce, Jacob, Russian general 182
Buch, Hinric 210
Bukk, Olav, bailiff 47, 92
Burgmeister, Hans, bailiff 177
Burke, Peter 191
Bäck, Kalle 207

C

Calonius, Matthias, professor 209
Carl Knutsson, king of Sweden 40–41, 44–45, 230
Carlsson, Gottfrid 73
Charles IX, king of Sweden (see also Duke Charles) 80, 153–156, 158–160, 167, 183, 195, 239–240, 249, 262, 267
Charles XII, king of Sweden 20, 183, 193, 242
Charles X Gustavus, king of Sweden 165–166, 171, 195
Charles XI, king of Sweden 166, 174, 178
Charles XI, king of England 241
Christian II, Union king 18, 49–50, 93, 239, 267
Christian III, king of Denmark 20, 49, 61, 63, 70, 79, 267
Christian IV, king of Denmark-Norway 103, 105, 111, 113
Christina, queen of Sweden 162, 164–165, 169, 171, 175, 178, 182, 195
Christopher I, king of Denmark 228
Christopher of Bavaria, Union king 48–49, 128, 228, 231, 235
Christopher of Oldenburg 49
Clemens 49, 267–268
Creutz, Lorentz, governor 172–173
Creutz, Ernst Johan, governor 173
Cruus, Anna Maria 174
Cruus, Jesper Mattsson 172, 174
Cuttler, S. H. 251

D

Dacke, Nils 51, 53, 56–57, 58–65, 67–77, 79–81, 85, 233

289

Index of persons

David 45–46
Didron, Eric Philip, judge 217
Dorothea, queen of Denmark 99
Døssland, Atle 114
Duke Charles (see Charles IX) 80
Duncan, Niclas Gustaf 216
Duncan, Catherine Birgitta 216–217
Dyri, Gudmundur 132

E
Eggertsson, Jón 138
Egil 32
Einarsson, Gissur, bishop 130
Einarsson, Oddur, bishop 140, 143
Engelbrekt Engelbrekstsson 39–41, 44, 48, 212, 230
Englund, Peter 244
Eric XIV, king of Sweden 153, 238–240
Eric IV, king 36
Eric of Pomerania, Union king 17, 37–42, 44, 47–48, 92
Eric Magnusson, king of Sweden 234
Eric, king of Sweden 33
Eric Mendved, king of Denmark 36
Eriksson, Hans, bailiff 104
Eriksson, Jöran 57, 62, 68
Erikssøn, Jens (Jösse Eriksson), bailiff 39, 44
Eve 260

F
Filipsson, Birger 227
Filipsson, Johan 227
Fincke, Gustavus 152
Fincke, Gödick, bailiff 157
Fleming, Claus 155–159
Fordell, Hans 155
Forselles, Ullrika af 212
Frederic III, king of Denmark 20, 136
Frederic II, king of Denmark 113
Frederic I, king of Denmark 49, 267
Fredric, king of Sweden 200

G
Gaas, Hans, bishop 90, 115
Galle family 102
Gardie, Jacob de la 178
Gerreksson, Jón, bishop 128
Gertorn, Sven, bailiff 68
Glipping, Erik 228
Gläuser, Jürg 120
Gothus, Laurentius Paulinus, archbishop 161
Gottrup, Laurits, sheriff 143–144
Gråtopp, Halvard 47–48, 91–92, 259–260
Gudmundur, syslumadur 128
Gudnason, Björn 131

Guðmundsson, Páll Gaddur 127
Guðmundsson, Ari 138
Gunnalugsson, Teitur 128
Gustavus Vasa (Gustavus I, Gustavus Eriksson), king of Sweden 19–20, 25, 50–51, 53–54, 56, 58, 60–74, 76–80, 105, 149–154, 183, 212, 230, 239, 245, 261, 265
Gustavus III (prince Gustavus) 190, 209, 211–212, 213, 215, 218–220, 243, 250
Gustavus II Adolph, king of Sweden 159–162, 164, 241

H
Halldór 132
Halvardsson, Rolf 90, 115
Hane, Måns 64, 69, 74, 76
Hans, king of Denmark 93
Hansson, Jösse 45
Harrison, Dick 42
Haukdælir family 121
Henry VIII, king of England 240
Henry, bishop 32–33
Hjort, Isak Birgersson 57
Hjärne, Harald 228–229
Hofman, Sven 188, 190–191, 193, 196, 198, 201, 203
Hollur, Einar 118
Holm, Poul 36
Horn, Henrik Classon 152
Horn, Arvid 193
Hugleiksson, Auðunn 126
Hus, Jan 260
Hyncze 45–46
Håkon, king of Norway 126, 131
Hästesko, Johan Henrik 243

I
Ilkka, Jaakko 156
Imsen Steinar 35, 47–48, 50, 95
Ingelsson, Torsten 45
Innocent III, pope 33
Innocent IV, pope 227

J
Jacobsson, Johan, clerk 173
Jagellonica, Catharina 153, 239
Johansson, Måns 57, 62
John III, king of Sweden 153–155, 195, 239
Jon i Gavlö 80
Jonsson, Sigurd 92
Jónsson, Jón, lawman 140, 142
Jónsson, Magnús Prúdi 131
Jónsson, Stefan, bishop 133
Jägerhorn, Reinhold 208
Jönsson, Bertil, judge 150
Jörensson, Bertil, bailiff 150–151

290

K

Kagg, Lars 179
Kálfsson, Vigfús 132
Karlsson, Anders, bailiff 62
Katajala, Kimmo 223–224, 234, 244
Knut, king of Denmark 35
Knutsson, Filip 227
Knutsson, Holmger 227
Koht, Halvdan 47
Kráksson, Jón 132
Kráksson, Haflidi 132
Krummedike, Henrik 93
Krämare Pelle 60
Kröpelin, Hans, bailiff 40, 44–45
Kurki, Axel 156
Kuronen, Henrik 217

L

Lalli 33
Larensson, Olof, bailiff 62
Larsson, Erik 70
Larsson, Lars-Olof 41–42, 59, 64, 66–67, 70, 72–74
Laurentius Andreææ 239
Lear, Floyd Seward 225
Lejonhufvud, Axel, governor 233
Lejonhufvud, Abraham Eriksson 61
Lenæeus, Johannes Canurti, archbishop 161, 163
Leppur, Lodinn 125
Lilliesparre, Jon Olsson 57
Loccenius, Johannes 161
Loðinsson, Bjarni 126
Lofthus, Christian 94
Loftsson, Thorvardur 128
Ludvigsson, Rasmus 53, 55, 58, 60, 62–65, 67–69, 72–73, 77–78
Luther, Martin 260
Lönnroth, Erik 41, 46

M

Maarbjerg, John 158
Macchiavelli, Niccolo 62, 85
Magnus Ericsson, king of Sweden and Norway 33, 102, 228, 230–232, 234, 237, 249, 251
Magnus Birgersson Ladulås, king of Sweden 227, 230
Magnus, son of Gustavus I 153
Magnússon, Ari, sheriff 136–137
Magnússon, Árni 143–144
Magnússon, Björn, sheriff 137
Magnússon, Gunnlaugur, syslumandur 127
Maitland, Frederic William 224
Margaret, queen of Denmark 37–38, 230

Mathisen, Runar 109–110
Matssen, Hartvig, bailiff 104–105
Mickelsson, Peder 80
Molteke, Herman, bailiff 91, 102
Montgomery, Robert, colonel 217
Multiainen, Ingi 152, 233
Munck, Ludvig, district governor 90, 103–104, 111
Mundt, Pros 140
Månsson, Sven, bailiff 68
Mårtensson, Hans, bailiff 44

N

Nackerej, Olof von, governor 218, 246
Natt och Dag, Måns Johansson 68
Nehrman, David 224, 226, 236, 245, 247
Nielsson, Krister 44–45
Nilsson, Jören 57, 80
Nilsson, Birger, governor 57
Nyrhi, Maunu 151–152, 233
Nyström, Per 83

O

Oddaverjar family 121, 132
Olaus Magnus 238
Olaus Petri 239
Olivecrona, K. 243
Olsson, Gustavus, councillor 58–61, 76
Órækja 118–119
Oxenstierna, Gabriel Bengtsson 175–176
Oxenstierna, Johan 172
Oxenstierna, Carin 172–174
Oxenstierna Axel, Chanchellor of the Realm 20, 172

P

Paakkunainen, Tuomas 179–180
Pálsson, Ögmundur, bishop 130
Patkul, Johann Reinhold 235
Persson, Bengt 243
Petersson, Filip 227
Petersson, Niklas, governor 99–100
Petri, Olaus 84
Petrus, archbishop 35
Philippus 45–46
Pining, Didrik, hirdstjóri 134
Polack, Otto Wilhelm, bailiff 216
Pollock, Frederic 224
Puke, Erik 39–40, 44

R

Ramsay, Anders Henrik, governor 213, 216
Reinholdsson, Peter 42–43, 92–93, 145–146, 245
Reuterholm, Gustav 209

Index of persons

Rian, Øystein 102, 106, 108
Rosenhahne, Schering, governor 177
Rosenhahne, Axel 177
Rudbeckius, Johannes, bishop 164

S
Salminen, Tapio 46
Saltza, H. H. von 246
Sandnes, Jørn 108
Sandvik, Hilde 113
Sæmundsson, Björn 132
Sætra, Gustav 112
Schedin, Gustav 199
Schriver, Christian, bailiff 131
Schulze, Winfried 113, 244
Scott, James C. 191
Sighvatsson, Sturla 118–119
Sigismund, king of Sweden (and Poland as Zygmunt III) 80, 153–155, 158–159, 235, 239, 241, 262, 267
Sigmundsson, Jón 131
Sihvo, Matti 168, 170–171, 182, 213
Skinnar Per Andersson 196
Skráveifa, Jón, hirdstjóri 127
Skrivare, Hans 57, 80
Skräddare, Erengisle, bailiff 68
Skåncke family 101
Somme, Germund Svensson, governor 57, 65
Sørensson, Søren, bailiff 105
Sprengtporten, Jacob Magnus, general 211, 213, 216
Stefan, priest 142
Stenbock, Gustavus Olsson, councillor 57
Stille, Sven, bailiff 179–180
Sture, Svante 60, 71, 81
Sture family 18
Sturesson, Jöns, bailiff 45
Sturla, son of Sighvatur 121
Sturlasson (Sturluson) Snorri 32, 118, 121, 132–133
Sturlungar family 121, 132
Sturluson, Thórdur 121
Sturluson, Sighvatur 121, 132
Styrmisson, Valgadur 132
Sune Hakonsson (Soini), bailiff 37
Suvanto, Seppo 46
Sven i Flaka 76
Svínfellingar family 121
Söfrringsson, Pehr, bailiff 173

T
Tagesen, Henrik 49

Tavast, Ivar 157
Tavast, Magnus, bishop 45
Tegel, Erik Jöransson 66–67
Thórdur 132
Thorðarson, Einar 133
Thórðarson, Sturla 119, 121
Thorleifsson, Björn 128
Thorleifsson, Einar 128
Thorsteinsson, Björn 126
Thorsteinsson, Jón 138
Thorvaldsson, Jón 142
Tigerstedt, Georg Fredrik 243
Tilly, Charles 191–192
Tord 'The Knight' 64, 76
Tordsson, Øystein, priest 97–98
Torfason, Sveinn 143
Tott, Klaus Åkeson 176
Trolle, Arffvet 62
Trolle, Ture 57, 59–60, 62, 65, 75
Tunne 32
Tyler, Wat 258

U
Ullrika Eleonora, queen of Sweden 193
Ungern, Gertrud von 167–170

V
Valdemar Birgersson, king of Sweden 227
Vidalin, Páll 143
Vigfússon, Jón, bishop 139, 143
Vogler, Günter 95
Voionmaa Väinö 37

W
Wallenius, Gabriel, bailiff 216
Wrangel, Wilhelm Gustav, major 199
Wrede, Henrik 167, 169, 171, 212
Wrede, Rabbe Gottlieb, count 212
Wrede, Casper 167, 169–170
Wrede, Fabian, baron 171
Wrede, Carl 167, 169–171
Wrede family 212

Y
Ylikangas, Heikki 46, 157, 160, 223, 244–245, 248

Å
Åqvist, Gösta 248

Ö
Örtken, Simon, bailiff 179
Österberg, Eva 160, 244–245

Index of places and names

A
Aalborg 49
Akershus 47, 92
Akureyri 136, 138
Allbo 63–64, 68, 75
Amsterdam 28
Anjala 168, 170, 182
Arboga 40–41
Arendal 94, 114
Aringsås 68
Árnessýsla 129, 140, 143
Árnesthing 121, 129
Aspeland 71, 75–76

B
Baltic provinces 178
Baltic Sea 231
Baltic 19, 159, 163, 167
Bardastrandsysla 137
Bergen 94, 105, 128, 135, 243
Bergkvara 53, 56–58, 60–62, 65
Bergslagen 39, 41–42
Bergunda 62
Bessastaðir, fortress 139–140
Biskupstungur 141
Blekinge 59–60, 65, 70, 72, 83
Bohemia 260
Bolmen, lake 80
Bologna 83
Boo 62
Borganäs Castle 39
Borgarfjarðarsýsla 143
Borgarsysla 97–102
Borås, town 188, 191, 201
Brandenburg-Prussia 30
Bratsberg 103, 106–108, 110, 114
Breiðafjördur 118
Bremen 135
Britain 24
British Isles 260, 262
Bro, town 192
Brúará, river 128
Bruges 259

C
Central Europé 13
Copenhagen 20, 39, 83, 107–108, 128, 134–135, 140, 143

D
Dalecarlia 39, 42, 44–45, 50–51, 182, 188–190, 192–193, 196–197, 199–201, 203, 220, 236
Dalir 119
Denmark 12, 16–30, 32, 35–38, 47–50, 53, 56, 59, 61, 65, 69–72, 83, 104, 111, 128, 130, 137–138, 145, 166, 182, 189, 197, 199, 211, 226, 228, 237, 239–240, 242, 251, 260–261, 263, 267–268
Denmark-Norway 12, 19–21, 25–26, 28, 30, 105, 109, 112, 130, 183, 243
Dittmarsken 82
Djúpavogur 138
Duchy of Schleswig 17

E
Eastern Gothia 30, 44, 58, 60, 63–65, 69, 71, 74–76, 226
Eastland (Finland) 17, 32
Ed 63
Egilsstadir 132
Egypt 38
Eidsberg 97
Elbe, river 21–23,
Elimäki 167–171, 212–214, 216
England 24, 35, 83, 153, 225, 240, 251, 260
Eskiholt, farm 132
Essex 259
Estonia 19, 45
Ettak, royal manor 64
Europe 11–14, 19, 21–22, 24–25, 27–29, 39, 43, 53, 74, 82–83, 95, 100, 115, 144, 152–153, 160, 162, 194, 207, 223, 231, 258–259, 262–263, 268
Eyjafjörður 121, 127–128, 132, 136, 145

F
Fagirskógur 132
Falun 189, 195, 199
Faroe Islands 16–17
Finland 11–12, 16–17, 19, 21–25, 29–30, 32–33, 35–39, 44–45, 47, 49, 57, 63, 111, 149–152, 154–156, 158–159, 167, 170, 172, 183, 189, 195, 208, 210–214, 216, 218, 220, 223, 233, 243, 248, 259, 261, 263, 265–268

293

Finnveden 54, 64–66, 71, 74–75, 78–79, 83
Flanders 258–259
Fljót 140, 143
Fläskjum 188, 201
France 11, 24, 27, 83, 249, 251, 259–260, 262
Friesland 82
Fyn 35, 48

G
Gardsvík 142
Gauldalen 104
Germany 19, 23, 27, 29, 43, 51, 65, 83, 95, 113, 138, 149, 222, 238, 260, 263
Gotland 48
Greenland 16–17
Grindavík 133
Grund 121, 126–127, 131
Gullbringusysla 143
Gästrikland 44, 80
Göstring 64, 75

H
Habsburg empire 113
Hackås 101
Hagi, estate 118
Halland 23, 35, 182, 218, 237, 243, 246–248
Hamar 93
Hamburg 135
Handbörd 72, 75–76
Hanekind 64
Haukur 118
Hedemark 93
Helsingör 135
Helsinki 11, 12
Hergranes 125
Herjedalen 99
Hesleby 62
Hólar 128, 130–131, 139, 142–145
Holaveden 71, 76
Holland 24
Hólmur 138
Holstein 17, 49
Hova 181, 192
Húnathing 127
Húnavatnssýsla 127–128, 143
Húsavík 136, 138
Hvammur 121
Hälsingland 39, 44, 80
Hämeenkylä 168
Hämeenlinna Castle 150, 215
Högsby 71

I
Iceland 12, 16–17, 19, 21–25, 27, 30, 85, 119–122, 124–132, 134–140, 142–146, 149, 261, 267–268
Ikalapori, barony 177
Ilomantsi 216
Indaselva, river 98
Ingria, province 160
Ísafjarðardjúp, fjord 118–119, 122, 136
Ísafjarðarsysla 136
Ísafjörður 136, 138
Italy 27

J
Jemtland 17, 39, 97–106, 108
Joensuu 210–211
Jokioinen 167, 172–175, 208–209, 211
Jylland 36, 48–49
Jäder ironworks 195
Jääski 37
Jönköping 61, 63–65, 71

K
Kaarlepori, earldom 176
Kalmar, town 37, 57, 64, 71, 75
Kalmar, province 56–58, 62, 75
Karelia 23, 33, 36–37, 45–46, 149, 159–160, 167, 178–179, 182, 216–217, 233, 235, 259, 263
Kiikala 233
Kinda 64, 71, 75
Kinnevald 63–64, 68, 75
Kirkholm 167
Kirkjubæklaustur 142
Kirkjuból 131
Kisa 63
Kitee 181
Kokemäki 36
Kolding 36
Kolshult 59–60
Konga 59, 62–64, 66, 68, 75
Korela (chf. Keksholm), town 159
Korsholma, earldom 175–176
Kronoberg Castle 59–60, 67–68
Kuhmo 248
Kurikka 157
Kymi, river 168
Kyrö 157, 233
Käkisalmi, province 19, 160, 167, 178, 182
Käkisalmi, town 179, 182
Käkisalmi, citadel 181
Köpinghus 39
Köyliö, lake 33

L
Lappee 150–153, 233, 239, 261, 265
Lapua 233

Leidarhólmsskrá 131
Leirá 143
Lekaryd 68
Linköping 61–65, 67, 77
Liperi 181–182
Livonia 19, 167, 235
Ljungsåkra 68
London 11, 28, 259
Loviisa, town 213–214
Lund 35
Lysings 75
Lübeck 48, 53, 135
Lützen 162
Långasjö 75

M
Malmö 135
Mark 195
Markaryd 61
Marstrand, fortress 243
Marttila 233
Memmingen 260
Mjøsa, lake 30
Moheda 63
Moisio 168
Mora 199
Motala 44
Munkathverá 143
Mälaren valley 30
Mälaren, lake 30, 44
Mödruvellir 128
Möre 75

N
Namdalen 104
Nastola 214–215, 247
Netherlands 48
Njudung 54, 75
Nokia 157
Norra Möre 64
Norra Vedbo 64, 70, 75
Norrköping 194
Norrland 21, 39
Norrvidinge 63–64, 72, 75
Northern Karelia 19, 216
Norway 12, 16–27, 29–30, 35, 37–39, 47–49, 51, 85, 90–91, 93–97, 100–103, 106, 109, 111, 113, 115, 120–121, 125–128, 130, 135–136, 138–139, 145, 149, 183, 226, 228, 251, 259–261, 263–264, 266–268
Nyystölä 157

O
Oslo 35, 47, 92–93, 97–98, 100, 106
Oslo Fjord 23, 30, 47, 91

Østfold 91, 97, 100–102
Ostrobothnia 23–24, 39, 155–159, 166–167, 175–177
Oulu Castle 155, 233
Oviken 105

P
Padasjoki 157
Paimio 233
Paris 11
Peippola 168
Pielisjärvi 180–183
Poland 80, 153–155, 159, 239
Poltava 183
Pomerania 19, 180
Porkkala, manor 46
Prussia 53
Pälkjärvi 216–217

R
Ragunda 98
Rakkestad 91
Rangárthing 121, 137
Rautalampi 156
Reval (Tallinn) 45
Reykholt 121, 127, 132
Reykjanes 133
Reykjavík 138, 144
Riga 167
Rogaland 103, 108, 109
Rome 38
Romerike 93
Ronneby 59, 69
Russia 153, 159–160, 176, 189–190, 196, 199–200, 206, 211, 220, 240, 268
Rydaholm 63
Ryssby 63
Rödeby 72

S
Sala, town 200
Sarpsborg 100
Satakunta 34–36, 45–46, 265
Sauðafell 119
Savonia 33–34, 156–157
Savonlinna Castle 150, 152, 157
Scania 17, 23, 35–36, 182, 211, 218, 237, 243, 248
Schleswig-Holstein 19, 29
Scotland 163, 240
Screffvaremåle 62
Seltjarnarnes 138
Sevede 71–72, 75–76
Sjaelland 48
Skagafjörður 121, 125, 128, 132, 142, 145

295

Skálholt 128, 130–131, 133, 140–141, 144–145
Skaraborg 192, 238
Skeda 65
Skien 92
Skutulsfjarðareyri 138
Slätbacka 65
Slätthög 63
Småland 25, 53–66, 69–72, 74–75, 77–81, 83–84
Snæfellsnes 121
Somero 233
Stavanger 103, 109
Stegeborg 60, 71, 75
Stockholm 11, 23, 29, 40–41, 44, 67, 69, 74, 80, 83, 150–151, 168–173, 175–177, 179–182, 188–191, 194–203, 208, 210–220, 234–238, 240–241, 247
Stranda 64, 75–76
Strängnäs 50
Strömsholm 195
Stånge, river 159
Sudreim (Sørum) 92
Suistamo 181
Sunnerbo 65, 85
Sunnmøre 93
Svartholma citadel 213–214
Sweden 12, 16–26, 28–30, 33, 35, 37–38, 40, 42, 44, 47–51, 53–54, 56, 63, 67, 73, 83, 92–93, 101, 105–106, 109–110, 145–146, 149, 153–154, 156, 159–161, 166, 172, 180–184, 188–189, 192–193, 195, 206, 218–219, 224, 226, 228, 230, 233–236, 239–240, 242, 244, 248–251, 259–265, 267–268
Switzerland 82
Söderköping 155, 234
Södermanland 40, 44, 60, 154
Södra Vedbo 64, 72, 75
Södra Möre 59, 63–64, 72, 75

Tammela 172
Tavastia 33–35, 45–46, 167, 172, 175, 233
Telemark 91, 103, 106, 111, 115, 261
Thingeyjarsýsla 136, 142
Thingeyrar 121, 144
Thverá 127
Thykkvibær 121, 140
Tjust 63, 66, 70, 75
Tohmajärvi 179, 182–83
Torsås 75
Trøndelag 23, 30, 91, 97, 100, 103–104, 110

Trondheim 19, 90, 104–106, 111, 128
Tuna 64, 70, 75
Tunsberg 91, 100
Turkey 183
Turku, town 38, 45, 156, 158–159, 169, 171, 180, 209–210
Turku Castle 36, 44–45, 156, 159, 265
Tveta 64, 75

U
Uezd of Korela (chf. Käkisalmi, province) 160
Ulvila 156
Upper Austria 259
Uppland 35, 39–40, 50, 60, 156, 231
Uppsala 32–35, 38, 40, 102, 105, 195, 199, 227, 238
Uppvidinge 63–64, 72, 75–76
Uusikaarlepyy, town 176
Uusikirkko 233
Uusimaa 37, 167

V
Vaasa, town 175, 217
Vadsbo 192
Vadstena 40, 71
Valkebo 75
Varne 98, 101
Vatnsfirðingar family 118
Vatnsfjörður 118
Vatnsleysa 141
Veden 190–191
Vesur-Skaftafellssysla 121
Videy 130
Vigfolka 75
Viipuri, town 149, 152
Viipuri Castle 37, 44–45, 150–151, 157, 169
Vimmerby 58, 62
Virserum 72, 80
Visby 230, 234
Vissefjärda 75
Vista 64, 75
Värend 54–55, 59–60, 63, 69–70, 74–75, 83
Värmland 45
Värtsilä 179
Västbo 59, 65, 85
Västervik 65
Västerås Castle 39
Västerås, town 39, 44, 164, 199
Västmanland 39, 44
Västra 64, 70, 72, 75–76
Vättern, lake 71
Växjö 59–60, 63–65, 67–69, 74, 76, 78, 80, 84

West Fjord peninsula (West Fjords) 118–119, 134, 136, 142
Western Gothia 25, 30, 51, 57–58, 61, 64–65, 71, 164, 195, 226, 229, 231–232, 239

Y
Ydre 72, 75–76

Å
Åland Islands 16, 39

Ä
Älvsborg 190
Äyräpää 151

Ö
Ögur 131, 136
Öland 75–76
Örebro 71
Örlygsstadir 121–122
Östbo 59, 65, 70, 85
Östra 62, 64, 70, 72, 75–76

Subject index

A
Academy of Turku 209
Act of Union and Security 220
Almenna bænaskráin 144
Almúgans samhykkt 126
Althing 120, 125–128, 130, 136–142, 144
Árnesingaskrá 129
Áshildarmýrarsamthykkt 129, 131

B
Bible 72
Bishop Árni's saga 125
Biärköa law 234
Borgläger 154–159, 183
British Empire 135
Bundschuch 260

C
Cap party (the Caps) 193, 198, 206
Church Ordinance 245
Club War 149, 153–154, 156–158, 160, 167, 183–184, 195, 223, 233, 259, 262, 265, 267
Commonwealth 262
communalism/communalistic order/ communal principles 13, 43, 81–82, 112, 183, 266
Counter-Reformation 153, 261
Coutumiers 83
Croquant uprising 13, 259, 263

D
Dacke War/uprising 25, 53–54, 56, 72, 80–81, 84, 149, 239, 261, 265, 267
Dackeland 55, 68, 79
Dalecarlia uprising 192–193, 203, 207, 236–238, 250–251
David's uprising 45–46, 231, 259, 265–266

E
enclosure movement 153
Engelbrekt uprising 39, 41–44, 46, 223, 231, 259–260, 264–265, 267
English Civil War 259
English Rising 1381 11, 258–260
Enlightenment 206, 211, 219
Eriksgata 84

European Union 11

F
Flanders uprising 258
Folkunga party 227
French Revolution 144, 219
Fronde 259, 262
fundamental laws 161

G
General Law (SRL) 211, 235
German law 251
Glossators 83
Godar 120–121, 125
Godord 120–121, 125
Great German Peasant War 13, 113, 153, 222–223, 260
Great Famine 180, 259
Great Reduction 166, 171, 174, 177–178, 184, 207–208, 212, 263
Great Northern War 110, 161, 171, 175, 182, 220

H
Halvard Gråtopp's revolt/uprising 47–48, 50, 259–260
Hansa, trade union 39, 41, 135
Hat party (the Hats) 193, 196, 206
Heimskringla Saga 32, 118
Hirdstjóri 126–127, 129, 134
Hofman uprising 190–193, 200, 203, 207
Holy Roman Empire 17, 43, 152, 222–223
Hussitie War 260
Hussities 49
Höfudsmadur 134, 137

I
Íslendiga bók 119

J
Jaquerie 258–259
Jónsbók 124–125

K
Kalmar Union 17, 29, 37, 41, 44, 47, 49–50, 105, 128, 130, 251
Kalmar War 109

Karelian tax-revolt (14th century) 37
Karelian tax revolt (15th century) 45
Karelian uprising 259
Kett's rebellion 153, 260
Kongespeilet 226

L
Lappee revolt 152, 183
law of Grágás 120
Law of the Realm (landslag) 161–162, 172, 223, 228, 230–231, 235, 237, 249–250
Lex Julia Majestatis 227
livres de pratique 83
Lofthus uprising 91, 94, 113
Lutheran Reformation 19–20, 25, 29, 51, 74, 97,103–104, 111, 115, 130–131, 134–135, 140, 146, 149, 152, 245, 260–261
Lönguréttarbót 128, 131

M
manorial law 166
monarchia mixta 161
Morgonstjärneupproret 181, 192

N
natural law 161, 206
Nordic war 105
Nordic countries/realms 16–17, 21–25, 28–29, 32, 35, 43, 50, 260–266
Nu-Pied uprising 13, 263

O
Old Finland 220

P
Philosophes 28
Pilgrimage of Grace 260
Píningsdómur 134, 138
political culture 13, 26, 42–43, 50, 92, 95, 111, 149, 159, 183, 202, 244, 266
post-glossators 234
Prayer Book Rebellion 260
provincial law 226, 228–230, 232
Pugachev's revolt 268
Puke uprising 44, 260

Q
quarter reduction 166, 176

R
Roman law 83, 85, 225–228, 230, 234, 238–239, 251

S
Sachsenspiegel 83
Scandinavia 12, 33, 95, 105, 128, 135, 192, 225, 227, 229, 231–232, 237, 251, 259–261, 264, 266, 269
Schwabenspiegel 83
Seven-Year-War 105, 109
Skálholtssamtykkt 127
Skipper Clemens revolt 267–268
Snapphanarna 182
St. Olav's law 114
Statute of Strängnäs 228
Statute of Örebro 235, 241
Statute of Skenninge 228
Statute of Telge 230
Statute of Skara 232
Stavnsbånd 22, 24,
Sturlung wars 121
Sturlunga saga 122, 132
Syslumadur 127–128

T
Telemark revolts 261
Thirty Years War 160, 263
town law 228, 230, 234–235, 242, 249
Tractatus de legibus 83
Treaty of Westphalia 263
Treaty of Stettin 105
Treaty of Stolbova 160, 178
Treaty of Teusina 154–155
Twelve Articles of Memmingen 153, 260

U
Uppland uprising 267

V
Vasa dynasty 238
Verrechtligung 113, 263
Vornedskab 22
Värtsilä mutiny 180

W
War of the Strils 91, 94, 113
War of Charles X Gustavus (the 'rupture') 176
War of the Counts 49, 53, 267